VITA COMMUNIS

In Tittmoning, Bartholomew Holzhauser wrote down his apocalyptic visions, but above all he deserves credit for having rediscovered and renewed the ancient policy of St Eusebius of Vercelli and Saint Augustine, of secular priests living in community ... The police station, therefore our home, was the most beautiful house on the town square, which had formerly served to house the community chapter.
Josef Kardinal Ratzinger, *Aus meinem leben*,
München, 1997, pp. 11–12

Cover picture: The Alte Kapelle at Regensburg, an ancient collegiate church rebuilt in the eighteenth century.
Back cover picture: The former community house at Tittmoning, Bavaria.
Title page vignette: Brass of Adam de Ertham, first Master of the collegiate church of Arundel, 1382.

VITA COMMUNIS

The Common Life of the Secular Clergy

Jerome Bertram

GRACEWING

First published in 2009 by

Gracewing
2 Southern Avenue, Leominster
Herefordshire HR6 0QF

All rights reserved. No part of this publication may be reproduced, stored in a retrieval system, or transmitted in any form, or by any means, electronic, mechanical, photocopying, recording or otherwise, without the written permission of the publisher.

© Jerome Bertram 2009

The right of Jerome Bertram to be identified as the author of this work has been asserted in accordance with the Copyright, Designs and Patents Act 1988.

UK ISBN 978 0 85244 201 2

Typeset by
Action Publishing Technology Ltd, Gloucester, GL1 5SR

Contents

Foreword ix

1	Some Definitions	1
2	Before the Council of Nicaea	22
3	From Nicaea to St Gregory	32
4	From Gregory to Charlemagne	52
5	The Carolingian Empire	77
6	The Viking Years, and a Longer Rule	95
7	Eleventh-Century Reformers	124
8	General Legislation, and Cathedral chapters in the High Middle Ages	140
9	Other Collegiate Churches in the High Middle Ages	163
10	After the Black Death: the Heyday of late Medieval Colleges	184
11	The Age of Reform, and the Wars of Religion	215
12	The Glorious Catholic Reformation	231
13	The Revolution and After	250
14	Reaffirmation and Renewal	273

Bibliography 291
Index 297

Abbreviations

AA.SS.	*Acta Sanctorum ex Latinis et Graecis aliarumque gentium Monumentis*, ed. J. Carnandet (Paris and Rome, Palmé, 1863–1925).
DI	*Die Deutschen Inschriften* (Düsseldorf, Göttingen, Heidelberg, Leipzig, Mainz, München, Wien, Akademien der Wissenschaften, 1942–date, 70 vols so far).
DS	Denzinger, H. and Schönmetzer, A., *Enchiridion Symbolorum Definitionum et Declarationum de rebus fidei et morum* (Barcelona, Herder, 1976).
IC	Institutio Canonica (ed. Bertram).
Mansi	*Sacrorum Conciliorum Nova et Amplissima Collectio*, ed. Mansi, J.D. (Venice, Antonio Zatta, 1759–98, 31 vols).
MGH	*Monumenta Germaniae Historica*.
PG	Patrologia Graeca.
PL	Patrologia Latina.
RA	Rule of St Augustine (ed. Verheijen).
RB	Rule of St Benedict (ed. de Vogüé).
RC	Rule of St Chrodegang (ed. Bertram).
RL	Rule of St Leofric or Longer Rule (ed. Bertram).
S.Th.	St Thomas Aquinas, *Summa Theologica*.
c./cc.	column(s) (re chapter end notes)

Foreword

This book has been long in the making, and has been overtaken in some areas by faster or better funded writers, but in its scope and intention is still, I venture to suggest, something new. Very many friends have collaborated in various ways, members of my own Oratory, former students and colleagues, librarians and custodians innumerable, far too many to list for fear some should be forgotten. In particular, though, I must mention Abbot Geoffrey Scott and Professor Henry Mayr-Harting who have examined the text in its final stages, and made useful comments and suggestions. In trawling through such a vast range of material, serendipity has often come to my aid, chance encounters with books or buildings that illuminated points previously obscure. The topic is so vast, and the possibilities for further research so boundless, that I cannot claim to have done more than skimmed the surface of what could be written. Doubtless others will continue to examine aspects of the story in greater and more critical detail. However I am confident that the broad historical picture is accurate, and that movements towards the Common Life did unfold according to the outlines here given.

Whether this historical picture will be helpful to form patterns of clerical life in the future remains to be seen. It is offered to the Church as a small contribution to the endless work of forming and deploying clergy for the mission to the world.

jfab, Oxford

Chapter 1

Some Definitions

The suggestion is often made that the celibate clergy of the Catholic Church would be healthier, happier and more holy if they lived in communities rather than in isolation. Practical solutions have been offered, but somehow the idea has been slow to find approval, and experiments have been made, but somehow they soon come to an end. It is often pointed out that priests lived in community in the 'early Church', but the history of the Catholic Church in the past forty years has shown us very clearly that there is no point in reviving something that was done in the early Church until we know why the later Church ceased to do it. Looking at historic experiments will help to clarify future possibilities, and to reveal the difficulties and obstacles that have been experienced in the past.

As a result, the bulk of this book is an investigation into what form the common life of the secular clergy really took, not only in the early Church but in all subsequent ages. We look at the different manifestations of community, ranging from something very like monasticism to loose associations, and we consider why in the majority of cases these forms of community life came to an end. In so doing I am inevitably drawn to focus on the Oratory of St Philip Neri, which is almost the only surviver of these forms of life into the modern world, besides being the institute in which I myself happen to have found community. Parallels and antecedents to the Oratorian way of life can be seen from the fourth century onwards, and it becomes clear that St Philip Neri and his first followers did not found something new but helped to codify a well-established way of life.

The purpose of examining the history of the *Vita Communis* is the hope that it will help to resolve the present debate over how 'secular clergy' should live. However to speak meaningfully on this topic we need to be clear about our terms, to define what 'clergy' are, and what is meant by calling them 'secular'. In particular we must be aware that the term 'clergy' has never been synonymous with 'priests', and that the term 'secular clergy' is not synonymous with 'diocesan priests'. To the casual reader, the idea of 'secularity' appears to contradict the very purpose of 'clergy', a confusion made much worse when secular priests remark that they are 'not religious'. The terms 'religious' and 'secular' as applied to 'clergy' are indeed misleading, and protests were made in the eleventh century when they first began to be used, but it is rather too late now to eliminate them.

It is often imagined that 'clergy' are, or have been, the only active members of the Church, and that all responsibility rests on them, for the maintenance of the church buildings, the care of the poor, the education of the young, the raising and managing of funds. Even in an age which fondly imagines that the 'laity' are for the first time allowed to become 'involved', most priests spend most of their time fundraising, talking to builders and attending school governor meetings, while the laity take responsibility for distributing the sacraments. This is a serious distortion of their respective roles, and one reason for the perceived decline in priestly vocations. In the past, at least until the French Revolution, the role of the priest, and of the many other grades of clergy, was seen entirely in terms of worship; they were the servants of the cult, spending their time in vestments, while leaving it to the active laity to look after investments. It was lay people who designed and built the churches, who donated and administered the money, and who directed the 'pastoral' work of almsgiving and education. When we consider what clergy did and how they lived in the early Church, and at all times up to the late eighteenth century, we must get away from the comparatively modern idea that their primary role was 'pastoral' – it was not, it was cultic.

Another fruitful area of misunderstanding is that of clerical celibacy or continence. While this book is not directly about celibacy, that aspect of the discipline of the Western Church inevitably affects the history of the common life, and some attention must be paid to elucidating what the tradition really is. Much more relevant is the question of apostolic 'poverty', since the long rivalry between 'secular' and 'religious' communities hinges entirely on that question. Chastity and obedience were never controversial (at least until the late twentieth century); poverty was controversial indeed.

Clergy

The distinction between clergy and laity, and the use of those two terms, arose at the very beginning of Christendom, and the former term in particular came to be invested with crucial significance for our discussion of the common life. The actual word 'clergy' and its cognates derives from the Greek word for 'lot', which was first used in the account of the choice of Matthias (Acts 1:15–26). The word Κλῆρος (klēros) is used in its literal sense of a lot drawn to settle which of the two candidates should be chosen, but it is also the word which St Peter chooses for the 'share' in the ministry, which Judas had relinquished: καὶ ἔλαχε τὸν κλῆρον τῆς διακονίας ταύτης – 'he relinquished the lot of this ministry'. It is a word which was very familiar in the Greek Old Testament, and its use by St Peter (or by St Luke in writing up the story afterwards), was to provide the Fathers of the Church with important material for exegesis.

St Jerome, in a passage which was to be enormously influential for centuries, introduces the idea that the word Κλῆρος, as applied to the Christian ministry, has two further applications: the cleric is one who is the Lord's allotted portion; and the Lord in turn is his portion:

> Therefore a Cleric, who serves the Church of Christ, should first understand the meaning of the word, and, once that meaning is defined, should strive to be what he is called. If the Greek word Κλῆρος means 'lot' in Latin, they are called 'clerics' either because they are the lot of the Lord, or because the Lord himself is the lot, or portion, of the Clergy. He who is the lot of the Lord, or has the Lord as his lot, must show himself to be such that he both possesses the Lord and is possessed by the Lord. He who possesses the Lord, and can say with the Psalmist 'the Lord is my portion' [Ps. 15:5, and 72:26] can own nothing apart from the Lord. For if he were to own anything apart from the Lord, the Lord would not be his portion. For example, if he has gold, or silver, or lands, or fine furniture, with such portions the Lord could not be his portion. If therefore I am 'the Lord's portion, and his allotted heritage' [Deut. 32:9], I do not accept a portion among the other tribes, but like the Levites and Priests I live on the tithes. As one serving the altar, I am supported by the offerings of the altar, having food and clothing I will be content with them [2 Tim. 6:8], and bare, I will follow the bare Cross.'[1]

All three meanings of the word Κλῆρος may be drawn upon to indicate what it means to be a cleric, what the clerical state implies, what risks it carries, and what privileges it enjoys. Firstly, the cleric is one chosen by lot. In the case of Matthias that happened literally: there were two candidates for the one vacancy, and the Apostles drew lots to see which one should be appointed. There may have been times in the history of the Church when her deacons, priests and bishops were chosen by lot in the same way, just as Saul was chosen for the kingship (1 Sam. 10:20–21), though that never became the standard practice. Nevertheless, there still remains something of the nature of a lottery in the choice of a candidate for the priesthood. Ordinands have never been selected in quite the same way as candidates for any secular task or office: there was always an understanding that they had to be in some way 'called' by God, that they should not put themselves forward, that on no account should they offer any financial inducement for ordination. The last in particular, the sin of Simony, was condemned so often by church councils that it indicates a widespread abuse which needed to be corrected over and over again.

Old Testament precedents can be cited for the principle that clergy should not be self-selecting, but instead be diffident in accepting ordination. Moses was sure that the Lord had mistaken him for his brother Aaron who was a much more fluent speaker (Exod. 4:10–17). Gideon knew well enough that he was altogether unsuited to be the liberator of Israel (Judges 6:15). In the case of David, not only his family but even the prophet Samuel were certain God had made a mistake this time (1 Sam. 16:11). The prophet Jeremiah flatly refused the ministry, pleading his youth and lack of experience, only to find that he could not escape, could not avoid the task laid on him. 'If I say, "I will not mention him, or speak any more in his name," there is in my heart as it were a burning fire, shut up in my bones' (Jer. 20:9, cf. Jer. 1:6).

The other two uses in the Greek Old Testament of the word Κλῆρος and the concept of a lottery were much more commonly applied to the priesthood. In choosing the word for that passage of Acts (1:15–26), St Luke calls our attention to these Old Testament roots, to demonstrate that already before Pentecost the priesthood of the New Covenant stands in a true succession to that of the Old. The repeated metaphor in Scripture is of the lottery as the means of distributing property. The Hebrew words חֵלֶק (*heleq*) for 'lot', and נַחֲלָה (*nahalah*) for 'portion' are frequently found together. When the world was created, the nations of the earth were allotted to various angels, principalities and powers, but Israel was the Lord's own lot (cf. Psalms 32:12; 134:4), just as of all the days of the week, the Sabbath is allotted to the Lord as his portion. Because one portion, one lot, belongs to the Lord, the rest share in a reflection of his holiness: the whole world is made holy, because one nation, one people has been chosen as the Lord's own lot. 'In you all the nations of the earth will bless themselves' (Gen. 12:3; 28:14). Then within Israel, the tribe of Levi is allotted to the Lord, and within the tribe of Levi the family of Aaron. A recurrent theme throughout the Scriptures is that of one portion being selected and made holy, so that the remainder is in turn made holy. The tithes and the first-fruits of the produce of the Land are made over to God, so that the entire produce, the whole Land, becomes holy. This is the root meaning of sacrifice: a sample consecrated to God so that the remainder may become holy. The priesthood, therefore, is a sacrificial portion taken from the people and made over specifically to God, so that the whole people are sanctified.

This idea did not change in the New Testament: the use of the word Κλῆρος for the Christian ministry indicates that the priesthood of the New Covenant is consecrated to God in the same special way, in order that the entire Church may become the people of God. In his first Epistle, St Peter calls the Church a 'priestly people', because the priesthood exists within her (cf. 1 Peter 2:9). In this he is quoting the Torah (Exod. 19:6), where the Lord refers to all Israel as 'priestly'. Neither Moses nor Peter understood by this that all the people were equally priests: long chapters of Exodus (28–9) and the other books of the Law demonstrate how only one family was selected and set aside to be priests, and their priesthood sanctified the whole nation, while others usurped the priesthood at their peril. The priesthood is necessary to the Church, because without that consecrated portion or lot, the holiness of God cannot be diffused throughout the remainder of the Church. There is therefore a responsibility on the priesthood to be holy, in order that all God's people may be holy.

The third implication of the word Κλῆρος is that in allotting the Land and its produce to the twelve tribes of Israel, no lot or portion is granted to the tribe of Levi, for the Lord himself is to be their portion (Deut. 10:9). They may live on the offerings of the faithful, but they are to have no inheritance or lands of their own. This too was brought forward and perfected in the priesthood of the New Testament. The priest is to have no inheritance, to leave no posterity. That is why from earliest times the practice of the Church was to call the priest to live without wife or family, to refuse to allow him to store up property to leave to his descendants. The Lord is his portion, and there is no other. The priest is dependent only on what comes from the people, whether for good or ill, for plenty or want. 'I know how to be poor', says St Paul, 'and I know how to be rich too' (Phil. 4:12). At the beginning of the Acts of the Apostles we find that the Apostles were all given great respect, and that people came willingly to offer them the proceeds of the sale of their property (Acts 2:44–7, 4:33–7). But it was not long before the same people were hurling stones at the Apostles, and they were flung into prison, while St Paul had to travel all over the eastern Mediterranean to raise funds to relieve their poverty.

It is this third meaning of the concept of 'clergy', the ideal of poverty or community of possessions, that was to be the major conscious driving force behind the many attempts and experiments in the common life of the clergy. Very early evidence for some sort of common fund for the Church in general is found in Justin and Tertullian, but this is not specifically for the clergy; it is a fund (*arca*) to which all contribute absolutely freely, and which is used for the relief of the poor.[2] The Apostolic Canons, of uncertain age but certainly pre-Constantinian, require a bishop to keep his property quite distinct from the collective property of the Church so that on his death neither his family nor the Church might be defrauded of their just inheritance.[3] It was a commonplace of church legislation from the earliest times to prohibit the clergy from being entangled in secular business. For example, the Apostolic Constitutions say of a bishop that 'he must not be involved in the commerce of life' (μὴ τοῖς βίου πραγματείας συμπεπλεγμένος).[4] This document also is of uncertain age, but appears to have taken its present form in the third century. An indisputably third-century witness is Cyprian, who writes that 'those who are occupied with divine and spiritual matters should not be entangled in worldly troubles and ties'.[5] To support the clergy, some sort of common fund for their food and clothing was therefore necessary. It would need to be entrusted to someone to administer it for them, as in the case of Rogation, to whom Cyprian writes enclosing a donation from his private funds for the needs of the clergy who have been imprisoned during the recent persecution.

> To assist them if they are in any need of clothing or food (*vestitum vestrum vel ad victum*) I have sent you 250 pounds out of my own funds which I have kept with me, and I will soon send another 250. Also Victor the lector, now a deacon, who is with me, has sent you 175 pounds.

This also makes it obvious that individual clerics, whether lector, deacon or bishop, were entitled to have their own funds (*sumpticulis propriis*).⁶ The common fund was distributed in the form of a monthly stipend (*divisio mensurna*), as shown by the note that subdeacons and acolytes who had lapsed during the persecution were not to receive their stipends until Cyprian had time to deal with them personally.⁷

Minor Clergy

A fruitful area of confusion has been the extraordinary collective amnesia that seems to have overtaken the Catholic Church on the subject of the minor orders. Those in minor orders were never bound by the same obligations as those in major orders; in particular they were never prohibited from marriage. When evidence is cited for 'married clerics', or for clerics employed in secular work, if the clerics in question are only in minor orders, it is quite irrelevant to any discussion of married priests or 'worker priests'. In discussing the development of church discipline, it is vital to keep the distinction in mind. Minor orders were only suspended in the West in 1973, and until the Council of Trent minor clerics were still commonly found in the Church at large. Throughout the Middle Ages, it was clerics in minor orders, married and living in ordinary homes, who served as civil servants and secretaries, so that the English derivative word 'clerk' came to mean what it still does. The distinctive hair style of the clergy, the 'tonsure', acted as a visible sign of belonging to the clerical state, and a ceremony of conferring the first tonsure became the moment marking transition to that state. (After 1973 the tonsure was abolished, and the clerical state deemed to begin only with the diaconate.)

The distinction between 'minor' and 'major' clerics and orders is found from the very beginning. For a long time the major orders were defined as those of deacons, priests and bishops, all of which titles are found in Scripture, although many authors repeat St Jerome's observation that priests and bishops were originally alternative titles for the same persons. In his commentary on the Epistle to Titus, he writes that a 'presbyter is the same thing as a bishop', and further on, 'at that time they used to call the same men "bishops" as those they called "presbyters"'.⁸ That passage was extraordinarily influential, and established the substantial identity of priest and bishop until the mid twentieth century. The deacons were specifically the servants of the bishop, which may explain why they were comparatively few in number at certain periods. The first epistle of Clement, generally accepted as a genuine document of the late first century, speaks of a distinctive ministerial class, using as a metaphor the need for officers in an army. (§37) He seems to speak of all three grades of Order, in drawing a parallel to the Old Testament ministry in which 'specific liturgical duties are appointed for the high priest, to the priests a specific place is assigned, and specific duties (διακόνιαι) to the levites.' (§40) The existence of bishops and deacons ('επισκόπων και διακόνων) he concludes, is nothing new but has been the practice from the beginning. (§42)[9] The letters of Ignatius also speak of the collaboration of priests around their bishop.[10]

Minor orders emerged gradually, developing out of the diaconate: hence their present occlusion can be interpreted as their re-absorption into the diaconate. The number and sequence of minor orders emerged between the third and sixth centuries. The Apostolic Constitutions define major orders as bishops, priests and deacons, and minor orders as cantors, lectors and porters.[11] By 397 the third Council of Carthage defines lectors, psalmists and porters as the minor clerics, though the fourth council in 398 speaks of ordaining subdeacons, acolytes, exorcists, lectors and porters, but explicitly not psalmists.[12] By the mid fifth century subdeacons crossed over to the status of a major order. The final sequence seems to have been well established by the end of the fifth century, with the four minor orders of porter, lector, exorcist and acolyte, and the three major orders of subdeacons, deacons and priests, while bishops were being recognized only as expanded priests, not an order in their own right. Although Isidore of Seville (560–636) still includes psalmists in his 'Ecclesiastical Offices', he notes that they are not ordained by a bishop but can be appointed by an ordinary priest.[13]

The traditional sequence was canonized at the Council of Trent, which defines the sacrament of Order as consisting in various grades so that those 'who are already marked with the clerical tonsure ascend through the minor to the major'. The Council recognizes that the order of subdeacon is considered major by some early writers, and minor by others, and lists the four minor orders in sequence. When it comes to the formal Canons of the Council, the decree is 'If anyone were to say that apart from the priesthood there are in the Catholic Church no other orders, both major and minor, by which one ascends towards the priesthood as if by a succession of steps, let him be anathema.'[14] All this was thrown into confusion in the late twentieth century, when it came to be taken for granted that the only grades of order were bishops, priests and deacons, and the subdiaconate together with the minor orders were virtually forgotten. No authoritative decree of any council lies behind this new definition of orders, and the suspension of the minor orders was only done in a *motu proprio*, on the initiative of the liturgical Consilium, not as a definitive act of papal supremacy.[15] The decrees of Trent are therefore still valid, as is shown by the continued existence of the subdiaconate and minor orders in the eastern Rites, and the 'extraordinary use' of the Roman Rite. This confusion awaits resolution at some future date.

The minor orders were certainly seen as stages on the way to the priesthood, even though it was recognized that many would never advance beyond any particular stage. Pope Siriacus (385–98) writes to his clergy setting out the normal process of advancement through holy orders. One vowed to the Church from infancy should be baptized and serve as lector until the age of puberty. From then until the age of thirty he may serve as acolyte and subdeacon, as long as he remains content with the wife whom he married as a virgin, and with a priest's blessing. At thirty, if he undertakes to become continent, he may be ordained deacon, and five years later priest. If of worthy life he could be a bishop ten years after that. Those who come late to the clerical state must wait two years before being ordained acolyte and subdeacon, and five years before the diaconate.[16] A very similar curriculum is proposed by the late fourth-century Councils of Carthage, and by Pope Zosimus in 417. Those ordained lector in childhood are to be ordained in turn as exorcist and acolyte, and at the age of twenty subdeacon; five years later deacon, five years again priest. Orders are not to be omitted but each one exercised for the proper time. 'Late vocations' are to serve five years as lector and exorcist, and four years as acolyte and subdeacon before the diaconate.[17] It is noticeable that these orders go in pairs, whether meaning that these older men were ordained to two together, or that the orders were not yet quite distinct.

A little later we hear that all minor clerics were required at the age of puberty to make a choice: either they should marry at once, or undertake a celibate life, in which case alone they could proceed to the subdiaconate at the age of twenty.[18] Those who married were still clerics, with certain responsibilities as well as certain privileges. It is probable that many lectors or acolytes at the age of puberty did choose not to proceed further in the clerical career, and would have lived with their wives and families in the secular world. However certain obligations remained; the Fourth Council of Carthage restricts the means by which minor clerics may gain their living to handcraft or agriculture, and requires that all should learn to read.[19] In later centuries they were certainly able to find ready employment as secretaries in royal, noble or even commercial houses. Even late in the Middle Ages we still hear of these married minor clerks, who are instructed to retain clerical dress and tonsure if they wish to retain the privileges of the clerical state.[20]

Minor clerics were often extremely young: a boy could be ordained lector as soon as he was able to read. Ambrose speaks of a child lector (*lectoris parvuli*),[21] and as we have seen Popes Siriacus and Zosimus consider it to be routine to ordain children to this office. In general these clerics were the schoolboys and adolescents who are frequently referred to in the various monastic and canonical Rules (e.g. IC 135). These young lectors were instructed by priests, and schools were established, presided over by an official known as the *Primicerius lectorum*.[22] This title was already claimed by St Pollio or Pullio, martyred in AD 304; when interrogated by the prefect, Probus, as to his rank. Probus asked 'which lectors?', and Pullio answered 'those who are accustomed to read divine eloquence to the people'.[23] Schools for lectors, which developed into song schools, became common throughout the Church, and survive in the form of cathedral schools today. Usually they were integrated into the clergy residences, though at different times different approaches prevailed, whether the senior were to sleep in the same dormitories as the juniors to maintain order, or should be kept strictly apart from them. At Rome there is evidence for communal clergy houses as early as the third century, when each *titulus* had to have at least one lector. Pope Cornelius speaks of forty-six priests in the city of Rome, supported by seven deacons, seven subdeacons, forty-two acolytes, and fifty-two exorcists, lectors and porters.[24] At Ravenna in the late fifth century there was a separate building for the minor clerics attached to the *episcopium*, the residence of the bishop. In 441 the Council of Orange required candidates for ordination to live with the bishop beforehand.[25]

To sum up, then; those in minor orders were never bound by any obligation of celibacy; indeed we have seen they were obliged to marry on reaching the appropriate age, unless they made a conscious and deliberate choice of celibacy. Such 'fast-track' ordinands were naturally expected to live lives of chastity. On reaching mature age, the married minor clerics could make the choice of separating from their wives and seeking major orders, possibly at a comparatively advanced age when their children were already independent in the world. This might mean that they could be as old as thirty, after fifteen years of marriage, and after their children had left home at the age of seven to become pages at Court, or minor clerics in their fathers' footsteps.

Clerical Continence

All this leads to the great question of clerical continence, often confused with celibacy. This was the second major force contributing to the ideal of community life, although in the earlier centuries it was not so much debated. The full history of clerical continence remains to be written; almost everything published on the subject has as a subtext the present controversy over celibacy in the Western Church, and evidence is selected and arranged accordingly. Confusion often arises through ignorance of the existence of minor clerics, who could perfectly lawfully marry and beget children, as well as because of confusion about the meaning of 'continence', which merely meant that married men must abstain from their wives after major orders. They did not dismiss their wives, or in any way pretend they had never been married, and they were expected to keep an eye on the children they had begotten before ordination, so that there was no scandal in meeting the wife and children of a priest or bishop, unless perchance the children were too young.

A number of recent studies have established beyond any reasonable doubt that from the late fourth century onwards the universal discipline of the Church, both in east and west, was for married men to separate from their wives on ordination to the diaconate (or later from the subdiaconate), and to live lives of continence.[26] It remains controversial how much earlier this discipline was observed. There is no clear positive evidence from before Constantine that it was acceptable for those in major orders to marry and beget children, nor is there any indisputable evidence against. Two key texts cited by the two sides both refer to the early fourth century. On the celibate side is the decree of the Council of Elvira, dated to AD 305, that 'Bishops, priests, and deacons, and all clerics holding office (*positis in ministerio*), are to abstain from their wives and not to beget children: anyone who disobeys is to be exterminated (*exterminetur*) from the honour of the clerical state.'[27] On the uxorious side is the frequently quoted story told by Socrates, writing in the *fifth* century, to the effect that a certain bishop Paphnutius accused the Council of Nicaea of introducing continence as a new discipline, and persuaded the council not to pass a similar canon against the marriage of major clerics.[28] The authenticity of both stories has been challenged. The canons of Elvira have been argued to date from much later in the fourth century, and the story of Paphnutius is implausible because of a total lack of contemporary evidence, including the fact that no bishop of that name appears in the list of Fathers at Nicaea. The idea that Abba Paphnutius, the 'Aurochs of Scete' whom we meet in Cassian could have intervened decisively in a council held in his early childhood is simply absurd.[29] For our purposes we may leave the two pieces of evidence to cancel each other out. Where there can be no doubt is that the discipline of clerical continence was in force by the end of the fourth century, and moreover at that period it was believed to be of apostolic origin. Given the fondness of fourth-century controversialists for accusing each other of innovating, the mere fact that no one accused any one else of having introduced continence as a novelty proves that there was no memory of any other discipline.

St Ambrose, in his book on the ministry of around 391, is in no doubt that a deacon, and therefore *a fortiori* a priest or bishop, must abstain from conjugal relations. He is aware that in certain remote regions (*abditioribus locis*) there are some who argue that the Old Testament permitted levites and priests to beget children, as long as they leave two or three days before offering the Sacrifice, but Ambrose considers that the New Testament demands a higher standard.[30] In a letter of about five years later he responds to an objector who has quoted St Paul about a bishop's one wife and well-educated children (1 Tim. 3:1-4), saying simply that the Apostle does not say he may beget children after consecration, only that he must still look after them.[31] His arguments may be weak, but he clearly believed the continence of the clergy to be an existing and long-standing obligation. His contemporary Pope Siriacus (385-98) also cites the parallel with Old Testament priests, but completes the argument by pointing out that they only served in the Temple for limited periods, whereas now 'All priests and levites are bound by an unbreakable law, that from the day of our ordination we should preserve our hearts and bodies in soberness and modesty, so that at all times we may please our God in these sacrifices which we offer every day.' He concludes by saying that transgressors will be degraded from their office. Further on in the same letter he also decrees the laicisation of even minor clerics who marry widows or who marry for a second time. The same point about daily offering is also made in a subsequent letter. Pope Siriacus is thus an interesting early witness to the practice of offering Mass every day, and the fact that it is called a 'sacrifice'.[32]

Earlier evidence is undoubtedly scanty, and there are apparent counter-indications. The Apostolic Constitutions require that deacons, priests and bishops must not marry after ordination, but that those in minor orders, here listed as cantors, lectors and doorkeepers, are free to do so. They do not explicitly say that the married men ordained to the diaconate must in future abstain.[33] One of the Clementine letters, presumably earlier than the fourth century, seems to recommend marriage to young priests to avoid fornication, but then goes on to recommend chastity, 'preserving the bride of Christ in prudence', which sounds like a non-consummated marriage.[34] The Apostolic Canons, one of the sources of the Apostolic Constitutions, actually forbid a bishop, priest or deacon from throwing out his wife on the pretext of piety, and they mention abstinence only in the context of prohibiting it if it is undertaken for the wrong reasons:

> If any bishop, priest or deacon, or anyone in the catalogue of hierarchy, abstain from marriage, flesh or wine, out of disdain rather than for asceticism, forgetting that God created all things very good, and man both male and female, but blasphemously slandering the demiurge, he shall be corrected or deposed and expelled from the church. This also applies to the laity.[35]

This is of course not incompatible with the later discipline, for the Church was always opposed to Gnostic or dualist disparagement of marriage, however often it re-surfaces among Christian writers. What does seem clear is that a cleric was to be 'the husband of one wife' (1 Tim. 3:2) in the sense that they may never marry a widow, and if widowed themselves may never marry again. Moreover the prohibition on marriage after major ordination seems to be ancient; those who wish to marry must do so before the diaconate. Only a few years after the supposed date of Elvira, a council at Neocaesarea in 314 decrees that a priest who marries (after ordination) should be deposed from his rank.[36]

A complication introduced into the situation before Constantine, is that Roman law, from the time of Augustus, made it an obligation on every citizen to be married. (The vestal virgins were an important approved exception to this rule.) The *Lex Papia-Poppeia* (denounced by Tertullian as *vanissima*) restricted the ability of the unmarried to receive gifts or legacies, and preferred the married for senatorial or magistral posts. Caracalla rashly extended to all inhabitants of the Empire the privileges, and therefore the responsibilities, of Roman citizens (*Constitutio Antoniana*, AD 212), which may have begun to cause problems for the clergy. Penalties could be incurred if a freeman lived openly in the city of Rome, or anywhere in the public eye, without a woman. Surely here we see the purpose of the *mulieres subintroductae*, women who shared the homes of the clergy, and would be considered their wives in the sight of the law, but who were not supposed to have marital relationships with them. Naturally such a system was open to misunderstanding, and to abuse. Hence the Council of Nicaea legislates for these *mulieres subintroductae*, that no bishop, priest or deacon, or anyone at all in the clergy, should have a *subintroducta* (συνείσακτον ἔχειν) unless she be his mother, sister, or aunt, who is beyond suspicion.[37] Very obviously this canon is not talking about the wives of higher clergy, obliging them to commit incest! In the event the canon was unnecessary, for Constantine had repealed the Augustan laws against celibacy in 320. Whether this was for any Christian motive is unclear, though twenty years later Eusebius praises him for this action, which freed from the 'threatening terrors of the laws' those who had chosen to be unmarried 'for love of philosophy'.[38]

The practice of unmarried men and women living together, boasting about their ability to remain chaste, is attested only in the context of condemnations, from the time of Ignatius of Antioch onwards. The Nicene canon, about mothers, sisters and aunts beyond reproach, continued to be quoted for centuries to come, to prohibit the settlement of a female servant or 'housekeeper' who might be a temptation to the priest, bishop or deacon. Pope Siriacus includes that canon in his letter to the clergy,[39] and St John Chrysostom amuses himself in a denunciation of those who claim that they allow poor, pretty, young women to live with them out of charity, suggesting that there are doubtless many ugly old women in similar need of charity.[40] The Council of Elvira, if it be genuine, allows a cleric to have living with him only his sister or his virgin daughter, and no woman from outside the family.[41]

After the clear evidence for the discipline of clerical continence in the letters of Ambrose and Siriacus, the tradition continues unbroken. A succession of regional councils repeats the legislation that deacons, priests, and bishops must abstain from their wives after ordination. We may begin by citing a spurious canon attributed to the Council of Arles in 314: it is certainly not that old, but fits in very well towards the end of the century, repeating the position that priests and levites should not cohabit with their wives, for they are occupied every day with their ministry.[42] The First Council of Carthage, AD 394, believes that the discipline is ancient: 'as the apostles taught, and antiquity has preserved, we too should retain the custom that they should abstain from their wives'. It also includes decrees that lectors, on reaching the age of puberty, should be compelled either to marry or to commit themselves to celibacy, and that nuns are prohibited from living with men outside the family.[43]

A rather different view emerges in the First Council of Toledo, AD 400. This implies that the discipline has only been established within recent memory, for it says that deacons may continue to serve even if they have wives, but those who have lived incontinently with them before the new rules were promulgated in Lusitania may never be advanced to the priesthood. Priests who begat sons before it was prohibited may never become bishops. A lector who marries a widow may not be ordained any further, except, perhaps, as a subdeacon, but a subdeacon who remarries is to be degraded to porter or lector.[44] This does give support to the idea that the oft-quoted canon of Elvira may indeed belong much later in the fourth century than usually claimed, and that the 'new rules in Lusitania' may refer to this later meeting at Elvira. The implication is that different rules may have applied in different provinces, and that the Iberian peninsula was out of step with Italy and Africa for a time. In Rome, a letter of Innocent I (402–17) repeats the ruling that priests and levites must not cohabit with their wives because they are occupied in the needs of the daily ministry.[45] The Councils of Telepte (Zella), and Carthage V, in the next two decades, repeat the same rulings.[46]

There are few relevant references from the East. The Cappadocian Fathers were committed to real monasticism, and in that context eschewed marriage altogether. St Basil did write to a priest named Poregorius, reminding him of the canon of Nicaea about '*subintroductae*'.[47] A council at Ctesiphon in Persia in AD 414 decrees that any bishop, priest, deacon, subdeacon, or cleric who lives with a woman is to be rejected, but this goes far beyond any contemporary Western legislation and may be referring to concubines rather than lawful wives.[48]

The discipline of continence was gradually extended to subdeacons. St Leo writes very explicitly, in the year 445, to extend the existing discipline:

> Although those who have not been promoted to the order of clerics may make a free choice to be joined in marriage and beget children, nevertheless to demonstrate the purity of perfect continence, not even subdeacons are permitted carnal intercourse, 'that those who have should be as those who have not' [1 Cor. 7:29], and that those who have not should remain single. If it is right to observe this rule

for that order, which is the fourth from the top, how much more should it be observed in the first, second or third order, so let no one be considered fit for the dignity of a deacon or priest, or the excellence of a bishop, if it is detected that he has not detached himself from the enjoyment of his wife.[49]

The series of conciliar documents continues unbroken. A new theme emerging is that the married higher clergy must not share accommodation with their wives, and should have another male cleric living with them to act as witnesses to their continence. These 'chamberdeacons' or 'chums' became a regular feature particularly for the episcopate, as it became more normal for bishops to be chosen from the knightly or noble classes rather than from clerics who had been educated from infancy for the continent life. This must be the background to the often repeated requirement in the later Rules that clerics living in community should all sleep in one dormitory (e.g. RC 3). In a society where most men slept in common in a great hall, all jumbled up together with the servants and dogs, such a requirement was no hardship and nothing unusual. Only the privilege of separate beds, also mentioned in many rules, would have distinguished the clergy from their lay contemporaries.

At Agdé in AD 506, we read that young married deacons must have separate bedrooms from their wives after their ordination. More importantly, the council insisted that the wives must consent before their husbands could be ordained.[50] In Gerona in AD 517 it was decreed that those married before ordination should live apart from their wives, or if they still share the same house they must have a brother as witness. The unmarried are not to have female servants, unless they have a chum. Their mother or sister may live with them.[51] At Tours in 567 we find that the wives of the clergy took titles reflecting their husbands' dignity. The bishop must treat his wife like a sister, and in order that there be no suspicion, he should have a chum to live with him wherever he is. A bishop who does not have a bishopess (*episcopus episcopam non habentem*) must not be attended by a flock of women. No priest or monk should allow another man to share his bed. Archpriests must have a lector from among their canons as chum. No priest may live with his priestess, nor deacon with his deaconess, nor subdeacon with his subdeaconess.[52] Again the Fourth Council of Toledo (AD 633), requires bishops, priests and levites to have witnesses to their way of life sleeping in the same rooms.[53]

Individual letters of popes, and decrees of local or regional councils, were given worldwide authority by being incorporated into the authoritative collections of canons circulated on papal authority, such as the Dionysio-Hadriana sent to Charlemagne by Hadrian I.[54] Until the end of the first millennium it remained common for married men to be ordained to the diaconate and onwards on the clear understanding that they were no longer to cohabit with their wives. The wives were not repudiated, but enjoyed their status as 'canonesses', eventually forming communities of their own. As long as the children still needed parental supervision, the clergy were obliged to keep an eye on them, and to ensure that they were properly brought up in the faith. The fact that council after council needed to repeat the laws about clerical continence is a clear indication that the rule was not always kept. This is not surprising: however no one in the West seems to have doubted that it was a good rule, and ought to be kept. As is now well-established by Cochini and others, it was the East that broke away from the former common discipline at the controversial Council *in Trullo,* thus perpetuating the existing difference between the eastern and western discipline.[55] Although the West never accepted the decrees of that council, it has never denied the easterners the right to follow their own discipline.

The western practice of requiring continence from previously married ordinands continued as the norm until the early second millennium, when an increasing realization of the sacredness of marriage as a sacrament in its own right, and the importance of marital relationships within that sacrament, led to the present discipline whereby it is a rare exception to allow a married man to be ordained and undertake continence, and nearly all ordinations are conferred on the unmarried or the widowed. In the first half of the twelfth century, Hugh of St Victor was one of the most influential theologians who developed the doctrine of the sacramentality of marriage, against the ascetic tradition of such as Peter Damian. Greater urgency was given to the topic by the Cathar crisis, since one of the central tenets of Catharism was that marriage was utterly evil and that the married could not enter heaven. Against this, Innocent III affirmed the sanctity of marriage, and the sacredness of its consummation. He carried this to the logical conclusion of strongly discouraging married men from leaving their wives in order to undertake a life of continence.[56] The rule of St Francis of 1223 (the *Regula Bollata*) says of potential recruits, 'if they have no wives, or, if they have, and their wives have already entered a monastery, or have, with the authority of the diocesan bishop, given them permission after having made a vow of continence, and if the wives be of such an age that no suspicion may arise concerning them', showing the precautions now taken about married men embracing a life of continence.[57] St Thomas Aquinas failed to complete the relevant part of the *Summa Theologica,* but his views on the subject were collected and systematized in the *Supplementum,* where he affirms the sanctity of the marriage debt, and agrees that it is on the whole wrong to separate from one's wife in order to undertake continence, and that it cannot be done at all unless she freely consents. 'No one can make an offering to God of what belongs to another. Since by the act of consummating a marriage, the body of a man is made the property of his wife, he cannot offer himself to God through a vow of continence, without her consent.'[58]

The Common Life of the Clergy

During the first millennium, the two principles of clerical poverty and clerical chastity were the greatest motives for urging clergy to live in common. The example of the Apostles is regularly quoted on both issues, and legislators for the common life almost invariably indicate that they believe they are restoring the ancient apostolic discipline, which had fallen into disuse in these decadent times. Motives that might be considered much more important in our own time, such as mutual support and encouragement, are not mentioned by any of the early writers.

Chastity was not controversial, but recognized to be in some cases difficult. If major clerics continued to live with their wives, or if they lived independently and unsupervised, there was the continual danger of scandal. This danger could be eliminated if clerics slept together in the dormitory within a securely enclosed building, from which they could emerge in the daytime for their pastoral duties, and to visit their wives and children. Other dangers could be avoided by ensuring that boys were properly supervised, and that everyone was entitled to a separate bed.

Poverty was much more controversial. The ideal of total renunciation of private property was established among monks at a very early date, and was consistently enforced. Extending this to pastoral clergy, however, was difficult, and not everyone agreed that it was necessary or even desirable. In practice even those who were most in favour of renouncing property seem to have been thinking about serious capital rather than personal possessions. Clergy living in common were always allowed to receive and own the necessities of life, *victum et vestitum,* whether in kind or in cash.

(The phrase *victum et vestitum* is not the usual Vulgate translation of 1 Tim. 6:8, but is used by St Cyprian as quoted above, and even by St Jerome.[59]) Capital in the first millennium, and for long after, meant land, including its livestock both 'animate and inanimate' (i.e. serfs and cattle). It was frequently held that individual clerics should not be landowners, and that they should not have the right to bequeath land to their heirs. Cloaks and books, on the other hand, even parchment ones (cf. 2 Tim. 4:13), could be privately owned, and given away or bequeathed to whomsoever the owners wished. In this the clergy were always distinct from the monks, who were prohibited from claiming ownership of anything at all.

Both monks and clerics could, of course, be considerable landowners on a collective basis, and indeed it was virtually essential for the maintenance of any community for there to be a solid endowment in the shape of lands. Such endowments were formally made over to the monastery or community, with a charter of ratification from the local prince, and were thereafter inalienable. At least in theory. The history of the common life of the secular clergy, like that of monasticism, consists of a succession of episodes of rich endowments followed by plunder and confiscation. In effect, communal life is only possible in a reasonably peaceful stable society, where lands are tilled and rents paid regularly. War and civil unrest almost inevitably cause the destruction of communal religious life.

In outlining the course of the various experiments in common life that have been tried, the recurrent theme will be found to be successful and hopeful foundations brought to ruin by invasions, wars, and rapacious lords. The simple answer to the question of why communal life did not survive is often 'Vikings!', but of course there were also internal causes of decay. No system is so perfect that it does not need to be reformed at regular intervals. In particular there was often a tendency of clerics to want to move out of the community and live on their own. However by far the greatest number of failures were caused by outside forces which prevented the communities from receiving the rents on which they depended. That is no reason for not trying again: no precautions can safeguard any way of life against war and revolution, but there is much to be learned from studying the past in order to help establish structures for the future.

In his article on the spirituality of the canon, Jean Chatillon comments aptly:

> All through the ages, numerous bishops, reforming clergy and founders have striven with burning hearts to create a form of

common life which is capable of sustaining and assisting secular clergy to live out their evangelical or apostolical ideals, without in the process transforming them into religious. The history of these attempts would be long in the writing.[60]

It has certainly taken a long time to assemble the material for this book, and a great deal more could still be discovered and incorporated, but there is enough in the following chapters to demonstrate the potential that has existed, and still exists, for community life among the clergy.

Notes

1. Jerome, Epistle 52, to Nepotian, 5; PL 22:531.
2. Justin, *Apologia* I, 67; PG 6:430; Tertullian, *Apologeticus* 39; PL 1:470.
3. Mansi I, c. 37.
4. Apostolic Constitutions II vi; PG 1:601.
5. Cyprian, Epistle 66, to the clergy and people of Furnae; PL 4:409–11.
6. Cyprian, Epistle 6, to Rogation; PL 4:411; cf. also Epistles 36 and 69.
7. Cyprian, Epistle 28, to priests and deacons; PL 4:308–9.
8. Jerome, *Comm. in Titum*, I, 5; PL 26:562–3; see also Epistle 156, to Evangelus, PL 22:1193.
9. I Clement, 37, 40, 42; PG 1:238, 289, 292.
10. Letters of Ignatius, PG 5:643–728.
11 Apostolic Constitutions VI, xvii; PG 1:957.
12. Carthage III (397) cap. xxi; Mansi III, c. 884; Carthage IV (398) cap. ii-x; Mansi III, cc. 950–2.
13. Isidore, *De Ecclesiasticis Officiis*, II, xii; PL 83:792.
14. Council of Trent, *De Sacramento Ordinis*, cap. 3 and canon 2; DS 1765, 1772.
15. Paul VI, apostolic letter *Ministeria Quaedam*, 15 August 1972; in A. Flannery, *Vatican Council II, The Conciliar and post Conciliar Documents* (Leominster, 1981), vol. 1, pp. 427–32. See also A. Bugnini, *The Reform* (sic) *of the Liturgy 1948–1975*, Liturgical Press, Collegeville, 1990, pp. 727–51, for the reasons alleged for suppressing the minor orders.
16. Siriacus, Epistle 1, ix-x; Mansi III, cc. 659–60 = PL 13:1142–3.
17. *Codex canonum Ecclesiae Africanae*, canon xvi; Mansi III, c. 717; Zosimus, Epistle 9, 1–3; Mansi IV cc. 347–8, = PL 20:672–3.
18. Carthage VI (419) canon xvii; Mansi IV c. 427.
19. Carthage IV (397), caps. xliv, xlv; Mansi III, c. 955.
20. Palencia (1388), canon iii; Mansi XXVI, cc. 741–2.
21. Ambrose, *de Excessu Fratris* I, 61; PL 16:1309.
22. Vaison (529); Mansi VIII, c. 726.
23. AA.SS., April III, p. 572.
24. Cited in Eusebius, *Historia Ecclesiae* 6, 43; PG 20:621.
25. Orange I (441), can. viii; Mansi VI, c. 437.
26. See, inter alia, Roman Cholij, *Clerical Celibacy in East and West* (Leominster, Fowler Wright, 1989); Christian Cochini, *The Apostolic Origins of Priestly Celibacy*

(San Francisco, Ignatius, 1990); F. G. C. van Leeuwen-van Sandick, *Die Priestervrouw* (Tegelen, St Petrus Canisiusstichting, 2000); and Stefan Heid, *Celibacy in the Early Church* (San Francisco, Ignatius, 2001).
27. Elvira (305 ?), canon 33; Mansi II, c. 11.
28. Socrates, *Historia Ecclesiastica* I, 11; PL 67:101b-4b.
29. See Cochini, *Apostolic Origins*, pp. 195–200. For the real Paphnutius see Cassian, *Collations* III, 1; PL 49:557–9; for list of bishops at Nicaea, see Mansi II, cc. 692–702.
30. Ambrose, *de Officiis* I, 50, 248; PL 16:98.
31. Ambrose, *Epistolae*, classis I, 63, 62; PL 16:1205.
32. Siriacus, Epistle I vii and xi; PL 13:1139, 1144; Epistle V, viii; PL 13:1160.
33. Apostolic Constitutions VI, 17; PG 1:957.
34. 'Clement' to James, I, 7; Mansi I, c. 116.
35. Apostolic Canons 5, 50; Mansi I, cc. 29, 39.
36. Neocaesarea I (314), tit. I; Mansi II, c. 539.
37. Nicaea I (325), canon 3; Mansi II, c. 669.
38. See Judith Evans Grubbs, *Law and Family in Late Antiquity* (Oxford University Press, 1995), pp. 103–39, 'The Repeal of the Augustan Penalties on Celibacy'.
39. Siriacus, Epistle I, xii; PL 13:1144.
40. Chrysostom, *Adversus eos qui apud se habent virgines subintroductas*; PL 47:495–514, esp. c. 504.
41. Elvira (305 ?), canon 27; Mansi II, c. 10.
42. Arles I (314 ?), tit. xxix; Mansi II, c. 474.
43. Carthage I (394), cap. ii, xvi, lxx; Mansi III, cc. 692–3, 718, 775.
44. Toledo I, ERA 438 (AD 400) cap. i, iii, iv; Mansi III, cc. 998, 999.
45. Innocent I, Epistle II, ix; Mansi III, cc. 1034–5.
46. Telepte (418), canon ix; Mansi IV, c. 381; Carthage V (438), cap. iii; Mansi III, c. 969.
47. Basil, Epistle 55; PG 32:401–4.
48. Ctesiphon (414), canon v; Mansi III, c. 1169.
49. Leo, Epistle IV; Mansi V, cc. 1281–2 = PL 54:672.
50. Agdé (506), canon 16; Mansi VIII, c. 327.
51. Gerona (517), cap. vi; Mansi VIII, c. 549.
52. Tours II (567), canons xii, xiii, xiv, xix; Mansi IX, cc. 795–7.
53. Toledo IV (633), canons 22 and 23; Mansi X, c. 626.
54. Dionysio-Hadriana, Mansi XII, cc. 859–84.
55. See note 26 above.
56. See Olsen, M., 'Body and Sacrament in the Age of Hugh of St Victor', in Olsen, G.W. (ed.), *Christian Marriage, a Historical Study* (New York, Herder & Herder, 2001), pp. 223–7 (Hugh); 229, 241 (Innocent).
57. Second Rule of the Friars Minor, §2, in Fr Paschal Robinson (ed.), *The Writings of St Francis of Assisi* (London, Dent, 1906), p. 65.
58. St Thomas, *Summa Theologica*, Supplement LX, I, respondeo.
59. Cyprian, Epistle 6; PL 4:411; Jerome, *Comm. in Matt.* cc. 34, 59; PL 26:43, 63.
60. J. Chatillon, 'La Spiritualité Chanoniale' in *Saint Chrodegang*, p. 122.

Chapter 2

Before the Council of Nicaea

Apostolic Precedent

All attempts to legislate for a common life of the secular clergy begin by citing the example of the Apostles, and claiming that it is time to restore the primitive discipline of the Church as described in the Acts of the Apostles. Augustinian canons in particular like to date their institute back to the very beginning of the Church. The major study by Eusebio Amort has to admit that not all Christians, and not even all clerics, did in fact undertake to renounce all private property, but maintains that before the fourth century there were communities of clergy who took vows of poverty and owned all things in common.[1] His evidence, however, is not convincing, and depends too much on documents of doubtful authenticity.

Not all that much material survives from before the time of Nicaea, at least not much that is of unquestioned antiquity. The copious and fascinating writings found in the early volumes of Mansi and Galland include a great deal that is certainly much later, at least in its present form. However a considerable proportion of the Clementine literature probably does date from the third or early fourth century, and while it cannot be cited as evidence of the time of St Clement, it will do very well for the immediate pre-Nicene era. Even the material reconstructed in the ninth century, and usually derided as the 'Forged Decretals' may preserve a kernal of authentic tradition, and need not be totally dismissed. Those who transcribed them certainly selected themes that were highly relevant to the circumstances of western Francia in the ninth century, and made no attempt to reproduce the phraseology and style of the second or third centuries, but they probably believed themselves to be reconstructing genuine documents which were now in the last stage of disintegration. Treated with caution, there is no reason why even the Donation of Constantine may not tell us something about the early Church. As Wallace-Hadrill writes, it is 'a Roman forgery in which there may well be elements of truth ... a literary composition by some member of the Lateran staff who knew how to make intelligent use of a much older composition'.[2]

The texts involved are few, and little can be deduced from them, but we must begin by examining the evidence of Scripture. Before the crucifixion we hear that St Peter and the other Apostles left their fishing boats and nets, the tax desk, and everything, to follow Jesus. Our Lord's words to St Peter imply that they had also left 'houses or brothers or sisters or father or mother or children or lands for my name's sake' (Matth. 19:27, 29). Moreover we know that they had a common purse, from the one episode of its being plundered by Judas (John 12:6). St Thomas Aquinas preserved the tradition that Christ lived a life of poverty in this world (S. Th. III, 40, iii), and that the Apostles 'are understood to have vowed what relates to the state of perfection, when they left everything and followed Christ' (S. Th. II-II, 88, iv ad 3). Nevertheless not all the disciples had abandoned their family and property, for Martha and Mary were able to entertain the Lord in their own house, and Joseph of Arimathea could provide an upper room, and a tomb. There were several women who provided for the Apostles out of their own resources, as well as being able to bring the spices for the Lord's burial. What is more, after the Resurrection, St Peter and the sons of Zebedee are able to return to their boats and fish once more (John 21). In leaving their boats, therefore, they had not lost all rights over them, but presumably entrusted them to other members of their extended families or acquaintances.

The famous passages about primitive communism in Jerusalem give us a description of a decisive renunciation of property: everything, we hear, was sold and the money was shared in common. 'All the believers were of one mind, and they held all things in common. They used to sell both their lands and goods, and distributed them to all, in accordance with what anyone might need.' 'Of the multitude of those who believed there was one heart and one soul; not one of them used to say that any of his possessions was his own, but all things were common among them' (Acts 2:44-6; 4:32-35). As it stands, this applies to the entire community of believers, not only to the small inner group of Apostles, the 'clergy', who are elsewhere clearly distinguished from the laity (e.g. in Acts 5:13, where the Apostles met privately in Solomon's Portico, and none of the rest presumed to join them). The sale and sharing of goods was not however compulsory, as illustrated in the story of the married couple Ananias and Sapphira. St Peter rebukes them for lying to the community, in that they pretended the value of the property they had sold was less than it really was, 'but while it remained unsold, did it not remain your own? And after it was sold, was it not at your disposal?' (Acts 5:4). That certainly implies that the renunciation of property was voluntary: they could have kept it if they had chosen; their sin lay in pretending to renounce their property but actually keeping some back in secret. The fact that Barnabas is specifically commended as having sold a piece of land and given the proceeds to the Apostles again implies that this was something exceptional (Acts 4:36–5:11). Even from the key chapters of the Acts of the Apostles, therefore, we must deduce that the idyllic picture of total communism was never more than an ideal.

When converts were numbered in the thousands, as they were from the day of Pentecost onwards, the logistics of administering so large a commune would have been extremely problematical. A significant proportion of the saleable property in Jerusalem would have been on the market all at once, and without a proportionate number of buyers. This of course could explain why St Paul found it necessary to spend so large a part of his ministry fundraising to help the impoverished Jerusalem community (Acts 11:29; cf. Acts 24:17; Rom. 15:26–8; 1 Cor. 16:1–4; 2 Cor. 8:9; Gal. 2:10). In reality it may be more likely that it was only the Apostles themselves who really practised communism to the full, while the ordinary faithful were encouraged to contribute to the common fund, and praised if they did so, but were not compelled. Even among the Apostles, the rapid squandering of capital resources would inevitably lead soon enough to a financial crisis, and it is not surprising that the primitive experiment was obviously of short duration – St Luke refers to it in the past tense as an example of the first fervour. It became a commonplace of late nineteenth-century exegesis to use the communist experiment as proof that the early Christians were obsessed by a vision of the end of the world as expected from day to day. More recent exegetes like C. H. Dodd and George Caird have challenged this interpretation, and seriously questioned whether the early Christians were quite so convinced that the world would end in their lifetime.[3] In any case, improvident dispersal of resources could just as easily be explained by over-confidence in the availability of Providence to look after daily needs.

Whatever the reason, it is clear that after the earliest days the renunciation of all property was not universally practised even by apostles, however much it might remain the ideal. St Paul tells us, with some self-satisfaction, that he earned his own living, and therefore managed his own finances, independently of any collective resources the Church might possess, though he allows that other apostles did, and could, accept a stipend from the Church (1 Cor. 9). St Paul is also concerned to keep hold of his personal possessions, asking anxiously about his books, especially the parchment ones, and about the cloak he left at Troas (2 Tim. 4:13).

In practical terms, while Christians were a persecuted, or barely tolerated, minority, fugitive and concealed, it was not easy to hold and administer any serious quantity of property for the benefit of the clergy or the faithful in general. The church funds we have already mentioned, recorded by Justin and Tertullian, were fed by the Sunday collection, and must have been quickly dispersed among the poor for whom they were principally intended. Large reserves of cash, or the lands and farms necessary to generate a steady revenue, must have been entrusted to one or more named individuals, who could be relied upon to administer it faithfully. They would, of course, be targets during any persecution. The story of St Lawrence, martyred in 258, shows that the government was aware that such reserves of cash did exist, and was determined to find them. After the death of his bishop, Pope Xystus II, St Lawrence took immediate steps to place the money out of the reach of the persecutor: as St Augustine comments, 'He gathered together crowds of poor people, and with loving devotion divided the church fund among them. What a profound and heaven-inspired scheme! That man of the Spirit both assisted those in need, and made it impossible for the persecutor to find what he had given away, because so large a crowd had consumed it.' St Leo adds that he 'concealed the property so that it could not be recovered, by feeding and clothing (*victu atque vestitu*) the innumerable poor'.[4]

The common funds, in any case, were not specifically for the clergy, although the clergy could expect to be supported by them. During the first three centuries it appears that Christians continued to think of the persecution as in some way abnormal for the Church; a phase of testing through which they expected to pass, and which they confidently believed would end one day. Conditions during this phase could not be other than provisional: when the persecution eventually ended they lost no time in establishing the Christian presence in the world on a more permanent basis. They never lost sight of the ideal that property should be held in common, and that individuals should renounce any claim to private property, but long before the end of the persecutions they had become aware that true communism was not practicable on the scale of entire congregations. The ideal was approached by encouraging generosity, so that rich layfolk and rich clerics alike contributed towards the relief of the poor, both clerical and lay, and took responsibility as trustees of the money dedicated to church purposes. The history of the rise of monasticism illustrates the conviction both that poverty was a noble ideal, and also that it was not to be required of everybody.

The Origins of Monasticism

The first monks or hermits were men who made a deliberate decision to cut themselves off from the modern world and withdraw into solitude, without possessions (monk deriving from μόνος 'alone', and hermit from ἐρῆμος 'desert'). The story of St Antony illustrates the gradual process of detachment from property.[5] Born in about 251, he was brought up in a devout but wealthy Christian family of Alexandria. At the age of eighteen to twenty he was left an orphan, with a considerable amount of inherited property, with which he supported his young sister. Coming to church one day, he heard the Gospel passage about the rich young man being read (Matt. 19:21), and understood the text as a personal call to renounce his property and follow Christ. His first reaction was to sell all his lands, and give most of the proceeds to the poor, keeping back sufficient for the needs of himself and his sister. The second call came when he heard the words, 'Do not be anxious about tomorrow' (Matt. 6:34), whereupon he gave away what remained, put his sister into a convent, and devoted himself to an ascetic life, working with his own hands to support himself, and giving all the excess to the poor. He was not, as commonly believed, the first, for he put himself under the direction of 'an old man who had followed the monastic life from his childhood': in other words from the very beginning of the third century. Eventually he moved away from the city, and settled in the desert, where he supported himself, growing his own vegetables. We are not told what work he did, but most later desert monks made palm-frond baskets which they could sell on occasional visits to the city, to provide for their own needs, and those of the poor.

Now this illustrates a number of points. Firstly, during the 'peace of the Church' in the late third century there were already such things as nuns, devout women living a common life and able to take charge of orphaned girls. Secondly, a distinction was already visible between those who followed the Christian faith in an ordinary way, and those who felt called to a closer following of the Lord. There is no hint of condemnation of those who did not follow Antony's example, and his own way of life would have been impossible unless there were good people ready to buy, first his lands, and later his baskets or produce. However the story does not in any way relate to the clergy: Antony was a layman, and remained so, and the monks and hermits who eventually followed him into the desert were also nearly all laymen. By the fourth century, a vocation to voluntary poverty and a life of prayer was widely recognized, but it was not seen as one relevant to the life of clergy, whose ministry was to celebrate the liturgy in the presence of the people. However monasticism was to be decisive in the future development of the Church, and would influence the life of the clergy on many occasions.

Clergy in the first three centuries

St Jerome tells us that under Mark the Evangelist the church in Alexandria still lived in the manner Luke describes, and 'the believers had all in common'.[6] The letters of Ignatius of Antioch, which are genuine witnesses to the practice of the second generation of Christians, speak frequently of the community which should exist between the three orders of clergy, for instance the priests form the 'council of God and the bond of union of the Apostles'. In the letter to Polycarp, he recommends that they should all collaborate, 'fight together, run together, suffer together, sleep together, rise together, as stewards of God, his coadjutors, his ministers'.[7] From such scanty evidence Poggiaspalla concludes that whenever possible the clergy lived together with their bishop around the church, although really it is not until the third or fourth century that there is any clear record of some sort of community living. Among the Clementine materials, for instance, we find the fifth Epistle of Clement recommending the 'common life as necessary for all, and especially those who desire to serve God without blame, and who wish to imitate the life of the Apostles and their disciples'.[8] The Apostolic Canons, as we have seen, require the higher clergy to provide for their wives, and not to repudiate them or drive them away after ordination.[9] This implies that the clergy do have funds with which to provide for them.

An important letter attributed to Urban I (222–30) admits that the full Apostolic Life is no longer being lived by all, but is still practised at least by the clergy:

> You are well aware that hitherto the common life has been in force among good Christians, and still thrives by the grace of God, especially among those who have been chosen as the lot of the Lord, that is the clergy, as we read in the Acts of the Apostles [quoting Acts 2 and 4 as above]. The chief priests, therefore, and the others, and the levites and the remainder of the faithful, saw that it would be more advantageous if their inherited property and land, which they had been selling, were given over to the churches over which the bishops presided; thus from their revenue they would be able to serve the faithful, who practiced the common faith, better and more efficiently, both at present and in times to come, than they would be able to from the proceeds of their sale. Therefore, instead of selling them, they began to make over their estates and lands to the mother churches, and to live off their revenue.[10]

Whatever the degree of authenticity of this text, there is no doubt that it was extremely influential in centuries to come, and later writers hold up Urban I as the first to promote the common life among the clergy. The extent to which the situation envisaged by this letter could really have existed in the third century remains unclear. It seems that it was sometimes possible for Christian churches to hold property as corporations, for in Roman law, the corporate ownership of property was quite normal. Three or more individuals could associate themselves into a *collegium* with a common purpose whose duration was not bounded by the lives of any of its members. It received the quality of a public institution, and was designated as a *corpus*, a corporate body capable of owning property. (This concept survives into modern Canon Law, see 1917 Code, canon 100; 1983 Code, canon 115.) Theoretically, therefore, there would have been no difficulty in incorporating churches as *collegia*, which could legally own the common property of the clergy, the building itself, and any lands or other endowments which provided an income. However, for incorporation as a *collegium*, it was necessary to obtain the consent of the Senate, if in Rome, or of the Emperor's representatives, if in the provinces. As long as the profession of Christianity was considered illicit, such consent could not be obtained, or if obtained inadvertently, could be withdrawn. The result was that common ownership of property was inevitably precarious. Nevertheless there is clear evidence for churches owning property in the third century, in that the Edict of Milan specifically provides for the restoration of such property which had been sequestrated during the early fourth-century persecution, *ad ius corporis eorum, id est ecclesiarum*, 'to their, that is the churches', corporate rights'.[11]

The situation described in the letter attributed to Urban I is therefore perfectly plausible: individual members of local churches could make over their inherited property, lands and buildings, to the ownership of the *Collegium*, and use the revenue for their own support and for the charitable works of the Church. This could apply whether or not individual members retained the actual ownership of any personal property. At least in Rome there were well-organized local churches, *tituli*, with up to four priests, and at least an acolyte and a lector; St Cornelius' catalogue of clergy has already been quoted. Though a church building and its residence might be communally owned, there is still no evidence on the manner in which the clergy shared the house. Nevertheless some sort of communal living seems likely.

It is less likely that there was any sense of obligation for the individual cleric to renounce ownership of property. Cyprian, whose letters are undoubtedly authentic, rather implies the contrary, for as we have already seen, he talks of sending a contribution from his own private income to subsidize a common fund for the support of the clergy, including the minor clerics. He and his deacon Victor were therefore comparatively wealthy men, who had not surrendered all their property, but made a voluntary contribution to the needs of their impoverished fellow clergy. The common fund is committed to a named recipient, Rogation, who is in effect the trustee for the clergy, and there is no mention of a *collegium*. The letters were, of course, written during a time of persecution, when Christian *collegia* might not have been able to exist.[12]

If there is no evidence that third-century clergy were obliged to divest themselves of all property whatsoever, including moveable possessions, in the manner of Saint Antony and the first monks, there are certainly indications that the concept of common ownership found in the Acts of the Apostles was still current among the clergy, though probably less so among the laity. The modification described in the Urban I letter, of retaining the property in common ownership and living off the revenue, rather than disposing of it and squandering the proceeds all at once, is eminently reasonable. Large-scale contributions to a common fund, as described by Cyprian, are certainly an indication that the wealthy felt themselves called upon to help the poor, coming close to the ideal that all wealth should be shared.

The monastic tradition remained suspicious even of commonly owned wealth. Cassian reports how Abba Piamun, the oldest of all the monks of Diolcos (and therefore probably born before the Edict of Milan), described to him and Germanus the gradual decline of the Church from its original communism. He quotes the familiar passages from Acts 2 and 4, and assures them that 'Such, I tell you, was the entire Church, as now only a few can be found living in monasteries. After the death of the Apostles the multitude of believers began to cool.' Since most Christians now considered themselves entitled to 'follow the way of Christ in full possession of their property', the more observant had withdrawn from civic society and moved into the desert to observe true poverty. Even the monks later grew decadent, and began to hold property, at least in common. Abba Piamun is very severe on these false monks, whom he calls Sarabites (possibly a derivative of Sybarites). They are considered utterly detestable, as St Benedict was later to quote, but significantly the places where they lurk are called *collegia*.[13]

Here we see the very beginning of that endless rivalry between the 'religious', those who take vows of poverty, chastity and obedience, and the 'seculars', those who take no vows, but merely keep them. The religious never seem willing to accept that it is lawful for communities of clergy to live together without the total renunciation of personal possessions; the seculars are constantly suspicious of any move to reform them into the semblance of religious. The controversies triggered by Peter Damian in the eleventh century, and Matthew Grabon in the fifteenth, are still stirred up by writers like Poggiaspalla, who roundly asserts that 'Experience has adequately shown that common ownership of property is an indispensable part of the discipline necessary for the common life.'[14] There is a distinction to be drawn between total communism, in which even clothing is owned in common, and the maintenance of a common fund to support a community of priests, who still retain ownership of their personal possessions, and even their inherited property, which they are free to bequeath to the community or not. The 'common life of the secular clergy', to be explored throughout this book, means the latter, and experience has adequately shown that such a life is indeed possible, and has often been very successful.

Notes

1. Amort, *Vetus Disciplina*.
2. See Wallace-Hadrill, *The Frankish Church*, p. 168.
3. See my *People of the Gospel* (Oxford, Family Publications, 2006), p. 147.
4. Augustine, sermon 302; Leo sermon on St Lawrence, both cited in AA.SS. August II, pp. 492–3.
5. See Athanasius, *Life of St Antony*, PG 26:844.
6. Jerome, *De Viris Illustribus* viii; PL 23:624.
7. Ignatius, Trall. 3, PG 5:677; Polycarp 6, PG 5:724.
8. Clement, Epistle 5; Mansi I, c. 143.
9. Apostolic Canons, 5; Mansi I, c. 29.
10. Urban II, Epistle; Mansi I, c. 749.
11. Waltzing, 'Collegia'.
12. Cyprian, Epistle 6; PL 4:411; see also Leclercq, 'Chanoines'.
13. Cassian, *Collations* XVIII, 5, 7, 10; PL 49:1094–5, 1102–8, 1111. Cf. RB 1.
14. Poggiaspalla, *Vita Comune*, p. 1.

Chapter 3

From Nicaea to St Gregory

The Fourth Century

While there may be little evidence for the details of clerical life before the Edict of Milan, and the establishment of Christianity throughout the Empire, we are on much more certain ground after that, largely because so much more of the writings of this period survive. It becomes more possible to distinguish between the monastic and clerical states, even though one influenced the other to a confusing extent. Monasticism thrived in the open country, the 'desert', but there is increasing evidence for a settled community life among urban clergy in the fourth century and later.

True monasticism was very well established in Egypt and Syria, and sources like the letters of St Jerome leave us in no doubt that monks were obliged to renounce all property, and to submit themselves to a life of total obedience to their *abba*, living chastely in seclusion and devoting themselves exclusively to the practice of prayer. Manual labour, while an essential element in primitive monasticism, was only a means to an end, that of purifying the mind. Several of Jerome's letters, those to Nepotian, Paulinus, Oceanus and Rusticus, together with his three brief lives of the hermits Paul, Hilarion and Malchus, give us a clear picture of what he considered to be the proper mode of life for a monk, and were later to be cited as evidence for a rule of life approved by him.[1] The later use of St Jerome's writings in canonical rules for clergy rather obscures the essential difference between monk and cleric. The role of the cleric, as we have already stressed, is to serve the people in a church, and this service is primarily liturgical. 'Pastoral' work in the modern sense of caring for those in need was not the task of the clergy in the early centuries, or indeed for long afterwards: it was the responsibility of the entire Christian community. Clergy were cultic: the minor orders were each defined by their function in the liturgy, the role of the priest was to immolate the sacrifice. Monks were not usually clerics at all. Each monastic community normally had one priest to celebrate Mass, and presumably a deacon or another in training, but such priests were not the monastic superiors. In the fifth-century writings of Cassian we find that a large group of hermits might have only one priest among them, and that even if there was a second priest he was content to serve only as a deacon.[2] The sixth-century Rule of St Benedict makes it clear that the abbot is not normally a priest, and that a priest in the community is entirely subservient to the abbot (RB 60–62).

St Jerome occasionally does mention clerics: he expects them to live a frugal life, for 'those who serve the altar should not drink wine or strong drink', and like monks they should not hold inherited property, but he says nothing of communal living.[3] Unlike monks, priests and bishops should live in cities, for the salvation of others.[4] Monks who aspire to the clerical state should begin by living the monastic life to the full, 'that you may deserve to be a cleric'.[5] On the other hand the letter to Heliodorus seems to be devoted to persuading him not to be a cleric, but a monk instead, for clerics have a heavy responsibility and are bound to be irreproachable: 'If a monk sins, the priest can pray for him, but if a priest sins, who can pray for him?'[6] He takes it for granted that the discipline of continence after ordination goes back to the Apostles,[7] but concedes that because of the scarcity of virgins, men who had formerly been married might have to be accepted for ordination.[8] Priests may live on the funds of the Church, but not luxuriate therein. They should be satisfied with their food and clothing, *victum vestimentumque.*[9]

If we search for evidence of the clerical life, as opposed to monastic life, there is not much to be found in fourth-century sources about the form of communal life, but enough to show that such a life was expected. Some of the Eastern bishops, like Athanasius and Basil, who came from a monastic background, established monasteries in their cities and continued to live as monks, but they cannot be said to have instituted the common life of the secular clergy in any sense. We should not be distracted, as Amort was, by the fact that St Basil uses the word κανόνικος (kanonikos), since it is clear from the context that he means monks living under rule, not 'canons' in the later sense. In writing 'for those canons living in community' (πρὸς τοὺς ἐν κοινωβίῳ κανονικοὺς) he is not talking about priests or clerics at all, but monks with rules of total renunciation of property. Indeed they are not to desire ordination.[10] In the few cases where Basil does mention 'secular' clergy, he does not expect them to renounce property. He commends a priest who earns his own living, but without implying that he lived in community. In a letter describing his building projects, he mentions a clergy house as something separate from his own dwelling, though near the church.[11]

Of the other great Greek Fathers, St Athanasius had very little chance to live at peace in his own city, and there is no direct evidence that he considered a common life desirable for clergy who were not bound by monastic customs. Chrysostom refers to the provision of food and clothing for the clergy who served the altar, but that does not necessarily imply any common life.[12] Gregory of Nazianzen actually left a will, showing that he was entitled to own and dispose of property, though it was to the church of Nazianzen that he left it.[13] Perhaps the most interesting Greek source is the fifth-century historian Sozomen, who speaks of the church in Rinocurura in Egypt, which had been an example of monastic observance in the mid fourth century, an observance which survived up to his own time, for the clergy have 'a common house, a common table, and all other things in common'.[14] Their bishop was a monk, and it was obviously on the monastic model that he instructed his clergy to live, but it is still a clear indication that clerics might be found living the common life.

The first real evidence in the West for a bishop living in common with his clergy is in the life of Eusebius of Vercelli (bishop *c.*340 to 370). St Ambrose, in his letter of 396 to the church at Vercelli, recalls the example of Eusebius, for 'There are two things which appear to be necessary for a bishop, the asceticism of a monastery, and the discipline of the Church. Eusebius, of happy memory, was the first in western lands to put these two different things together, and to observe the monastic rule while living in a city, and to govern a Church under a strict regime of fasting.'[15] Eusebius had received his training as a monk, and during the vicissitudes of the Arian crisis had spent some time in the East, which gave him a chance to learn the ways of eastern monasticism. On appointment as bishop he preserved his monastic way of life, and expected the other clergy of the city to do the same. They are to be real monks, their clerical duties interfering as little as possible with the monastic life. In this, we are told, he was following the example of the great Athanasius himself. The monastic discipline stood him in good stead when he had to witness to the faith as the Arian persecutions reached western Europe. Very little of Eusebius' own writings survive, and nothing directly to the point, but his second letter does express his solidarity with the clergy, 'our most holy priests and deacons, and the other brothers who are with me', and 'our brethren who are with me, that is to say the priests and deacons'.[16]

There is here a danger of confusing the monastic and clerical vocations. It is implied that Eusebius expected all his clergy to live like monks, practising fasting and vigils, and presumably renouncing their right to private property, though nothing is said specifically on this point. What was original was the attempt to live the monastic life within a city. This is rather different from the decision of his younger contemporary St Martin of Tours (bishop 370-97), who chose to continue his monastic life outside the city, in a proper monastery at Marmoutier, governing his diocese from a distance, visiting the city only on Sundays and feasts, just as the desert monks of Egypt travelled to the central church for Mass on such days. Presumably at Tours the other clergy of the diocese remained in the city, and were not expected to join Martin in his rural retreat.[17]

St Ambrose himself, who praises Eusebius for combining the monastic and clerical life, does not seem to have felt drawn to follow his example. In writing to his clergy he certainly encourages them to live in community, but without requiring the renunciation of property. 'Two are better than one, and a threefold rope will not fray ... it is good therefore for one to join with another.'[18] He recommends that clerics should decline invitations to parties, and should refrain from visiting the houses of virgins and widows, 'for we have one house which is large enough for all, and anyone who needs us can find us there'.[19] Clergy are expected to despise material possessions, but not necessarily to give them up: 'If anyone has been ordained to the priesthood or another ministry, and does not wish to be a burden on the Church, he need not give away everything that he has, but let him live respectably in accordance with what his duties require: that does not seem wrong to me.'[20]

Ambrose expects a high standard of his clergy, and that they should be distinct from the laity – his main argument for the prohibition on ordaining those who had been twice married is to make this distinction. 'Otherwise what difference would there be between people and priest, if they are bound by the same rules? The life of a priest should be exceptional, just as his grace is.'[21] As we have already seen, he considers the reason for the rule of perpetual continence among priests of the New Testament to be that they are to serve all year round, priests forever, unlike the Old Testament priests who served only for a month at a time. Nevertheless, like every Christian writer at every age, he believes the men of his own time to be decadent, fallen far below the standard set by the brave days of old. 'In the ranks of the church you will find nothing so scarce as a man who follows the instructions of the fathers.'[22]

Communities where bishops lived with their clergy seem to have been not unusual in northern Italy by the end of the fourth century. We hear that at Aquileia in 374 the clergy 'were considered a choir of the blessed', and Zeno of Verona, an older contemporary of Ambrose, speaks of the 'workers who are with me' implying that his clergy lived around him. Further north, in Trier, excavations suggest that the church of St Maximin was served by a large community of clerics in the second half of the fourth century.[23] The urban monastery that Augustine found already functioning in Milan, and the community of clergy gathered around Ambrose, were well-established precedents for Augustine's later experiments in Africa.

The Fifth Century: St Augustine

Ambrose himself was of course the mentor and inspiration behind Augustine (354–430), that giant figure whose influence stretches over all subsequent church history, for good or ill. In discussing Augustine we must tread carefully, for the status and authenticity of the 'Rule of Saint Augustine' is crucial in the later history of the canonical life, though it has been much debated.

Commentators vary depending on their own background. Augustinian authors are agreed that the Rule of St Augustine codifies the existing practice among clergy, as well as monks, and that it was observed at least in some places at all subsequent periods. In their view, therefore, 'secular' canons, who fail to observe the Augustinian precept of total renunciation of private property, are corrupt. Benedictine authors, on the other hand, tend to doubt the very existence of the Rule, and consider it is not so much that secular canons are corrupt as that they demonstrate a worldly compromise from the very beginning, never matching the example of the true monks. Authors from among the secular clergy prefer to defend the independence of the clerical order, and see all attempts to make them live a community life as an unwarranted imposition of monasticism on the free clergy. Bellarmine (1542–1621), a Jesuit and therefore a sort of regular cleric, seems to have been unsure about whether the 'Rule of Augustine' is genuine at all.[24]

The Rule exists in three forms: the best authenticated is the rule for women, and the masculine version is clearly adapted from the feminine, though whether by Augustine or by a later author (even as late as Benedict of Aniane in the early ninth century) is unclear. The third form, the *Ordo Monasticus*, certainly appears to be later than the time of Augustine, possibly composed by his friend and disciple Alypius. In any case it is intended for a community of unordained monks, not for clergy in holy orders.

None of these texts can be accepted as the rule of life used by Augustine as a bishop, living with his clergy in Hippo, although the subsequent users of the 'Rule' always take it for granted that it was.[25] Negotiating the minefield, we can agree that the text on which the Rule of St Augustine is based is a perfectly genuine letter of the saint, to his sister, giving an outline rule of life for nuns.[26] This letter is quoted in a number of subsequent monastic rules, and is specifically incorporated in the *Concordia Regularum* of Benedict of Aniane.[27] An 'Augustinian' way of life for monks did spread through Africa, and he certainly had an influence on Gallic monastic legislators like Caesarius and Hilary. But all these citations or references to a 'Rule of St Augustine' are specifically applied to monks. At no point before the eleventh century was it cited or used in the context of clergy: whenever earlier writers or legislators refer to Augustine as the founder of the communal life, they do not mean that they had a written text to follow, but only quoted him as an example.[28] They never mention the Rule, but refer instead to his two sermons to the clergy.[29] Although his clergy are not equated with monks, the sermons do contain the implication that at first his clergy took a formal vow of poverty. Later in life Augustine seems to have thought better of this; *muto consilium*, he writes, 'I have changed my mind'. He now permitted them to retain a certain amount of private property, though he still disapproves, and is shocked at a priest who makes a will.[30]

There is no doubt that Augustine did expect some of his clergy to live with him in a quasi-monastic life when he became Bishop of Hippo in 393. In other words, Augustine, like Eusebius and Martin, was continuing the monastic life he had already begun before he was appointed bishop. As soon as he was ordained priest, in Thagaste, he had set up a *monasterium*, and 'began to live with others in the manner of the Apostles'.[31] Here presumably not all the other members of the community were priests, and some may have been lay scholars, like those who had gathered around Augustine back in Cassiciacum. When he became a bishop, he published the two sermons to the clergy as an explanation to his people of why he insisted on his clergy living like this, as if the practice were controversial. He treated country clergy quite differently, for they lived scattered around the villages, but those in training, all the minor clerics, were expected to stay in the city with the bishop. Even among the city clergy, the numbers living in the community were small, out of the five hundred clerics who lived in Carthage at that time. A common life for such a great crowd would have been a very different matter, and Possidius implies they were not properly provided for. Augustine's community consisted of only three priests, seven deacons and one subdeacon, but they had a common house and table, and fed and dressed in common. Nevertheless they were not monks, and were even permitted to eat meat on occasion, and to have wine regularly. Indeed a forfeit of the regular allowance of wine was the usual punishment for misdemeanours. The *Life* by Possidius describes this community as a 'monastery of clergy', *monasterium clericorum*, and makes it clear that the clerics were expected to renounce all private property.[32]

This passage of Possidius was used as the reading at Matins on the feast of St Augustine, and so kept the ideal of 'Apostolic life' before the eyes of subsequent generations. Thus the example of Augustine was to be crucial for centuries to come, and whatever the true status of the Rule of St Augustine, there can be no doubt that Augustinian influence, particularly in the south of France, continued to encourage bishops to live in community with their clergy. St Augustine's own community was of course to be vandalized and extinguished not long after his death in 430.

The Augustinian tradition was brought to Europe by Julianus Pomerius, a native of Mauretania, fleeing before the Vandal invasions. Described as the 'last of the rhetors of Gaul', he taught in Arles, where he may have founded a community, and numbered Caesarius among his pupils. He brought Augustine's works with him, and himself wrote at least four works, of which the only survivor is *De Vita Contemplativa*, long attributed to Prosper of Aquitaine.[33] It is addressed to a bishop, probably Julianus of Carpentras, and is in effect the first pastoral instruction that survives in the West. In this he speaks of how the clergy should combine the contemplative and active lives, making the distinction not so much on the manner of life as on the state of the soul. In the second book he treats of the question of whether the cleric should renounce all property or not. He begins by enquiring whether it is expedient for the Church to possess goods to provide for the community life of the brethren and their support, and concludes that the Church should certainly own property collectively. Far from trying to reduce the Church's holdings, a diligent bishop will seek to increase them, for they are held in trust for the poor. An individual priest may laudably give away all his property, in which case he is entitled to be supported by the Church in a suitably frugal manner. On the other hand, one who retains property, if he do not accept a church stipend, is effectively giving to the poor and is therefore also laudable. However if he has retained his own property it would be sinful to accept any stipend from the Church, for in so doing he is effectively robbing the poor. Pomerius provides for the eventualities both that a priest will be living alone, or that he will be living in community, and that in either case a poor priest may be supported by the Church.[34] In other words Pomerius, like many Christian writers, upholds the principle of 'from each according to his means, to each according to his needs'. He cites with approval the examples of Paulinus and Hilary, who gave up their own property, but strove to increase the common holdings of the Church, as property held in trust for the poor.

These chapters of Pomerius entered the common heritage of the secular clergy, and are quoted directly in the later canonical rules. They are not truly 'Augustinian', since the renunciation of property is optional, but they do provide the basis of what was to emerge as the life of secular canons. The principle of poverty is maintained, for there is to be no extravagance, and the funds of the Church are to be treated as the heritage of the poor. In fact Pomerius addresses the often quoted rebuke that a vow of poverty can absolve one from any further anxieties over money, or any further duties to the poor. Those who have a private income are obliged to live on it rather than to expect a stipend from the Church, and they are still bound by the common obligation to almsgiving.

Exiled African bishops established the common life in their new dioceses, like Gaudiosus of Abitene, and Fulgentius of Cagliari, who each had 'a common table, common cellar, common clothing and likewise reading'.[35] In Italy, St Peter Chrysologus at Ravenna and Paulinus at Nola had common dwelling places, as did Hilary in Arles. Meanwhile in Rome, Gelasius I is credited with instituting 'regular canons' in about 495, and promulgating the common life of the clergy. He is considered the founder of the Canons of the

Lateran, although there is no clear contemporary evidence.[36] He also facilitated the ordination of monks, implying a convergence between the clerical and monastic vocations.[37]

The Sixth Century

Pomerius' pupil Caesarius, Bishop of Arles (503–543), seems to have adopted the same manner of common life with his clergy. He too had been a monk before being called to the episcopate, though he still owned enough property at his death to make a bequest to his sister's nunnery in Arles. It was for these nuns that he wrote his celebrated Rule, which is fully monastic, and not relevant to the life of the clergy. Nevertheless he did encourage some of the clergy to live together in a quasi-monastic community, eating with them in a common refectory, listening to the readings at meals and examining the younger clerics on them. He also followed the practice of having a 'chamber deacon' or 'chum', a young cleric to share his room as a witness to his way of life.[38] Writing to the bishops of Gaul in April 534, he refers to the traditional discipline of the clergy as based on the 'precepts of the 318 bishops', in other words the Council of Nicaea. This was to become a commonplace in later canonical writings, as was the reference to the foolishness of Eli the High Priest in being over-indulgent to his sons, (1 Sam. 1–4) in the same paragraph.[39]

The sixth century was above all the age of Western monastic rules, among which the Rule of St Benedict stands out, effortlessly superior. Benedict unites the eastern and western traditions, consciously influenced by Cassian, and just possibly with some unconscious influence from Augustine. (Despite assertions that Benedict is based on Augustine, there is only one passage where there might be a literary dependence, or a common source, where both draw attention to the fact that an Oratory is by etymology a place of prayer.)[40] Among contemporary rules one was specifically drawn up by a diocesan, Saint Ferreolus, Bishop of Uzès in Occitania, around AD 558, though it is clearly intended for monks in vows, not ordained clerics.[41] Like the other monastic legislators, he draws on earlier sources, including the writings of Cassian and Augustine (though he never refers to his 'Rule'). Private property is strictly forbidden, and the rule of the Abbot is absolute. The day is spent in psalmody, reading and manual work. Of the many monastic rules, the most ferocious is an anonymous one *cujusdam patris*, believed to be of Celtic origin, with unremitting fasts, and quite savage penalties against erring brethren.[42] It is obvious why the Rule of St Benedict, with its wise moderation and flexibility, was to survive when all the others are rightly forgotten. The vexed question of its relationship to the 'Rule of the Master' is, happily, outside the scope of our enquiry.

Those rules were for monks, but at the same period we have evidence for sixth-century bishops and kings introducing the common life among their clergy. Childebert is supposed to have gathered 'clerics who lived a common life' around the tomb of Saint Severinus at Saint-Séverin de Château-Landoin as early as 506.[43] St Frigdian of Lucca (d. 588) fostered the common life, beginning a long tradition of canonical life in that city. Gregory of Tours tells us that Baudin, the sixth Bishop of Tours, 'instituted the canonical table' or common fund, and mentions in passing that Saint Patroclus, when a young clerk in Bourges, was so abstemious that he 'did not come to eat together at the canonical table with the rest of the clerics'.[44] He assumes, therefore, that a common lodging and common meals were a normal part of clergy life. At Trier also the common life and common fund were well established by the time of St Nizier (525–66).[45] Nearby at Longuyon in 634 we hear of a 'monastery or hospice', *monasterium sive xenodochium*, established with sixteen places for poor men, to be served by clerics under an abbot; something similar existed at Tholey at the same period.[46] This form of community, founded specifically to serve the poor and sick, was to become widespread. Saint Valentinian, Bishop of Chur, built a community house by 548, which later grew into the Augustinian Abbey of St Stephen and St Lucius. Excavations suggest that they celebrated the Divine Office in common grouped around a sarcophagus which was used as an offertory table. Here and elsewhere in the Alpine region there seem to have been several churches within one enclosure, used for different parts of the Office.[47] The convergence of clerical and monastic life in Gaul is illustrated by the foundation of Agaunum under King Sigismund of Burgundy in the early sixth century, where the ceaseless round of psalmody and manual labour was somehow combined with the public celebration of the Mass and sacraments.

Canonical Legislation after Nicaea

By referring to the Council of Nicaea, Caesarius draws our attention to the ever increasing body of legislation, the *canones* passed by successive Church Councils, as well as the decisions incorporated in decrees from the popes, known as *decretals*. The canons of Nicaea were effectively the earliest known, (until the emergence of the Isidorean Decretals in the ninth century) and are always quoted at the head of the whole sequence. There are very many canons relating to the clerical life, particularly to the obligation of continence, but comparatively few genuine ones referring to the common life, which can be found in the pages of Mansi.

The famous Third Canon of Nicaea, which prohibits priests from sharing their homes with women other than mothers, sisters or aunts, effectively assumes they will not be living in community, since the sister of one priest would naturally be an occasion of scandal to all the others.[48] However the existence of a common fund for the support of the clergy is reasonably well attested in canonical legislation. A decree attributed to a Council of Rome in AD 324, under Pope Silvester I, orders the division of revenue into four parts, for the bishop, the other clergy, the poor, and church maintenance.[49] However unreliable this particular document is, the principle was available for Pope Gelasius I to quote at the end of the century, and had become commonplace by the time of St Gregory two centuries later.[50] The same Pope Silvester is reported to have subsidised poor clergy with rich ones.[51]

By the very beginning of the fifth century the idea was already current that clergy living according to the canons, *canonici*, might be indistinguishable from monks: Toledo I in 400 urges them to make a clear distinction, *vel veri monachi sint, vel veri canonici*.[52] The contemporary synod of Ctesiphon, at the opposite end of Christendom, urges priests, deacons and subdeacons to have their own refectory and not to intrude on the food being served to the poor. The clergy are not to take food out of the refectory. Here is the opposite problem, of the clergy being assimilated to the people they serve, but the legislation presupposes an organized communal life.[53] The same is attested by the Syrian canons of 405, which require those supported by the Church to live together in the bishop's residence, *in domo*, under the authority of a *majordomus*, and to eat together in the refectory.[54] In 436 the Fourth Council of Carthage says that while the bishop should sit in a higher place in church, he should remember when he is at home that he is truly a colleague of the priests.[55] The Council of Orange in 441 decrees that no one may be ordained unless they have lived in the bishop's house for a period, so that it has now become normative for the bishop to share his house with the ordinands, and presumably with some at least of the major clergy of the city.[56] However not all were required to live in community, for a council at Venice in 465 requires all clergy resident in the city to attend Matins, implying that as well as those living in the bishop's house, there were others who would have to come in specially.[57] The same requirement for clergy who lived away from the main community to come back together on occasion is found in the Council of Agdé, over which Caesarius himself had presided: those serving private chapels must attend the cathedral church on great feasts.[58] A similar canon was decreed at Tarragona in 516, calling all diocesan clergy to meet for Mass once a week, and to celebrate Matins and Lauds daily.[59] Similarly a French council in 535 called on country priests to gather in the city and celebrate together with the bishop on major feasts, when the leading citizens should also attend.[60] Many clergy, then, lived in separate houses, or in small communities away from the centre of the diocese, but they were expected to keep closely in touch with the bishop and his community, the *Domus*. There the bishop lived with his senior clergy, and some of those in training, and it was inevitable that the community of the *Domus* came to undertake a legislative role over the diocese.

Not all of those in training were in the central community, however, for we find that the Council of Gerona in Spain expects all priests wherever they live to have a 'witness to chastity' sleeping in the same room, and a council in 529 at Vaison-la-Romaine in what was about to become France states that it is the universal custom in Italy for priests living in their parishes to have junior clerics living with them, who would assist them in the liturgy, and whom they were obliged to educate.[61] The implication is that what was done in Italy was normative, and should be imitated this side of the Alps. At the age of eighteen such minor clerics were to choose whether to marry or not. The same concern for the rights of juniors to choose at eighteen is found in Toledo in 531, which continues that if they decide not to marry they can be ordained subdeacon at twenty, deacon at twenty five and priest at thirty. These canonical ages were to remain the norm for a long period. The council also speaks of the canons running a school 'in the house of the church under the control of the bishop', so here the training of the young ones was obviously envisaged as being in the central community.[62]

Early Merovingian councils already speak of clergy as divided between those who live 'canonically', in communities in cities, and country clerics who live alone and unregulated. The Council of Clermont in 535 mentions the latter as 'those who are not recognized as canonical clergy, either in the city or in parishes, but who live in villages'.⁶³ The Third Council of Orleans in 538 refers to *canonicos clericos* who are to be directly supported by the bishop, as opposed to rural clergy supported by their landlord. The latter must obtain the bishop's approval before appointing a cleric to his private oratory. Continence is now enjoined on subdeacons.⁶⁴ Meeting again at Orleans in 541 the council introduces the word *matricula*, 'register', for it states that the clerics, wherever they come from, should be 'emancipated' at the altar, and their names written in the *matricula*.⁶⁵ This implies that the minor clergy, once enrolled, are supported by the Church. Here is the very beginning of a prebendal system: only those whose names are on the roll are entitled to a share of the provender. The same idea was apparently mentioned at a Synod in Auxerre in 567.⁶⁶

The major motive given for gathering the clergy into a common dwelling appears to be the preservation of chastity. The council at Orleans in 541 requires priests and deacons to live in a common dwelling, and specifically prohibits them from living with their wives.⁶⁷ The Second Council of Tours in 567 applies this also to the country clergy. The archpriest, the head of a small community serving a *vicus* and its surrounding countryside, is to be chaperoned, sharing a house with his clergy, and with a companion even at night. That is why these country clergy must come to town and celebrate with the bishop on major feasts, so that they are regularly under the bishop's eye. The major clergy, who are bound to continence, are strictly regulated in the times at which they may visit their wives, even although the wives, who are also committed to perpetual continence, are still an important part of the Church. All clergy must share a common dormitory under the supervision of an abbot or provost. Moreover the council prohibits the clergy from sleeping in the same beds, so as not to scandalize the laity. The council repeats the rule that bishops in particular should have priests, deacons or minor clerics to share their rooms and bear witness to their continence. The bishop is to live with his clergy in the *domus ecclesiasticus*, and his wife is to live quite separately in her own house; neither she nor her servants is to enter the *Domus*. In the same way, 'if any priest be found with his priestess, any deacon with his deaconess, or a subdeacon with his subdeaconess, they shall be excommunicate for a whole year, and degraded from all clerical functions.'⁶⁸ To this extent, some sort of common life appears to be virtually compulsory. By the end of the sixth century the Third Council of Toledo is able to take it for granted that the clergy are living together, for it decrees that there should always be readings in the refectory.⁶⁹ At the extreme edge of civilization, we hear that St Kentigern of Glasgow had 'a great community living according to the form of the primitive Church' by the year 600.[70]

Throughout the fifth and sixth centuries therefore, the same picture emerges all over Europe; the central city clergy normally lived in community with the bishop, slept in a common dormitory and ate in a common refectory. Other clerics, in charge of subordinate parishes, might well live in separate houses, though always with 'witnesses' to share their rooms, but they had to attend the bishop's church frequently. Country clergy also formed small communities, particularly with boys and youths to be educated and to serve as minor clerics. They too had to come to the city regularly to take part in the celebration of the great festivals with the bishop. Under no circumstances could any priest live completely alone: any household was bound to include servants and retainers of various descriptions as well as the actual clerics, both major and minor. Only married minor clerics, those who chose not to aspire to major orders, could live in their own family homes, but even they were still ranked as clergy and could be expected to attend the bishop's church on great occasions.

Since the bishop's church was the one adjacent to the bishop's house where he lived in community with his clergy, it was known as the 'church of the house', *ecclesia domūs*, from which derives the common word for the bishop's church in Italian (*Duomo*), German (*Domkirche*) and other languages. It is not difficult to imagine the routine of life in these communities. Like most men of their class, they slept in a common dormitory, and rose together to begin the day with prayer. Each priest would celebrate Mass, either in the 'church of the house' or in a nearby church; all would be together for the chanting of the Divine Office. The main meal was taken together, accompanied by readings. Priests responsible for the catechizing of the laity, or administration of the sacraments, would go about their business. Others might study or write, or teach the minor clerics living in the house. At some time, presumably in the afternoon, the married major clergy would call on their wives, and make sure the children were behaving themselves. All were back in the community house by nightfall. The bishop would be in charge, and make all decisions, assisted by a community superior, whom he would appoint. This superior might be called an 'archpriest' or an 'archdeacon', a 'provost' or even an 'abbot'. Presumably from time to time the community would be gathered to listen to the bishop's exhortations and receive his instructions either from him in person, or from the community superior.

The major differences from the way of life in monasteries are the pastoral care of the laity outside the house, and the fact that clergy still retained ownership of their property. The running of the house, its maintenance, and the provision in the refectory, required a common fund, for which an administration was necessary, so some sort of treasurer or bursar must have existed. This fund was already kept separate from the bishop's income. If the rich were expected to contribute to the common fund, the poor were subsidized from it. Apart from that, clerics could spend their money as they pleased. There was obviously a standing temptation for the rich ones to acquire more comfortable lodgings for themselves, which is why the councils repeatedly legislated to encourage them to keep returning to the bishop's church, and to incorporate the minor clerics into their households.[71]

St Gregory the Great

The pattern of common life for the secular clergy was thus well established by the time of St Gregory the Great (Pope 590–604), whose copious letters give us a vivid picture of Church life of the period. He himself appears to have taken inspiration from the apostles to live in common with his clergy, both monks and clerics:

> The most devout monks could be seen in the Pope's company together with the most learned of the clergy, and members of different [religious] professions shared the common life. Thus the Church in the City of Rome under Gregory was such as St Luke says it was under the Apostles, such as Philo says it was in Alexandria under the evangelist Mark.[72]

Many of the same concerns that we have seen in conciliar legislation appear in St Gregory's correspondence – we discover for instance that the rule of continence was in some areas only now being applied to subdeacons, but that those ordained before the new rule were exempted.[73] Many of the letters are concerned with making proper provision of clergy for particular churches: in most cases he expects there to be a 'cardinal priest' (presumably a bishop) and two deacons, with a couple of parochial priests to serve the outstations. Nothing is said specifically about whether they should all live together, though he writes to Agnellus of Rimini asking him to appoint a provost (*praepositus*) to look after the brethren and their dwelling (*cella*) which does look like some sort of communal establishment.[74]

It is the celebrated letters to St Augustine of Canterbury that are most revealing about the relationship between monks and secular clergy in community. Augustine was a monk, as Gregory himself had been, and came accompanied both by monks and by priests, at first simply with a monastic title, 'Augustine, your provost (or prior), whom we wish to make also your abbot'.[75] Once consecrated bishop, of course, Augustine had crossed the divide between monk and cleric. He is then described, in all the commendatory letters, as 'our brother and fellow-bishop'.[76] When Gregory wrote to the missionaries, only Augustine himself and Laurentius were addressed as *presbyteri*, the remainder still being *monachi*. When Augustine wrote to ask how he should live with his clergy, he received a reply that drew attention to his unusual position. The normal rule, writes the pope, is to divide the income into four, one for the bishop's household, one for his clergy (implying that there are two separate funds), one for the poor and one for the maintenance of the church buildings. Augustine, however, being a monk, ought to live in common with his clergy, 'and you should follow the practice of our Fathers in the earliest days of the Church, when none of them said that anything they had was their own, but all things were held in common among them'.[77] In other words, Augustine himself ought to follow the example of Athanasius, Eusebius and Augustine of Hippo, and continue to live as a monk among monks, although the normal practice was by now something different, for as Gregory himself complains, bishops were already becoming entangled in secular affairs, and might often be called away from the community and from their devotional duties.

In making two separate foundations in Canterbury, then, Augustine seems to have gone slightly against the pope's letter. The Cathedral foundation, later Christ Church, seems to have begun as a community of secular priests, and remained so for much of its history, whereas the foundation of St Peter and Paul (later St Augustine's), was monastic from the start. It looks as if Augustine decided to keep up the monastic life outside the city, like St Martin, while leaving the priests and other clerics to form a clerical community within the walls. Later bishops, who were not monks, would have lived at Christ Church among the clergy, not at St Augustine's among the monks. St Bede never refers to Christ Church as a 'monastery' but simply as a *mansio*, unlike St Peter and Paul which was a real monastery.[78]

Meanwhile in Rome, St Gregory lived together with his clergy, and continued the practice of grouping the city clergy into little communities or 'urban monasteries', of which up to sixty were to appear within the next few centuries. Despite the attempts by fifth and sixth-century councils to distinguish monks from canonical clergy, there was a great assimilation of the clerical life to that of the monks, and the inmates of these communities are sometimes called *monachi canonici* as if their status were something in between true contemplative monks and pastoral clergy.[79] St Gregory's own monastic history, and his great interest in promoting the Rule of St Benedict, must have been a major factor in this assimilation. As always, therefore, the strict monks considered life in these urban communities to be terribly lax, whereas the pastoral clergy resented the constrictions of too monastic a model of life.

In reality, this mixed vocation, although admirable in its first fervour, was bound inevitably to lead to a slackening of the monastic side of life under pressure from pastoral concerns. Clergy engaged in serving the sacramental needs of their people have to be available at unpredictable times for the anointing of the sick, for funerals and other sacramental ministries, as well as the predictable round of Mass and the Divine Office. There must always be at least one able to leave the enclosure at night to visit the sick. Outlying areas of the mission need visiting, and bad weather, floods or snowfall must occasionally have made it unavoidable that they stay the night away from the enclosure. Preaching, catechizing, hearing confessions and giving spiritual direction bring priests into constant contact with laymen and women, in a way that militates against the detachment proper to a monk. If the ideal is too closely based on monasticism, tensions must continually arise. As a result we find almost immediately that church councils try to make a clear distinction between the clerical and monastic way of life, and urge priests to make up their minds whether they were monks or clerics.[80]

Since the word *regula* was understood to mean a rule for real monks living in monasteries, the word *regularis* was applied to those living such a monastic life, and the priests, deacons and minor clerics who were true monks and ministered only within the monastery came naturally to be called the 'regular clergy'. A different name was required for clergy who were not monks. They were expected to live in accordance with the *canons* or legislative decrees of church councils, and as a result came to be called canonical clergy or *canonici*. It is unfortunate that in English the clergy themselves are called 'canons', exactly like the decrees they are supposed to observe. To avoid too much confusion, I shall often use the less familiar phrase 'canonical clergy' for them, while dealing with the first millennium. After that the confusion deepens, as only certain senior members of the communities preserved the title *canonicus*, while the members collectively acquired the paradoxical soubriquet of 'secular' clergy. In fact, of course, κανών, *canon* is simply the Greek for *regula*; *regula* the Latin for *canon*. (The suggestion has also been made that canonical clergy are so called because their names were inscribed in a register or *canon*, but there seems to be no early evidence for this, and the Latin word for 'register' is *matricula*, as we have seen.)

Notes
1. Jerome, Epistles 52, 58, 69, and 125; PL 22:527, 540, 690, 1038; *Lives of Hermits*, PL 23:17–60. In the fifteenth century these were spun together to make a 'Rule for Monks'; PL 30:319–92.
2. e.g. Cassian, *Collations* IV, 1; PL 49:585.
3. Jerome, Epistle 52, *Ad Nepotianum;* PL 22:536.
4. Jerome, Epistle 58, *Ad Paulinum;* PL 22:582–3.
5. Jerome, Epistle 125, *Ad Rusticum;* PL 22:1082.
6. Jerome, Epistle 14, *ad Heliodorum*; PL 22:353; cf. *Dialogus adversus Luciferanos*; PL 23:159.
7. Jerome, Epistle 48, *ad Pammachium*, PL 22:493.
8. Jerome, *Adversus Jovinianum* I, 34; PL 23:257.
9. Jerome, *Comm. in Michaeam*, I, iii; PL 25:1182.
10. Basil, *Monastic Constitutions* xviii; PG 31:1381–1427; cf. Amort, *Vetus disciplina*, I, p. 75 sq.
11. Basil, Epistles 81 and 94; PG 32:437 and 488.
12. Chrysostom, *Hom. in Matth.*, 67, cap. 21; PG 58:631–40.
13. Gregory of Nazianzen, *Testament;* PG 37:389–96; cf Amort, *Vetus Disciplina* I, part I, qu. 2.
14. Sozomen, *Hist. Eccles.* 6:31; PG 67:1380.
15. Ambrose, Epistle 63, §66; PL 16:1207.
16. Eusebius, Epistle II, ii, xi; PL 12:949, 954.
17. Severus, *Vita B. Martini*, 10; PL 20:166.
18. Ambrose, Epistle 81; PL 16:1274.
19. Ambrose, *De Officiis Ministrorum* I, 20; PL 16:49–50.
20. Ibid., 30; PL 16:68.
21. Ambrose, Epistle 63 §64; PL 16:1206.
22. Ambrose, *De Officiis Ministrorum* I, 44; PL 16:88.
23. Siegwart, *Chorherren*, p. 22 (Aquileia); Poggiaspalla, *Vita Comune*, p. 37 (Verona); Crusius, *Weltlichen Kollegiatstift*, p. 15 (Trier).
24. R. Bellarminus, 'De Scriptoribus Ecclesiasticis, in Augustinum', in *Opera Omnia*, ed. J. Fèvre (Paris, 1874), XII, p. 395.
25 See Verheijen, *Règle de Saint Augustin*.
26. Augustine, Epistle 211 (109); PL 33:958–65.
27. Benedict of Aniane, *Concordia Regularum*; PL 103:701–1380.

28. Verheijen, *Règle de Saint Augustin*, II, p. 46.
29. Augustine, *Sermones de diversis* 355 and 356 (49 and 50); PL 39:1568–81.
30. Augustine, *Sermo* 355, 3–5; PL 39:1570–1.
31. Possidius, *Vita Augustini*, PL 32:37.
32. Ibid., cc. 54–5.
33. Pomerius, *De Vita Contemplativa*, text in PL 59:411–520; translation and introduction by Sr. Mary Josephine Suelzer, Ancient Christian Writers no. 4, Westminster MD 1947.
34. Pomerius, *De Vita Contemplativa*, Book II, 8–16; Suelzer edn, pp. 72–85.
35. Crusius, *Weltlichen Kollegiatstift*, p. 14; Life of Fulgentius in PL 65:138.
36. Dereine, 'Chanoines', c. 358; cf. Poggiaspalla, *Vita Comune*, p. 62; Dugdale, *Monasticon*, VI, p. 39.
37. Gelasius I, Epistle 9, § 2; Mansi VIII, c. 37.
38. Life of Caesarius, II 6, 31–4; in Klingshirn, *Caesarius of Arles, Life &c*, pp. 45, 58–9.
39. Caesarius, Letter 14b, in Klingshirn, *Caesarius of Arles, Life &c*, p. 112, cf. RC, Preface. See also Klingshirn, *Caesarius of Arles, Making of a Community*, chapter 10 (pp. 273 sq.), for his subsequent influence.
40. RB 52, cf RA 2,2; see also de Vogüé and Neufville, *Règle de Saint-Benoît* I, pp. 34–9.
41. S. Ferreolus, *Regula ad Monachos*; PL 66:959–76.
42. *Regula cujusdam Patris*; PL 66:987–94.
43. Veissière, *Saint Quiriace de Provins*, p. 13.
44. Gregory of Tours, *Historia Francorum*, Lib. X, § 16; PL 71:570 (Baudin); *Vitae Patrum* cap. ix; PL 71:1053 (Patroclus).
45. *Gesta Trevirorum*, MGH Script. VIII, 161.
46. Crusius, *Weltlichen Kollegiatstift*, pp. 41–3.
47. Siegwart, *Chorherren*, pp. 32–5.
48. Nicaea I, 318, canon 3; Mansi II, c. 669.
49. Amort, *Vetus Disciplina* I, part I, qu. 2; Mansi II, cc. 624–5.
50. Gelasius, Epistle 9, para. 27; Mansi VIII, c. 45; Gregory, Epistle XI, 64; PL 77:1184.
51. Amort, *Vetus Disciplina* I, part I, qu. 5.
52. Toledo I, ERA 438 (AD 400); Mansi III, c. 1012.
53. Ctesiphon (*c*. 410) canon 10; Mansi III, c. 1169.
54. Syrian Canons, xviii; Mansi VII, c. 1184.
55. Carthage IV (398), canon xxxv; Mansi III, c. 954.
56. Orange I (441), canon viii; Mansi VI, c. 437.
57. Venice (465), canon xiv; Mansi VII, c. 955.
58. Agdé (506), canon xxi; Mansi VIII, c. 328.
59. Tarragona, ERA 554 (AD 516), canon vii; Mansi VIII, c. 542.
60. Clermont (535), canon xv; Mansi VIII, c. 862.
61. Gerona (517), canon vi; Mansi VIII, c. 547; Vaison (529), canon i; Mansi VIII, c. 726.
62. Toledo II (531), canon i; Mansi VIII, c. 785.
63. Clermont (535), canon xv; Mansi VIII, c. 862.
64. Orleans III (538), canons ii and xi; Mansi IX, cc. 12, 15.

65. Orleans IV (541), canon xiii; Mansi IX, c. 115.
66. Auxerre (567), canon 13, cited in de Clercq, *Législation Religieuse*, II, p. 30.
67. Orleans IV (541), can. xvii; Mansi IX, c. 116.
68. Tours II (567), canons xii-xiv, xix; Mansi IX, cc. 795, 797; cf. also de Clercq, *Législation Religieuse*, I, 41, 93.
69. Toledo III (589), canon vii; Mansi IX, c. 994.
70. AA.SS. Jan. I, p. 817.
71. For example, see the Carolingian legislation described in chapter 5 below.
72. John the Deacon, *Life of Gregory*, II, 12; PL 75:92.
73. Gregory, Epistle IV, 36; PL 77:710.
74. Gregory, Epistle VII, 10; PL 77:864.
75. *Augustino proposito vestro quem et abbatem vobis constituimus*, Gregory, Epistle VI, 51; PL 77:836.
76. *frater et co-episcopus noster*; Gregory Epistle XI, 57–62; PL 77:1176–81.
77. Gregory, Epistle XI, 64; PL 77:1184.
78. See Brooks, *Church of Canterbury*, p. 88–9; Deanesley, 'Familia at Christchurch', pp. 1–13.
79. Schüster, *Sacramentary* III, ch. 2, p. 14.
80. e.g. Toledo I (already mentioned, note 52 above); Ver (755), described in chapter 4 and Carolingian Councils of 813, in chapter 5 below.

Chapter 4

From Gregory to Charlemagne

The Seventh Century

Although detailed evidence is still scarce, it appears that throughout the seventh century clerical life remained much the same as before. A bishop would normally live in his own *familia*, surrounded by the clerics of his household, often with a second establishment for the city clergy, equipped with a school for the young minor clerics in training. All were expected to eat and sleep together, and to celebrate the Divine Office in church. Married minor clerics lived in their own homes in the city, and country priests had their own establishments, with one or more minor clerics living in the priest's house as pupils. Real monks, taking vows of poverty, lived in real monasteries in the countryside, but the urban clerical establishments were commonly called *monasteria,* their superiors often called abbots. It can be very difficult to know what sort of establishment is being referred to in contemporary accounts, and later writers often become hopelessly confused. Some monasteries of vowed monks included priests with a pastoral mission to the people around them, although in strict rural monasteries there need not have been more than one or two priests to provide the sacraments for the other monks. Real monks would undoubtedly have observed the traditional counsels of perfection, and would predominately not have been clerics: real clerics would have been expected to serve the people in the cult and the pulpit, and need not necessarily have practised evangelical poverty. No doubt many of them would have been selected from among married men, and remained in touch with their wives, however faithful they were in observing the law of continence.

True monastic houses followed one of the many rules for monks, of which those of St Benedict and St Columbanus came to predominate. Whichever rule they followed, all professed monks were considered to belong to one 'order', the *ordo monasticus*, as opposed to the *ordo canonicus*. The word *ordo* was still used in a classical way, to signify a recognizable status in society, quite different from the modern use of the word 'order'. To distinguish them from clerical communities, they are sometimes called 'ascetic' monasteries. Without direct evidence, we cannot assume at this period that any particular monastery followed a particular Rule, even though at a later period almost all would come to adopt the Rule of St Benedict.[1]

A peculiarity of Irish church organization was that bishops and priests normally continued to live as monks among monks, and that non-monastic clerics were unknown.[2] Elsewhere the majority of clerics were not monks, and only partially attached to the ideals of poverty and chastity, to judge by continuing conciliar legislation attempting to call them back to a more regular way of life. In England in the seventh century there seem to have been few real monastic houses, but many houses of clerics, living apparently to a reasonably high standard. In Merovingian France we hear of a falling away from high ideals, which must have been precipitated by the troubled times when it was difficult to secure the regular income necessary for stable community life. In Rome, the urban communities of clergy continued in the form established in the time of St Gregory. Rome and Italy went into a period of relative decline, but still remained the administrative centre of the Church, so that visitors from all over Europe could witness the pattern of clerical life there, a model for imitation elsewhere.

England in the Age of Bede

Many communities of clerics were formed in the seventh century in south-eastern England, and have been extensively studied. Those in cities were founded and regulated by the bishops; those in the countryside might be founded by kings, or by local lords, all but independently of the bishops. This could lead to conflicts. It is unfortunate that St Bede, our principal source for the period, disapproved of clerical houses so strongly, as did Dom David Knowles, who sees them as 'merely clerical establishments'.[3] Bede knew what a monastery ought to be like, and was unsympathetic to communities of property-owning clerics, especially when they were founded, and therefore patronized, by laymen. Yet whenever Bede talks about establishing a 'church' he means some sort of community, as opposed to a 'prayer place', *locus oratorii,* which was a chapel or open-air site marked with a cross, to which clergy travelled for occasional liturgies. Such a community was called, to his disgust, a *monasterium,* which was Anglicized as *mynstre.* It has become a useful shorthand to reserve the word 'minster' for a community of clerics, and keep the word 'monastery' for ascetic establishments following a mixture of monastic rules (*regula mixta*), thus introducing a clarity which is not to be found in the original sources.[4]

As we have seen, Christ Church, Canterbury, began as a community of clerics, and the arrival of St Theodore in 667 with the latest Roman practices in mind must have confirmed this status. It was thus distinguished from the contemplative or 'ascetic' house of SS Peter and Paul, which had no pastoral mission. The mission of Augustine began in Kent, and it is here that we first hear of rural communities of clergy. Dover, for instance, was founded around 640 by Eadbald, son of Ethelbert I, as a community of secular priests, though it was called a *monasterium.* It appears that rural minsters were usually constructed and endowed by the local landowner, who was considered responsible for the maintenance of the church which was to serve his people. Several of these 'old minsters' are mentioned by King Wihtred (696–716), in his charter of privileges safeguarding the minsters from lay domination.[5] He therefore confirms Bede's fears that the lay patrons could become too possessive, and seek to treat churches as their personal property. A royal charter was eventually the means of incorporating the rural communities so that they could be independent of lay control, in the same way that the episcopal communities in cities tried to be. Some of these minsters survived into the later Middle Ages as the central churches of groups of parishes, and can still be identified by certain archaic privileges, such as the right to the payment of 'chrism money'. Rural minsters could contain women as well as men: Eadbald's sister Ethelberga founded a double community at Lyminge, called a *basilica* as well as a 'venerable monastery' (*illo venerabile monasterio*). In 741 Cuthberth was named as its 'abbot', but the area under its pastoral care was termed a *diocesis,* at this stage meaning a subordinate part of the bishop's jurisdiction – to add to the confusion the area under the bishop was termed a *paroechia.*[6] Eadbald's daughter Eanswith made a similar foundation in Folkestone, mentioned as a 'nunnery' in around 630. Reculver had a minster for men in 669, while in around 670 both Minster in Sheppey and Minster in Thanet were communities of women with a *familia* of clergy to evangelize the neighbourhood.[7] (The community of nuns at Minster in Thanet, which became Benedictine after the first Danish wars, still survives, after a period of exile in Germany.)

In the neighbouring Kingdom of Sussex, minsters were found all along the coastal strip, from Bosham to Bexhill, leaving the forested interior, the Weald, to the wild men and travelling missioners.[8] Further west, the area that was to become Wessex was first evangelized by St Birinus or Beren, a Lombard from Milan, sent by Pope Honorius to penetrate central England. Excavations in Winchester have revealed the groundplan of the very first church, the 'Old Minster', built in 648, during the lifetime of St Beren under King Ceawlin (645–77). The Milanese influence is obvious, with its precisely ruled squared cross-shape.[9] It would not be surprising, therefore, if the Milanese model of clergy life was also introduced at Winchester, as at Dorchester, the other foundation associated with St Beren.

In the south midlands W. J. Blair and others have established a pattern of church settlement, whereby each minster would be responsible for an area of a radius of no more than two hours' walk from the centre. Thus in the Oxford region, minsters can be detected at Dorchester, Oxford, Bicester, Cropredy, Bampton and Abingdon. Vague traditions of devotion to local saints help to indicate these minsters, the saints probably being in each case the founders or foundresses: Sts Beren, Frideswide, Eadburg, Freomund, Beornwald and Ebbe respectively.[10] From surviving evidence of land tenure and boundaries, the minster pattern has begun to emerge, though direct historical references are few. Only St Beren's arrival at Dorchester in *c.*640, and St Frideswide's foundation in Oxford in *c.*700, have left any literary trace. Beren was a Lombard, but Frideswide was a Saxon, daughter of a petty king. Most of the other putative founders have Saxon names. An intruder is found in the shape of St Diuma, associated with Charlbury, and apparently of Irish origin. He (or she) presumably would have followed the Irish tradition, and established a proper monastic community with obligations of poverty as well as chastity and obedience, with the priest or cleric of the outpost subordinate to the monastic superior. Two models of community life, therefore, could co-exist in the same area at the same time. We find this also in Sussex, where St Wilfred apparently established a community on the Roman model at Selsey, while the Irish monk Dicul was already well established at Bosham nearby.[11]

Further north, we hear of similar foundations by obscure local saints, such as St Osburg who made a foundation in Coventry, and Wlfer in Stone.[12] Many later collegiate churches claimed early Saxon foundations, and in the absence of authentic charters it is impossible to be sure, but undoubtedly there was a comprehensive network of minster parishes covering the settled parts of England by the end of the seventh century. Complaints about excessive lay influence on churches indicate that the prevailing opinion was that all these churches, served by communities, should properly be under the control of local bishops, as indeed were the true ascetic monasteries. In this they differed from the country chapels on private estates, which from the beginning were the property, and the responsibility, of the local landowner. Conciliar legislation often returns to the problem of the solitary priests serving these private chapels, and attempts to integrate them into the minster system.

Throughout southern and central England, then, it is probable that the normal form of Church organization was one based on clerical minsters, enclosing communities of clergy, both major and minor, often with nuns as well, and a sufficiency of servants. The nuns would have devoted themselves to prayer, needlework and writing, the major clerics to preaching and the administration of the sacraments, the minor clerics to study, and the lay servants to the practicalities of daily life. All the indications are that it was the women who dominated, and directed the entire enterprise. In many places the names remembered as foundresses are those of highborn ladies, who fled from arranged marriages to positions of independence and influence as abbesses of minsters.

Bede's description of certain 'monasteries', meaning real ascetic monastic houses, includes the information that the priests of the monastery went out regularly among the people to preach and celebrate the sacraments, including regular confession.[13] St Cuthbert, indeed, often went out of his monastery for up to a month at a time in order to evangelize the populace. This may be very different from the original ideal of a monastery as a place apart, where the monks lived within the enclosure, but Benedictines have never found it difficult to adapt to different circumstances, and there is no reason to doubt that the southern 'monasteries' mentioned by Bede were beginning to follow the Benedictine Rule, just as many of the northern ones followed a more primitive Irish rule, which was also tolerant of monks going out to preach and celebrate the sacraments. Bede had no problem with this, and commends the clergy of St Cuthbert's time because they 'all observed the rule, along with their bishop'.[14] Nevertheless there clearly was a tension between two different ideals: when king Ethelwald of Deira wanted to found a monastery where he himself and his people could go to pray, to hear the word of God and to bury their dead, St Cedd promptly made his foundation in a remote mountain site among thieves and wild beasts, just like any Syrian or Egyptian monastic founder.[15]

Because real monks could have a pastoral or missionary role, it made it difficult to appreciate the value of the communities of unvowed clerics, the 'minsters'. The probability is that many of the 'old minsters' of seventh- and eighth-century England consisted of clerics, who did not consider themselves to be monks, but were often confused with monks by the populace, and compared unfavourably with them by writers such as Bede. Married minor clerics, and major clerics still responsible for the wives they had renounced on ordination, were considered a scandal to those accustomed to real monasticism, whether Irish or Benedictine. If in addition they retained ownership of private property, even only in the form of moveable property, the scandal was compounded. Reformers, therefore, were already at work casting doubts on the whole concept of property-owning clerics living in community.

Seventh-Century Communities outside England

In Ireland and Scotland the older, fully monastic type of community continued to be the norm, although with a pastoral mission unknown to the original monks of the Egyptian desert. Church order consisted of a pattern of monastic centres, in which the abbot (maybe not ordained) would direct the community and have authority even over the bishop. This pattern was spread by the Irish missionaries who entered England from the north. Side by side with the true monks, there were communities of *Celi Dé*, 'people of God', who were not bound by the same vows of poverty, and like clerics elsewhere might have been married men who were supposed to keep apart from their wives after ordination. They had a consistently bad reputation, and were gradually to be reformed out of existence, but it rather looks as if the *Celi Dé* were simply the local form of secular community.[16]

There is no reason to suppose that the pattern was any different on the continent of Europe in the seventh century. In northern Gaul there were non-episcopal communities, rural minsters, where the clergy lived together in a *monasterium*, whereas small country chapels did not have parish status, but had resident clerks 'not reckoned to be canons'. As in the sixth century, we hear they were expected to come to the city for great feasts.[17] St Ouen, *referendarius* to King Dagobert, issued writs on the endowment of St Denis under Bishop Landri as a 'mixed' house of clerics, Martinian monks, and devout paupers, *matricularii*. At Rouen in 640–50 he supported genuine monasteries like Saint-Wandrille. Priests and 'abbots' could pass between the 'clerical' and 'ascetic' life very easily.[18] The superior of either type of house could be styled an 'abbot'. 'Double' communities with both nuns and clerics seem to have existed in Merovingian Francia, and certainly the idea of a community of clerics remained commonplace in Italy. The terms *monachi* and *canonici* were often used interchangeably. A number of seventh-century bishops are said to have promoted the communal life, such as St Amand of Utrecht who founded 'many colleges of canons'.[19] Around 640 Bishop Sindulfo of Vienne lived an 'apostolic life', which was later taken to mean that he followed the Augustinian model, and about 700 Bishop Tetradius of Besançon restored the 'regular discipline' with the help of the Prior of Luxeuil, building a common refectory and dormitory for the canons.[20] St Paul, Bishop of Verdun (632–49) found his church all but destitute, with no clerics to celebrate the Mass and Office: only a rural priest turned up occasionally to perform the Mass 'rapidly and without decency', rushing back home as soon as he had received his stipend. With the help of King Dagobert, Paul succeeded in endowing the church so that the clerical order would serve Divine worship, and the canons could live canonically, in the Church of St Saturninus.[21] Evidence for community life can also be found on inscriptions, such as that to the priest Crescentius at Andernach, which mentions his 'companions in office' (*consortes officii*) who placed the monument to him.[22]

The last Spanish councils continue to legislate for clerical life in much the same way as before. At the Fourth Council of Toledo in 633, existing legislation is repeated about the proper qualifications and age for ordination, and it is made clear that some sort of community life is compulsory. Every bishop must have 'the witness of reputable persons in his bedroom', and priests and deacons likewise must either sleep in the bishop's room, or, 'if their health and age make this impossible, must have witnesses to their life in their own cells'. In the same way, teenage minor clerics 'must all live in the same dormitory, under the authority of a most reputable elder'. Furthermore, if the bishop discovers that any clerics have women living with them illegally, the bishop is to take them away and sell them.[23] The Sixth Council of Toledo speaks about the problem of property: those who receive an income from the Church must make their property over to the Church by means of a *precaria*, a deed of gift.[24] This is not the total renunciation desired by the Augustinians, but the principle already expressed by Pomerius, that no one should become rich at the Church's expense.

In the year 666 the Council of Mérida decreed that every bishop must appoint an Archpriest, to supervise the priests, an Archdeacon to supervise deacons and church property, and a *primiclerus* or *primicerius* to look after those in minor orders. Parish priests, presumably meaning those in country parishes, must choose clerics from the 'family of their church' and educate them, providing them with food and clothing, *victum et vestitum*.[25] The function of these dignitaries is explained by Isidore of Seville, who wrote copiously on the different ranks of clergy, and the offices for which each was responsible. The Archdeacon is in charge of deacons and subdeacons, the Primicerius in charge of acolytes, exorcists, psalmists and lectors, the Treasurer in charge of porters, and the sacristy.[26]

The Eighth Century: the Anglo-Saxon Mission to Germany

The pattern established in the seventh century continued to flourish in England for some generations, during the great age of the Anglo-Saxon Church. Pope Constantine I (708–15) granted privileges to minsters at Woking and Bermondsey, showing that these were minsters of canonical clergy with the cure of souls. They were to pay one third of their revenue to the bishop, who had the right to ordain priests and deacons, and to consecrate the 'abbot' whom the clergy could elect. The bishop also had the duty of visitation, to enquire 'of any faults contrary to the sacred canons', implying that there was no specific rule of life other than the existing decrees or canons of internationally recognized local councils.[27]

The distinction still needed to be drawn between monks and canons, and between clerics under episcopal authority and those living on their own. St Egbert's 'Extracts', compiled in the middle of the eighth century, make it clear that clerics are never to dress like monks, but should have their own distinctive costume, the *colubium* or *cappa*.[28] Although some of the extracts imply that priests commonly lived alone, each priest having his own church, others emphasize the importance of living under rule and canon. Even the isolated priests, the *acephali*, must obey the common rules laid down by the councils of old, especially those on continence after ordination to major orders.[29] Egbert himself is quite clear that the word *canonicus* derives from *canon*, the rules by which the 'canons', that is the 'regular clergy', ought to live. The phrase 'regular clergy' of course here means those who live according to the rules: only later was it to become the preserve of those who followed *monastic* rules. Egbert was Archbishop of York from 732 to 767, and must have made his collection of canonical legislation in the first instance for his own diocese, but it circulated widely in western Europe as a handy compendium of priestly life.

Frequent references can be found in conciliar legislation to the importance placed on living according to the established canons, *canonice*. The Council at Cloveshoe in 747 speaks of 'monasteries of seculars' and urges clerics to live together in such *monasteria*. It also prohibits any superior from aggregating more members than he can support. In 786 another council repeats the common injunction that 'all canons should live canonically'.[30] When we hear of bishops establishing the canonical life, it is always with the implication that they were restoring something well-known, which had fallen into disuse through negligence or war, rather than starting something new.

The policy of using communities of priests, whether under the Rule of St Benedict or not, as centres for evangelizing the surrounding countryside was brought back to the continent of Europe by the Anglo-Saxon missionaries who penetrated Germany in the first half of the eighth century. St Boniface himself was a Benedictine, but obviously never felt bound by any principle of enclosure, as he and his followers travelled widely and organized the Church over a large territory. This freedom to travel was presumably justified by the overriding importance of the mission. It seems also to have been applied to nuns, though his correspondents Eangyth and Bugga still feel slightly uncomfortable about travelling, since 'canons of councils prescribe that everyone shall remain where he has been placed; and where he has taken his vows, there he shall fulfill them before God'.[31] Writing back to England, St Boniface addresses 'canonical clerics' as well as monks, though there is no explicit mention of such canons existing in the German mission field.[32] At the end of his life he refers to the poverty of the missionary priests, 'living near the border of the heathen', and appeals to Pippin, the new king of the Franks, for help. The implication is that they are not living in community, but in isolated stations.[33] Accordingly Boniface, in the statutes he issued in 741, requires all bishops within his jurisdiction to ensure that in every *paroechia* there should be a monastery of monks, living in a regular manner, and also that where the canonical life exists they should live well and canonically.[34]

Community life depends on reasonably stable social conditions, and was therefore less likely to flourish on the Edge of the Wild than in the more settled territories further west. In western Germany, therefore, and along the Rhine, minster communities must have been established in the same way they were in southern England. Rigobert, for instance, the eighth-century Bishop of Reims, established the communal life for his clergy: according to Flodoard, 'He restarted the canonical religion for his clergy, and established an adequate source of supplies, giving them certain lands, and a common fund for their use. He allotted them servants (*famulos*) as well, and their lands, to serve the needs of the canonical clergy.'[35]

Here then we find stable, endowed canonries, giving the community life a more permanent basis. No longer dependent on freewill offerings as they came in, the communities drew a regular income from their lands and the *famuli* who tilled them, in effect feudal serfs. From then until the French Revolution, institutes of common life, like monasteries, were to live on the income from their lands, and were responsible for the wellbeing of the people on the land. Such income might be lost in times of war, plundered in times of anarchy, or depleted in times of famine, but the principle remained unchallenged. Canonical clergy, like monks, might be good or bad landlords, but no one doubted their right to be landlords. It may have taken a long time to become established in different areas, but it is clear that everyone believed that the system was theoretically ideal, and the basic principles of the canonical life were well understood and well known.

Popes Gregory II and Zacharias, in writing to St Boniface, instruct him to divide the revenues into four parts: for the bishop's household, for the clergy, for the poor, and for the maintenance of the church, in exactly the same manner that Gregory the Great had prescribed for St Augustine.[36] As elsewhere, we hear that the clergy are to be provided with food and clothing – it was the lack of provision for clothing that prompted Boniface to appeal to Pippin – and with accommodation. They are to be closely under the supervision and authority of the bishop, however difficult that might be in the vast territories administered by some northern bishops. They are bound by the law of continence after major orders, which they should not receive until the appropriate ages; twenty-five for a deacon and thirty for a priest. Those in minor orders, though married and maintaining their own households, were still to be under the bishop's authority and were expected to lead exemplary lives. No cleric was to be given to frequenting taverns, or attending wild parties. However the crucial point remains that only those who were professed as monks were obliged to renounce all personal property: the clerics who wore the *colubium* or the *cappa* could still own property, in the form of lands and livestock as well as portable personal possessions. Communities established by Boniface included Ohrdruf, Fritzlar, Würzburg, Buraburg, Erfurt and Eichstätt: the two latter have maintained continuous religious life since their foundation in 741–2.[37] At Erfurt a letter of Bishop Lul in 755–6 mentions a number of priests among the first canonical clerics, Denehard, Eamberth, Wienbert, Sigeher and Sigewald, at least two of whom must have been Anglo-Saxons.[38] The same Lul is also claimed as the founder of the community at Bleidenstadt in the Rheinland, which was to survive until 1802.[39] Evidence for community life in Trier is furnished by an eighth-century inscription to Ludubert, who 'handed over all his property to St Peter and made himself a cleric'.[40] Eventually six colleges were to emerge in Trier, as well as a ring of rural houses, with the duties of hospitality to pilgrims and the sick.

While Boniface was working in the East, St Pirmin (d. 758) evangelized southern Germany, in a more monastic style, although as he left few writings we have less idea of his priorities. In his *Scarapsus* he urges all to be contented with their food and clothing, *victum et vestitum*, that familiar phrase.[41] Communities associated with Pirmin were located in Murbach, Strassburg, Basel and Reichenau. Sidonius, a monk of Reichenau, took a number of monks with him when he became Bishop of Konstanz (746–59), forming a community which was to mutate into a canonry in 826. At Strassburg Bishop Hedde (736–60) was a friend and associate of Chrodegang, and his successor Remegius left money to the canons to encourage them to pray for him, implying that they could possess at least some of their own money. The canonical life is mentioned in Basel under Bishops Wala and Baldebert in the 740s.[42]

As an indication of the way of life observed in these Merovingian communities, there survives a single manuscript, dating from *c.*830, in the library at Berne.[43] It preserves a curious text which the editor dated to the early eighth century if not before, written in the most atrocious Latin. 'The reader finds himself plunged into total barbarism, that is to say an epoch when the natural forms of Latin, vowels and consonants alike, dissolve into utter uncertainty.' It consists of extracts for reading in the refectory of a community of clerics, with some prayers. The introduction is clearly derived from the Rule of St Benedict, giving a general tone to the work, but the legislative material is quite unparalleled, either before or since. The community is governed by a *magister* or *princeps*, with authority to command or punish, but he is elected by the others, who form a college of twelve. Each one possesses his own means of subsistence, but owes obedience to the Master. The note of the common life is joy, *laetitia, gaudium,* even *hilaritas,* in the practice of charity, and their principal work is the psalmody of the Divine Office and the celebration of Mass. On feast days they are all entertained to dinner together in the house of one of the members, showing that they did not inhabit a common dormitory, nor had a refectory in common. During the meal there is to be silence for the readings; the bursars (*dispensatores*) are to distribute food to the poor, to orphans and widows. Further legislation covers the illness and burial of any of the brethren.

It concludes with a litany of saints. The latter is what betrays the origin of this document: the French monastic editor was convinced that such atrocious Latin could only come from the Anglo-Saxons,[44] but the selection of saints includes Saints Denis, Germanus, Rémi, Vedast, Amand, and Geneviève, all of Frankish origin, and no English saints are included at all. It is certainly French, and certainly gives the impression of dating from the period before Anglo-Saxon scholars travelled to Aachen to teach the Franks how to write proper Latin. However it has been pointed out that it includes a long quotation from the hymn *Ubi caritas*, which the same editor, Dom Wilmart, himself dated after the year 807.[45] In that case, we have evidence for an isolated Frankish community that had remained untouched by the 'Carolingian renaissance' and oblivious to the influence of the Rule of Chrodegang, preserving an older tradition of community life into the century after the Council of Aachen.

Chrodegang and the Carolingian Reform

By the middle of the eighth century the tradition of a 'canonical' way of life for the clergy, with at least the ideal of that life being lived in common, was well established. It is hardly surprising, therefore, that during the programme of church reform instigated by the newly crowned King Pippin, we should find our first extensive documentary evidence for the common life of the secular clergy, in the rule written by St Chrodegang.

Chrodegang (712–766) was Bishop of Metz, the most important city in Austrasia. (His name is variously spelt Chrodegandus, Hrodegandus, Rodigangus, Rothigandus and, by Pope Stephen II, Drochtegangus). Born in an important noble family, closely related to Pippin, and possibly also to the Merovingian dynasty, he was brought up in the entourage of Charles Martel, and educated in the Benedictine monastery of St Trond, although it does not appear that he was ever a monk. He became *referendarius* to Charles Martel, and Bishop of Metz shortly after Pippin succeeded Charles as Mayor of the Palace, before he acquired the title of King.[46] When Pippin persuaded the pope to depose the last of the Merovingians, and grant him the kingship, Chrodegang was sent to Rome in 753 to meet the Pope, Stephen II, and escort him across the Alps for Pippin's anointing and second coronation at St Denis.

Chrodegang's Roman visit inspired him with the desire to introduce Roman liturgy and chant, and he founded at Metz a school of church music that was to remain famous for centuries. His liturgical reforms are represented by the version of the Gelasian Sacramentary associated with Gellone; his work also extended to the embellishment of his Cathedral of St Stephen. He also promoted Benedictine monasticism, founding an abbey in the cathedral parish dedicated to St Peter, and another in 748 at Gorze, where he was eventually buried, and supporting the Abbey of Lorsch.

At a Synod held in Metz in 753 Chrodegang was evidently responsible for drafting the canons on disciplinary matters, which are clearly in the same inimitable style as his foundation deed for Gorze and his Rule.[47] When St Boniface was martyred in 754, the post of Archbishop of Germany was passed on to St Chrodegang, presumably by Stephen II who was still in Francia. As Archbishop, Chrodegang presided over further reforming councils, including the important synod at Ver in 755. In 756 or 757 he promulgated privileges for the Abbey at Gorze, witnessed by bishops, and 'our brethren of the congregation of St Stephen'. Among these brethren are Anghilram, later to succeed him as Archbishop, and Richerus Wasco, a deacon.[48] In 760–62 he presided at an assembly in Attigny, where forty-four bishops and abbots made a union of prayer (a *Totenbund*) which was originally an Anglo-Saxon practice.[49] There is no evidence of any conflict of interests between Chrodegang and his predecessor Boniface, or his contemporary Pirmin; in general the bishops of the entire region seem to have been conscious of their existence as a confraternity. Nevertheless

Chrodegang began a tradition of close involvement with the monarchy which was to cause difficulties later.

On succeeding to power in 742, Pippin and his brother Carloman were determined to reform the Church in Francia, and in this they were encouraged by the pope. They summoned their first council in 747, attended by both St Boniface and St Chrodegang. In 751 Pippin wrote to the pope asking for an authoritative text of the canons. St Zacharias (741–752) obliged with a selection of canons taken from the collection attributed to Dionysius Exiguus, as a guide to the reforms necessary, and included in his covering letter some recommendations of his own. Among these was a reference to the possibility that bishops and priests might choose to live together under monastic discipline.[50]

It is worth observing that Pippin and Carloman did not imagine that in reforming the Church they were beginning anything radically new, or that they dismissed the previous centuries as wholly barbaric. Church councils had been held regularly under the earlier Merovingian kings, though none had been held since 660, and the concerns for clerical discipline expressed in the Carolingian councils were all addressed by the previous dynasty.[51] By 714 St Beregisius of St Hubert had already established a minster of 'clerics, serving in the canonical order', though the seventeenth-century editors of his life, unable to believe in the existence of secular canons, insisted that these must have been secretly vowed Augustinians, an error which survived into the 2004 edition of the Roman Martyrology.[52] The councils of the 740s encouraged the clergy to live and dress distinctively, and ordered monks and nuns to follow the Rule of St Benedict. There was clearly a need for a parallel Rule for the pastoral clergy.

Chrodegang's authentic Rule (henceforth RC) may well have been written in response to the letter of Pope Zacharias mentioned above, and to Chrodegang's visit to Rome in 753, in which case it is not the result but the cause of the Council of Ver (Verneuil) on 11 July 755, which uses very similar language in its call for a reform of the way of life of the clergy. (Indeed, the fact that RC refers always to the 'bishop', never 'archbishop', could be taken to mean that it was written before the death of Boniface in 754, when Chrodegang became Archbishop.) Like several other councils, Ver asks 'all who are consecrated to God to choose whether they are to live as monks, under a regular order, or under the hand of the bishop in the canonical order'. The council laments that this would be unnecessary if only people observed the canons of the ancient Fathers, in words very similar to those of the prologue to the Rule.⁵³ If only the canons of the 318 Fathers of Nicaea and other councils had been observed! These canons, included in the collection sent by Pope Zacharias, show how successive church councils had legislated for the clergy, urging them to live exemplary lives and work for the evangelization of the people, and gradually becoming more insistent that some form of common life was the best, or the only way to ensure these reforms. The motive was still to a large extent the preservation of chastity, as deacons, priests and bishops who had separated from their wives were again strongly encouraged to share their homes with other clergy as 'witnesses to chastity'.

St Chrodegang wrote in the first instance specifically for the clergy of his own cathedral, St Stephen in Metz. The oldest surviving manuscript appears to be part of the actual Chapter Book of the Canons of Metz, containing not only the Rule but also a Martyrology and Necrology, and a selection of sermons.⁵⁴ The superiors mentioned are the ordinary diocesan officials, archdeacon and primicerius, not offices specifically invented for the community. The earliest manuscripts of the Rule contain frequent references to St Stephen's and the other churches within the *domus*, as well as to the outlying estates from which supplies might be expected, including estates controlled by 'our abbots', the superiors of extra-mural and country churches. This does not mean that Chrodegang did not intend his Rule for a wider audience: by writing a specific example he provided a pattern for others to imitate. In one of the later manuscripts all the specific references to Metz have been omitted; it is doubtless a copy made for some other diocese. Another later manuscript includes additions attributed to Anghilram, who succeeded Chrodegang at Metz: these passages do include the word 'archbishop' (RC 34).

At the first glance it is obvious that Chrodegang drew very heavily on the Rule of St Benedict, which must be considered his primary source. Some chapters are repeated almost in their entirety, and there are few chapters in RC that do not at least echo the language of St Benedict. As he was educated by the monks of St Trond, he must have been familiar with the Rule of St Benedict from childhood, and his two Benedictine foundations show how he valued that Rule in its original form. Like many readers, he was obviously struck by the flexibility of St Benedict's approach, and saw that an adaptation of the Rule could be suitable for his diocesan clergy. Far from confusing clerics and monks, he makes a clear distinction between the two vocations. Otherwise, apart from Scripture, there is little direct borrowing from earlier writings, although existing conciliar legislation is clearly in mind. The only named source is Julianus Pomerius (named as Prosper of Aquitaine). It is perhaps significant that he made absolutely no use of the 'Rule of St Augustine', and there are only very brief echoes of the language of the monastic reformers Gregory the Great and Caesarius.[55]

Work and Prayer

The service of the Church meant, above all, the daily round of the Divine Office. In his Rule for monks, St Benedict legislates for it in detail, calling it, famously, the 'Work of God', *opus Dei*. Well before the time of St Chrodegang it had already become understood that priests also should pray the entire Divine Office. We find Caesarius of Arles instructing his clergy that they should celebrate the Day Hours (Prime, Terce, Sext and None) so that the people may attend, as well as the great night hours, Vigils and Matins, Vespers and Compline, which he assumes they are already celebrating.[56] The eight 'hours' of the Office could well occupy eight hours of time, if they were sung in full, and they can really be seen as the principal work of a cleric's day. The remaining time would be used either in study and manual work within the enclosure, or in pastoral work outside. One of Archbishop Anghilram's additions to the Rule (RC 33) provides for the possibility that the night Vigils might be celebrated in another church of the city as well as the cathedral, but normally one would assume that the Office was sung, and most sacraments celebrated, in the cathedral. The only sacrament specifically mentioned by Chrodegang is Confession, which clergy and laypeople must make twice a year unless there is need to confess more often (RC 14 and 34). The practical care of the poor and the sick, which we might consider to be essentially 'pastoral' work, was still the responsibility of all Christians, not specifically of priests.

The bulk of St Chrodegang's Rule is devoted to what we might consider 'internal' matters, particularly the housing, feeding and disciplining of the clergy. He begins by reminding the clergy of the importance of humility, and of keeping to their order within the community (RC 1-2). On accommodation, Chrodegang insists that the canonical clergy should all sleep together within the enclosure (RC 3). Most are to sleep in the common dormitory, the seniors interspersed with the juniors to keep order. Nevertheless some, with the bishop's permission, can have lodgings (*mansiones*) of their own, still within the walls of the enclosure. In this case they again need the bishop's specific permission to have junior clerics as assistants or servants, and the bishop is to keep a strict eye on their behaviour. Other than members of the community, no other men are to enter the enclosure except occasional guests for meals (leaving their weapons at the door), and workmen as necessary. Women are never allowed in. Minor clerics from outside may come in to serve the older ones, for chapter on Sundays, and for the Office (RC 8).

When the first bell rings for Compline, all the clergy are to return home, in time for the second bell. This is the moment when the enclosure shuts for the night: silence is to be kept, as in a Benedictine house, and no one is to go in or out until after Prime. The exception is that outsiders may come in for Vigils, which is the only opportunity for those locked out to get back in. Clerics who stay out deliberately, or with contrived excuses, are to be punished. Leaving the enclosure at night may only be for 'a reason so compelling that whoever is in charge can explain it to the bishop', presumably visiting those in danger of death (RC 4).

The Night Office is made up of two parts, 'Vigils' and 'Matins'. Vigils begins well after midnight, so that the clergy have had sufficient sleep, for they will not be going back to bed again. The interval between Vigils and Matins is to be used either for reading or meditation: it is to last for as long as it takes to recite forty or fifty psalms (a usual way of measuring time). Then they are to celebrate Prime in the Cathedral of St Stephen (RC 5, cf. RB 8). During the day, the clerics have their duties either in the enclosure or in the city, but when the bell rings for Office, they are to come back to the cathedral if they are near enough. Failing that, they are to celebrate the Office wherever they be (RC 6, RB 50). Chrodegang emphasizes the need for proper reverence and attention during the Office, repeating chapter 19 of the Rule of St Benedict almost verbatim, and adds a special prohibition of carrying clubs or staves into the church unless they are really necessary (RC 7, RB 19).

After Prime all are to return to their lodgings to vest for chapter, and the non-resident ones are also to be 'vested in chasubles and the usual vestments' before they come to Sunday chapter. Senior clergy who have juniors to serve them are to ensure that these juniors have chasubles (RC 3). Chrodegang's clergy are expected to attend chapter daily, if they are resident within the enclosure, and once a week if they are resident outside (RC 8). This is an occasion for instruction, 'to hear the Word of God', and practical administration. A chapter of the Rule is to be read every Monday,

Tuesday, Thursday and Saturday, and suitable homilies on the remaining days. That of course is why the meeting is called 'chapter', and the term 'chapter' thus came to be applied to the corporate body of canonical clergy themselves.

After chapter the clergy are to go to work (RC 9). In a passage drawing heavily on St Benedict, Chrodegang urges the necessity of each cleric to have some occupation, either personal or communal. He also follows St Benedict closely in his provisions for those going on a journey (RC 10, cf. RB 50), on the good zeal which the servants of God should have (RC 11, cf. RB 72), and that it is the duty of the superiors to maintain discipline, so that no one should take it on himself to punish or to defend another (RC 12–13, cf. RB 69–70).

The chapter on confession is important (RC 14), as a witness to the development of this sacrament. After quoting Scriptural and Patristic texts, Chrodegang decrees that each of his clergy must make a sacramental confession at least twice a year, and more often if necessary. He may confess only to the bishop, or to another priest specifically delegated by the bishop: it is strictly forbidden to choose another confessor in the hope that he will be more lenient than the bishop. The almsfolk of the city also are expected to confess twice a year (RC 34). Clergy, including those who are in minor orders, are expected to receive Holy Communion worthily on every Sunday and major feast.

Chrodegang's chapters on serious faults (RC 15–19) incorporate many passages and themes from St Benedict's equivalent chapters (RB 23–28, 43–46), but they have been considerably rewritten and rearranged. He considers it possible that his clerics will be guilty of serious sins and crimes, murder, adultery and burglary not excluded, and provides for a prison sentence, followed by a period of penitential life within the community. He also includes St Benedict's provision that the really incorrigible should be subjected to corporal punishment (RC 17, cf. RB 23). St Benedict is explicit in other contexts that he is thinking of the boys and youths, rather than the senior members of the community here (RB 30 and 45). Chrodegang uses St Benedict's metaphor of the superior as a skilled doctor, treating each patient as an individual with specific problems and needs; 'the medicine should be tempered to the disease, for not even a saintly doctor can cure injuries any other way' (RC 19, cf. RB 28).

From the specific penance imposed on sinners, Chrodegang turns to the collective penitential seasons of the Church's year (RC 20). Lent is to be kept by the clerics as a sort of annual retreat: they should eat sparingly, with only one meal in the day, and always in the refectory with the others. More time is to be devoted to study, and they are not to go out of the enclosure more than necessary. It is forbidden to eat meat at all in Lent, but they are permitted to eat meat on certain days at other times. From Easter until Martinmas they have two meals, but between Pentecost and St John's Day they abstain from meat. After Martinmas comes the second Lent, or extended Advent, lasting until Christmas, when they have one meal a day, without meat. Between Christmas and Lent they have one meal on Mondays, Wednesdays and Fridays, and two on the other days, with meat.

As an afterthought, Chrodegang allows the bishop to moderate the abstention from meat as he may consider best. A further addition, found only in the Vatican MS, is specifically attributed to Archbishop Anghilram, and introduces the Octave of Pentecost as a festal season, a 'second Pasch', when all may eat meat.

Thought of food turns St Chrodegang's attention to the refectory, the rations and the rota of cooks. The refectory is arranged in seven tables, for the clergy in their several degrees, the seventh being for those canonical clergy living out in the city, who come in on Sundays and festivals. All are to arrive on time, and enter together. Grace is said, and silence preserved, as they listen to the readings. Readers and servers may have a morsel to sustain them before the meal, the implication is that they eat their meal after the others have finished. Clerics are not to frequent the refectory other than at meal times, nor take anything out of it. Guests, lay or clerical, may only be admitted with the superior's permission. This provision is explicitly extended to minor clerics who live outside but enter the enclosure to look after the older ones.

The measure of food and drink varies depending on the time of year. Quantities are not specified: they receive 'enough' bread, a 'dish' of pulse, a 'portion' of meat, and another dish (*cibarium*). If the latter be wanting, it is made up with more meat or bacon. On days of abstinence they have a 'portion' of cheese instead of meat, and fish if available. When supplies are short, the bishop is to compensate as best he may. When it comes to drink, the priests are allowed three 'cups' (*calices*) at each meal, the deacons three at dinner and two at supper, the subdeacons two at each meal, the others two at dinner and one at supper. If wine is in short supply, it is to be replaced with beer, and the brethren are not to grumble. Those who abstain from wine are expected to drink beer. This chapter ends with a warning against drunkenness, quoting St Benedict again, with the wistful thought that in an ideal world they would not drink wine at all (RC 23, cf. RB 40). The chapter on the cooks, and how each are to take a turn in the kitchen, follows St Benedict very closely, except that the superiors, the cellarer and the wardens of the three churches within the enclosure are exempted (RC 24, cf. RB 35).

The Rule then turns to the Archdeacon and the Primicerius (RC 25). (The latest manuscript of the RC substitutes *propositus* (provost) for *primicerius*, providing an internal superior for the community, as in IC.) Here there is a major difference from St Benedict, for the latter envisaged his abbots being elected by all the monks, or at least, notoriously, by the wiser among them (RB 64). Moreover he is to consult them, even the youngest, and be guided by their advice (RB 3). Chrodegang's clergy, on the other hand, are governed by officials appointed by the bishop alone, and there is no mechanism for consultation at all. Chrodegang does, however, incorporate a whole paragraph of St Benedict into his text, on the encouragement and admonition of the brethren, as well as one urging prudence and restraint. The bishop himself also has functions to play with regard to the community directly.

The Cellarer is described almost exactly in the same terms as by St Benedict (RC 26, cf. RB 31), as is the Porter (RC 27, cf. RB 66), although Chrodegang gives more practical instructions about locking up the enclosure after Compline and handing the keys to the superior. The chapter on the sick (RC 28) makes similar provisions to those of St Benedict, though there are only very brief quotations from the older Rule (RB 31 and 36). The responsibility lies on the superiors in turn, from bishop to archdeacon to primicerius, unless the sick cleric has private resources sufficient for his needs. An infirmary is to be provided within the enclosure.

A chapter follows on the clothing and shoes of the canons, and their firewood, to the value of four pounds a year (RC 29), to be paid out of the revenue of the country estates. Clothing and shoes are also to come from these rents, or from the common fund of the house: excess income can be used for other necessities or kept for the future; any deficit must be made up by the bishop. However a cleric with sufficient private income should provide his own clothing and shoes.

A chapter follows on Office and meals on the feasts of saints, which seems to be displaced; it may be one of Chrodegang's afterthoughts (RC 30). The feasts specified are those of Our Lord, the Blessed Virgin, the Apostles and local saints: on these days all the clergy should celebrate Office together, and they should then be entertained to dinner. The bishop himself is to provide the dinner, in his own house at Christmas and Easter, and in the common refectory on certain other feasts: on saints' days it is the archdeacon's responsibility. The former custom of the canonical clergy dining in local monasteries on these feast days is to be discontinued: since one of the tables in the refectory is allotted to abbots (RC 21), they were presumably invited in on those days.

There follows a lengthy section about the personal income and property of the canonical clergy, which is the crucial difference between Chrodegang's legislation and that for monks (RC 31-2). He begins with the usual reminder that in the early Church all things were held in common, citing the Acts of the Apostles. However he concedes that this is now impractical for clergy who are not monks, and that therefore he needs to suggest ways to approximate to the primitive spirit of abnegation and sharing. In this he is influenced by Pomerius, whom he believed to be Prosper of Aquitaine.

The first suggestion is for the clerics to make over all their property to the Church, reserving only the use for their lifetime. The second option, for those unable to go so far, is for the clerics to retain ownership of their property, but to be entirely self-supporting. This is still a form of charity, since it relieves the Church of the necessity of supporting these clerics, leaving funds available for other purposes. What Chrodegang will not tolerate is that a wealthy propertied cleric might expect a stipend from the Church. He gives specific regulations about the way in which a deed of gift is to be drawn up, and handed to the bishop in person in the Church of St Paul (probably the private oratory of the community). Making over the property here keeps it quite separate from the cathedral revenue. The bishop can then give him a voluntary mandate (*precaria*) for the usufruct of the property during the cleric's lifetime. The third option remains that on joining the community a cleric might renounce all property whatsoever, in which case the bishop must provide for his needs entirely. In each case, the reference seems to be only to immovable property, lands and buildings. Moveable property remains his to do as he likes with, as long as he pays his way, and after his death it is to be divided among the poor and the clergy: he has the right to appoint an executor to arrange this.

Donations made by the faithful may be kept by the priests, if they are given to a specific priest, as what we now call a Mass stipend. Donations to the community are to be held in common. What appears to be another afterthought is the provision that there is a limit on how many such donations a priest may accept personally, rather than sharing the donation, and with it the obligation of prayer for the donors, among the whole community. Chrodegang does not specify the limit, but leaves it to the superiors to moderate (RC 32).

Another section which must be an afterthought makes further provision for the way canons, including non-residents, are to appear for chapter and Mass on Sundays and major feasts (RC 33, cf. RC 8). It provides for Vigils being celebrated in churches outside the enclosure, but insists that all the brethren must still get back to the enclosure for chapter.

The final part (RC 34) turns its attention to the laity, the *matricularii* who live in *matriculae* in the city. The most probable explanation is that the poor were registered on a roll (the original meaning of *matricula*), and lived in almshouses which came themselves to be called *matriculae*. Chrodegang is concerned for their spiritual welfare, which had been neglected. Twice a month they are to come to the cathedral for spiritual instruction. They have the opportunity for confession, and must in any case go to confession twice a year. Failure to attend is to be punished, even to the extent of expulsion from the *matricula*. A final paragraph, which is missing from the earliest manuscript, provides a dole for these *matricularii*. Rations of bread, bacon and cheese were to be given out regularly, and wine, curiously, during Lent.

The Rule of Chrodegang is a carefully structured and planned treatise, on the essential requirements for community life. Although the obvious source is the Rule of St Benedict, Chrodegang uses the material in his own way. Some sections in the earliest manuscript look like additions, and the later manuscripts include paragraphs attributed to Chrodegang's successor in the see of Metz. That indicates an attentive pastor modifying the Rule as a result of experience. The Rule was obviously drawn up for a specific place, the city of Metz, but that does not mean that Chrodegang did not intend it to be copied and adapted for other dioceses. The latest manuscript, dating from the tenth century, eliminates all specific references to churches in Metz, and must have been intended for use elsewhere, even though the Institutes of Aachen were by now well established.[57]

If the structure of the Rule is admirable, the language and grammar are not. Latin is here well on the way to becoming a modern language, with the appearance of a definite article (still hovering between *ille* and *ipse*) and very hazy ideas about case endings for nouns and adjectives. There is also some very peculiar vocabulary, with vulgar words like *formaticum* for 'cheese' which were to reappear in modern languages. The two later manuscripts make attempts at improving the grammar and vocabulary from time to time, but they are still very far from classical standards. Chrodegang was a competent organizer, well acquainted with the Scriptures and the Rule of St Benedict, but clearly not classically educated: much what we should expect from an upbringing in an Austrasian monastery. He refers often to the 'fathers', but never quotes them. It is this lack of erudition, one fears, that is the reason for the failure of Chrodegang's authentic Rule to become widespread. The new classical learning promoted at the Court of Charlemagne meant that a new and much more erudite rule was required, as was to be provided by the Council of Aachen in 816.

Notes
1. See Foot, *Monastic Life*, pp. 51–7.
2. Blair and Sharpe, *Pastoral Care*, esp. chapters 1–5.
3. Knowles, *Monastic Order in England*, pp. 23, 32–3. See also Bede, Epistle ii, to Bishop Egbert, PL 94:663.
4. For 'minsters' see the works of W. J. Blair, especially *The Church in Anglo-Saxon Society*, and Foot, *Monastic Life*, pp. 283–9.
5. Deanesley, 'Early English & Gallic Minsters', p. 44.
6. Ibid., pp. 41, 32.
7. Ibid., p. 41; Douglas, *Domesday Monachorum*, pp. 9–10.
8. Page, 'Domesday Survey', pp. 61–101.
9. Kjølbe-Biddle, K, and Biddle, M., *The Anglo-Saxon Minsters of Winchester*, Winchester Studies 4.i (Oxford University Press, 2008).
10. See Blair, *Anglo-Saxon Oxfordshire*, especially chapter 2.
11. Bede, *Eccl. Hist.* IV, 13; PL 95:192–3.
12. Steven Bassett, *Anglo-Saxon Coventry and its Churches* (Dugdale Society, 2001); Dugdale, *Monasticon*, VI, p. 225 (Stone).
13. Bede, *Eccl. Hist.* III, 26 and IV, 27; PL 95:163–5, 220–1.
14. Bede, *Vita S. Cuthberti* 16; PL 94:754.
15. Bede, *Eccl. Hist.* III, 23; PL 95:154.
16. For Ireland and Scotland see, again, Blair and Sharpe, *Pastoral Care*.
17. Deanesley, 'Early English & Gallic Minsters', p. 35.
18. Ibid., pp. 39–40, 48.
19. Amort, *Vetus Disciplina*, II, vi, p. 216 sq. and see his references for other such bishops.
20. Poggiaspalla, *Vita Comune*, p. 68; Siegwart, *Chorherren*, p. 40.
21. AA.SS. Feb. II, p. 177.
22. Crusius, *Weltlichen Kollegiatstift*, p. 39.
23. Toledo IV (ERA 671, AD 633), canons 22, 23, 24 and 43; Mansi X, cc. 626, 630.
24. Toledo VI (ERA 676, AD 638), canon 5; Mansi X, c. 664.
25. Mérida (666), canons 10 and 18; Mansi XI, cc. 81, 85.

26. Isidore, *De Ecclesiasticis Officiis*, II, i-xv; PL 83:777-94; Letter to Leudefrid, Mansi X, cc.1232-3.
27. Deanesley, 'Early English & Gallic Minsters', p. 51.
28. Egbert, *Excerptiones*, cap. 154; PL. 89:399.
29. Ibid., cap. 160; PL. 89:399-400.
30. Cloveshoe I (747), in Hadden & Stubbs, *Concilia* III, 360 sq; Cloveshoe II (786), Ibid. III, 450, c. 4. See also Simon Keynes, *The Councils of Clovesho* (Brixworth 1994).
31. Boniface, *Letters*, vi, p. 17.
32. Ibid., xxxvi, p. 52.
33. Ibid., lxxvii, p. 148.
34. Hartzheim, *Concilia* I, 74, can. xii, cf. can. xvii; cf Mansi XII, c. 383 bis.
35. Flodoard, *Hist. Eccl. Rem.*, Lib. II, cap. 11; P.L. 135:113.
36. Boniface, *Letters*, x and lxvii, pp. 21, 132.
37. Siegwart, *Chorherren*, p. 61.
38. Sonntag, *St Marien zu Erfurt*, p. 2.
39. D.I. 43, *Rheingau-Taunus Kreis*, p. xx.
40. D.I. 70, *Stadt Trier* (2007), no 22; also illust. J. Higget, *Roman, Runes and Ogham* (Donington, Shaun Tyas, 2001), pl. 46.
41. Pirmin, *Scarapsus*, PL 89:1029-50.
42. Siegwart, *Chorherren*, p. 63 (Pirmin); p. 69 (Sidonius); p. 79 (Hedde); p. 82 (Wala).
43. Berne library MS AA 90 fragm. no. 11; Edition and commentary by Dom A. Wilmart, 'La Règlement Ecclésiastique de Berne', in *Révue Bénédictine* 51 (1939), pp. 37-52.
44. Wilmart, 'Règlement Ecclésiastique', p. 39.
45. Julia Barrow, 'Chrodegang, his Rule and its Successors', *Early Medieval Europe* Vol. 14 (2006), p. 203.
46. The life of Chrodegang is preserved by Peter the Deacon in *De Gestis Longobardorum*, written *c*.783, during the time of Anghilram, successor to the saint. Text in AA.SS. (6 March) March I, pp. 451 sq., also MGH SS II, 267-8. See also my *Chrodegang Rules*, Claussen, *The Reform of the Frankish Church*, and Langefeld, *Enlarged Rule of Chrodegang*. This near simultaneous publication is called 'morphic resonance'.
47. P.L. 89:1119-21 (foundation of Gorze); Mansi XII, c. 571 (synod of Metz).
48. de Clercq, *Législation Religieuse*, p. 137; PL 89:1121-6.
49. Wallace-Hadrill, *Frankish Church*, p. 172.
50. *si monastica vita velle habeant vivendi*, MGH Epist. III: *Epist. merov. et kar.* i (Berlin 1892), 479-87; also Mansi XII, c. 326.
51. See Klingshirn, *Caesarius of Arles, Making of a Community*, pp. 275-7.
52. AA.SS., Oct. I, p. 494, cf *Martyrologium Romanum*, 2004, p. 550.
53. *Sufficerunt quidem priscorum patrum regulae, sanctae aecclesiae catholicae rectissimae normae ad mortalium correctionem prolatae, si eorum sanctissima iura perseverassent inlesa.* MGH Leg. II Capit. I (1883), *Capitula Regum Francorum* p. 33.
54. Bern MS 289; see Ebner, 'Zur Regula Canonicorum des Hl. Chrodegang', *Römische Quartalschrift* V (1891) pp. 82-6.
55. For quotations from Gregory, Caesarius and Pomerius see Claussen, *Frankish Church*, pp. 170, 177 and 198 respectively.

56. Klingshirn, *Caesarius of Arles, Life &c.*, I, p. 15.
57. For the full text and translation see Bertram, *Chrodegang Rules*. For a discussion of the context of the RC in the reform of the Church in Francia, see Claussens, *Frankish Church*.

Chapter 5

The Carolingian Empire

Chrodegang's Rule in Use

There is little definite evidence that the Rule of St Chrodegang in its original form found many followers. Clearly it was observed in Metz itself, as the modifications by Anghilram demonstrate, and for some considerable period after the time of Chrodegang. The existence of the edition omitting all specific references to Metz shows that it was used in other dioceses. From the late eighth century onwards there are a number of royal *capitula*, which require that clergy and monks should remain each in his proper state of life, and that canonical clergy should live according to the canons.[1]

Among the capitula of Charlemagne promulgated at Aachen in 789 we hear that those 'who attained the clerical state, which we call the "canonical life", must live in all things as canons according to their rule, and the bishop shall govern their life just as an abbot does that of monks'.[2] The reference to their 'rule' (*regula*) does seem to imply that a known text was available, and the immediate reaction is to assume this must be the Rule of Chrodegang. The same capitula of Aachen also include the reminder that all monks should learn to sing in the Roman way, as established under King Pippin, in other words by Chrodegang.[3] However Charlemagne also says the allowance of food should be equal for everyone, contrary to Chrodegang, and, as we shall see, the same word *regula* used at Mainz in 813 appears to refer to the writings of St Isidore.[4] Charlemagne regularly sent envoys (*missi*) to inspect the behaviour of the clergy, with instructions to see that the clergy lived 'canonically'. By 802 the Emperor was insisting that all those consecrated to God had to follow either the 'regular' way of life (i.e. the Rule of St Benedict), or the 'canonical'. Solitary priests, and above all wandering priests, were to be constrained to join communities of one or other form. Nevertheless there is still provision for 'country priests', whose community life was shared only with minor clerics and no other priests.[5]

Further afield, it has been suggested that Bishop Leidrad reorganized his see of Lyons in 797 with a *schola cantorum* on the lines of what Chrodegang had done at Metz, and that the buildings erected there by his successor Agobard were modelled on the canonry of Metz.[6] It is rumoured that the Rule of Chrodegang was still used in Hungary after 816, though I have not been able to verify this.[7] In the alpine regions, there were communities at Schönenwald and Basel in the late eighth century.[8] Würzburg also had a canonical house under Bishop Berowelf (794–800) where bishop and clergy lived in common.[9]

The use of the Rule of Chrodegang in England has often been posited for the late eighth century. Reforms in Canterbury under Archbishop Wulfred in the early ninth century are also often compared to the provisions of Chrodegang, though there is no clear evidence for a connection, or for the existence of copies of the original Rule in England at all.[10] The legates of Hadrian I came to England and presented twenty *capitula* for the synods of 786-7, including the injunction that the clergy should live 'canonically': Dom David Knowles considered that they also brought the Rule of Chrodegang to England, though is little trace that anything came of it, save possibly at Canterbury. He admits that it is superior to 'merely collegiate communities', but sees it as already part of the slide down the scale of observance from real monasticism.[11] The Council of *Calchuthae* (probably Chelsea) in 787 repeats the requirement that bishops are to ensure that all their canons live canonically, their monks monastically, and that they be clearly distinguishable. The canons are not to wear precious garments dyed with Indian colours.[12] A charter of 805, signed by Archbishop Ethelheard, is signed by two *praepositi*, eight other priests, one archdeacon, one deacon and two minor clerks, implying the existence of a full range of clergy.[13]

A definite reference to a 'rule of life' is in the decree of Archbishop Wulfred in 813, in which he ordered his canons to attend the canonical hours, and to use a common refectory and dormitory, permitting them to bequeath property only to other members of the *familia*. This charter was signed by a priest-abbot, eight other priests and three minor clerics.[14] This is certainly not incompatible with observance of the Rule of Chrodegang, but not even the use of the word 'rule' is indisputable evidence that Wulfred was aware of that particular text: these provisions were part of the common heritage of what was understood as the proper way of life for the pastoral clergy, and Brigitte Langefeld thought he could just as easily be referring to the Rule of St Benedict.[15] Again, the witnesses to the charter include a *presbyter abbas* as superior, rather than a more Chrodegangian *primicerius*. Wulfred's achievement seems to have lain in bringing his clergy back together from their own scattered houses to live within an enclosure.

The indications are that the canonical life was already being widely observed at the time of Chrodegang and afterwards, but there is no clear evidence for any attempt to impose a uniform written rule before that of Aachen. Observant canonical clergy in England would doubtless have considered the canons of Metz to have been living, like themselves, in accordance with ancient tradition. Observant canonical clergy in eastern Austrasia, as at Toul and Verdun, would have welcomed the text of Chrodegang's Rule as a useful codification of principles they already knew well. The name of Chrodegang was not even to be remembered in England: in the eleventh-century Missal of Leofric there is no mention of his feast day (6 March) even though Leofric certainly used the 'Longer Rule' which incorporated portions of that of Chrodegang.

An innovation, which was to prove far-reaching, was the establishment of the Imperial Chapel in Aachen as a community of secular priests, not under the direct control of the bishop, but that of the Emperor. Community life in this *Hofkapelle* was apparently in every way comparable to that in an episcopal community of clergy – it is sometimes called a *monasterium canonicorum*, but the clerical superior, the Provost, was an imperial appointment. In 794 Anghilram was brought from Metz to become first Archchaplain to Charlemagne at Aachen, with the clear implication that his experience of the Rule of Chrodegang would be useful. The purpose of the community was explicitly the performance of the Divine Office, and the celebration of Mass and the sacraments for the imperial household. This was the first of a long series of imperial, royal and noble foundations which existed in parallel to episcopal foundations, using the same manner of life and fundamentally serving the same purpose.[16]

The Council of Aachen

The programme of consolidation and reform begun by Pippin was continued with unbroken zeal by his successors Charles the Great and Louis the Pious, always in close communication with the pope, and under considerable influence from England. As ever, the maintenance of a high standard of conduct of the clergy was seen as the key to enlivening the entire Church, and a succession of local synods or councils prepared the way for the definitive Councils of Aachen in 816–7. The calling of councils, which had slightly fallen into abeyance under the later Merovingians, was a revival of the standard Roman practice.

In response to Charlemagne's admonitions, five regional councils were held in 813, at Arles, Reims, Mainz, Châlons and Tours, all concerned with church discipline, and all coming to much the same conclusions about the need to enforce community life on the clergy. Bishops should see to it that canons and monks live each 'according to their proper order, whether canonical or regular', and in every monastery or minster the bishop should sort out those who wish to be real monks and those who wish to be canonical clergy and make them live accordingly.[17] Canons are to know their rule of life 'according to the decretals of Pope Innocent' — startling evidence for some knowledge of these early popes long before the Isidorian corpus was published.[18] 'Canonical clergy must live canonically, observing the teaching of sacred Scripture and the writings of the holy fathers ... they should eat and sleep together, where funds make this possible, or where they can receive a stipend from the property of the Church; they are to live within their enclosure, and come at dawn every day to the reading to hear what is enjoined on them.' Again '[the canonical clergy] must all sleep in a single dormitory, and eat in one refectory, so that they may the more readily hasten together to celebrate the canonical hours, and to be admonished and taught about their life and behaviour; they are to receive their food and clothing according to the resources available to the bishop.' At table they are to hear readings, and 'they are to display obedience to their masters according to the canons.'[19] Wandering priests (*acephali*, a word taken from Isidore) are to be rounded up and brought into community life, but no one should be tonsured underage and against his will, which seems to oppose the existing practice of being brought up as a cleric from infancy.[20] Nevertheless schools are to be maintained, so the young boys remain under the care of the canonical clergy without being clerics themselves.[21] The number admitted to community life must be proportionate to the revenue available; all candidates for priesthood must be at least thirty years old and have lived in the bishop's community, *in episcopio*.[22]

All this looks exactly like the provisions in the Rule of Chrodegang, including the daily chapter meeting, but there is no mention of a written source other than scripture and the early fathers. The only authorities quoted by the councils are St Jerome, citing his letter to Nepotian, and St Isidore, on the clerical life; they make no mention of Chrodegang.[23] In making a clear distinction between those who live in the world and those who have left it, the latter are to be marked by living 'according to the rule of clerics' (*regula clericorum*). 'Abbots' of monasteries or 'minsters' in which the canonical life existed long before must ensure that there is a dormitory and refectory, that the canonical hours are kept, and that food and clothing are made available as resources permit. This is in contrast to abbots of 'monasteries of monks in which the rule of our holy Father St Benedict was once observed', where they should restore it.[24] All five councils reported to a preliminary general council at Aachen in September 813, which coincided with the coronation of Louis as Emperor.[25]

The great Councils of Aachen (Aix-la Chapelle, Aquisgranae) were summoned a few years later, that of 816 to deal definitively with the clergy, that of 817 for the monks. Our concern here is with the session of 816, concerned exclusively with the 'canonical clergy'. The council met in August, and began by making the familiar distinction between the 'canonical life' and monasticism. They asserted that ancient precedents were well-known, and all that was necessary was to remind the clergy of their existing canonical obligations. The emperor opened his palace library to provide the necessary evidence, and the council went into recess for a month to allow time for the document to be drafted. They reconvened in September to acclaim and approve the resulting text, the *Institutio Canonica*.[26] The accompanying document was a rule for women living according to the canons, making a distinction between these 'canonesses' and the real nuns who followed the Rule of St Benedict. (These canonesses might reasonably be supposed to include a number of the wives of ordained clergy who had separated from their husbands on their ordination to the diaconate.)

At the second session, in 817, the emperor presented an authentic copy of the Rule of St Benedict, sent from Monte Cassino for the purpose, and the Council made that Rule normative for all monks of the empire. St Benedict of Aniane was commissioned to draw up a comparative edition of the Rule of St Benedict, showing how it related to other monastic rules, the *Concordia Regularum*.[27] Prior to this time all monastic rules had been considered more or less equivalent, even the horrific 'Scots' ones with their unbelievably harsh discipline, and a novitiate served in any house was accepted for any other. St Benedict of Aniane's work effectively ensured the occlusion of all rules other than the Benedictine, and although he quotes the Rule of St Augustine, we must assume that it too was disused. Despite the wishful thinking of later Augustinians, it is quite clear that in the ninth century, as before, there were no such things as 'canons regular', meaning non-monastic clergy with vows of personal poverty. Canons were all what would later be called 'secular'. A key difference that emerges at this time between monks and canons is that monks were not permitted to teach boys other than their own oblates, whereas canons were expected to run schools for the general public.[28]

The Canonical Institute

One thing which must be made clear is that the *Institutio Canonica* is not in any sense a new edition of the Rule of Chrodegang, although even quite reputable historians continue to state that it is.[29] There is not one word, not one phrase, that can be shown to be a quotation from Chrodegang, and there is really no evidence that the compilers of the Institute were influenced by the Rule of Chrodegang at all. The only verbal echoes come when both texts quote the same original, usually the Rule of St Benedict. Although St Chrodegang quotes St Benedict very much more than Aachen does, there is at least one place where Aachen quotes more of the Benedictine Rule than Chrodegang (the provision for a light in the dormitory, IC 136, RB 22), showing that it approaches St Benedict independently. Where provisions are similar, they are commonplaces of canonical legislation (the use of dormitory and refectory, keeping enclosure, etc). There are many places where the provisions of the *Institutio Canonica* differ considerably from those of Chrodegang, and many areas treated by Chrodegang that receive little or no consideration in the later rule. Because of the variety of sources there is a variety of title used at Aachen for the superior: the ultimate authority is the *praelatus*, usually a bishop, who appoints either a *praepositus* or a *prior*, translated as 'provost' or 'superior' respectively. The *primicerius*, so often mentioned by St Chrodegang, is never mentioned. Examination of the text really makes one doubt Morhain's confident assertion that 'The work of Aix la Chapelle remains a magnificent homage paid by the best qualified representatives of the episcopate of the whole Empire to the work of the Bishop of Metz.'[30] It would seem strange if the bishops at Aachen were really unaware of the work of Chrodegang, but they display remarkably little evidence of such an awareness.

The texts and canons which make up the *Institutio Canonica* were chosen to reinforce existing legislation, not to make any new provisions. Only the Emperor's personal intervention about food and drink is truly original — and this was to be the area most attacked in later centuries.[31] The rule was drawn up by a single author for approval by the Council. It runs to one hundred and forty-five chapters, one hundred and eighteen of which are lifted from earlier sources, found in the palace library at Aachen. The most peculiar is the *Libri Sententiarum* of Taio of Saragossa, itself a catena of extracts from St Gregory. Other sources, apart from Scripture, are the Rule of St Benedict, Isidore of Seville (*Libri Sententiarum* and *De Ecclesiasticis*), St Jerome's commentary on the Epistle to Titus, and a selection of his letters, Julianus Pomerius, and sermons by Augustine of Hippo on the Shepherds and on the Common Life of the Clergy. Conciliar and papal decrees come from the collection known as the *Dionysio-Hadriana*, but out of order. In all, out of one hundred and forty-five chapters, there are sixty-three taken from the Fathers, fifty-five from conciliar decrees or papal decretals, and only twenty-seven of original material, including the final summary. Even these original chapters are full of quotations from Scripture and the Fathers. And in all this, not a word can be shown to be directly quoted from the Rules of Augustine or Chrodegang.

The document opens with a prologue, describing the process by which the Rule came to be written, and the purpose it was intended to serve. The emperor urged the council to have a selection drawn up, both from the fathers and from existing canons of past church councils, which could act as a guide to the proper mode of conduct for superiors and subordinates in the clerical life. For this purpose he gave them access to the Imperial Library.

This prologue is followed by a very long catena of patristic and conciliar texts, with which the compiler spun together a useful manual for the clergy, and in particular for their superiors. It begins by describing each of the eight degrees then acknowledged of holy orders (IC 1–8), and then looks critically at the bishops, and their possible misbehaviour (IC 26–38). There then intervenes a selection of conciliar canons, drawn from the collection of canons sent by Pope Hadrian I to Charlemagne in 774, the so-called 'Dionysio-Hadriana' (IC 39–93).[32] Presumably the canons selected are the ones the compiler considered were not being observed, and of which the clergy and their superiors needed to be reminded. They are particularly concerned with the problem of wandering clergy, leaving their own dioceses and appearing in others without episcopal control. There are also concerns about clerical behaviour, continence, sobriety, fasting and detachment from worldly ambitions, as well as possible lawsuits, and the preservation of due order and respect. It is perhaps worth noting that only one canon is quoted about continence, the famous third canon of Nicaea (IC 38), which prohibits women living in clergy houses except for the very closest relatives: this would imply that incontinence was not a common problem among clerics in the early eighth century – rather the opposite, since they saw the need to include a canon warning against being too proud of one's virginity (IC 67). Obviously the compiler was far more worried about clergy wandering from place to place. However he did choose two canons prohibiting clergy from going to public houses (IC 60, 90), two more prohibiting banqueting in churches (IC 59, 80), and one telling then not to plunder the bishop's property when he dies (IC 88). The text then turns to select passages from the Fathers concerning the life of the ordinary clergy. Extracts from St Jerome, Isidore, Gregory (via Taio), and pseudo-Prosper, are concluded by the two long rambling sermons by St Augustine (IC 112–13), which consist largely of accounts of how the various named clergy of Hippo have given up all their property to live with Augustine.

There follows a fresh start, with a new prologue, and the rubric *Regula Canonicorum*, the Rule for Canons. Although the paragraph numbering continues it is obvious that we have here almost a self-contained document, the actual Rule of Aachen as opposed to its supporting documents. It consists of thirty-two chapters, of varying length, describing the way of life to be observed among the secular clergy of the Empire. It is worth describing it in detail, if only to show how it differs from the Rule of Chrodegang.

It opens with a very long chapter (IC 114), almost entirely composed of New Testament quotations, but based on a letter of St Augustine.[33] This is intended to make clear the distinction between the vocation of the monk, which is one of perfect self-denial, with the renunciation of all private property, and the common vocation of every Christian to charity, frugality and the observance of the Commandments. This theme continues in the following chapter (IC 115), which claims that the life of canons, who are not monks, 'excels all other institutions'. A chapter on the possessions of the Church (IC 116) stresses the importance of being scrupulous in accounting for the money entrusted to the Church. None of this has any parallel in Chrodegang.

From church funds, the Rule now turns its attention to the actual communities of canons. It begins with the enclosure itself (IC 117), specifying that there should be a strong wall surrounding the dormitories, refectories and other domestic buildings, with only one gate. This is similar in principle to Chrodegang (RC 27). The next two chapters speak of the members of the community, and the discretion needed in choosing them (IC 118–9). Provosts are not to admit too many canons, nor are they to confine themselves to admitting only members of the *familia* of the Church. The implication is that canons are recruited in adult life. We then have another chapter dealing with clergy income (IC 120). Quoting the pseudo-Prosper yet again, the rule distinguishes between those who have a private income, who are entitled only to food, drink and a share of the free-will offerings, and those who have nothing, and will therefore need a stipend from church funds. The fact that the canons can legitimately own private property has been seen as contradictory to the intention of the two sermons of St Augustine included in the catena, but we cannot conclude that a distinction was therefore made between 'renunciant' and 'non-renunciant' members of a single community, as Amort seems to imply.[34] The *Institutio Canonica* does not even recommend such a degree of renunciation of poverty as Chrodegang does, nor is there any question of making property over to the church, a fact which Poggiaspalla sees as a clear sign of decadence.[35]

In the matter of the provision of food and drink, whereas the Rule of Chrodegang provides a graduated scale of drink depending on seniority, and rations the food in vague terms (RC 22–3), the Council of Aachen insists that all the canons must receive the same amount with no favouritism (IC 121). The only variation is from house to house, depending on the prosperity of the neighbourhood. In a long and complicated chapter (IC 122) the council, after the personal intervention of the emperor, suggests that in an ideal situation every canon should receive five pints of wine a day, which is to be made up with beer if insufficient wine is available. In case there is disagreement over quantities, the emperor has provided standard weights and measures, to be found in every city, province and mine. This Gargantuan allowance of wine was to lead to much adverse comment during the eleventh century, not least from Peter Damian.

As if to raise our minds from this Bacchanalian chapter, the next returns to themes already found in Chrodegang. The provost has the duty of feeding the minds as well as the bodies of his subjects (IC 123), and for this purpose a daily chapter meeting is envisaged. We are again reminded of the importance of a common dormitory and refectory, with readings and mutual service. Two chapters on clothing (IC 124-5) give no detailed instructions, but are concerned to warn canons against the opposite tendencies of dressing fashionably, or of pretending to be monks. The implication is that there is a recognized form of clerical dress, and that this should be worn, without ostentation either in finery or squalour. Moreover the canons are evidently expected to acquire their own clothing, unlike Chrodegang's clergy.

Five chapters on the Divine Office (IC 126-130) are lifted verbatim from St Isidore,[36] and two newly composed chapters (IC 131-2) give instructions for the manner of celebrating the Office, including the prohibition on carrying staves into choir, as in Chrodegang (RC 7). The chapter on readers and cantors (IC 133) seems unique to this Rule: the topic is treated at greater length further on (IC 137). Two very long chapters on discipline (IC 134-5) use the familiar metaphor of the physician, and the Gospel recommendation of admonishing two or three times before punishing (Matt. 18:13-17). The punishments envisaged are fasting on bread and water, separation from community life, corporal punishment if of a suitable age, imprisonment, and eventually expulsion from the community. Boys are to be housed separately from the adults, under strict supervision, whereas Chrodegang had suggested they should share the same dormitory as the older canons (RC 3). The duty of all to come to Compline, and the arrangement of the dormitory (IC 136), is followed by a long chapter on the cantors in church (IC 137). Despite Chrodegang's known interest in church music, there is no parallel to this in his Rule.

Chapters follow on the officials of the community, beginning naturally with the superior. In the choice of a deputy to govern the canons, bishops are advised in words closely related to St Benedict's advice on choosing a dean or prior (RB 21), with no similarities to St Chrodegang's equivalent chapter (RC 25). The title of provost (*praepositus*) is defined (IC 139), and it is emphasized that he bears only a delegated authority. This title was used by St Benedict (RB 65), who was less than enthusiastic about the institution: his warnings against the institution of provosts are echoed by Aachen (IC 139). The chapter on the cellarer (IC 140) quotes St Benedict again, independently of Chrodegang (RB 31, cf. RC 26). It appears that the cellarer here is to be in charge of domestic servants, drawn from the *familia* of the Church, and that these include the cooks. Here is another major difference from the Rule of Chrodegang which insists that all should take their turn at cooking (RC 24).

The next chapter speaks of the need for a guesthouse, and a guestmaster, to care for the poor, both the local indigent and wandering beggars (IC 141). The guesthouse is not an integral part of the establishment, as it is for St Benedict, but it should not be far away, so that the canons can visit it, and at least during Lent pay attention to the poor. There are echoes of St Benedict (RB 53) but the situation in a city will be very different from that around a rural monastery, and the scale of provision for the poor must be much greater. Considerable sums of money will be involved, which explains the stern admonition against misappropriating funds. The chapter on the sick (IC 142) tells us in passing that canons are entitled to have their own lodgings within the enclosure. Nevertheless an infirmary is to be provided, particularly for those without sufficient means of their own. No specific infirmarian is appointed, however.

The next two chapters deal with the porter (IC 143–4) and the securing of the enclosure. The porter is described in words reminiscent of the Rule of St Benedict (RB 66), but with the provision that after Compline the porter is to surrender his keys to the superior: this last point is also found in Chrodegang's Rule (RC 27). The canons are to be restrained in their behaviour, both within and without the enclosure, and women are on no account to be allowed inside (IC 144). This provision too is the same as in the Rule of Chrodegang, but whereas the earlier rule does not encourage even lay men to enter the enclosure (RC 3), the Rule of Aachen makes no such provision, and indeed seems to expect lay servants and cooks as a matter of routine.

The final long chapter is a summary or epitome of the whole of the preceding Rule, designed to be memorized so that the canons may be reminded of all the important provisions of the Rule they are to follow. It is the only part that has previously been translated into English.[37]

After this comes the Rule for Canonesses, with similar provisions to those for the canons (indeed many chapters follow much the same text), though they are expected to keep more strictly within their enclosures.

The whole text, therefore, with the catenas of patristic readings and the two Rules, comes to a very considerable length. It is accompanied by a circular letter from the emperor, which was directed to all the Archbishops of the Empire who were not personally present at the council, directing them to summon a provincial synod and have the entire document read out and explained. Copies are then to be made for every bishop and provost, and the Imperial envoy will supervise this. The emperor warns the archbishops that he will send another envoy on the coming first of September to check up on their compliance with his requests. Since he says this gives them a full year, the first mailing of the text must have taken place in the autumn of 816. He concludes with a severe warning against noncompliance, and a note that the standard weights and measures are also enclosed.

Traditionally the Canonical Institute has been attributed to Amalarius of Metz, and it is under his name that the text is printed in the Patrology.[38] It is possibly because of the coincidence that Amalarius was born in Chrodegang's diocese that it has been so confidently stated that the Institute imitates the Rule of Chrodegang. However Albert Werminghoff challenged the attribution, suggesting instead that the author was Ansegis of St Wandrille.[39] His key evidence is that the author of the Institute was apparently familiar with the works of St Gregory only through the medium of the obscure Taio of Saragossa, and that a copy of Taio existed in the library at St Wandrille. A third candidate for authorship is St Benedict of Aniane himself, who was certainly the prime mover behind the monastic reforms of 817, but it is unlikely he would have been concerned in both. In reality, the authorship must be left in doubt.

What is most noticeable about the text of the *Institutio Canonica*, as opposed to the Rule of Chrodegang, is the immense superiority of its prose style. An improvement in Latin scholarship was, of course, a characteristic of Charlemagne's new Imperial style, and it was clear that the rough and ready dog-Latin of Chrodegang would not do. Courtiers around the Emperor vied with each other in composing Latin verse as well as prose, and in offering each other their verses for criticism and correction. The English, of course, had been doing this sort of thing two generations earlier – St Boniface and his correspondents regularly sent each other verses for criticism – but it would have been quite beyond the capabilities of poor Saint Chrodegang. It may even have been the barbaric quality of his Latin that deterred the compiler of the *Institutio Canonica* from taking any notice of his Rule, though it has also been pointed out that, as a recent writer, he would have had no authority compared to that of the fathers and councils.[40]

Application of the Aachen Rule, to the Treaty of Verdun

Louis' achievement as a reformer of the clerical and monastic life was celebrated in interminable verse by Ermoldus.[41] The emperor certainly intended the decrees of his reforming councils to have far-reaching and long-lasting effect throughout his dominions. He outlined stringent measures to ensure that the new Canonical Institutes would be observed in every cathedral and collegiate church throughout the empire, with the promise of regular inspections by Imperial *Missi*. It was even suggested that if the local church could not afford to build and endow a canonry, the emperor would pay for it himself.[42] This certainly did happen occasionally; an example is when Charles the Bald gave land at Châlons-sur-Marne for the Canons in 859.[43] In reality, however, it is unlikely that the emperor was able to achieve this uniform observance for any length of time, or throughout the whole of the Carolingian empire. The political unity and stability of that empire was already crumbling, and the ninth century was to see Charlemagne's legacy disrupted and fragmented. For the canonical way of life to thrive, a stable political and economic climate was essential, and this was not to be granted. Nevertheless the Aachen Institutes were certainly observed in many houses, and they remained the standard rule of life for canonical clergy for centuries to come, as evidenced by the enormous number of surviving manuscripts collated by Werminghoff.[44] Among the earlier manuscripts is one from Cheltenham (no. 6546), in Lombardic script, indicating that interest in the decrees of Aachen extended outside the Empire. The *Institutio Canonica* continued to be copied until the fifteenth century, which suggests that the way of life it envisages did not die out in the eleventh century, as generally considered, but continued to form the background to later collegiate life. It was first printed in the sixteenth century, but thereafter it appears only among collections of conciliar texts, as if it no longer had any value other than historical.

There is certainly evidence that the emperor's wishes were carried out in many different places. Dereine gives a long list of dioceses where the canonical life was properly observed, and alludes to the foundation of many collegiate churches apart from the cathedral houses, seven in Liège alone. He affirms that for a period at least after 816 the *Institutio Canonica* was properly observed, without decadence.[45] Semmler concurs in the success of the Aachen rule during the lifetime of Louis the Pious, citing foundations across the Pyrenees in Urgel and Barcelona.[46] Archbishop

Ebbo of Reims directed the observance of the Canonical Institute, and was one of the first to introduce the title of dean (*decanus*) alongside that of provost, for an official whose duty was to supervise the clergy, including those living in country parishes in small groups. The emperor gave him permission to block a street in the city in order to build his canonical enclosure.[47] Bishop Hetti of Trier wrote recommending the same Rule to Bishop Frotarius of Tulle, and he himself ordered the construction of a *claustrum* in Trier, as well as establishing a collegiate church in Koblenz in 830.[48] The community at Konstanz, originally monastic in inspiration, was definitely canonical by 826, when it had 35 members, including twelve priests and seven deacons: by 839 it had risen to 67 members. At Chur, however, the *domus episcopi* with its almshouse and hostel was destroyed and the canons scattered, in 823.[49] Although there are frequent references to the decadence of canons in the subsequent two centuries, there was no doubt that it was the Aachen Institutes that set the standard from which they had decayed. Later legislation always refers back to Aachen. The only certain evidence for use of the *Institutio Canonica* outside the empire, in England, is provided by the earliest statutes of St Paul's, London, which incorporate chapters 98–100, 124, and 131-3 verbatim, following the text of Aachen exactly (and not, as usually stated, the abbreviated text found in the 'Longer Rule').[50]

It is in Lotharingia, where all the surviving manuscripts originate, that we find the only convincing evidence for the survival of Chrodegang's Rule after the date of the Council of Aachen. During the second quarter of the tenth century there was a remarkable flowering of monastic life, centered on the Benedictine houses of Gorze near Metz, St-Evre near Toul and St-Maximin outside Trier – Gorze had been St Chrodegang's own foundation. Among the reforming monks and abbots we find many that had formerly been officials among the canonical clergy of the cathedrals of Metz, Toul and Verdun: three of them had held the office of *primicerius*. As Nightingale comments, 'these cathedral communities were able to provide a seedbed for the reform because the transition from them to full monastic life was not that big a step.'[51]

In Le Mans, the canonical life was established by Aldric, who became bishop in 832, having already been *primicerius* of Metz 'according to the Roman order'. He built an enclosure for the canonical life, gathering together clerics who had been living here and there throughout the city, and were thus unable to be regular in attendance at Divine Office. He also endowed the canonry with lands, and ensured a regular income sufficient for their food and clothing. Two *hospitia* were founded, one to be a guesthouse for visiting bishops, abbots and counts, so that they would not intrude on the life of the canons; the other to be a refuge for the poor. In all this he was clearly inspired by the instructions of Aachen. Nevertheless, after the death of Louis the Pious in 840 everything was destroyed in the ensuing turmoil, and the new buildings of the close were 'devastated and destroyed to their foundations'.[52] Yet shortly after this, Hermanus, Bishop of Nevers, was able to establish canonical life, in almost exactly the same terms, in 849, providing for sixty canons in the city and sixteen at St Martin's.[53]

It did not take long for it to become necessary for Louis to summon another reforming council, which met at Paris in 829. The council complains 'with great and swelling indignation' that modern bishops are still not following the example of their predecessors, for they should live with their clergy and celebrate the office with them. Moreover, in order that 'rectors of churches' may prepare and educate new 'soldiers of Christ', schools should be established throughout the empire.[54] Returning to Aachen in 836, the assembled bishops urged each other to keep a close eye on the congregations of canons, and the 'abbots' of non-cathedral canonries likewise, 'according to what is contained in the book which was compiled about their life'.[55]

However the times were troubled, and the common pattern was the gradual secularization of church property. To begin with, the lands and properties of the Church might be taken into lay control 'for the duration of the emergency' only, and nominally still belonged to the minsters or monasteries concerned. Once in lay hands, however, the lands proved difficult or impossible to recover, and, with the loss of the regular income, community life disintegrated. As always, the same lay proprietors were ready to welcome priests and other clerics to serve on their own lands on their own terms, so that the dispersed canons found homes waiting for them in the service and under the protection of powerful laymen. During the ninth century, for instance, the cathedral canons of Trier, Speyer, Worms and Mainz were all dispossessed, and community life came to an end. Various bishops tried in vain to reverse the trend.[56] Whereas in a city there were sizeable communities not only at the cathedral but attached to other great churches, in the country a parish might be served by a single priest with a deacon or two and some minor clerics. Ninth-century councils reiterate the prohibition of subdeacons and above marrying after ordination, and extend the Nicene ban on women living in priests' houses to include all, even close relations. Again, if they are living in these little communities, the priest's sister could be a source of temptation to the deacon or even the subdeacon.[57]

Despite the constant encouragement to distinguish canonical clergy from monks, there were examples of mixed communities, where property-owning clerics lived side by side with monks. At Corbie the statutes of c.830 speak of 350 monks, 150 prebendaries, and 12 poor men. The 'prebendaries', meaning those who were provided with provender, were mostly laymen, but included nineteen clerics, under the *praepositus* of the Church of St John. Nevertheless the predominant ethos was clearly monastic.[58] Rabanus Maurus, although of genuine monastic origin, did write a treatise on the clerical life for Archbishop Haistulf of Mainz in around 819. This is an excellent treatise on the training of priests and their liturgical ministry, but says nothing at all about the Common Life.[59] St Radulphus of Bourges, who became archbishop in 841, had been a member of a clerical institute, but his own foundations were purely Benedictine.[60] If contemporaries were confused, it is hardly surprising that later writers have found it very difficult to tell whether a given community was a 'monastery', a 'minster' or a 'canonry', and there is a continual tendency to project the later institute of 'canons regular' back into an age where canons might be very irregular indeed.

Notes
1. e.g. Capitula of Aachen (789), caps. xxv, lxxi; Mansi XIII, appendix cc. 163, 173; Council of Frankfurt (794), Mansi XIII, c. 908; Capitula of Aachen (802), Mansi XIII, c. 1101; see also MGH Legum II, cap. I, 60, 103, 95; also the Capitulary of Herstal (779), MGH Cap. I no 20; and the statutes of Theodulf of Orleans (*c.* 802), PL 105:192.
2. MGH Legum II cap. I p. 73, 74; Mansi XIII, appendix c. 173.
3. Ibid., cap. 78; Mansi XIII, appendix c. 174.
4. Mainz (813), canon x, Mansi XIV, cc. 67–8.
5. *Capitulare Missorum*, in MGH Legum II capit I, 95–102; Mansi XIV, cc. 1–5.
6. Wallace-Hadrill, *Frankish Church*, p. 359.
7. R. Beckefi, *A magyarországi kaptalanok megalukasa és Szent Chrodegang regulaja* (Budapest, 1901).
8. Siegwart, *Chorherren*, p. 81.
9. Ibid., p. 66.
10. See Deanesley, 'The Familia at Christchurch', pp. 1 sq; and Edwards, *English Secular Cathedral*, p. 4.
11. Knowles, *Monastic Order in England*, p. 139.
12. Calchuthae (787), canon iv; Mansi XII, c. 941.
13. Kemble, *Codex Diplomaticus Ævi Saxonici* I, 231.

14. Kemble, *Codex Diplomaticus Ævi Saxonici* I, 251, cf W. de Grey Birch, *Cartularium Saxonicum*, London 1885, no. 342, pp. 478–9.
15. Langefeld, *Enlarged Rule of Chrodegang*, pp. 16–17.
16. Crusius, *Weltlichen Kollegiatstift*, pp. 110–4.
17. Arles VI (813), canon vi; Mansi XIV, c. 60; MGH Legum II Conc. II, 251; Mainz (813), canon xxi; Mansi XIV, c. 71.
18. Reims II (813), canon viii; Mansi XIV, c. 78.
19. Mainz (813), canon ix; Mansi XIV, c. 67; MGH Legum II Conc. II, 262; Tours (813), canon xxiii; Mansi XIV, c. 86.
20. Mainz (813) canon xxiii; Mansi XIV, c. 71.
21. Châlons II (813), canon iii; Mansi XIV, c. 94.
22. Tours III (813), canon xxiv; Mansi XIV, c. 86; MG Leg. II Conc. II, 289.
23. Mainz (813), canon x; Mansi XIV, cc. 67–8. The text from Isidore cited here (*de Officiis* II, 2), reappears as chapter 100 of the IC.
24. Tours III (813), canon xxv; Mansi XIV, c. 87.
25. de Clercq, *Législation Religieuse* I, p. 245 sq.
26. For text and translation, see Bertram, *Chrodegang Rules*.
27. *Concordia Regularum* auctore S Benedicto Anianæ, ed. Fr Hugo Menard (Paris, 1638), PL 103–701 sq.
28. MGH Cap. I, 346.
29. e.g. Claussen, *Reform of the Frankish Church*, p. 18 ('in the ninth century [the RC] was made the basis of the rule by which all Canons in the Empire had to live'), also Brooks, *Church of Canterbury*, p. 156.
30. Morhain, 'Origine et histoire', p 183.
31. de Clercq, *Législation Religieuse* II, pp. 12–13.
32. Text in Mansi XII, cc. 859–82.
33. Augustine, Epistle 157; PL 33:674–93.
34. Amort, *Vetus Disciplina*, part II, cap. 8.
35. Poggiaspalla, *Vita comune*, pp. 105–6.
36. Isidore, *On Ecclesiastical Offices* book 2, chapters 19–23; PL 83:757–60.
37. Wulfstan, *Homilies*, ed. D. Bethurun, Oxford University Press, 1957, Xa.
38. PL 105:816. See also Van Waesberghe, *De Akense Regels*, pp. 29–34.
39. Werminghoff, 'Die Beschlüsse des Aachener Concils'.
40. H. Leclercq, 'Chanoines', p. 245.
41. Ermoldus, *In Honorem Hludovici Pii;* MGH Poetae II, 1 ff.
42. Capitula for the Missi in 819, cap. vii; Mansi XIV Appendix, c. 417.
43. Amann & Dumas, *L'Eglise au Pouvoir des Laïques*, p. 255.
44. The MSS are collated in MGH *Legum, Sectio III, Concilia II pars i* (Hannover 1904), pp. 307 sq.
45. Dereine, 'Chanoines', pp. 366–7, 370.
46. Semmler, in Crusius, *Weltlichen Kollegiatstift*, p. 79.
47. Lesne, *Propriété Ecclesiastique*, p. 18.
48. Mansi XIV, cc. 311–2; Crusius, *Weltlichen Kollegiatstift*, p. 53, Lesne, *Propriété Ecclésiastique*, p. 18.
49. Siegwart, *Chorherren*, pp. 69–70, 90–1.
50. Sparrow Simpson, *Registrum Statutorum Londiniensis*, part III cap. 14, pp. 40–3.
51. Nightingale, *Gorze Reform*, p. 97.

52. Morhain, *Origine et Histoire*, p. 179; cf *Gesta Aldrici*, in PL 115:29–93, esp. c. 32.
53. Mansi XIV, cc. 925–6.
54. Paris VI (829), canons xx, xvi and xxx; Mansi XIV cc. 553, 554 and 558–9.
55. Aachen II (836), caput I, canons vii and xi; caput II (ii), canons i and xv; Mansi XIV, cc. 675, 676, 679–80 and 683.
56. Amort, *Vetus Disciplina*, II, ch. 9.
57. de Clercq, *Législation Religieuse*, Book IV, p. 391 sq.
58. Ganz, *Corbie and the Carolingian Renaissance*, p. 26.
59. *Rabani Mauri De Institutione Clericorum libri tres*, ed. Dr Aloysius Knöpfler (München, 1901).
60. AA.SS. June V, p. 101.

Chapter Six

The Viking Years, and a Longer Rule

The Empire breaks up

After the death of Louis the Pious, the empire of Charlemagne broke up. The Treaty of Verdun in 843 foolishly divided the territory between three quarrelsome brothers. France and Germany discovered their separate identities, and the long straggling Middle Kingdom emerged to be a bone of contention and a cause of war for over a thousand years to come. As rivals squabbled for the Imperial Throne, and lesser rivals for lesser dignities, the Church suffered, and community life in many places became impossible. A new and potent threat from the North failed to unite the divided legacy of the Franks, and brought more confusion and disruption to the Church.

Conciliar and Imperial Legislation in France

We hear most about the western division, which was to become France. Charles the Bald attempted to preserve the full rigour of Carolingian legislation about community life. A council in Meaux in 845 repeated the injunction for canons to observe their rule, whether they lived in the city or in rural minsters. They were to have a common dormitory and refectory, and be tended as necessary in a common infirmary. Whether in sickness or health they were to dress as canons, and to be present in their enclosures in order to celebrate the canonical hours. Bishops were ordered to provide suitable dwellings for them, and the Emperor undertook to confiscate land for their use, and pay for the buildings if necessary (as had already been agreed by Louis the Pious).[1] There was always the possibility of transfer between the two orders, the monastic and the canonical, and at intervals during the next few centuries we find one or other alternately in favour with the ruling powers. Monasticism was usually considered superior, as being more demanding, but canonical clergy were more useful for the care of souls and the spread of the Church. In 848 the canons of St Martial in Limoges petitioned Charles the Bald to allow them to become monks, which he did gladly. However their bishop, Stodilus, was most displeased at losing his clergy to monasticism.[2]

The local Council of Soissons in 853 urged bishops 'not to neglect their sees, but to live in their cities, together with their clergy, in a canonical manner. They are to compel the priests entrusted to them to reform themselves in learning, chastity and sober living, as well as hospitality'.[3] Following this, Charles sent *missi* to visit the canonical communities, and to inspect the revenues of the superiors, and the *mensa* of the canons.[4] At Châlons-sur-Marne in 859, Charles gave the canons enough terrain to pay for the building of their *mansiones*: these mansions were allocated by the chapter, but thereafter descended like private property from one canon to the next. This implies that they no longer slept in a common dormitory, but they did still dine in common.[5] A council at Châlons-sur-Saône in 873 issued a charter to confirm the rights of the canonical clergy over the Church of St Lawrence, on the plea of Leuterius, who is described as 'provost and advocate of the canons'.[6] However by 881 the situation had deteriorated, and the Council of St Macra (Fîmes), had to deplore the decadence of modern clergy because of the political situation and the confusion of worldly affairs: it urges the *missi* once again to inspect 'all monasteries, whether of canons, monks or nuns', to correct abuses.[7]

Charles the Bald and his successors developed the concept of the dynastic chapel and mausoleum which Charlemagne had commenced at Aachen. Louis the Pious had already built a new *capella* in his palace at Diedenhofen (Thionville), and another in Frankfurt. With the division of the Empire, Lothar took possession of the original *pfalzstift* at Aachen, Louis II used Frankfurt and Regensburg, and Charles the Bald founded a new community at Compiègne. The foundation charter for this illustrates very clearly what was the intention in establishing these dynastic communities.

> Our grandfather Charles constructed a chapel in the palace at Aachen, to the honour of the blessed Mother of God, the Virgin Mary, and he established clerics there, for the healing of his own

soul, the absolution of his sins, and for the dignity of the Imperial house; he also accumulated there a great collection of relics, and adorned it with all sorts of ornaments: we too intend to imitate his style and that of the other kings and emperors who have preceded us, and since by the fortune of Partition that part of the realm has not fallen to us, we have constructed anew a minster (*monasterium*), called the Regia, in the palace of Compiègne within our jurisdiction, to the honour of the blessed Mother of God, the ever-Virgin Mary; we have endowed it with many gifts, with the help of the Lord, and established clerics there to the number of one hundred, who are to entreat the mercy of the Lord for the good estate of the holy Church of God, for our parents and ancestors, for ourselves, our wife and children, and for the stability of the entire realm.[8]

This document is of enormous importance for the understanding of the purpose of these royal foundations, which were to remain a feature of Europe until the Revolution. It is essentially an establishment for prayer, not only for the founder and his kin, but for the entire Church and realm. Although under the direct control of the emperor, the establishment had the constitution of a community of canonical clergy. The chapel at Compiègne was octagonal, on the model of Aachen, and became the centre of several other royal chapels in the Oise valley. It was governed by a provost, with a dean, treasurer and cantor under him, and had ample provender free from tax. Even after Charles succeeded in recovering Aachen, Compiègne remained his winter palace.[9]

From then on, the principle was well established that a secular lord, whether emperor, king, duke, or country squire, could make a collegiate foundation for clergy to serve as his household chaplains, to minister to his dependents, but above all to pray, for the good estate of the Church, the stability of the realm, and, of course, for the founding family, living and dead. Foundation charters continue to express the same intentions until the eighteenth century. In all internal matters the clergy were to govern themselves according to the *Institutio Canonica*, but the entire community remained under the personal control of the founder and his family, who could appoint the provost and other officials, and select new members for the community. This domineering lay control could mean that a pious and reform-minded lord might ensure a devout community of pastoral clergy, but it was much more likely to mean that worldly princes and landowners would treat the community as their private property, and distribute positions within it as a means of disposing of young relations who were unlikely to be of much use in war or administration, thus ensuring them a comfortable income for life. At times of strong central government, these lay-dominated communities of clergy were subject to inspection, by Imperial *missi* or diocesan archdeacons, while in times of unrest the property and revenues of the communities were a standing temptation to impoverished local war-lords.

Episcopal Legislation

At the same time, other communities of canonical clergy existed under the direct control of the bishops, in France as in all areas of Europe. Some bishops were evidently more concerned about the common life than others, though as legislation always tends to be drafted in reaction to difficult situations, silence about community life may simply mean that it thrived with no problems. However in many cases it is clear that community life had effectively ceased. Despite Aldric's efforts in Le Mans earlier in the century, after the death of Louis the Pious the '*episcopium* was devastated and reduced virtually to nothing ... the enclosure of the canons and the mother church in the centre of the city ... with the other properties ... were destroyed to the foundations and despoiled'.[10] On the other hand, we hear from Hincmar of Rheims that when Charles the Bald plundered Laon, he spared both the *domus episcopi* and the *clericorum claustrum*.[11] The emperor was at least consistent to his own principles in preserving and promoting the canonical life. One of the earliest MSS of the *Institutio Canonica* is preserved at Laon, with annotations about canonical life there in the 870s.

A number of late ninth-century bishops produced 'Episcopal Statutes' in order to reform the clergy of their dioceses, which are informative about the expectations and requirements of the clergy, but are singularly silent about any form of the Common Life. Such are those of Radolphus of Bourges, Wulfrad of Bourges, Riculf of Soissons, Hincmar of Reims and Hérard of Tours.[12] Like contemporary councils and papal letters, they reiterate the long-established canons on the dress and decorum of the clergy, clerical continence, episcopal authority over the clergy, the requirement to celebrate Mass in consecrated churches and to use those churches for no other purpose, never to celebrate Mass without at least one server, always to maintain a minor cleric as apprentice, and so on, much of which is also mentioned in the Canonical Rules.

Hincmar of Rheims (845–82), who lived very closely with his

canons, produced an important set of statutes on 1 November 852, including a twenty-point questionnaire for the deacons, a consultation document on priestly manners, and a confidential note to the deans. Hincmar required all priests to attend a meeting on the first day of the month. The main purpose of these monthly meetings was the instruction and correction of the clergy, but it also had a social aspect, for he tells them, after Mass had been celebrated, not to sit too long over their lunch, and to return to their flock once they have finished the third cup.[13] The monthly deanery meeting, gathering all the clergy for prayer, instruction and recreation, dates from this period. In 874 Hincmar turned his attention to the rural 'mother churches' which served small chapels or 'field churches' in the neighbourhood, and sends archdeacons or deans to supervise them. Rural priests are expected to attend monthly meetings like their city colleagues, but Hincmar remarks that the vocations of monk and pastoral priest are quite distinct, and should not be confused, implying that he does not even consider a common life desirable. 'It is clear and certain that no one is able to maintain the enclosure and duties pertaining to a monastery at the same time as doing what is necessary for the people in rural parishes.' Despite the good bishop's earnest desire for a holy and pastoral clergy, he does not value community life, for clearly the rural priests are expected all to live separately from one another – though they do not live alone, for they are all to maintain at least one minor cleric.[14] Walter of Orleans also instructs 'each of his clergy to maintain his own minor cleric, and to ensure his religious education. If at all possible he should not neglect to hold a school in his church'.[15]

In contrast, other French bishops obviously did desire a common life, and attempted to establish it. In 849 Hermanus, Bishop of Nevers, took steps to restore community life after all canonical houses had been destroyed by war. He established sixty canons inside the city, and sixteen at St Martin's outside, as well as communities of monks and nuns, and two hospitals, one for the poor and one for noble travellers. All this was ratified by Charles the Bald.[16] A generation later, in 873, Bishop Willibert of Cologne speaks of communities of canons other than the cathedral community, and affirms their independence.[17] In 875, Odo of Beauvais made grants of land sufficient to support fifty canons at St Peter's, Beauvais.[18] Bishops Anselm of Laon, Manasses of Troyes and others strove to maintain the canonical life, as did Benno of Meissen and the synod of Trosby in 909. The lives of various saints testify to their desire to promote community life, such as St

Odulfus of Utrecht (*c.*865), and St Madalrée of Verdun. St Everard of Cysoing (ob. 867) founded a community, described as 'canons regular', which at this period can only mean canons living according to the Aachen rule.[19] Some communities were evidently flourishing: in 885 a charter of Charles the Fat attests there were sixty canons at Toul, and they were well endowed.[20] In 888 at Herrieden, the bishop 'ejected the monks and established canons there, granting them provender (*praebendum*) out of a few revenues, while he retained the remaining income for himself to distribute to the serving clergy'.[21] Here is a prime example of the canonical life being preferred to the monastic, in the service of a pastoral bishop.

Common Life outside France

In the Middle Kingdom similar legislation existed, but is less well recorded. At Mainz in 847 the council ordered priests to live canonically, and continued at some length about the importance of not being involved in secular business.[22] A council at Metz in 888 reaffirmed the importance of clerical continence, and went further than before in forbidding any woman, even a priest's mother or sister, from living in the clergy house. They are to live an 'angelic life'.[23] In other regions about the same time, we hear that new buildings for the canons, 'most apt for the regular life', were constructed by Bishop Altfried at Hildesheim in 872. Similar buildings were constructed at Halberstadt between 853 and 886, and the canonry at Barcelona was restored after its virtual destruction.[24]

The common life was promoted even more in Italy. A council in Rome under Eugenius II in 826, and another attended by sixty-seven bishops in 853 legislated for the common life. The latter required an enclosure for the clerics to be established beside every cathedral church, containing a refectory and a dormitory, and that suitable superiors be appointed. Bishops are to be restrained from admitting more clerics than they can reasonably support (cf. IC 118), and every bishop is to maintain a school.[25] Shortly afterwards a decree of Nicholas I (858–67) ordained that there should be no building in the atrium of a church save for the clergy house.[26] A council at Pavia, attended by John VIII and Charles the Bald in 876, and ratified the same year at Pontignone, urged bishops to live with their clergy in closes, and not to allow priests to be absent from their churches. It further insisted that women should never enter the houses of priests.[27] A synod in Ravenna the next year prohibited laymen from treating the clergy houses as hotels.[28] A community of pastoral clergy was founded in San Elpidio near Fermo in 884, and the deed witnessed by eight priest-canons, five deacon-canons, five subdeacon-canons and four acolyte-canons.[29]

The ideal of a common life for the secular clergy was therefore very much alive south of the Alps to the end of the ninth century. In France and Germany, which were in the process of separating from each other, the idea was remembered but in practice was difficult to put into action. In many places it was impossible, in some it was considered undesirable, in others it was well established and survived. The implication is that the institute of community life continued to be favoured and to spread, despite setbacks such as occasional Viking raids.

In England, in the meantime, the ideal of the minster was already beginning to fade before the first Vikings landed, and the high culture of the age of Bede was yielding to a lower and simpler level. Minsters tended to dwindle to small communities, just of priests, without the deacons and minor clergy which would feed their future development. Powerful laymen began increasingly to take control, and the confusion of the Danish wars gave them an opportunity to extend that control. Once the raids became widespread, conditions became quite impossible. The raiders targeted the minsters deliberately, knowing that they served as repositories for the portable wealth of the neighbourhood, and virtually all the pre-war clerical establishments were wiped out. Some were able to make a fresh start: at Ely the surviving clerics after 870 'lived here as secular priests under the government of provosts or archpriests', which implies that some sort of regular life lingered on.[30] Beverley, Winchcombe, Leominster and Chester-le-Street also seem to have found new life as secular communities after a wartime interlude. The common judgement may not be quite true, that by the end of the ninth century priests were few, scattered and ill-educated, and all regular common life, whether of monks or canons, was extinct. Knowles talks of 'a complete collapse of monasticism by the end of the ninth century',[31] but at the time Fulco was able to write to King Alfred to congratulate him on the diligence and industry by which he had restored the ecclesiastical order, which had indeed largely collapsed, not only because of pagan raids, but also through 'the lapse of time, the negligence of bishops and the ignorance of their subjects'.[32] In Alfred's laws we hear that a church building may not be the most suitable place for a fugitive, because the community might need to use it; and that a murderous priest must pay his weregeld out of the place in a minster that he has bought himself.[33] This implies both that there were existing communities, and that places in them were already being treated as personal property which could be bought and sold.

The Longer Rule

At some stage in the late ninth or early tenth century, a third rule for canonical clergy was written, and so successfully passed off as the Rule of Chrodegang that even now historians continue to treat it as an eighth-century document. This text, which draws heavily both on the Rule of Chrodegang and the Institute of Aachen, is that usually known as the 'Interpolated' or 'Enlarged' Rule of Chrodegang, first published by d'Achery in 1657–77, and reprinted by Migne as if it were Chrodegang's original version, with the genuine text (RC) treated as an abridgment.[34] I have preferred to name it simply the 'Longer Rule' (RL, which may also stand for *Regula Lotharingica* or *Regula Leofrici*). Many historians, noticing the identity of certain passages with parts of the Rule of Aachen, believed that Aachen came later, and consciously incorporated the Rule of Chrodegang, or expanded it for wider use. There can be no doubt, however, that this third text is later, probably considerably later, than the date of the Council of Aachen. There are two versions of the text, one English, and the other, probably, from Lorraine, which uses the entire prologue from the Rule of Chrodegang, including the title which names both Pippin and Chrodegang, whereas the English version has a shorter Prologue, omitting the title and names. All in all, it is more likely that the Lorraine version is the first.[35]

In composing the text, the author used both his main sources very freely. Sometimes an entire chapter is reproduced virtually unchanged, but often lines or paragraphs are omitted, inserted, or rearranged. Of the text of the original Rule of Chrodegang only about forty per cent survives into the new Rule, making the title 'Enlarged Rule of Chrodegang' somewhat inappropriate. Of the Rule of Aachen (excluding the preliminary catena) forty-six per cent survives. The remainder of the document is made up of a very wide-ranging selection of extracts from conciliar decrees, papal and episcopal letters, liturgical texts, and some sources still unknown. There are a number of places where additional material from the Rule of St Benedict appears: this implies that the compiler was brought up in a Benedictine environment. Moreover three chapters (15, 18 and 23) draw on a reformed Benedictine text, the *Ordo Qualiter* which originated in Monte Cassino in the late eighth century.[36] Some of the sources are certainly mid ninth century: the latest positively identified is the Capitula of Hérard of Tours (858), used for IC 67 and 73.[37]

It is difficult to see much structure or order to the Longer Rule as a whole, and at times it seems that one chapter leads to another simply by association of ideas rather than according to any plan. As a composition, it must be said that this Longer Rule is very inferior both to the genuine Rule of Chrodegang and to the Institutes of Aachen, though by including so many extra topics it does provide a much more complete guide to the clerical life.

The context of this document must be a moment of reform, under a bishop determined to reinstate the canonical life for his clergy, and probably with some link to England. It appears to be an episcopal document, rather than a royal one, but has no specific reference to any one church. The author clearly had access to both the original Rule of Chrodegang, and the Canonical Institutes of Aachen. His other sources include Gregory, Bede, Alcuin and Egbert of York, Conciliar decrees, the Benedictine *Ordo Qualiter*, and the Capitula of Theodulf. One possibility is the church of Reims, which flourished under the two reforming bishops Hincmar and Fulco, and the latter's Chancellor, Grimbald. The church of Reims would have been familiar with the institutes of Aachen, being part of the Empire, but Reims is also close enough to Metz for the memory of St Chrodegang to be familiar, and his original Rule to be accessible. A bishop and his chancellor who had been Benedictines would have known the Rule of St Benedict so well that half-conscious quotations and echoes of its wording would have come naturally to them. The link with England is amply provided by St Grimbald, who was sent with a letter of recommendation from Fulco to assist King Alfred of Wessex in the reconstruction of the English Church following the first Danish Wars. Grimbald must be considered seriously as either the author or the disseminator of the Longer Rule.

Another possible source is the North Italian region, where many colleges of clerics were founded or reformed during the mid tenth century, such as those directed by Ratherius of Verona. Langefeld considered a western French origin more probable, possibly in the Loire valley. A possibility there is the group of dispossessed canons of Le Mans who may have been responsible for the Isidorian literature. If so, the Longer Rule is the only one of their productions which has continued successfully to pass itself off as a writing of an earlier century, for it is still cited by recent respectable historians as the work of Chrodegang. Because of this, and its later influence on England, it is worth looking at the text to see how it differs from the two preceding Rules. (Langefeld accepts Professor Bischoff's dating of the earliest manuscript of this Rule, the only one that names Chrodegang, to the second quarter of the ninth century, but it must surely be later than 858. Curiously even she thinks that the Rule of Aachen incorporated passages from Chrodegang, which as we have seen is not the case.)[38]

The Rule of Life

The first half of the Longer Rule consists almost entirely of extracts from the original Rule of Chrodegang and the legislative part of the Institutes of Aachen. The chapters dealing with the question of property all come from Aachen, and maintain the principle that those who have ample private property must support themselves, while those who have not may be supported by the Church. On domestic matters, the chapter on food and drink is more specific than Chrodegang, less detailed than Aachen, and concludes with a severe warning against drunkenness, despite preserving Aachen's allowance of five pints of wine per day. The cook and the provost are described precisely in Chrodegang's words, the porter and the enclosure in extracts from both earlier rules, the cellarer largely in original terms.

The cycle of prayer (RL 14–27) draws heavily on the *Ordo Qualiter*, for the sections on what to do on first rising (RL 14), on Prime, on manual labour, on silence after Compline, and most of the section on meetings for chapter. More about the daily chapter is taken from Chrodegang (RL 18, RC 8); the remaining Offices of the day are described in extracts from St Isidore out of the Aachen catena, much abbreviated. The section on how to behave in church is put together from both Chrodegang and Aachen. Chapters on discipline (RL 28–33) are largely taken from Chrodegang, who here closely follows St Benedict, to which is added an order of confession and of reconciliation on Maundy Thursday taken from an eighth-century source. Frequent confession is recommended, every three weeks for the canons, and every week for monks: this is a great advance on the original Rule of Chrodegang which only envisaged confession twice a year. Three chapters (RL 34–6) deal with the different times of year and the seasons of fasting or celebration, mostly taken from Chrodegang.

After this, the Longer Rule appears to disintegrate, and there is no obvious order or pattern in the sequence of chapters. From chapters 37 to 55 the remaining chapters of the Chrodegang and Aachen Rules are inserted in random order, with sections on similar topics separated by other material. What is more informative is to see which chapters of the older Rules are not represented. From St Chrodegang, the whole section on the keeping of enclosure and remaining within bounds at night is omitted (RC 3–4), as also the chapter on manual labour (RC 9). A large part of chapter 14, on Confession, is omitted, and the whole of chapters 16 and 19, on association with the excommunicate. The chapter on the arrangement of the refectory (RC 21) is totally omitted. That on clothing (RC 29) is drastically reduced, and there is no mention of firewood. The long and complicated chapter 31 on making over property to the community is totally omitted, as is chapter 33, on attending chapter and Mass on Sundays. The whole chapter on the care of the poor, their spiritual instruction and feeding, is reduced to a few lines.

Turning to the Canonical Rule incorporated in the Institutes of Aachen (IC 114–145) no part is used of the Imperial preface, or the long chapter defining the difference between monks and canons, and the status of church property (IC 114–16). The chapter on food and drink is drastically abbreviated, and the whole of the section on weights and measures disappears (IC 122). The chapters on how angels are present during the Divine Office (IC 132), on the care of the sick (IC 142), and on fortifying the enclosure (IC 144) are all omitted, and the epitome (IC 145) is not used at all in the Longer Rule. Those chapters that are used, especially those which are extracts from St Isidore, are again abbreviated. The implication is that life is more complicated than in the previous century, but that more can be taken for granted (such as Sunday Mass). There is less interest in the details of feeding, clothing and safeguarding the community, perhaps feeling that more can be left to the initiative of the local superiors.

From chapter 56 onwards, the Longer Rule rambles through a series of extracts from a variety of sources. Some of these are similar, or identical, to chapters in the catena prefixed to the Rule of Aachen (IC 1–113), though with variations, and sometimes a major re-arrangement of material. A long chapter on drunkenness (RL 62) is taken from an unknown source, which quotes St Jerome and St Basil. There follows a run of conciliar canons (RL 66–80) on a the behaviour expected of a priest, and how this should be enforced. Most of these come from collections such as the Dionysio-Hadriana, sent by Pope Hadrian to Charlemagne, and the capitula of Hérard of Tours. Nothing is directly attributable to the Pseudo-Isidorian Decretals.

After this come two long pastoral letters. The former incorporates part of a letter by Gregory II introducing the canons of the Council of Rome in 721, the latter has been identified by Langefeld as by Alcuin. They are full of salutary, if rather predictable, advice, and designed more to encourage the bishops in pursuing their known duty than to suggest anything new. Then comes another chapter of Isidore, also used in the catena to Aachen (RL 83, IC 23), and two more canons, one of which may come from the Isidorian atelier. Finally comes an odd chapter warning the clergy to be on their guard against the illusions of the devil, citing two cases, one of which comes from St Gregory's Dialogues. There the Rule ends, abruptly, with no conclusion.

The Isidorian Decretals

One of the most influential features of the ninth century was the emergence of the huge body of canonical literature known as the 'Isidorian Decretals' and associated material. The first section consists of a Capitular attributed to Anghilram, which is presented as a text sent by Hadrian I to the Archbishop of Metz (PL 96:1055–68). Then follows an Imperial capitular, attributed to Benedict of Mainz (PL 97:699–911). The major corpus, attributed to Isidore (PL 130), is the only one to incorporate ante-Nicene material: it was this which first, in the sixteenth century, raised suspicions about the authenticity of the whole collection. It was probably produced in or around Le Mans in the late 840s, in other words soon after the extinction of canonical life there, and possibly as a result.[39] The first two collections were probably produced very quickly, in response to an immediate need; the Isidorian corpus properly so-called was composed with greater skill and plausibility. By 852 Hincmar is able to quote them, and they were known in Italy by the time of Nicholas I (858–67) and Hadrian II (867–72), both of whom refer to them.

They should not be ignored or dismissed out of hand, for they represent a valiant attempt to restore a body of legislation which was believed to have existed, and needed to be reconstructed. As Newman commented, they 'embody existing opinions in writing.'[40] Documents on papyrus were disintegrating, and the gist of their content had to be restored from the fragments or memories which survived. Like most fabrications of earlier church documents, they are not designed to deceive so much as to provide the missing but necessary evidence for what was believed to be the true legal position. It is untrue to say that the primacy of the papacy is based on these Decretals: it was well established long before, and was the occasion of their composition rather than the result. Nevertheless they did lead to centuries of confusion, and gave the enemies of the Church an easy weapon in controversy.[41] But perhaps we should acclaim the authors as among the first great European novelists, who composed plausible letters from such a variety of early popes. If we are looking for an identity for these novelists, they may well have been the canons of Le Mans, dispersed after the sack of their canonry, but still active and eager to reassert the rights of the Church against the nobility, and to restore the community life they had lost. The occasion may have been the Diet of Épernay in June 846, which represented a challenge to the church by the lay nobility: the dominant theme, especially of the letters and decrees attributed to the popes of the first three centuries, is the exemption of the clergy from lay control, which was obviously an urgent concern of the dispossessed canons of Le Mans.

The Tenth Century

The tenth century was a time of turmoil and of restoration, of corruption and of reform. Baronius begins his account of the century by warning his readers not to be dismayed at the decadence and worldliness of the papacy.

> Lo, here begins the nine hundredth year of our Redemption, which begins a new century, one which is often called an 'age of iron' for its harshness, devoid of all good; or an 'age of lead' for its depravity, oosing evil; a 'dark age' for the lack of written sources. Poised on its brink, before we go any further I feel I must warn the Reader in advance, because of the terrible things we have found ourselves researching as the century opens, so that he will not suffer any scandal to his tender conscience, when he sees the 'abomination of desolation in the Temple', but rather will be struck with amazement as he recognizes the power of God watching over it for its protection.'[42]

Baronius of course saw things from a Roman perspective. Others write feelingly about the 'Tenth Century Reformation', celebrating the great monastic movements associated with Cluny, Gorze and

Glastonbury. On the whole it was a difficult time for communities of secular clergy, since during the more lawless and decadent periods they were seized and secularized by powerful laymen, and the canons were dispersed, while in periods of restoration the great reforming bishops tended to expel canons in order to replace them with monks.

In addition, the tenth century saw the rise of the *prebendal* system, which was to threaten the essence of community life. Bishops were not always reliable in passing on the proper share of the church revenue to the canons, so that some communities broke up for lack of income. To resolve this, canonries came to be endowed separately from the dioceses. A specific fund was allocated for food and clothing, the *praebenda* or 'things to be provided' (provender). Donations were made by the faithful directly to the canons, rather than to the bishops, because 'it was on the canons, not the bishop, that they relied on for prayer, day and night, in the church, and for singing the Mass and office on the anniversaries of the dead'.[43] Although to begin with this was administered as a single fund, and the canons allocated their food and clothing as in the *Institutio Canonica*, by the tenth century the revenues came to be divided among individual canons, as wartime conditions drove them to live in separate establishments, and the refectory could no longer be maintained. A donor would give a property for the maintenance of a specific additional canon, who would thus feel a proprietorial right over that land and its revenues, and feel entitled to treat it as his own. The divisions were equal to begin with, but since each *praebendum* was linked to a particular source of revenue, differences soon arose. The prebend came to be seen as an honour to which the canon was entitled, then as a proprietorial right. At first the chapter allocated them — in 971 Gérard of Toul decreed that the primicerius and dean should do so with the consent of the rest of the chapter — but after that canons began to treat them as property which they could bequeath, exchange or even sell. A fee, *xenium* or *servitium*, was payable to the bishop on the occasion of any such exchange of prebend. Prebends could also be given to monasteries, which began to collect them as sources of income.[44] The land remained inalienably 'church property', but it could easily be held by a married minor cleric, with no intention of performing divine service, or it could be bequeathed to a monastery, who would enjoy the revenue without any direct involvement in the life of the cathedral or collegiate church.

The dominance of the laity meant that patrons frequently

appointed unsuitable youths to clerical positions, for the sake of the potentially lucrative prebends. Inevitably, the perennial problems of Simony and Nicolaism resurfaced in the tenth century, and triggered many conciliar and episcopal rebukes. Condemnations of clerical concubinage continue to be a feature of reforming local councils, such as those at Mainz in 888, Trosby in 909, Augsburg in 952, Winchester in 975, Calne in 978, Aure in 994 or Poitiers in 1000, with the usual requirements to send the women away. For instance, at Augsburg the last canon reads, 'A bishop, priest, deacon, or subdeacon, must abstain from his wife, as has been established by many Councils, because he serves the Mysteries of God.'[45] Nevertheless, canon law of the time considered clerical marriages merely illicit, not actually invalid: it was only in the twelfth century that marriage after ordination was declared to be invalid. In some areas, such as western France, major clerics lived more or less openly as married men. Subdeacons, deacons, priests, and bishops ignored their obligation of continence and either continued to live with the wives they had married before ordination, or took new partners on a temporary or permanent basis. Councils and episcopal statutes might well deplore the situation ('the priests are rotting in a dungheap of decadence', says Trosby), but in some areas it was recognized that little could be done: St Ratherius of Verona remarked that if he applied the canons strictly and deprived all unchaste priests of their priestly functions, he would have virtually no clergy left.[46] Neither he, nor Atto of Vercelli, nor the successive reform councils had much effect, and most bishops settled for exacting a fine for concubinage which in effect became a licence fee for marriage. Adalberon II of Metz (984–1005) even agreed that the sons of priests could be ordained, contrary to former legislation, which inevitably led to clerical positions becoming hereditary. This was counteracted rather strongly by the councils of Goslar in 1019 and Pavia in 1023 which declared such children to be serfs. As long as the papacy remained under the domination of the laity, little could be done to correct the abuses.[47]

Ratherius of Verona, in his famous 'Rant', the Synodal Address of 932, issued a long and eloquent rebuke to the clergy, giving them many salutary instructions. 'Let your dwelling be next to the church, and do not let women into them. Rise for vigils every night, sing your way through the office at the proper time ...'[48] While very critical of the way in which the cathedral canons had embezzled the funds due to the minor clergy, he met the problem by encouraging the formation of a number of *scholae*, which seem to have been canonical communities on the Aachen pattern. Such *scholae* continued to multiply in Verona during the next two centuries. Moreover Ratherius was so confident in the validity of the canonical way of life that he reformed the decayed monastery of Maguzzano by expelling the monks and establishing a *schola* of three priests, one deacon, one subdeacon and several minor clerics.[49]

In this, Ratherius was going in the opposite direction to many other contemporary bishops, who saw 'reform' as a process of changing secular canons into monks. Different bishops had different priorities; some actively suppressed canonries, or mutated them into monasteries, some actively suppressed monasteries and gave their endowments to canonical clergy; far too many did nothing and let the Church rot around them.

Tenth-Century Reformers in Europe

Nevertheless, many important canonical foundations are attested in early tenth-century Italy, Spain, France, and Germany. A diocesan synod in Bergamo in 908 established a 'canonry for the refection of priests and clerics who serve in the same holy church of God'. The canonry was to be attached to the church of St Vincent, and a primicerius was appointed to supervise the ration of food and drink. The decision was witnessed by the bishop, the archdeacon, the archpriest, eleven priests, four deacons and seven subdeacons. Interestingly, the primicerius is one of the deacons, not a priest.[50] In Italy the Institutes of Aachen certainly remained in favour. Indeed by the tenth century, all the urban monasteries of Rome had been changed by the 'spirit of dissolution' into 'as many canonical chapters', as Schuster puts it.[51]

Meanwhile the Council of Trosby near Soissons (909) urged a reform of the clerical life according to the canonical rules. It recognized that much of the chaos had been caused by Viking raids (*a Paganis succensis et destructis*) and even more by the intrusion of laymen 'living among the priests and other religious men, like lords and masters; they order them about like abbots although they are totally ignorant of their origins, their way of life or their Rule'. These 'lay abbots with their wives, their sons or daughters, their men at arms and their dogs' are to be expelled forthwith.[52] It was not intrinsically necessary for the superior to be a priest or deacon, any more than a Benedictine abbot needed to be, so a powerful lay landowner could manipulate the existing canonical rules to the extent of getting himself accepted as a member of the congregation in minor orders, and being elected or persuading the bishop to appointing him superior. He could then take up residence in the community home, with his household and his hounds, without technically infringing any of the canons. Frequent references to 'clerics' with wives and children does not necessarily mean that these were subdeacons, deacons or priests breaking their obligation to continence: it was scandalous enough if married clerics in minor orders were living within what was meant to be the enclosure and absorbing the income that was intended for the support of the entire body of clergy. What was in effect the seizure of church property by robber barons could be done with a veneer of respecting legal form. This deceived nobody, and was the natural target of reformers, whether they intended to restore canonical life or substitute monastic. On the other hand, paradoxically, there were laymen who were more concerned for reform than the clergy, and who used their position to impose a stricter way of life on their unwilling subjects.

Fifteen years later the Archbishop of Sens wrote to his 'canons and secular clerics' to encourage the observance of the canonical rules. He is particularly scornful of the dubious wandering clerics known as the 'sons of Golias', who are to be shaved all over to remove any trace of their tonsure.[53] When John XIII established the new metropolitan see of Magdeburg in 968, he set it up 'according to the custom of the Roman Church' with twelve priests, seven deacons, and twenty-four cardinal subdeacons wearing sandals and *lisanis*.[54] Later in the tenth century we hear of communities of secular canons being re-established at Reims in 975, la Bisbal in the diocese of Gerona in 977, and St Pierre at Troyes in 991.[55]

Increasingly, the number of canons came to be fixed, often at twelve or twenty-four, but including large houses such as Chartres with seventy-two, or Nevers with sixty, and certain *abbatiolae clericorum* with only three.[56] In Germany collegiate communities began to multiply in the tenth century, often outside the walls of cities. By the middle of the century there were six at Cologne, three at Mainz.[57] Many of these extra-mural communities stood on the sites of much earlier cemetery chapels. At Trier, Archbishop Radbod (883–915) reorganized his diocese, under Viking threat, and divided it into five archdeaconries, each archdeacon presiding over a community of clergy. A generation later, Archbishop Heinrich I (956–64) built 'a close with *regulares officinae*, regular offices, and an enclosure around the great church, and decreed that the full vigour of the regular life should be lived there'.[58] By 'regular' life he did not mean following a monastic rule, but following the canonical rule strictly. Nevertheless by so doing the canons began to look more like monks to the lay observer. From this spread a general reform of canonical churches throughout Lotharingia. Archbishop Theoderic (964–77) reaffirmed full community life in Trier, building a refectory and dormitory, as did Wolfgang of Regensburg (972–94) who had formerly been Dean of Trier. Similar restorations were effected at Koblenz, Mainz, Worms and Speyer.[59] At Magdeburg in 968, Otto I erected a chapter of twelve priests, seven deacons and twelve subdeacons, known as a *Kardinalskolleg*.[60] The royal and imperial chapel communities continued to flourish, actively supported by the later monarchs and the popes who did their bidding. In 997 Gregory V appointed seven cardinal priests and seven cardinal deacons to Aachen, and Compiègne remained in use as the coronation church until the end of the Carolingian dynasty with Louis V in 979.[61]

Siegwart lists a very large number of German cathedral and canonical communities, under their dates of foundation, of which fifteen were founded in the ninth century, *after* the Treaty of Verdun, and no less than fifty-eight during the tenth century, showing that the ideal of common life was very far from being extinct. One of the best documented is Zürich, reformed in 951, as *fratres* living the *regularis vita* under a dean, and exercising supervision over a number of daughter houses.[62] Similarly, Deraine lists a great number of flourishing canonries in France at the same period.[63] In part it was because many of the best priests were becoming monks that bishops felt driven to reform and improve the life of the secular clergy.

However in other places, reformers were less sympathetic. The hermit Grimlaic of Metz refers to the Rule of Chrodegang as still in use there in the early tenth century, but it seems to have fallen out of use by the middle of the century.[64] Bishop Adalberon I, though coming from a canonical tradition, preferred to promote the reforms associated with St Chrodegang's Benedictine foundation at Gorze rather than the same saint's canonical foundation in Metz itself. Expelling lay proprietors, he called on former officials of cathedral canonries to take the lead in restoring strict monasticism.[65] In 933 he took possession of the royal palace vacant since the death of King Zwentibold in 900, to assist his monastic foundations.[66] In 941 he referred to the minster of St Arnulf as a 'conglomeration of headless clerics, who exist under the pretence of observing the canonical rule'. After consulting 'our clergy, namely the abbots of both Orders', he drove them out and substituted monks. The dispossessed canons appealed to the emperor and to the pope, both of whom supported Adalberon.[67]

Communities could go backwards and forwards between the two ways of life. At a local council in Mont-Sainte-Marie in 961 it was reported that the monastery of St Vincent at Laon had decayed, and that Bishop Adalmus had put in 'twelve canons who lived devoutly', but that they had also decayed, so Bishop Rorico was putting the monks back in.[68] Eleven years later another council in the same place approved the move by Archbishop Adalberon of Reims to instal monks in Mouzon, a house that had originally been for nuns, and had been turned into a canonry by Bishop Herive. But it had become impossible to allow them to contine, for their 'infamous behaviour and utter neglect', so Abbot Ledald was instructed to begin regular monastic life there.[69] Similar vicissitudes are recorded in Reims. In Aachen in 966 the monks were replaced by canons. The ancient secular community of Bleidenstadt was reconstructed as a Benedictine monastery under the influence of Gorze.[70] Although reform often meant replacing canons with monks, the reformers themselves mostly came from canonical backgrounds. The first 'reformed' Abbot of Gorze had been the primicerius of Toul, and other reformers had been canons of Metz and Verdun. Existing members of canonical communities often seem to have been happy to stay on as monks, and in some cases the principal reform was the wresting of financial control away from the lay families who had dominated for generations.

The interchange between the two ways of life gradually led to the reformers achieving a proper distinction between monks and seculars, as had been so often desired. By the end of the tenth century, contemporaries were probably quite clear in their minds about the two ways of life, the 'two orders', and could choose between them, whichever they preferred.[71] Later writers, however, have not been so clear, particularly those from a monastic background. Some denigrated the seculars as 'rustic illiterates', who 'though they wore the garb of monks, practised no regular observance'. This however must be an exaggeration, as is so common when monastic reformers look back on the canonical life. Many of those who lived in communities of canonical clergy doubtless lived exemplary lives, observing the requirements of community life and prayer, as well as serving their people in a pastoral role. 'These cathedral communities were able to provide a seedbed for the reform, because the transition from them to full monastic life was not that big a step.'[72]

Reform in England

In England, unlike the rest of Europe, the tenth century is remembered as a time of reform, though the reform party, partly inspired by the Gorze reform, often set themselves sternly against the canonical clergy. After the first Viking wars, King Alfred embarked on a programme of reconstruction, including the reform of the secular clergy. Churches were as far as possible situated within fortified towns or *burhs*. The number of West Saxon dioceses was increased from two (Winchester and Sherborne) to seven, adding Sonning, Ramsbury, Wells, Crediton, and St German's. Grimbald, already mentioned as a possible author of the Longer Rule, is closely associated with Winchester, where he seems to have been established in a small community during Alfred's lifetime. In the early years of the reign of Edward the Elder the important canonical foundation in Winchester called the 'New Minster' was endowed, with Grimbald as its first superior, even though he appears to have died just before the buildings were ready, in the summer of 902.[73] Like the 'Old Minster', the original cathedral founded by St Beren in the seventh century, the 'New Minster' certainly began life as a house of secular canons, although both were to be 'regularized' later in the tenth century. Moreover, the English translation of the Longer Rule is associated with New Minster, even though it must have been done well after the Benedictines had been established there.

After the time of Alfred, there was an urgent need to reconstruct church life that had been devastated by the first Danish War. Because of the long-established English tradition of minster churches, the common life among secular clergy was a familiar phenomenon in pre-war England, so that it would have been quite natural during the reconstruction process to found, or refound, a number of collegiate churches. Many such colleges do seem to have been founded, and during the first half of the tenth century the kings and bishops were obviously happy with the idea of secular canons. King Athelstan (924–39) in particular was remembered as the founder or restorer of many canonical bodies, and he is addressed as *pater clericorum* by Radbod, provost of St Sampson at Dol, who promises that he and twelve canons will pray for him.[74] The fact that this commendation comes from overseas illustrates the extent to which England was able to look to other nations for help in reconstructing church life. Coenwald, Bishop of Worcester, travelled extensively in the German lands to study monastic customs.

As well as the New Minster in Winchester, which we have already mentioned, we hear of canonical foundations between 900 and 950 in Bury St Edmunds, Crediton, Chester, Gloucester, St Buryan, Exeter, Tettenhall, Evesham, and Malmesbury. Many others can be conjectured, such as the second Oxford foundation, at St Peter's, which was probably founded outside the then city walls during the time that Oxford was under the rule of Alfred's daughter Æthelflæd. (Since she commonly attributed her actions to her father, and any collegiate foundation would have included an educational function, this is probably the origin of the tradition attributing Oxford University to King Alfred.) She also founded the community which became St Oswald's, just outside the walls of Gloucester, as a house of secular canons.[75] It appears that the old pastoral pattern in rural areas was effectively reconstructed, based on minsters at the market towns, each serving an area with a radius of two hours' walk, although not all the new minsters were on the same sites as those that had existed before the war. Many of them were probably small, possibly with only a single priest accompanied by a deacon or two, and some minor clerics.

There are a number of passing references to minster communities, such as the Fifth Code of Athelstan, which asks 'all the servants of God at every minster' to sing fifty psalms for the king; and the will of Theodric, Bishop of London (951–3) who makes bequests to the secular communities at Mendham, Hoxne and Bury in Suffolk, as well as to the monks of Glastonbury.[76] In 940 the ecclesiastical laws of Hywel Dda, Prince of Wales, refer to the *hospitium sacerdotis et clericorum*, a dwelling-place for priests and clerics, which implies some sort of communal establishment even in Wales. A portion of the *dirwy* or weregeld due for crimes of violence was to go to the 'priests and canons who serve God'.[77] In 942–3 Archbishop Oda of Canterbury promulgated some Constitutions on the rights and duties of the clergy, in which they were encouraged to live 'canonically, with all honour and reverence according to the decrees of the holy fathers'.[78] In conjunction with the province of York, these were reissued as the set of laws known as 'I Edmund'. Oda seems to have been a monk of Fleury, an associate of Dunstan, Oswald and Æthelwold.

A charter of Athelstan, of 947, refers to Folkestone as a place where there was formerly a monastery, and an abbey of sacred virgins, and makes provision for its restoration.[79] Many of the late medieval colleges claimed Athelstan as their founder, and he certainly seems to have promoted the common life, not only copying the Carolingian model, but also respecting the alternative

Scots model, the *Celi Dé* or 'people of God'. At York on his way back from an expedition to Scotland, he made a grant of wheat to the *Colidei* (neatly Latinizing the Gaelic term!) who were so admirably looking after the poor. At the same time he endowed Beverley for seven canons.[80] The use and dissemination of the Longer Rule in England most naturally fits into this phase, during the reigns of Edward and Athelstan, before the Benedictine revival. However throughout the century there was a tendency for bishops to come from monastic backgrounds, and to favour monasticism over the secular life.

The familiar abuses of simony and clerical concubinage still remained to be tackled in the middle of the century. Successive royal law codes and episcopal statutes prohibit clerical marriage, pointing out that there was a well-known and unbroken tradition of continence after ordination to major orders, and refuting the fatuous arguments being put forward to the contrary.[81] Ælfric of Eynsham's two pastoral letters, issued both in Latin and English, deal with the question at length. A number of these rebukes were issued in English, 'for not all of you can understand Latin': part of the reform programme was the provision of better education. Writing to bishops Wulfsige III of Sherborne (993–5), and to Wulfstan of Worcester, Ælfric encourages them to reform their canonical clergy. He argues for clerical continence from the example of the Apostles and the seventy-two others who left their wives to follow the Lord, and cites the third Canon of Nicaea against 'you who say you can't live without women'. For poverty he cites the five thousand converts in Acts who sold their property and lived the common life for thirty years under St James, until the Apostles dispersed. He lists the seven orders of clergy (bishop and priest counting as one), and says all are obliged to sing the seven canonical hours, as decreed in the four great synods.[82] Incidentally, Ælfric uses the term *canonici regulares* to mean secular canons following the existing Rules.[83] However there is very little in all this body of legislation directly bearing on the question of a common life. Nevertheless the fact that Wulfstan translated the last chapter of the *Institutio Canonica*, the Epitome, indicates that he was using it as a means of introducing more regular observance to his canons in Ripon, Beverley and Gloucester.

A significant change of policy came with the strong rule of Edgar (944–75), and the period of dominance of St Dunstan (924–88). Most tenth-century writers agree with the author of the life of St Dunstan, who tells us that 'the clerical order at that time was exceedingly corrupt, for canons and parish priests were enslaved to the desires of the flesh'. The answer, as Dunstan and Edgar saw it, was to abolish communities of secular clerics altogether, and to enforce proper Benedictine monasticism. Backed by the authority of Pope John XII, Dunstan got the king to decree that canons 'who were unwilling to live chastely should be expelled from the churches they occupied, and that monks should be introduced in their place.'[84] 'Houses of clerics,' says Edgar, 'may be considered as the lodges of harlots, the spawning ground of jugglers ... it is time to rise up against those who dissipate the Law of God'.[85] Pope John's letter is just as vehement in its denunciation of the secular clergy as 'vessels of the devil', and of their 'hateful way of life', concluding with 'Let them be thrown out, along with their provost, like very devils.'[86]

The most dramatic account of the new policy in action tells how they set about the reform of Winchester Old Minster: Bishop Æthelwold had warned his canons several times that they should 'change their ways, repudiate their women, and embrace a more correct way of life', but they kept on postponing their acquiescence. Eventually he appeared in church with an armful of monastic cowls as they were singing the Communion verse, *Servite Domino in timore, et exultate ei cum tremore: apprehendite disciplinam, ne pereatis de via iusta* (Ps. 2:11–12). 'If,' he declaimed, 'you truly wish to "serve the Lord with fear" and "rejoice unto him with trembling", then you should "embrace discipline", in other words the monastic habit, lest, as you have been singing, "you perish from the just way".' Some of them did as he said, but others fled from the church, and appealed to the king, who of course upheld Æthelwold's decision, as did the Witan. Some of the expelled canons went further and appealed to the Scots for help, but at the subsequent Council of Calne called to settle the matter, the collapse of the floor was taken to indicate divine approbation of St Dunstan's party.[87]

Having dealt thus with the canons of the Old Minster, Æthelwold found little opposition when he did the same to the canons of St Grimbald's New Minster next door in 966. Edgar, who was by now calling himself *basileus et imperator*, claiming the imperial titles of both East and West, wrote some more denunciations of the 'nests of vicious canons', the 'lascivious clerics', who 'abound beyond measure in the aforesaid sins'. His mandate for the reform of New Minster claims that 'as Vicar of Christ, I have eliminated the nests of vicious canons from various minsters in our realm, and joyfully established nests of monks who are pleasing to God', and he goes on to warn the canons that if they try to return they will suffer the fate of Ananias and Sapphira.[88] In 964 Edgar had boasted that he had already founded forty-seven regular Benedictine monasteries or nunneries, and hopes to live to make it fifty. With this aim he encouraged St Oswald of Worcester to 'eliminate the clerics with their filthy and decadent music' and instal monks who will be 'devout servants of God.'[89] In the event Oswald proceeded much more diplomatically than Æthelwold, but no less effectively. Oswald himself had begun his career in a secular community, 'like Lot in Sodom', but travelled to Fleury to learn true monasticism. He expelled the 'deacons and *struciones*' from Ripon and substituted monks, and once he had been installed in Worcester he gathered around him many faithful clerics, whom he settled as monks in Westbury, Ramsey, Worcester and Winchcombe.[90] In 974 the clerics were expelled from Malmesbury in the same way, with the same sort of violent denunciations, as 'idiot clerics'.[91] At Glastonbury, also, Dunstan was able to drive out the canons, and establish true monasticism, for before the time of Edgar there had only been two real monks in Glastonbury. At one of his reforming councils in 969 he decreed that 'All canons, whether priests, deacons, or subdeacons, must either live chastely, or else surrender the churches which they hold.'[92] The process was completed at the end of the century, when Wulfsige turned the canons of Sherborne into monks in 992, and Archbishop Ælfric (995–1006) did the same at Christ Church, Canterbury. After the expulsion of the secular clerics from so many minsters, there was a tendency to recruit bishops from the newly established Benedictine communities, thus perpetuating the monastic bias into the eleventh century. One of the results was the peculiarly English institution of monastic cathedrals.

It has been debated whether the cathedral monasteries established by Dunstan and his associates were completely innovative, or whether they were simply restoring what had existed before the monasteries had 'slipped down the scale to merely collegiate communities'. Although Dom Thomas Symons believed that Christ Church, Canterbury had been truly monastic at an earlier period, Dom David Knowles seems to accept that it only began to be monastic in Dunstan's time, and indeed maintained some secular traditions until the Conquest.[93] Capgrave's account of the process introduces what is probably an anachronism: he says that the canons had abandoned the common life in order to live on their prebendal lands, employing vicars to take their place in the cathedral choir. Edgar's first move was to deprive the canons of their places altogether, and give the vicars possession of the property. It was only when the vicars turned out to be just as bad that he put in monks.[94] However this reflects the problems of Capgrave's own fifteenth century, not the time of St Dunstan. Although as we have seen, the separation out of 'prebends' had begun on the Continent, there is no evidence for it as early as this in England, still less for 'vicars'.

Nevertheless, there was to be something of a reaction after the death of the King-Emperor in 975. Almost immediately afterwards we hear that Alfer of Mercia had succeeded in expelling some of 'the abbots and monks from the monasteries in which King Edgar had peacefully located them, and introducing clerics with their wives'. This was resisted by Æthelwine, Duke of Essex, who defended monasticism in his territory.[95] 'The clerics were delighted, because their time had come. Abbots and monks were expelled [from Westbury], and the clerics arrived with their wives, so that the last error was worse than the former.'[96] However other sources are less critical, and many new communities of canonical clergy were founded in the last decades of the century, such as the major minster of Wolverhampton, founded by Wulfram. It has been estimated that ten times as many secular communities as real monasteries existed at the end of the millennium. Thus, contrary not only to the common modern view of the period, but even to that of near-contemporary monastic historians, the institution of secular community survived the tenth-century reformers with renewed vigour.

Curiously it was only after the expulsion of the canons from Winchester that the cult of St Swithin began to develop. His tomb was located outside the west door of the Old Minster, apparently in reference to the practice of lying in penance at the western door of the church in the Rule of Chrodegang (RC 15). In the same way St Anghilram had been buried outside the west door of St Riquier. More surprisingly, it was a generation after the Benedictines arrived that the Longer Rule was translated into English in Winchester, for the personal names used in the English version are all to be found in the New Minster at the end of the tenth or the beginning of the eleventh century.[97]

A succession of councils were held, at Winchester, Kirtlington, Calne and Amesbury, which presumably continued to debate the whole issue, though tantalizingly little is recorded of what actually transpired, save that in Winchester the crucifix on the wall intervened decisively in favour of the monks, and at Calne the floor collapsed leaving Dunstan perched precariously on a beam, and his enemies thrown down below.[98] A number of cathedral chapters did survive with secular canons, notably Dorchester, which was to become Lincoln. Bishop Æscwig of Dorchester witnessed some of Edgar's more extreme documents, in 966 as Abbot of Bath, but in 974 as bishop. He was still bishop in 993.[99] This means he must have presided at the 'Great Council of Kirtlington' in 977, and evidently succeeded in preserving his chapter as one of seculars, despite anything Dunstan could say. It was presumably for this reason that the canons of Dorchester remembered him as a saint hundreds of years later, when a fourteenth-century effigy (which still survives) was made to commemorate Æscwig.[100] Dorchester was always closely associated with Winchester, where they evidently possessed a text of the Longer Rule, and some bishop desirous of maintaining the canonical life must have commissioned the translation, to prove that canons did possess a respectable rule of life attributed to a saint. This agrees with our hypothesis that the Rule was introduced into England by St Grimbald, founder of New Minster, and fits with our speculation about the role of St Æscwig in preserving the canonical life, for if the Bishop of Dorchester was so inclined, he might well have requested a text from Winchester, however much Winchester itself had transferred its loyalties to St Benedict. One of the significant collegiate churches founded at the end of the tenth century in England was at Cholsey, in Berkshire and therefore in the then Diocese of Ramsbury, but only just across the river from Dorchester.

Notes

1. Meaux (845), canon liii; Mansi XIV, c. 831; cf Louis' capitula of 819, c. vii; Mansi XIV appendix c. 417.
2. Mansi XIV, cc. 917–20.
3. Soissons (853), additional canon; Mansi XIV, c. 995.
4. de Clercq, *Législation Religieuse*, p. 391.
5. Amann & Dumas, *L'Eglise au pouvoir des Laïques*, p. 255.
6. *Charta Restitutionis*, Mansi XVII, cc. 273–4.
7. Fîmes (881), canon iv; Mansi XVII, cc. 540–1.
8. D KdK 425 s. 451, cited in footnote to Crusius, *Weltlichen Kollegiatstift*, p. 139.
9. Crusius, *Weltlichen Kollegiatstift*, pp. 141–7.
10. *Aldrici Cenomanensis Episcopi vita*, liii; PL 115:93.
11. PL 125:1037, quoted in Lesne, *Propriété Ecclésiastique*, p. 7.
12. PL 119:703; 121:1135; 131:15–24; 125:773–804; 121:763–74 respectively. See also McKitterick, *The Frankish Church*.
13. Hincmar of Reims, capitula of 852; Mansi XV, cc. 475–91. The monthly meetings are in capit. xv; Mansi XV, cc. 478–9. See also J. Devisse, *Hincmar, Archevêque de Reims 845–882* (Genève, Droz, 1976), Tome II, pp. 862–89.
14. Hincmar of Reims, capitula of 874; Mansi XV, cc. 493–9.

15. Walterus Aurelianensis, capitula vi, Mansi XV, c. 506.
16. Hermanus of Nevers, Mansi XIV, cc. 925–7.
17. de Clercq, *Législation Religieuse*, p. 391.
18. Mansi XVII, cc. 303–4.
19. Amort, *Vetus Disciplina*, II, cap. 9; MGH Script. VIII, 431; *Martyrologium Romanum*, 12 June (Odulphus); 11 December (Everard).
20. Nightingale, *Gorze Reform*, p. 98.
21. Siegwart, *Chorherren*, p. 215n.
22. Mainz (847), canon xiii; Mansi XIV, cc. 906–7.
23. Metz (888), cap. v; Mansi XVIII, c. 79.
24. Crusius, *Weltlichen Kollegiatstift*, pp. 86–99; MGH SS 30 (ii), p. 944 (Hildesheim).
25. Rome, Council of 67 Bishops (853), canons vii, ix, xxxiv; Mansi XIV, cc. 1003, 1004, 1008.
26. Nicholas I, *Decreta*, Tit. XV, i; Mansi XV, c. 444.
27. Pavia (876), capit. x, xi, xii; Mansi XVII, c. 327; Pontignone (876), capit. viii; Mansi XVII, c. 312.
28. Ravenna (877), capit. xix; Mansi XVII, c. 340.
29. *Diploma Theodosii, Firmani episcopi*, for the Minster of the Holy Cross in Fermo; Mansi XVIII, cc. 53–8.
30. Tanner, *Notitia Monastica*, p. 35; cf. Foot, *Monastic Life*, p. 342.
31. Knowles, *Monastic Order in England*, p. 33.
32. Whitelock, Brett & Brooke, *Councils* I, p. 4.
33. Ibid., I, p. 7.
34. PL 89:1057 sq; RC is 89:1097 sq.
35. Texts in Bertram, *The Chrodegang Rules*. For a critical edition of the Old English version, see Langefeld, *Enlarged Rule of Chrodegang*.
36. *Ordo Qualiter*, printed in D. Bruno Albers, *Consuetudines Monasticæ*, Vol. III (Monte Cassino, 1907), pp. 26–49. It is quoted also in the *Regularis Concordia*.
37. Capitula of Hérard of Tours, cap. 49 and 89; Mansi XVI, cc. 681–2.
38 Langefeld, *Enlarged Rule of Chrodegang*, pp. 11–12.
39. See note 10 above on the sack of the community house at le Mans.
40 J. H. Newman, *Letters and Diaries*, XIII (1964), pp. 282–3.
41. Amann, *l'Epoque Carolingienne*, pp. 352–65.
42. C. Baronius, *Annales Ecclesiastici*, Venice 1603, X, p. 439.
43. Amann & Dumas, *L'Eglise au pouvoir des Laïques*, p. 257.
44. Ibid., p. 263.
45. Mainz (888), canon x; Trosby (909), cap. ix; Augsburg (952), caps. i, iv, xi; Winchester (975); Aure (994), Poitiers (1000), in Mansi XVIII, cc. 67, 288–94, 435–8; XIX, cc. 61–4, 63–6, 177–80 and 265–8 respectively.
46. PL 136:585–6. See also Amann & Dumas, *L'Eglise au pouvoir des Laïques*, pp. 476–82.
47. Ibid., pp. 476–82.
48. Rather's Rant (932), Mansi XVIII, cc. 365–72.
49. Miller, *The Formation of a Medieval Church*, pp. 42–50.
50. Synodus Bergamensis Dioecesana (908); Mansi XVIII, cc. 259–62.
51. Schuster, *Sacramentary*, III, p. 24.

52. Trosby (909), canons iii, ix; Mansi XVIII, cc. 270–2, 288–94.
53. Constitutions of Walter of Sens, canons viii, ix and xiii; Mansi XVIII, cc. 323–4.
54. *Bulla ad Adalbertum Magdeburgensem archiepiscopum*, Mansi XIX, c. 5.
55. Poggiaspalla, *Vita comune*, pp. 134n, 144.
56. Ibid., p. 122.
57. Crusius, *Weltlichen Kollegiatstift*, p. 10.
58. *Gesta Trevirorum*, MGH SS 8, 169, cited in Siegwart, *Chorherren*, p. 107.
59. Crusius, *Weltlichen Kollegiatstift*, pp. 54–7.
60. Siegwart, *Chorherren*, p. 110.
61. Crusius, *Weltlichen Kollegiatstift*, pp. 125–6.
62. Siegwart, *Chorherren*, pp. 95 (Trier); pp. 99–147 (list of houses); pp. 106, 169–200 (Zurich).
63. Deraine, 'Chanoines', p. 366.
64. Dom Gougoud, *Ermites et Réclus*, Ligugé 1928, p. 62; A. Prost, *La Cathédrale de Metz* 1885, pp. 332, 367; both cited in Morhain, 'Origine et histoire'.
65. Both Knowles and Deanesley give the impression that Adalberon restored the canonical life (*Monastic Order* chapter ii; *Pre-Conquest Church* 287–9), but Nightingale has shown that the Gorze movement was purely Benedictine (*Gorze Reform*).
66. Lesne, *Propriété Ecclésiastique*, p. 9.
67. Mansi XVIII, cc. 391–4.
68. Mont-St-Marie (961), Mansi XVIII, c. 457.
69. Mont-St-Marie (972), Mansi XIX, cc. 31–2.
70. Amann & Dumas, *L'Eglise au pouvoir des Laïques*, p. 255 (Reims); Siegwart, *Chorherren*, pp. 193–4 (Aachen); D.I. 43, p. xx (Bleidenstadt).
71. Nightingale, *Gorze Reform*, p. 11.
72. Ibid., pp. 16–17, 96–7.
73. See Philip Grierson, 'Grimbald of St Bertin' in *English Historical Review* 55 (1940), pp. 529–61.
74. Whitelock, Brett & Brooke, *Councils* I, p. 9.
75. Blair, *Anglo-Saxon Oxfordshire*, pp. 112–3; Dugdale, *Monasticon* VI, p. 82.
76. Whitelock, Brett & Brooke, *Councils* I, pp. 14 and 21.
77. Leges Ecclesiasticae Hoeli Dha, Mansi XVIII, cc. 385–6.
78. Mansi XVIII, cc. 393–8; Whitelock, Brett & Brooke, *Councils* I, p. 20.
79. Douglas, *Domesday Monachorum*, p. 11.
80. Dugdale, *Monasticon* VI, pp. 608, 1307.
81. e.g. I Edmund, par. 1, in Whitelock, Brett & Brooke, *Councils* I, p. 17.
82. *Die Hirtenbriefe Aelfrics*, ed. B. Fehr; see also Whitelock, Brett & Brooke, *Councils* I, pp. 40, 46.
83. Dickinson, *Austin Canons*, p. 24 n.
84. 'Vita Sancti Dunstani, auctore Eadmero', in Stubbs, *Memorials of St Dunstan*, p. 211.
85. *Oratio Edgari Regis ad Dunstanum*, Mansi XVIII, cc. 527–30.
86. John XII, *Epistula ii, ad Edgarum*, Mansi XVIII, c. 483, cf Whitelock, Brett & Brooke, *Councils* I, p. 29.
87. 'Vita Sancti Dunstani, auctore Eadmero', in Stubbs, *Memorials of St Dunstan*, p. 211.

88. *Charta Regis Edgari novo Wintoniae Monasterio*, caps. viii and ix; Mansi XVIII, cc. 494–5, cf. Whitelock, Brett & Brooke, *Councils* I, p. 31.
89. *Edgari Regis Anglorum Charta de Oswalde*, Mansi XVIII, cc. 479–80.
90. *Vita Sancti Oswaldi*, in Rame, *Historians of the Church of York*.
91. *Charta Edgari Regis, Malmesburiensi coenobio confecta*, Mansi XIX, c. 47.
92. Whitelock, Brett & Brooke, *Councils* I, p. 33; Concilium Anglicum a Dunstano (969), Mansi XIX, c. 15.
93. Knowles, *Monastic Order in Britain*, pp 696–7; cf. Foot, *Monastic Life*, p. 346.
94. Capgrave, in Stubbs, *Memorials of St Dunstan*, p. 341.
95. Concilium Wintoniense (975), Mansi XIX, c. 62.
96. *Vita Oswaldi*, in Whitelock, Brett & Brooke, *Councils* I, p. 34.
97. Förster. 'Lokalisierung und Datierung der altenglischen Version der Chrodegang Regel', in *Sitzungsberichte der Bayerischen Akademie der Wissenschaften, Philosophische-Historische Abteilung*, Schlussheft 7–8, 1933.
98. Mansi XIX, cc. 61–3.
99. Whitelock, Brett and Brooke, *Councils* I, 31, 39; Mansi XIX, c. 48.
100. J. Leland, *The Itinerary*, ed. L. Toulmin Smith (Carbondale, Southern Illinois University Press, 1964), I, 117.

Chapter 7

Eleventh-Century Reformers

The eleventh century is usually spoken of with respect as the age of the great 'Gregorian' reforms, when 'the world, as it were, shook itself awake, threw off its old garb and clothed itself everywhere in a white robe of churches'.[1] The implication is that everything beforehand had been corrupt and in urgent need of radical reconstruction, but now at last the 'Dark Ages' were over and the 'Middle Ages' could begin. As we have seen, the story is nothing like as simple as that, and the tenth century had in some areas been an age of reform just as much as the eleventh was to be. It was however in Rome itself that reform was needed more than elsewhere, which may be why the 'Gregorian' reform has become so famous.

Certainly the personal life of the clergy needed reform, as it does in every century, but the area that needed reform in particular was the dominance of the Church by the rich and powerful, characterized by the Investiture Dispute. This did not impinge very much on the topic of the common life of the secular clergy, for princes were just as anxious as popes for their clergy to be men of godly life, and the process of keeping them up to the canonical standard was furthered by both parties. Just as in the previous centuries, some pursued this end by insisting on canons living canonically, while others turned them into monks.

Canonical Foundations in England, before and during the Gregorian Reform

There seems in fact to have been something of a revival of the canonical life in England at the beginning of the eleventh century. The Council of Ænham in 1009 strongly recommends it, insisting on a common refectory and dormitory, and alluding to an obviously already well-known Rule:

Let the Canons in their minsters keep such watch on themselves that they may serve the Lord in pure continence and full chastity according to the Rule. Let them celebrate the divine office together in churches at the proper times. If there is sufficient income in that place to feed them, they should eat in their refectories every day, and they should sleep in their dormitories every night, as the authority of the Rule teaches them. If they neglect to observe these things, they must either amend according to the Rule, or be thrown out of their minsters and deprived of their inheritance from God.[2]

Reforms of the canonical life in cathedrals are attributed to bishops Wulfsige of Sherborne (991–1001/2) and Wulfstan of York (1003–23). It was for this Wulfstan, when Bishop of Worcester, that Ælfric of Eynsham had composed his pastoral letters in English already mentioned (p. 116 above). He again affirms the ancient discipline of celibacy, and claims that the four great early General Councils had taught that 'no bishop, nor mass-priest, nor deacon nor minster-priest should have any woman neither in his bedroom nor anywhere in his house'.[3] The title 'minster-priest' seems to represent those in minor orders, the junior members of a community of clergy. Wulfstan was responsible for the text known as the 'Canons of Edgar' (1005–8), tightening up on clerical discipline, though with no specific mention of the common life. However the Laws of Æthelred are explicit about the duty of canons to frequent their refectory and dormitory and to hold their minsters with right observance and charity 'as their rule directs'.[4] They are also to celebrate the Divine Office regularly in choir, and to celebrate a Mass daily for the king and people of the realm. A few years later Æthelred speaks of various grades of church, the 'Head-minster, medium minster, lesser minster and field-church'.[5] The last is presumably the country church served by a single priest ministering to a rural estate; the three grades of minster are evidently communities of some nature. A Mass-priest who lives according to rule is granted higher status than one living alone. It is evident that the status of secular priests living in community was fully recognized and valued in the first half of the eleventh century in England.

The Archbishops of York followed this recommendation by establishing a common refectory and dormitory in the 1020s at York, and also in Beverley and Southwell.[6] When a group of bishops from Lorraine were appointed to Exeter, Hereford, Wells, and Sherborne with Ramsbury, they may well have been familiar at home with the canonical life according to the Institutes of Aachen, or the Longer Rule in its Lotharingian edition, but they found that way of life already well established in England. Leofric of Exeter (1046–72), who may have studied in Liège, certainly used the Winchester translation, and the copy made for him at Exeter for use in chapter meetings is the one that survives. It was probably included in the same volume as the now fragmentary *Capitula of Theodulf* and copies of the sermons of Ælfric and Wulfstan, intended for spiritual reading at chapter as the Rule itself provides.[7] Evidence for an educational role for the canons, in accordance with the Institutes of Aachen and the Longer Rule, is that a contemporary copy of Ælfric's Grammar is among the Exeter manuscripts.[8] A copy of Cassian now in the Bodleian Library (Oxford) may also have been at Exeter in Leofric's time.[9] William of Malmesbury famously claimed that Leofric introduced something foreign, *contra morem Anglorum*,[10] but he was obviously mistaken, although many subsequent writers have seized on that phrase as evidence that the common life of the secular clergy was an undesirable import. He was also responsible for the widespread misconception that most of the monks of England were hardly distinguishable from seculars in the early eleventh century.[11]

A large number of collegiate churches were established in the first half of the eleventh century, particularly in the West Country, no doubt under the influence of St Leofric. He reversed the trend under Dunstan and Edgar by expelling the Benedictines from their church in Exeter, and moving the seat of his diocese there, to be staffed by secular canons. The original endowment of the monastery at Exeter had been lost, but Leofric ensured that a sufficient new endowment was made, including some manors from his own property. The manuscript with the English translation of the Rule was only one of many books he gave to his new foundation, which in turn became a major centre of book production. Among other things the canons turned their hands to reconstructing the lost charters giving them title to the endowments of the original monastery at Exeter. There were at least five canons in the original foundation, possibly more: by 1072 the income would have supported twelve, and by the late thirteenth century it was believed that the foundation had been intended for twenty-four canons and as many vicars. The names in the obit rolls include deacons, subdeacons and minor clerics, with both Lotharingian and Anglo-Saxon names.[12]

Other English cathedrals certainly followed the example of Leofric. Archbishop Ealdred of York (1061–70) had to re-establish the common refectories in York, Beverley and Southwell, *ubi canonici simul vescerentur*, which had already fallen into disrepair.[13]

A rule of life was produced, probably at this time, for St Paul's in London, incorporating several chapters from the Rule of Aachen.[14] Remembering that Bishop Wulfstan had translated the last chapter of the Aachen *Institutio Canonica* into English, this use of the same document at St Paul's acts as a warning not to assume that just because St Leofric used the Longer Rule, other canonical foundations followed the same text. Clearly both texts were well known in England, and could be used equally well in the establishment of a reformed canonical community.

Bishop Giso of Wells (1061–88), another Lotharingian, also seems to have reformed his cathedral chapter on the same lines. He records that he found only four or five canons there, and needed to 'prepare for them an enclosure, a refectory and a dormitory, in the style of my native land'.[15] The probability is that Walter of Hereford (1060–79) and Herman of Sherborne and Ramsbury (1045–78), who also came from Lotharingia, did the same.[16] These Lotharingian bishops were all closely associated with Edward the Confessor; both Leofric and Herman arrived with him in 1041, the others being royal chaplains. Waltham Abbey, when first founded by Earl Harold in 1060, was probably also a house of secular canons. When Edward the Confessor confirmed the foundation, he referred to 'a community of brothers subject to the Canonical Rule according to the authority of the holy Fathers', which could apply equally well either to the Institutes of Aachen or to the Longer Rule.[17] The see of Sherborne, which had become monastic in 992, was transferred to Sarum in 1075, but the monks remained behind, and when the chapter was established it was of secular canons.

The foundation of new collegiate churches continued throughout the eleventh century, and rural areas seem still to have been served by a network of small secular 'minsters'. Where subordinate churches split away to begin the process of forming separate parishes they were usually still tied to their original minster centres by certain obligations, such as the payment of 'chrism-money' and the collection of 'Romscot'. The pattern of these mother minsters can still be detected in Domesday, from which it appears that there were enough in each county to provide cover for the whole territory.[18] Many minsters were probably originally very small, without the legal structure of a corporation following a written rule, but increasingly they came to be incorporated as properly endowed collegiate churches. This represents a trend towards making a greater distinction between ordinary secular diocesan priests, and secular canons, who lived in an incorporated community which could legally own land. The smaller, unincorporated, minsters came to be treated in the same way as rural chapels, as real estate which could be owned by a lay or ecclesiastical patron. Actual lay ownership of churches, as opposed to the right of advowson,* was prohibited in the middle of the century, and the subsequent tendency was to grant the ownership of small minsters to major monasteries or colleges, which would accept the income and provide a vicar to serve the people. This served to break down any tradition of hereditary benefices, but it made it increasingly difficult to distinguish a former 'minster' from an ordinary 'parish'.[19]

Not all went according to plan, however, in a century of conquest and dramatic change of land ownership. At Wells the community broke up because the bishop moved his seat to Bath, and the provost left behind in Wells so oppressed the canons that they moved out of the common lodging and set up individual households. The new bishop, John of Tours, obviously approved of this dispersal, since he proceeded to order the demolition of the newly constructed communal refectory and dormitory.[20] In other cathedrals there seems to have been a serious disruption at the Conquest, since the work of founding chapters had to be started all over again at the end of the century. Only in London does there seem to have been no break, and elements of the Saxon *Regula Sancti Pauli* survived to be incorporated into the later medieval statutes. A few houses of secular canons were made monastic, like St Mary's at Coventry, refounded as a Benedictine house in 1043, but the same founders, Earl Leofric and Lady Godiva, also endowed a minster of secular priests at Stowe ten years later, to have the same service as that in St Paul's, London, and food and clothing provided from the earl's estates.[21] Both types of community, the truly monastic and the secular, remained in favour in England throughout the period of the Gregorian reforms and the Norman conquest, and it is quite untrue to maintain, as Morhain does, that the growth of the prebendal system meant that common life in England 'disappeared without trace'.[22]

Canonical Foundations on the Continent, before and during the Gregorian Reform

Communities of secular clergy were still being founded on the Continent in the same way as in England. For instance, the Council

---

* The right of presentation to a vacant benefice.

of Compostella in 1056 decreed, in very familiar terms, that the clergy around a bishop should all eat and sleep together, and must celebrate the entire Divine Office in church.[23] New collegiate foundations are noted at Barcelona (1009), Urgel (1010), Fresile (1032), and Turin (1057).[24] At Troyes, we find the institution exemplified in the life of St Aderaldus. He joined the clergy as a boy in the late tenth century, and was enrolled as a canon of St Peter's church, where at that time the clergy lived *secularissime*. He supported Bishop Manasses in reforming the community until they lived almost like monks. He then went on pilgrimage to Jerusalem, where he was captured by Islamic terrorists, but insisted on preserving the rule of silence after Compline, which, his biographer notes, was required by the Canonical Institute. Eventually released, he died at home as a revered archdeacon in around 1015. The implication is that St Peter's in Troyes was by then an exemplary observant house, following the *Institutio Canonica* or the Longer Rule. (It is true that IC 136 implies this silence after Compline, but it is much more explicit in the Longer Rule, RL 23.)[25] At Volterra the true canonical life was restored around 1070, for an Archdeacon, Provost and all ranks of clergy.[26] The letters of Gregory VII reveal that even he was by no means unappreciative of communities of seculars, though he did expect them to be observant. In particular he writes to the canons of Lucca urging them to live a common and regular life, as it had been established by St Leo, and as the Roman Church understands it, namely that all *church* property should be brought into the common use, and expended in common.[27] This says nothing about the canons' *private* property, but does follow the letter of the older canonical legislation about church property. However, a little later, Paschal II (1099–1118) does seem to expect true community of property in his *Tractatus* on the clergy.[28]

It is in the German-speaking lands that we find most information about reformed communities of secular clergy throughout the eleventh century, as a result of the work chronicled by Crusius and Siegwart. Many mixed communities, containing both monks and canons, had existed in the Empire for some time, and bishops were continually losing their best priests to monasteries, so there was a real incentive to re-organize and reform the life of the secular canons. A key figure seems to have been the sainted emperor Henry II (973–1024), who founded the see of Bamberg in 1007, with a chapter modelled on those at Liège and Hildesheim. The emperor was sufficiently realist to avoid imposing vows on his canonical clergy, but ensured that they were to live together, sharing dormitory and refectory, to dress alike, and to celebrate the Office together in choir. At the same period Bishop Burchard of Worms (1012–22) collected canons about clerical life, including many from the Isidorian corpus, and established the communal life in his cathedral. Similar action was taken by bishops such as Erlwin of Cambrai, Meinwerk of Paderborn, Bernwald of Hildesheim, Heinrich of Würzburg and Abalbold of Utrecht.[29]

The reform initiated by Henry II spread throughout the Empire, including Burgundy and Italy. Siegwart gives a very long list of foundations that were established or reformed at this period. Of these the best documented is the canonical foundation of St Felix at Zürich, reformed in 1006. The Great Minster, governed by a dean, formed the centre of a number of churches, including some communities of nuns who were under the direction of the canons. Here again we find the phrase *disciplina regularis*, not to be understood as implying a vowed monastic rule like that of the later canons regular, but simply the strict observance of the existing Canonical Institutes.[30] There is no indication that anyone considered the unvowed life reprehensible in itself, and not even Benedictines disapproved in principle of secular canonries. St Godehard became Bishop of Hildesheim in 1022, having been a Benedictine monk at Altach; while encouraging his clergy to live an observant religious life, he did not compel them to become monks, but instead fostered the canonical life. In the Church of Our Lady and St Epiphanius he established 'a congregation of canons of great reputation and benefit, united in the fear of God; he purchased buildings for them and gave them sufficiency of food and clothing'.[31] In the very middle of the 'Gregorian reform' the rebel Emperor Henry IV founded a collegiate church on the Harzberg, though this may have been a deliberate tease against his opponent Gregory VII.[32] St Gualterius of Lestirps (d. 1070) ruled as 'abbot, rector or provost' over a community of secular clergy, and was able to rebuild it after a local warlord burnt it down.[33]

Peter Damian's Rant

Despite the flourishing collegiate life observed in different parts of Europe, and its apparent approval by popes and emperors, Benedictines and seculars alike, historians from an Augustinian background like Poggiaspalla are adamant that the canonical life was in full decadence, and that a thorough reform was needed, which could only be done by imposing monastic vows on all communities of clergy. Hence much attention has been given to the sustained attack on the whole idea of the common life of secular clergy on the part of Peter Damian and his circle.

Damian wrote an intemperate tract against 'canons who own property' in which he denounces the permission granted in the *Institutio Canonica* for canons to own private property.[34] He appears to be the first to express the belief that all canonical clergy had formerly undertaken a life of evangelical poverty, before the time of the Council of Aachen (or maybe that of St Chrodegang), so that the permission for them to own private property is a decadent innovation. He is indignant that canons not only own property but even have the effrontery to claim that they have a legal right to do so. He quotes Augustine's sermons on clerical life as evidence for this, as well as passages from Julianus Pomerius, even though the very same texts are incorporated in the *Institutio Canonica* itself. He denies in fact that the *Institutio* has any authority: 'this so-called Rule is one of which we strongly disapprove, and to which we attribute no authority whatsoever.'[35] He proceeds to make game of the provisions for food and drink: 'If a boy of two or three can be admitted as a member of the clergy, and gets his ration of five pints of wine and four pounds of bread, he will not merely vomit, he will burst!'[36]

Returning to the sources, he quotes the texts from Acts about primitive communism, and concludes that canons have no right to own property at all. Ownership of property makes clerics disobedient, clerics belong peculiarly to God, owning property is like building a shrine to Mercury, no ecclesiastical honour should be given to a rich cleric, 'A cleric who is a slave to money can never be fit to administer the Word of Truth.' He concludes by demanding that the pope enforce a rule of strict apostolic poverty on all who call themselves canons.[37]

His argument is somewhat spoilt by the fact that he has already conceded that clerics who do not call themselves canons are not bound by this doctrine, but only 'those who call themselves canons and live in community'.[38] In effect he makes a new distinction. On the one hand there are ordinary secular 'diocesan' priests, who live scattered around the city or countryside, each attached to his own church. They are perfectly entitled to own and bequeath property as much as they like, and to live on their own resources. On the other hand are the 'canons' who live in community, and are to become in all but name monks with a pastoral duty. Yet all his arguments from Acts apply equally to 'diocesan' priests, and indeed to lay Christians. His objection appears to be solely to any form of communal life which is lived other than according to the three evangelical counsels, later to be formulated into the familiar vows of poverty, chastity and obedience. This would mean that priests and other clerics have to choose between living in full community with no property of their own, or living in complete isolation, with none of the support which community life can offer. Although 'canons' would continue to exist, the distinction between them and monks would henceforth be merely academic: there was already plenty of precedent for monks being ordained, and having a missionary pastoral role among the people.

What is particularly noticeable is that nowhere in this tract does Peter Damian refer to any text called the 'Rule of St Augustine'.

The Rise of the Canons Regular

Although Pope Leo IX (1049–1054) strongly defended the rights of canons to own property,[39] Damian's strictures were taken up in two reforming councils held in Rome under the two succeding popes, in 1059 and 1063, both of which pass the same decree about the common life. After condemning simoniacal clergy, and those living with wives or concubines, the councils proceed to speak to the obedient clergy, urging them to a fully apostolic life. The *Institutio Canonica* was read out, and it was agreed that it needed reform, particularly chapter 115, which asserts the superiority of the canonical life, and 122, which gives the generous measure of food and drink. Hildebrand, not yet pope, recommended the form of vow already in use among the clergy of Rome, 'I offer myself to the Catholic Church, to Saint N. in the house N., and to its provost, according to the canonical rule to be faithfully kept ... with the offering of my property as a portion for the use and consumption of the canonical brothers ... so that henceforth it shall not be lawful for me to remove my neck from the yoke of the rule.'[40] This is, in effect, to vow poverty and stability as much as any Benedictine, but the Council did not follow Hildebrand all the way. The eventual decree reads,

> Let them eat and sleep together, close to the churches for which they were ordained, as is fitting for religious clerics. Whatever comes to them from the churches they should hold in common. Moreover we urge and entreat them to make all efforts towards arriving at an apostolical way of life, in other words the common life.[41]

This leaves a distinction between more and less observant canons.

All clerics are now obliged to have a common refectory and dormitory, and to treat all their ecclesiastical income in common, in other words to live by the Chrodegang or Aachen Rules. In addition it is strongly encouraged that they should go one step further, and adopt a totally common life, with no private property at all, thus satisfying Peter Damian. Pope Nicholas II (1059–61) wrote to the Bishops of Gaul, Aquitaine and Gascony using the same words, thus making it clear that the decree of the Roman council was not intended to be a local legislation for Rome only, but should be applied throughout the West.[42]

Here then begins the real distinction between canons 'regular' and 'secular'. A new type of clerical life emerged from now on, for those henceforth called the 'canons regular'. They themselves and their supporters believed (and still do) that this was a restoration of an earlier structure, one which dated back well before St Augustine, if not before Adam. Abbot Lietbert of St Rufus by Avignon, for example, taught that Moses, Aaron and Samuel lived as canons regular.[43] From now on, writers condemn those living by the Rule of St Chrodegang as unwarrantably decadent, and communities living by the Institute of Aachen or the Longer Rules as in desperate need of reform. The holding of private property in particular was decried as an 'innovation'. In reality, however, we must admit in the light of all the preceding evidence, that it is the institution of regular canons which is the innovation. It involved a commitment to the total renunciation of private property, so that in future all lands and goods were to belong collectively to the canonry, to be distributed by the bursar according to the needs of individual canons.

In contrast to the new 'canons regular', communities of canonical clergy, including cathedral chapters, which did not adopt the rule of absolute poverty, came to be known as 'secular canons', usually with an air of disapproval. It should be remembered that before the eleventh century, canons who lived according to the 'rule' either of Chrodegang or of Aachen, had been known not unreasonably as *regulares*. The new distinction was still considered rather offensive by 'secular' canons in the fourteenth century.[44] A more reasonable distinction was made between the *ordo antiquus*, with which most communities in fact remained content, and the *ordo novus*, to which a number of houses attached themselves in the eleventh and twelfth centuries to form what became the Augustinian canons. We must, however, be more cautious to disentangle the two ways of life than many subsequent writers: it is commonplace for historians, even recent ones, to imagine that they have seen the later Augustinian way of life in earlier centuries, or to speak of all communities of priests as 'Augustinians' even where there is clear evidence that they never adopted community of possessions, which is the defining characteristic of the Augustinian reform.

The degree to which communities were willing to adopt the new ideal certainly varied. At the very time of these reforms, during Hildebrand's reign as Gregory VII (1073–85), the sixty houses of 'canons' in Rome, already mentioned, were presumably still living happily under the *Institutio Canonica* or something similar. They seem to have renounced their inheritance, but they still retained the use of their income, exactly as Pomerius and Chrodegang had recommended, but falling short of the full 'apostolic' ideal.[45] Elsewhere we hear of reformed communities which did adopt total community of property; at Lucca according to some reports they had already done so from 1048 onwards, to be followed at St Germans in 1050, and later at Milan by decree of Alexander II (1061–73), where they based their life on the letter of St Jerome to Nepotian, and explicitly on the 'rule of Saint Augustine'.[46] Bishop Anselm of Alicante (ob. 1086) entreated his canons that they should actually live as their name implies, being called 'canons' because they were governed by rule. They were somewhat reluctant to do this, so he agreed to share their common life himself. With nothing kept private, he was willing to hold all his property in common with them.[47]

The history of canons regular has been given sufficient attention, mostly by their own historians. The new institute, or the reform, is commonly attributed to Bishop Ivo of Chartres in the late eleventh century, who gathered his cathedral chapter into a canonry with community of property, and fine new stone buildings. The example of St Augustine was continually quoted, as well as that of the Acts of the Apostles, and by the end of the century we find increasing references to a 'Rule of St Augustine'. To begin with, however, mention of the rule of life of St Augustine was not to any specific text, but to the general precedent set by him in Hippo, and familiar from the vigil readings in the Divine Office for his feastday. If any further reference was required, it was given to the two sermons incorporated in the *Institutio Canonica*. The well-known text of St Augustine's 'Rule', although it had been quoted centuries earlier by St Benedict of Aniane, was not apparently available in the earlier stages of the Gregorian reform. A curious false start is represented by one manuscript of the *Institutio Canonica* surviving in the Vatican, which farces the chapters of the *Institutio* not only with chapters from the original Rule of Chrodegang but also with large portions of the text of the Rule of St Benedict, including the most stringent demands for absolute personal poverty. Liturgical evidence points to this manuscript being a Roman production, probably for a reformed community of canons at S Lorenzo in Damaso, after the Roman synods of 1059 and 1063 quoted above.[48] This lengthy and inconsistent document obviously enjoyed little favour, and was readily superseded by the Augustinian Rule. But at the same period Peter de Honestis drew up another *Regula Clericorum*, still in ignorance of the existence of the Rule of St Augustine.[49]

In 1092 Urban II wrote in confirmation of a refoundation in Rettenbach, where Welfo, Duke of Bavaria, and his wife Judith had established 'a canonry of brothers living according to the rule of blessed Augustine'. The pope gave thanks that the noble duke had renewed the approved life of the Holy Fathers and the discipline established by the Apostles, which arose in the early Church, but had virtually disappeared as the Church grew. Two forms of life were established for the sons of the early Church, says the pope: one for the weak and one for the strong, the ways of the canons and of the monks. Whereas monks were meant to be ascetic and far removed from the world, canons were to be more in touch with ordinary people, and to have a liturgical role among them. Nevertheless it was an abuse that they claimed the right to private property, and that abuse has now happily been corrected.[50] Reform of the canonical life was so significant a movement at the time that Pope Urban had probably chosen his name in homage to Urban I, who was credited with beginning the Canonical order (p. 28 above). Urban II certainly believed that the communal life is not viable without total community of possessions. Yet it was only in 1124 that a brother of Rettenbach travelled to Rome to search of the actual text of the 'Rule of St Augustine', which from then on became the foundation document for all orders of Canons Regular, and a number of subsequent Orders of great importance for the Church.[51]

From the beginning of the twelfth century, it became common for reforming popes or princes to encourage, persuade or force communities of secular canons to embrace the Rule of St Augustine. Various communities and congregations of canons regular, both black and white, grew and flourished from this date onwards, all over Europe. Of the 'white canons' the most important are the Norbertine or Praemonstratensian congregation, contrasted to the 'black canons' or Austin canons, who at first lived in autonomous communities under the direction of the local bishops, and only later were grouped into congregations with some degree of exemption from local control.

In England the first community of secular clergy to make a conscious change seems to have been that in Colchester, in 1105, followed rapidly by a large number of other houses, some ancient, and some newly founded. In Oxford city, for example, the eighth-century foundation of St Frideswide's became Augustinian in around 1120; St George's College, only founded in 1074, was regularized in 1149, becoming an appendage of the vast new foundation of Osney, begun in 1129. In the county of Oxford, the very early foundation of Dorchester became Augustinian in 1140, and new Augustinian houses were founded at Cold Norton (*c.*1160), Bicester (1182) and Wroxton (*c.*1215).[52]

The same pattern can be observed in most other English counties. Several of the greatest pre-Conquest minsters became Augustinian during the twelfth century: Carlisle and Cirencester in 1133, Twineham (Christchurch) around 1150, Harald Godwinsson's collegiate foundation at Waltham in 1177.[53] After the mid twelfth century there were fewer conversions, but new houses of Augustinian Canons continued to be founded on new sites into the fourteenth century. So common, indeed, did Augustinian houses become, that the impression can easily be given that the history of 'secular canons' had effectively come to an end.

Exactly the same process happened throughout the continent of Europe. Many new foundations were made, which were vowed Augustinian houses from the start, and many existing ancient communities were converted into Augustinian houses by one means or other. The process of division between secular and regular canons has been exceptionally well documented for the Church of St Quiriace in Provins, in the County of Champagne, by a secular canon, Michel Veissière.[54] He begins, as do so many historians, by lamenting the paucity of works on collegiate churches: Saint Quiriace was only one of five collegiate churches in the small hill-top town of Provins. It had been founded around 1030 along with many other communities in the county. The superior was called an abbot, but was not necessarily in priest's orders, and they presumably lived by the *Institutio Canonica.*

In the first half of the twelfth century the Rule of St Augustine was introduced into Champagne. Under the patronage of the counts, several new houses of canons regular were founded, and some existing chapters induced to adopt the Rule of St Augustine.

Nevertheless eight new houses of canons secular were also founded during the same period. In 1143 Count Thibaut II attempted to regularize St Quiriace, by introducing canons regular from his new priory of Soisy. The existing canons refused to accept the Rule of St Augustine, complaining that the regulars had been 'violently intruded', and two rival communities struggled for possession of the canonry. Thibaut suggested the seculars should live out their lives as they were, in a mixed community, to be replaced gradually by regulars, but neither side was happy with this. In 1151 Thibaut died, and was succeeded by Count Henri the Liberal: the secular canons appealed to him, and to Pope Hadrian IV, and it was decided that the regulars should move out and form a separate community, leaving the seculars at St Quiriace.

The two communities then lived happily side by side until the Revolution. The secular college of St Quiriace was reorganized, under an elected dean, who had the right to enfranchise serfs who wished to join the community. Below the dean was a provost, and there was also a cantor with the function of supervising schools. Up to a hundred prebends were available, and an enclosure was constructed with various buildings. In the last years of Henry the Liberal the number of prebends was reduced to forty-four, but a junior rank of *marguilliers* appeared. After that Veissière found little to record, because '*les peuples heureux n'ont pas d'histoire*' (p. 93). The other secular colleges that emerged in Provins at this time included the palace chapel, founded in 1176–81, for four canons and a chaplain, with a two-storey chapel. There was also a 'maison-Dieu' for the poor, founded in 1183, Nôtre-Dame du Val, around 1190, and Saint Nicolas in 1218. The surviving Church of St Quiriace was built in 1157–66; it remains unfinished, but is a spectacular monument to the vigour of the secular collegiate ideal after the Gregorian reforms had spent their course. All that survives of Nôtre-Dame du Val is the tower, but that indicates a building of significant size. It is obvious that communities of secular clergy survived the 'Gregorian Reforms' undimished, and were able to co-exist contentedly with the canons regular as with the Benedictines and the other orders that emerged in subsequent centuries.

Notes
1. Rodulfus Glaber, *Historiarum Libri Quinque*, III, 4, ed. J. France, Oxford University Press, 1989, p. 116.
2. Council of Ænham (1009), canon 1; Mansi XIX, c. 306.
3. Whitelock, Brett and Brooke, *Councils* I, p. 279.

4. See Æthelred Laws V and VI, issued at King's Enham in 1008, and the Edict of the Great Army (1009); Whitelock, Brett & Brooke, *Councils* I, nos. 49–50. The quotation is from Æthelred V, no 49, p. 348.
5. *Heafodmynstre, medemran mynstre, laesa mynstre 7 feldcirca*, Æthelred VIII (1014), Whitelock, Brett & Brooke, *Councils* I, no 52, p. 390.
6. Darlington, 'Ecclesiastical Reform', p. 404.
7. cf. RL 18; the manuscript is now Corpus Christi College, Cambridge, MSS 191 and 201, edited by A. Napier for the Early English Text Society (no. 150, 1914); and again by Langefeld, *Enlarged Rule of Chrodegang*.
8. now Camb. Univ. Library MS Hh,1.10.
9. now Bodleian MS Auct. D, infra 2–9.
10. William of Malmesbury, *Chronicle of the Kings of England* (Rolls Series, London, 1847), p. 201.
11. cited in Darlington, 'Ecclesiastical Reform', p. 403n.
12. See Drage, 'Bishop Leofric and the Exeter Cathedral Chapter', p. 195.
13. Rame, *Historians of the Church of York*, pp. 353–4; also Darlington, 'Ecclesiastical Reform', p. 404.
14. See Sparrow Simpson, *Registrum Statutorum*, pp 39–43; cf. IC 98–100, 124, 131–3; also Gibbs, *Early Charters of St Paul's*, p. 18, n.1.
15. J. Hunter (ed.), *Ecclesiastical Documents*, Camden Soc. 1st ser. VIII (1840), pp. 9–28.
16. Drage, 'Bishop Leofric', p. 275; Edwards, *English Secular Cathedrals*, p. 9; J. A. W. Robinson, 'The First Deans of Wells', in *Somerset Historical Essays*, (London, 1921), p. 55 sq.
17. W. Stubbs (ed.), *The Foundation of Waltham Abbey*, Oxford 1861, p. viii and chs. 12–15; Dugdale, *Monasticon* II, p. 11.
18. Douglas, *Domesday Monachorum*, pp. 14–15; also Page, 'Churches of the Domesday Survey'.
19. See Blair, *Minsters and Parish Churches*, and *Church in Anglo-Saxon Society*, esp. pp. 354–67.
20. Drage, 'Bishop Leofric', p. 194; Darlington, 'Ecclesiastical Reform', p. 404.
21. Whitelock, Brett & Brooke, *Councils* I, p. 540.
22. Morhain, 'Origine et Histoire', p. 183.
23. Council of Compostella (ERA 1094 = A.D. 1056), canon 1; Mansi XIX, c. 855.
24. Poggiaspalla, *Vita Comune*, pp. 134–5.
25. AA.SS. Oct. VIII, p. 980.
26. Synod of Volterra (*c.* 1070), Mansi XX, cc. 3–6.
27. Gregory VII, Epistle VI, xi; Mansi XX, c. 265.
28. Paschal II, *Tractatus ad Clerum*, Mansi X, cc. 1087–92.
29. Poggiaspalla, *Vita Comune*, p. 138; Siegwart, *Chorherren*, pp. 122, 155.
30. Siegwart, *Chorherren*, pp. 113–40, 169–204.
31. AA.SS. May I, pp. 506 sq.
32. John Bowden, *Life of Gregory VII*, II, p. 13.
33. AA.SS. May II, p. 699.
34. Peter Damian, *Contra Clericos Regulares Proprietarios*, PL 145:479–90.
35. Ibid., c. 484.
36. Ibid., c. 485.

37. Ibid., c. 490.
38. Ibid., c. 482.
39. Dickinson, *Austin Canons*, p. 23.
40. Poggiaspalla, *Vita Comune*, p. 161.
41. Council of Rome 1059, canon 4; Council of Rome 1063, canon 4; Mansi XIX, cc. 898, 1025.
42. Mansi XIX, c. 873.
43. Siegwart, *Chorherren*, p. 231.
44. See the comments of a canon of Utrecht quoted in Edwards, *English Secular Cathedrals*, p. 1.
45. Schuster, *Sacramentary*, pp. 24, 70.
46. Poggiaspalla, *Vita Comune*, pp. 150–1, 164.
47. AA.SS. March II, p. 649.
48. Codex Vaticanus 4885, printed in Mansi XIV, cc. 283–312; see Werminghoff, 'Aachener Concils', p. 637.
49. Dickinson, *Austin Canons*, p. 62.
50. Urban II, *Epistola LVIII*, PL 151:337–9.
51. Verheijen, *La règle de Saint Augustin*, II, p. 47.
52. Tanner, *Notitia*, pp. 413–430.
53. Dugdale, *Monasticon*, VI, p. 56 (Waltham), p. 141 (Carlisle), p. 176 (Cirencester), and p. 302 (Twineham).
54. Veissière, *Saint Quiriace de Provins*.

Chapter 8

General Legislation, and Cathedral Chapters in the High Middle Ages

Secular Communities after the Gregorian Reforms

Despite all the efforts of Peter Damian, and despite the popular conception, new colleges of secular canons, or 'collegiate churches' as they came to be called, were founded in increasing numbers all over Europe from the late eleventh century onwards, and were to remain a normal feature of ecclesiastical life until the Great Revolution. So normal are they, in fact, that few bothered to comment on them, which means that little attention has been paid to this form of institution, save for the most obvious cases of the cathedral chapters. Former collegiate churches are found all over Europe, and their architecture has long been observed and studied, but the institutions that they were designed to serve have been surprisingly neglected until very recently. When Fr Sonntag of the Leipzig Oratory studied the collegiate church of Erfurt in 1962, he complained that very little material was available anywhere on these medieval colleges – by the time Irene Crusius published her overview of research on German secular colleges in 1995 she was able to list seventy-five monographs on the subject.[1] In the same way, when Nigel Saul produced his study of Cobham College in 2001 very little had been published in England on medieval colleges, but since then a series of conferences and their attendent publications have raised awareness of the existence and nature of medieval communities to a new level.

Attempts have been made at different times to categorize late medieval colleges, in the few older works devoted exclusively to them, notably by A. Hamilton Thompson.[2] Distinctions have been observed between 'prebendal' colleges, where a fixed number of endowments were available for a fixed number of canons, and 'non-prebendal' communities where the revenues were held in common, and the individuals were paid only an equal stipend. Some colleges are characterized as 'chantry foundations', where the explicit purpose of the foundation was to pray for the souls of individuals. Others are classed as 'hospital' or 'educational' foundations, with a specific mandate to benefit certain classes of people. A distinction is noticed between episcopal foundations and those established by lay nobles. While all these distinctions do have a certain validity, we must remember that they are entirely the creation of later observers: during the Middle Ages themselves no such categories existed. Collegiate churches were a recognized institution, but no two were exactly alike. All had the responsibility to pray for the dead, to care for the sick and to educate the young; *praebenda* were necessary, whether they were equal shares of a common fund or unequal revenues from specific sources; bishops and lay nobles lived similar lives and were served by clergy in similar ways. Nevertheless, in an attempt to impose order on an otherwise unwieldy subject, it may be useful to look in turn at cathedral foundations, both major and minor, rural colleges, those attached to great households, hospital and educational colleges and informal communities or hermitages, all of which had appeared before the convenient turning point of the Black Death.

Conciliar and Papal Legislation

Despite the strictures of Peter Damian, the Chrodegangian Rule and the Rule of Aachen legislated for a fairly demanding way of life. This legislation was confirmed in many twelfth- and thirteenth-century local councils. It is obvious that the ideal of a real common life with religious observance was far from extinct at this period. Canonical clergy were still expected to observe some form of religious poverty, though without the total renunciation of property: certainly they were forbidden to grow rich on the proceeds of the common fund, and the 'share in the donations' was not envisaged as amounting to anything on the large scale. They were expected to keep enclosure except for necessary pastoral visits, and to devote a large proportion of the day and night to the choral offices. The insistence on a common dormitory and a common table enforced an equality among the canons. The only inequalities admitted are based entirely on age and ecclesiastical degree, not on civil status or wealth. At times it could be very difficult to tell the difference between canons, even 'secular' ones, and monks, especially as it became increasingly normal for most choir monks to be priests. It was still possible for married men to join canonries, but it was made clear that after this their children had no claim on their ecclesiastical income. If we read of prebends or canonries being granted to 'laymen', it should be noted that they were under the obligation of proceeding at least to minor orders immediately.

The common life of secular clergy not only survived the Gregorian reforms and the spread of Augustinian houses, but it actually revived and flourished, until in the later Middle Ages it became a vital feature of clerical life everywhere. The impetus for founding new Augustinian canonries, or converting older secular ones, was spent by the end of the twelfth century. The thirteenth century is usually seen as the day of the Friars, but it was also marked by the foundation or re-foundation of many secular communities. The fact that this happened after the great reforming Fourth Lateran Council does not mean that it was an explicit recommendation of that council: it wasn't, but the general atmosphere of reform led logically to a reform of the life of the clergy which in turn led to the revival of common life.

Nevertheless, not all went smoothly in every case. Prebends may have been equal to start with, but inevitably some lands gained in value while others declined, and a rich prebend could come to be worth very much more than a poor one. The word 'canon' came to designate a coveted honour, rather than being a description implying a regular way of life. Already in the early twelfth century, St Bernard was able to speak of a canon as a dignitary almost equal to an abbot or bishop: 'a canon is invested with a book, an abbot with a staff, a bishop with a ring'.[3] Too often positions in cathedral or greater collegiate churches were granted to the idle sons of the gentry, who only with difficulty could be restrained from taking advantage of their position. The problem of non-residence recurs incessantly, and was met by a variety of legislation. In the cathedrals this was only partially successful.

If we look at a selection of decrees passed between the time of Gregory VII and the Black Death, we can compile a picture of the general expectation of the life of canonical clergy.

The Council of Esztergom in 1114 speaks of canons in their closes, and chaplains at court, who are encouraged to speak Latin, and confirms that the livelihood of the canons is the responsibility of the bishop.[4] In 1118, Pope Gelasius II approved the customs of the canons of Lucca, as did Callistus II those of Vienne in 1120.[5] St Ubald, Bishop of Gubbio (d. 1160) found the clergy without any significant religious observance, living each in his own house, and leaving the cloister open to all, men and women alike. Ubald set to work to make them live more regularly, and keep enclosure, diligent at table, in the dormitory, and at choir. Eventually he brought a Rule for them from S. Maria in Portu, near Ravenna, which was a vowed Augustinian house, and so gradually mutated them into canons regular.[6]

Various rulings concern the allocation of dividends to canons, including the distribution of Candlemas candles.[7] In 1134 Archbishop Thurstan of York decreed that on the death of a canon his income was to continue for one year to clear his debts, and to provide Masses for his soul.[8] Eugenius III granted a quarter of the revenues of St Peter's to the canons in 1153, because 'they serve God night and day for the benefit of the living and the dead'.[9] A few years later, when the canons of Hildesheim were replaced by monks, the same Pope ensured that the surviving canons could retain their prebends for life.[10] Alexander III (1159–81) granted a stipend of four marks a year to non-resident canons of Paris, except for those in royal service, and the same pope wrote sternly to Archbishop Henri of Reims, on receiving reports that his canons were living with women: those under the rank of subdeacon must marry their women, subdeacons and above must send them away.[11]

The Third Lateran Council of 1179 insisted that every cathedral must maintain a master to teach the clergy and poor scholars, thus keeping up the educational and training role of the chapters. Canons, specifically including *seculares*, are obliged to keep residence in their churches, and lepers and other hospital inmates are also expected to form communities of prayer.[12] Two years later the local council at Aquileia ordered the clergy 'from henceforth to maintain the common life, sleeping all together in one common dormitory, eating all together in one refectory, and none should receive food or drink from the common fund except in the refectory'. All are to receive an equal share of food, though curiously the Dean and Magister Scholarum receive a double share of clothing: those who are studying should get an extra mark and a half per year; all other goods are to be held in common. On the death of a canon, his prebend should be applied for the good of his soul for one year.[13] At the end of the twelfth century, Celestine III wrote to the canons of Langres, insisting on long periods of continuous residence, on pain of forfeiting all income.[14]

In the early thirteenth century, conciliar and papal documents continue to attest to the vigour of the secular tradition, despite the usual judgement that secular canons, with some notable exceptions, had become altogether more comfortable, more worldly. At

Paris in 1212 the decree on the life and behaviour of clerics insisted on their duty to be present at Mass and Office daily, to have readings in the refectory, and to have respectable chamberdeacons as witnesses to chastity: similar decrees were passed at Rouen, Bourges, and London in 1214.[15]

At no stage has the Church in any place expressed herself satisfied that everything is going well, particularly when it comes to the behaviour of the clergy. A great movement of reform throughout the Church found expression in the Fourth Lateran Council (1215), which did not deal explicitly with the common life of the clergy, but was followed by a very large number of local councils, continuing into the fourteenth century. All of them have a chapter *De vita et honestate clericorum*, dealing over and over again with the same questions, and usually couched in the same phrases. There are few explicit recommendations of common life, but many passing references to collegiate churches and beneficed canons. It is quite clear that the common life of the secular clergy was still very much alive, and there is no evidence at all that the Church officially acquiesced in non-residence and canonical sinecures. This implies a singular unity of purpose throughout Europe – but it also implies continual falling away from the high standards expected, and the ceaseless need for reform. It is clearly taken for granted that there are collegiate churches in every diocese, as well as the cathedrals, and that some form of common life is to be expected. Often we hear the old call for 'one dormitory and one refectory', though in other cases it is obviously accepted that the clergy live in separate lodgings within the close.

Archbishop Konrad of Cologne issued a long set of statutes for secular clergy (as well as some for monks) in 1260. He begins by lamenting the fact that some churches do not have dormitories, or that if they do the canons sleep elsewhere, and are frequently absent from the Divine Office. Now, 'all these things are to be reformed, and once reformed they are to remain in full vigour, as it was instituted long ago'. From now on, he continues, dormitories and refectories are to be built for every collegiate church, and the canons are to sleep in the one, eat in the other, and attend the entire Divine Office in church.[16] Other councils agree that the canons must sleep within the enclosure, and that no women should do so.[17] Continuous residence is insisted on by every council and synod, and there is a repeated call for absent canons to return immediately or lose their prebends. Those who are lawfully absent with permission are responsible for finding someone to take their place at Mass and Office.[18]

Attendance at the daily conventual Mass and the Divine Office was enforced by many councils by the simple expedient that those who fail to do so may not receive their daily stipend. Minor clerics are to attend at least Mass, Matins and Vespers; major clerics the entire round of the Hours.[19] The canonical dress of surplice and cappa, now supplemented with the biretta, is obligatory in choir, and the cappa must be worn whenever canons go out of doors. After the beginning of the fourteenth century we begin to hear of the almuce, and at Paris in 1346 it was specified that canons wear black almuces trimmed with squirrel fur (*forratis minutis variis*), and vicars the same but without the fur.[20] The Martyrology and Necrology are to be read in choir, and there is to be reading in the refectory.[21] In every college at least one in ten clerics must attend a *studium generale*, to study theology, canon law or the arts.[22] That, of course, contradicts the call for perpetual residence, but it soon became established that a good and beneficial use of prebendal income was to subsidize university studies, and that permission for a canon to be absent for study was readily given.

Clerics in minor orders, many of them married, were still very much in evidence. They are reminded that they should still dress as clergy if they wished to retain their privileges, and are encouraged to attend at least the public Offices.[23] They may not, however, attend chapter or vote.[24] Although the married clerics do not live within the close, and are engaged in secular work, they should take only suitable employment. Lists of forbidden trades include butchers and publicans, actors, jesters and the like. In particular they are not to be goliards or wandering poets (known in Mainz as 'Eberhards'). The constitutions of Francesco, Bishop of Gubbio, explicitly forbid all clergy from possessing or playing a guitar.[25] (There is no evidence that the prohibition on guitar-playing has ever been repealed.) Married clerics may not be enrolled as recipients of church charity (*matricularii*).[26] Local councils in Hungary in the late thirteenth century still envisaged married men leaving their wives to be ordained subdeacon, and suggested that their children should be taken into the *familia* of the greater Church (in effect to become serfs of the diocese). Those ordained after marriage must make a public resolution of future continence, with the agreement of their wives, who are not to live with them any more. Sons of priests may not be ordained unless they become monks – this was obviously to prevent property being passed on from father to son.[27] In western Europe it seems that by now a greater respect for the sacrament of marriage had led to it becoming a rare occurrence for a married man to be ordained in this way.[28]

English Cathedral Chapters

In the late eleventh century it appears to have become necessary to re-constitute most of the cathedral chapters of western Europe. Much attention has been given to this topic in England, where the reconstruction was largely the result of the policies of the new Norman dynasty. In some cases episcopal seats were moved from ancient but decayed cities like Sherborne, Dorchester or Selsey into the larger new cities, Sarum, Lincoln or Chichester. In other cases the devastation wrought by the Danish and Norman invasions necessitated a new start, as at York, and most of the Welsh dioceses. In the process, in most cases, the statutes or rules previously followed seem to have been eclipsed, and throughout the twelfth century there was considerable variety in customs and practice. No clear written rules of life for any cathedral chapter date from earlier than the thirteenth century, but the haphazard structures were gradually reduced to a degree of uniformity with new statutes promulgated in the thirteenth and fourteenth centuries, all of which clearly copied each other, and duly take account of conciliar legislation. As well as the cathedrals, there were a certain number of major 'minsters' which survived the Conquest to become collegiate churches, some as large as cathedrals, and following almost exactly the same pattern of life; the most important of these were the three in the Diocese of York, namely Beverley, Ripon, and Southwell, with St Oswald's, Gloucester, which was for long a detached possession of York.

The earliest cathedral statutes to be formulated in England seem not surprisingly to be those of London, which were taking shape by 1060, and, as we have seen, demonstrate some continuity with the earlier period.[29] William I sent greetings to *mine canonicas on sancte Paules mynstre*, and they were clearly intended to be a resident corporate body.[30] In the late eleventh century, Bishop Maurice seems to have reorganized the prebendal system on a stabilized territorial basis, and the foundation was apparently able to support thirty canons. The dean presided over the four archdeacons, and the other officials were a cantor, a *Magister Scholarum*, and a *Custos Bracini* or seneschal. The magister was responsible for all schools in the City of London except for the collegiate establishments of the Arches and St Martin le Grand. In the twelfth century the structure at London was brought into conformity with the usual English pattern of four officials or 'dignitaries', the dean, precentor, chancellor and treasurer, the thirty vicars of the thirty canons became more influential, and the unusual rank of twelve 'petty canons' emerged. By the time of the statutes of Dean Baldock (fl. 1305), the establishment comprised the four dignitaries assisted by the subdean, succentor, and sacrist, the four archdeacons, thirty prebendaries or major canons (from whom the dignitaries and archdeacons were chosen), twelve petty or minor canons (from whom the subdean and the two 'cardinal canons' were chosen), thirty vicars, an almoner, innumerable chantry priests, three virgers or *custodes ecclesiæ*, two *garciones*, librarians, bookbinders, brewers and other such domestics.[31]

As already mentioned, chapters from the Institutes of Aachen formed part of the pre-Conquest statutes, the *Regula Canonica Ecclesiae Londoniensis*, found embedded in the later statutes of 1305 (p. 90 above). These later statutes make provisions about allowances of food and drink, *de pane et cervisia*, in language reminiscent of the *Institutio* and the Longer Rule. The ration for all canons is to be one loaf and one *laguna* of beer (*cervisia*) a day. A later chapter (21, p. 173) makes provision for the residents: a canon is to receive two large and two small loaves, adding up to nineteen and a half marks (156 oz. Troy), although it is noted that the ration was formerly seven marks for a major canon and half that for a minor.[32] The beer is computed as sixteen measures of the best bitter, and two of the worst, each measure being eighty *ciphi Sancti Pauli* defined as gallons. This allowance, 1,280 gallons of beer per week, is presumably for the entire establishment, canons, vicars, choristers, servants and all.[33]

Each canon is to maintain two unbeneficed clerics, and to supply three meals daily for two minor canons, two chaplains, four vicars, virgers and bellringers, and to qualify for a share of the dividend at all must reside for at least a full quarter. He must never live far from the cathedral, for he is to attend all the Hours, and after a year's probation will be granted a house in the close in which he is to accommodate the two minor clerks and a vicar. Being a canon of London was far from a sinecure, and involved considerable expenses, afterwards limited to 300 marks per year. At London the vicars began to reside together after 1273, with a common hall, and two senior priests resided with them to keep order.[34]

If the London statutes preserve some of the oldest texts, it is those of Lincoln that have been studied in greatest detail, thanks to the massive edition by Henry Bradshaw and Christopher Wordsworth. They begin with the foundation charters, dating from the move from Dorchester to Lincoln, when Bishop Remigius established a chapter in September 1090 with the four dignitaries, seven archdeacons and a subdean. He described the community as an *abbatia*, 'in which as a mother church the canons who serve God should live justly, chastely and Catholicly'. He divided the income between the cathedral church and the community house, and forbade the exchange of prebends for money.[35]

The chapter of Lincoln seems to have served as the model for others, which adopted the 'four-square' structure of dean, precentor, chancellor and treasurer. Archbishop Thomas established a similar chapter in York in 1090, and St Osmund did the same in Sarum a year later, in each case with the same four dignitaries. Bradshaw believed that the model for this was found in Normandy, though in the later edition Wordsworth pointed out that of all the chapters in Normandy, Bayeux alone had that precise structure.[36] When it came to the customs, however, by which the chapter canons were to live, it seems that St Osmund of Sarum provided the model, copied in turn from the customs followed at Rouen. In his 1091 foundation charter, Osmund is emphatic that 'Nothing can excuse the canons from keeping residence in the church of Sarum except for reasons of study, or the service of the King in his chapel.' Those who are not present at Mass and the Hours must beg pardon in chapter.[37] The customs, including instructions on the celebration of divine worship, bellringing, the night watch, and the entertainment of junior clergy by the prebendaries, were presented to newly elected canons who had to swear to uphold them. Until a prebend was available, the newly elected canon would receive his ration of wine, but nothing else.[38] The estate of a deceased canon would continue to receive the revenue from his prebend for a year, to clear all debts, and provide for the repose of his soul. The house must be left furnished and in a suitable condition for his successor. Here again, therefore, the presumption is that canons do not live in a common dwelling, but each has his own, in which he is to entertain various minor clerics as well as domestics. Among the earliest customs is found that of distributing the Psalms among the Canons, so that every day the entire Psalter would be recited between them, for their benefactors. At Lincoln the psalm references are still written up in the stalls.

In secular cathedrals, the functions of the four dignitaries became standardized in the later Middle Ages. The dean was the president of the chapter, responsible for government and correction, to visit the sick and provide for the poor. The precentor or cantor was to direct the singing and train the boys. The chancellor was to rule the school of theology and preach, correct books and appoint servers. At York, 'The chancellor, who was anciently called the master of the schools, must be a Master of Theology, and should lecture actively near the church, being also in charge of the schools of grammar.' The treasurer was to guard the vestments and plate, and was responsible for the bells, clocks, lights and all sacristy equipment including altar bread and wine. Archdeacons, being obliged to peregrinate their archdeaconries, were told that at York they need not keep residence more than three months of the year.[39] It certainly seems that Remigius intended his canons and dignitaries to be resident at Lincoln, and to serve God within the cathedral church, though here too the archdeacons had duties in the far-flung diocese that must always have obliged them to be absent for long periods. Indeed in the foundation charter William II instructed Remigius to ensure that the canons live canonically, which implies that something like the *Institutio Canonica* was intended to be used. Nevertheless he also instructed Remigius to convert Earl Leofric's secular canonry of Stowe into a Benedictine monastery, which in the event moved to Eynsham.[40]

England, it will be remembered, was unusual in that certain cathedrals were staffed by Benedictine monks rather than canons. Pope Alexander II wrote to Archbishop Lanfranc to support him in maintaining this peculiarity. It appears that certain nefarious laymen had been manoeuvring to have the monks expelled and secular clerics substituted at Canterbury, as a preliminary to effecting the same change in the other cathedrals. The pope quoted his predecessors Gregory the Great and Boniface I as authorities for the English custom.[41] Tensions between monks and canons continued during the eleventh and early twelfth centuries, with some cathedrals changing sides more than once. Some dioceses settled the difference by having two cathedrals. In 1191 Pope Celestine III noted that the monks had been expelled from Chester Cathedral in favour of secular canons, and ordered the Archbishop of Canterbury to replace the monks, and to move the diocese to Lichfield.[42] Lichfield remained secular, alternating with Coventry which (after two secular interludes) remained Benedictine. Similarly Bath and Wells both served as cathedrals for the Somerset diocese.

During the twelfth century, chapters of canons grew in autonomy against the bishop, and customs developed, eventually being written down as statutes, agreed by the dean and chapter and ratified by the bishop. During the thirteenth and fourteenth centuries there is a growing uniformity, and statutes tend to quote each other. In 1214 the customs of Lincoln were written down at the request of Brictus, Bishop of Moray, who intended to set up his own miniature cathedral chapter of eight canons, and the resulting

Consuetudinarium records the titles and functions of the four dignitaries, in language very similar to the Sarum institutes of St Osmund, as well as those of Chichester. There was evidently a great deal of copying and lending of statutes and customaries between the dioceses. The Dean and Chapter of Glasgow also wrote to Lincoln in 1259 to ask for a copy of the statutes and customs.[43]

Bishops continued to keep a close interest in their canons. At Lincoln, St Hugh ordered non-resident canons to maintain a deputy, a vicar, at their own expense, and in 1321–2 Bishop Robert Grosteste fixed the annual stipends at six shillings and eightpence (half a mark) for residential canons, three shillings and fourpence for non-residents, as much as thirteen shillings and fourpence (one mark) for vicars, twenty-two pence for poor clerks, and eighteenpence for boys, as a share out of the offerings made at the shrine of St Hugh.[44] It is noteworthy that the vicars are allowed considerably more than the canons, because the canons already enjoy their prebends. At Hereford the existing customs and statutes were collected in the time of Dean Aquablanca, c.1280, because they had fallen into disuse and needed to be restored. All canons are granted a ration of wheat and twenty shillings per year as commons, but those who attend Mass and Matins in their habits get a further daily distribution of bread, beer (*sereuisia*) and cash.

Several of the statutes mention the importance of proper dress and behaviour in choir. At Hereford they are told to 'wear decent and appropriate clothing, neither soiled nor torn' and that 'no one is to give way like a child to loud and immoderate laughter in choir, nor confer together, except for some reasonable and necessary cause'. They are to wear processional cappas. Outside the times of divine worship, all are to behave respectably and avoid taverns and suspicious places, and they are not to be out at night, 'which could cause scandal'. There follows a warning against scandalous behaviour in public, for which 'blessed Augustine, the founder of our religious life, excluded men from the common table' (cf. RA 37). Although there is no doubt that the canons of Hereford were 'secular', they still acknowledge St Augustine as their inspiration.[45] At York, the four dignitaries are allowed silk copes, and must keep residence. A canon receives a cloth cappa, or twenty marks to buy one, and a vicar is to have a red mantle, and his own palfrey, or ten marks to buy one. They must wear clerical dress when in the city, without resorting to extravagant fashions. On the death of a canon, his choir dress is to be given to his vicar, whereas his remaining linen goes to the minor clerics.[46] The York statutes were codified in 1291, when the vicars were beginning to form their own collegiate life. At Lincoln we hear, 'There must be no murmuring among the clerics, but they should behave decently and bear themselves without raucous laughter and joking, speaking rarely and only in a low voice about what is necessary.' The canons are to wear a white linen surplice, a grey almuce and a black woollen cappa, neither too short nor too long, according to the weather, and they should be properly shaved.[47]

Cathedral Chapters outside England

In a similar way we find that chapters of canons developed in cathedrals on the Continent, and very similar statutes were promulgated and codified for them, although they have not been studied so systematically. For instance, St Bertram of Aquileia in 1335 combined the canonries of St Odoricus and St Maria in Castello at Udine to provide a chapter for his new cathedral there, changing the warden into a dean.[48]

The medieval statutes of the chapter at Paris include a detailed ritual for the admission of a new canon.[49] He kneels before the dean, who admits him as a canon and brother, and presents him with 'the book of rules (*canonum*) which is read every day in Chapter after the Necrology, at the end of Prime'. The new canon swears obedience to the Dean and Chapter, and is then vested in the alb and black hooded cappa, before being literally in-stalled to his place in choir. If it is summer he may then take off the heavy black cappa. The Rule, *De Vita Canonici*, requires that all the canons reside continually in the church, in obedience, chastity, charity, prayer, reading, psalmody, contemplation and sobriety. They include priests, deacons and subdeacons: the priests are to take their turn celebrating Mass at the High Altar, and the deacons and subdeacons to assist. The canons are wholly responsible for the goods of the Church, which they must administer in common, and there should be a just distribution for their victualling.

Detailed instructions follow for the conduct of Divine Office. The cappa is to be worn for the Midnight Office, and from St Denis' day (9 October) till Easter at the day Hours. Daily chapter after Prime includes the reading of the lives of the saints (the Martyrology) and the list of anniversaries of the dead (the Necrology) before the reader reads with some solemnity a chapter of the Rule. This can only be the *Institutio Canonica*, which all the canons must hear with reverence. At the choral hours, only the cantor may carry a staff, *baculus*. The old prohibition in the Rule of

St Chrodegang of carrying staves or clubs has mutated into the staff becoming the badge of office of the cantor: late medieval incised slabs of Paris cantors show this baton as a thick man-high staff, topped with a moulded finial.[50]

Canons are to have their hair decently cut, their dress neither too long nor too short, their gait dignified and stately. They are to have little contact with women, particularly in church. During processions they are to look down, and must not gossip, and they must not wander around the church when they are supposed to be in choir. During chapter and at table the canons must behave reverently; women should not be allowed to enter the enclosure. Every Friday there is to be a chapter of faults, examining and correcting any failure in public duties. The dean is particularly charged to look to his own faults before presuming to correct those of others. A canon who has to leave the city, or spend a night outside the enclosure, must obtain a blessing from the dean, and after a long absence must report back to the dean, to hear what has happened while he was away. The dean is to resolve differences among the canons; difficulties with the dean are to be brought to the bishop. The dean, despite his many responsibilities, must still observe the usual hours in choir, but he is always given a double portion. (This presumably refers to shares of the money, rather than two helpings at every meal.)

Any income from legacies, or the sale of any property including carvings (*de sculpturis*), is not to be divided up but must remain common property, to be used particularly for the adornment of the church. The canons must remain devotedly obedient to the bishop, remembering that they form one body with him, even though his revenues and *mensa* are now kept separate. It is unfortunate that Martène gives no date for these statutes: they must be fairly early, but the implication is that they long remained in force as the governing document of the church of Paris. It is noticeable that the canons are vested only in alb and cappa, as we see them on thirteenth-century incised slabs, not in the almuce which appears in the first quarter of the fourteenth century.[51]

Prebends

A problem which was frequently addressed by reforming bishops or councils was the inequality of income that derived from the prebendal system. To recapitulate, from the eleventh century onwards, lay benefactors preferred to give a specific parcel of land for the support (*praebendum*) of a specific canon. The canon would thus feel indebted to the family concerned, and would naturally come to take a proprietorial interest in the land they had allotted him. The natural temptation, encouraged by the lay landowner, was to move out and live on it, to serve a separate church there. Frequently this must have been what the lay benefactor intended in the first place. On the death or resignation of such a 'prebendary' canon, his prebend would be bequeathed, allotted or simply sold to the next canon to be appointed. Obviously these prebends varied enormously in value, depending on the original donation and the subsequent management of the property. The history of cathedral and collegiate chapters for the next few centuries was to consist of the losing battle against prebendaries detaching themselves from community life, and trafficking in the more lucrative prebends. The reforms of Trent legislated against non-residence, but in countries like England and northern Germany which resisted these reforms, the institution of non-resident and unequally paid prebendaries was to continue until the twentieth century.

Once the idea had arisen of individual parcels of land being allotted to individual canons, it was extended, so that possessions formerly held in common for all the canons came to be divided up into separate prebends. This practice seems to have begun in France in the first half of the eleventh century, and was adopted in England a century later. To begin with, some effort was made to ensure that the prebends were equal, so that the remuneration of each canon would be much the same. This preserves the principle found in the earlier canonical rules that all should have a share of the *eleemosyna*, the donations given to the community. In addition the daily ration of bread and wine continued to be given, known as the *commune* or 'commons'. A canon joining a college would therefore find himself in possession of a regular income in cash from his prebend, a regular ration of food and drink distributed in the house, and also an unpredictable amount of free offerings given for the celebration of Mass. Again, however equal the prebends might have been to start with, subsequent management of the land could make them very unequal after a century or so. Prebends were usually identified by the place from which the money came, although in some cases the best prebend in a cathedral as called simply the 'Golden Prebend', whereas conversely one in Lincoln was named *Consumpta per mare*, 'lost to the sea'.

The position of canon in a cathedral or a greater collegiate church could, therefore, become extremely lucrative, and would be much sought after for the younger sons of the gentry. The old rule forbidding provosts from recruiting exclusively from within the family of the church, and excluding the freeborn or noble, became somewhat redundant. In some cases, indeed, cathedral chapters were composed exclusively of the nobility.

Canons Resident and Non-Resident

Indications are that the idea of the true common life rapidly fell out of favour, and the canons of cathedral chapters usually lived each in his own home, with his own household of servants. The prebendal income enabled the canon to build and furnish his own house, near the cathedral church but not necessarily enclosed within the close. He could also build a residence in his prebendal manor, in conjunction with the church there, and might be tempted to spend an increasing amount of his time residing there rather than in the city centre. To provide for the two incompatible pastoral responsibilities of cathedral choirstall and country parish, it was the responsibility of the canon to find another priest, to act as deputy or *vicar* during his absence from the cathedral city. This arrangement became institutionalized, with the canon being considered fully responsible for providing a vicar to represent him in the cathedral choir, and frequently also another vicar to represent him in his prebendal parish or parishes.

Legislation frequently addresses the need to pay these vicars properly. As we have seen, St Hugh of Lincoln (1186–1200) insisted on the duty of non-residents to provide suitable vicars and make an honourable and sufficient provision for them, which was later fixed at thirteen shillings and fourpence (one mark) a year.[52] His contemporary, Hugh of Lichfield (1185–98) did the same, and when the Lichfield statutes were re-issued by Bishop Pateshul (1239–41) the annual amount specified there was that a canon was obliged to pay his vicar at least twenty shillings, and if for any reason he did not have a vicar, the same stipend was to be paid to the common fund.[53] Thus the canon fulfilled his obligations of ensuring that divine worship continued without interruption in both city and country parishes. The fact that he ensured this was of greater importance than his personal attendance in choir. The vicars responsible for divine worship in the cathedral would naturally find accommodation in the canon's residence, among his other servants and retainers.

If the canon had satisfactorily provided suitable vicars to maintain divine worship both in the cathedral and in his prebendal parish, there could in theory be no objection to him being employed elsewhere, for the benefit of the Church or the realm at large. There was, indeed, no reason for him to be resident even in the same country as his chapter or prebend, so that it became perfectly regular for cathedral canonries to be treated as a source of revenue for royal and papal functionaries. The revenue from the prebend, after the salaries of the vicars had been paid, served as a satisfactory salary for a hard-working civil servant or papal secretary. Since in many cases the income from the prebend might leave little over after the salaries of two vicars had been paid, it sometimes became necessary for a canon to be presented to another prebend to augment his income to the extent that he could fulfil his obligations. Few voices seem to have been raised in protest against this system in itself, and indeed if it is considered simply as a rather roundabout way of raising money from the people to pay for the administration of Church or State, it is no more objectionable than raising income tax to pay for the Civil Service, or taking a collection in church to cover the administration of the diocese. There were indeed frequent objections to the adding of one prebend to another, and the gradual collection of considerable portfolios of benefices, but objections were usually quelled by ensuring that sufficient vicars were sufficiently paid to ensure that in every case divine worship was satisfactorily carried out.

Nevertheless, there were frequent calls for canons to be more often resident in their cathedrals, with the implication that at least in some cases the non-resident was not engaged in useful administration at all, but idling his time away at Court or in some locality more congenial than his cathedral city. As we have already seen, St Osmund issued a stringent decree about residence in the church of Sarum except for the reasons of study, or service to the king (p. 148 above). Later a distinction was accepted between residentiary canons, who were obliged to be in attendance at least for a significant part of the year, and non-residentiaries, who might never appear at all, and had a greatly reduced share of the emoluments. A new canon who expressed the intention of becoming a residentiary was expected to make a substantial payment on installation. Both types of canon would be expected to maintain vicars. Concern over non-residence is expressed in the twelfth-century statutes of St Paul's, which rule that non-residents could receive a common dividend, the *solanda*, but were not entitled to any share in the offerings, pittancies or distributions of incrued income from the *bracinum* (brewery) or *camera*.[54] Those who wished to become residentiaries were expected to appear on the vigils of Michaelmas, Christmas, Easter or St John's Day, and protest their willingness to reside: their duties were to include providing for the unbeneficed clerics. Residence requirements were a full quarter, less a maximum of six days, and no more than three weeks and six days absence during the remaining three quarters: this adds up to a total of thirty-three days' leave a year, which is not really excessive. A residentiary was expected to attend all the canonical Hours, and not to live too far from the cathedral church; after the first year a house would be allotted to him, in which he had to accommodate two minor clerics and a vicar, and entertain the remaining clergy for whom he was responsible. Because of the considerable expenses involved, the number of residentiaries was limited by statute, varying according to the income available to the foundation: in the thirteenth century St Paul's had eleven residentiaries, whereas in 1417 there were but five, rising to six in 1520. On the death of a residentiary (or his profession as a monk) his executors continued to receive the income for a year, to discharge all debts and provide for his dependants: this is doubtless why the house would not become available to a new residentiary until a year after his election.[55] At the very end of the Catholic period, the statutes of St Paul's were revised twice, firstly by Dean Colet, who expected residence to be taken literally, and permitted no absences at all, and secondly by Cardinal Wolsey, who allowed the canons nine months' absence a year.[56]

At Lichfield the statutes were codified in 1240–1 by Bishop Pateshul; he insisted that the vicars must attend day and night Hours under pain of dismissal, and that the minor clerics must sign on every morning before Mass. A few years later Bishop Meuland or Moland (1256–95) observed that the canons should obtain vicars for their prebendal parishes, rather than serving them themselves, because 'canons ought to worship not in them but for them, serving in the greater churches'. Residentiaries would forfeit their dividends if they were absent for more than thirty days in any one quarter.[57]

Besides the regular stipend offered to canons, there was a further distribution of commons for those actually present in choir on any specific day. It was usually expected that it was essential to attend Matins, Mass and Vespers to earn this dole, unless the canon were prevented by genuine illness. Originally the commons was in the form of bread and beer, as in the earlier Rules, but this was gradually converted to a money allowance by the thirteenth century: Bishop Moland allows twelve pence a day, two shillings on greater feasts, and ten shillings at Christmas, Easter, St Chad's day and the Assumption. At Hereford, in the time of Dean Aquablanca (*c*.1280) there were three types of commons: the 'small commons' distributed to everyone consisted of a ration of wheat as well as twenty shillings per year; residentiaries were to receive the 'greater commons' in wheat and cash; and then there was a daily distribution in bread and wheat, Mass pennies, and a 'consolation of beer' (echoing the language of Chrodegang), for all canons who attended Matins in choir, wearing their cappas.[58] At York, the vicars received tempence a day in 1216, and a bonus of ten shillings at Pentecost and Martinmas, whereas in the statutes of 1294 there is a fine of a penny for any Hour if they arrive late, and a similar fine of a penny for chattering in choir.[59]

If canons could sometimes be non-resident without incurring the charge of dereliction of duty, the same could not be said of dignitaries or vicars, to say nothing of choristers and the other minor members of the foundation. The dean in particular was necessarily resident: the Moland statutes begin with the requirement for a newly appointed dean to swear that he will be continually resident, and defining his task as that of 'correcting the excesses of the canons, vicars, clerks and servants'. The Pateshul statutes had already been insistent about the duties of vicars to attend choir regularly day and night, and appointed one to call the roll and notify the chapter about absentees. The same is required of the minor clerics.[60] In practice it appears that even the canons were often resident for more than the required minimum period, and the popular image of idle absent prebendaries is not justified by the facts. Only the canons could meet for the legislative chapter (and in some cathedrals the dean was excluded), and the impression is that cathedral business continued to be conducted reasonably efficiently throughout the Middle Ages.

Minor Corporations

'Residence', in the first three centuries after the Norman Conquest, did not mean life in community for the entire establishment, as we have seen, but simply being resident in the city near enough to the cathedral for it to be possible to attend the Night Offices. After the gradual abandonment of the common dormitory, each individual canon's dwelling (*mansio*) preserved something of the common life, with the vicars and minor clergy sharing his house and table, but by the fourteenth century it appears that in many places the vicars and minor clerics were commonly living, not in the households of their canons, but in private lodgings scattered about the city. The danger to morality, as well as the inconvenience of this practice led to the formation of 'minor corporations' in most English Cathedrals, bringing the vicars back together again to live in something much closer to the Common Life than had been seen since the eleventh century. By the end of the thirteenth century there were some 350 vicars choral serving the nine secular cathedrals, with numbers ranging from fifty-eight to twenty-five. Although supported by individual canons, they enjoyed a security of tenure independent of the lives of their canons. As corporate bodies, they began to be granted and to hold property separate from that of the cathedral chapters. Closes were constructed, reasonably near the cathedral church, which provided small individual lodgings for the vicars, and a great hall for communal dining. The common dormitory prescribed by the earlier Rules was now an anachronism, when even Cistercians had put up partitions in the dormitory, but the gathered vicars were certainly expected to eat together and recreate together as well as assembling regularly for divine worship.[61]

Thus at York, the vicars are first mentioned in 1138–43, and were beginning to act as a corporation in the second decade of the thirteenth century. An enclosure, the Bedern, was constructed for them at the time of the statutes of 1252, largely as a result of a bequest from William of Laneham. The vicars elected a *custos*, and a chamberlain to keep records of attendance. Later the Bedern staff included a *custos domorum*, a bursar, maltster and kitchener. The statutes of 1291 grant a stipend of forty shillings to each vicar.[62] York was the first English cathedral to have a common residence for the vicars, and has been the most studied, but others soon followed. In fact the institution of vicars choral probably emerged at all the major cathedrals at about the same time.

As early as 1293, the bishops of Lincoln insisted that the vicars should have a common building, with refectory and kitchen, but with separate bedrooms. They are to choose their own provost, and meet every Saturday for chapter. After 1305, the vicars were obliged to swear that they would 'take up residence in the new buildings, with the other vicars, and share their table unless for an overriding reason'. This college for senior vicars was complemented by a second building for the juniors in 1328. Similarly, the minor clerics or 'poor clerks' of good character were 'to live in the house granted to them, to provide proof of their respectability and good behaviour, and not to live separately as they have hitherto done, in a disreputable manner'. There are further points about liturgical custom, the night watch may play the flute to tell the hours if he likes (*et horas noctium per fistulam sufflabit si velit*), and canons are not to enter the church unless accompanied by a vested cleric as server. There are also to be twelve boys, two of them thurifers, and 'they should live together in one house and live in common under a Master, who shall give them a fixed stipend and ensure their expenses are paid'.[63]

At Lichfield statutes for vicars were drawn up in 1241, requiring permanent residence and regular attendance at the Offices. One member of the community was charged with keeping the register. At least five of them were to be priests, attached to the resident canons. The stipend was twenty shillings a year payable by the canons, and a daily commons of one penny, raised to a penny-ha'penny in 1311. Other benefices included chantries served by the priest vicars. They were responsible for the fabric of the cathedral, and they acted as clerks to the chapter. To begin with they had a house somewhere in the city, and a retirement home in the adjacent parish of Stowe, but a purpose-built vicars' college was established in 1315.[64]

At London by the end of the thirteenth century there were already three junior bodies of clergy, namely the minor canons, vicars and chantrists. By 1273 the vicars had a common hall in which they were obliged to eat, and a communal residence certainly existed soon afterwards, though remarkably little is known about the buildings around the cathedral of the capital.[65] At Wells the famous vicars' close was not begun until 1348, although some consideration had been given earlier to the disciplinary problems caused by vicars living remotely in the town. In 1243 the chapter decreed that no vicar could live alone, but must share his lodgings with at least two others.[66] None of the other secular cathedrals acquired vicars' closes until after the Black Death.

Outside England a slightly different pattern can be observed.[67] Cathedral chapters were augmented with clergy from urban colleges, which had become common in France and the empire, so that on major occasions considerable numbers of additional clergy could be brought in to add dignity to the functions. Two remarkable surviving examples are in Regensburg. Immediately outside the west end of the cathedral is the Collegiatstift of St John. It was constituted as an Augustinian canonry by Bishop Kuno in 1127, and granted privileges by Urban III in 1186, with the right to elect its own Provost out of the Cathedral chapter. In 1290 Bishop

Heinrich II transformed it into a college of secular clergy, with which status it survives.[68] At the other end of the cathedral, just across the square, is the Altkapelle, which claims an unbroken history from Roman times. It was certainly mentioned by King Ludwig in 875 as a collegiate establishment, and was reconstituted by St Henry II in 1109 as part of the establishment of his new Diocese of Bamberg. Thus the canons did not relate to the adjacent cathedral, but to Bamberg, 150 kilometres away. Only after surviving the turmoil of 'secularization' was the community's existence in Regensburg guaranteed by Ludwig I in 1830.[69]

At Angers in 1103 the members of the collegiate church of St Maurille were ordered to attend the nearby cathedral to boost the choir during major festivals. More significant, perhaps, was the endowment in the same year of two chaplaincies within the cathedral. This set a precedent for junior clergy in cathedral corporations, which spread rapidly in France and Flanders. By the middle of the twelfth century there are references to vicars or chaplains (*capellani*) in many western European cathedrals, and they were found in the Empire by the early thirteenth. They were not merely deputies for absentee canons, but had specific functions of their own, performed even while their supporting canons were in residence. Apart from the basic duties of attendance in choir and the celebration of Mass, they might be responsible for schoolteaching, fundraising, sacristy and church maintenance and secretarial duties. Their income and support came from a variety of sources, but property endowments with chantry duties seem to have predominated. This in turn demanded the incorporation of the junior clergy to hold property in perpetuity. The number of clergy of different ranks circling around the great cathedrals of Europe was very large indeed.

Notes
1. Crusius, *Weltlichen Kollegiatstift*, pp. 294–7.
2. Hamilton Thompson, 'Notes on Colleges of Secular Canons in England'; *Cathedral Churches of England*; *The English Clergy and their organization*.
3. Bernard, Sermon I in Coena Domini, *De Baptizmo* cap. 2; PL 183:272.
4. Esztergom (1114), canons 5 and 27; Mansi XXI, cc. 100, 103.
5. Gelasius II *ad canonicos Lucenses*, Mansi XXI, c. 173; Callistus II, Epistle 3, Mansi XXI, c. 191.
6. AA.SS. May III, p. 625.
7. Callistus II, Epistle 13, Mansi XXI, cc. 197–9.
8. Mansi XXI, cc. 495–6.

9. Eugenius III, Epistle 9; Mansi XXI, cc. 632–3.
10. Eugenius III, Epistle 61; Mansi XXI, cc. 662–3.
11. Alexander III, Epistle 14 *ad Decanum et capit. Parisiensis*, Mansi XXI, cc. 1067–8; Epistle *ad Henricum Remensis*, Mansi XXI, c. 1076.
12. Lateran III (1179), capit. 18 and 23; Mansi XXII, cc. 227–8 and 230.
13. Aquileia (1181), Mansi XXII, cc. 471–4.
14. Celestine III, Epistle *capitulo Lingonensi* (1197); Mansi XXII, c. 623.
15. Paris (1212), Mansi XXII, cc. 817–54; Rouen (1214), Ibid., cc. 897–924; Bourges (1214), Ibid., cc. 931–4; London (1214), Ibid., cc. 933–6.
16. Cologne (1260), cap. vii; Mansi XXIII, cc. 1016–8.
17. e.g. Meaux (1245), cap. vi; Mansi XXIII, c. 686; Lombardy (1287), cap. vi; Mansi XXIV, c. 883.
18. e.g. Cologne (1260), cap. ix; Mansi XXIII, c.1018; Ravenna IV (1317), rubric ix; Mansi XXV, c. 609; Etruria (1327), Mansi XXV, cc. 821–3; Florence (1346), Mansi XXVI, cc. 38–9.
19. e.g. Gubbio (1303), Mansi XXV, cc. 1145–6; Ravenna IV (1317), rubric 10, Ibid., cc. 609–10; Etruria (1327), Ibid., cc. 821–2; Trier (1337), cap. 7, Ibid., c. 1084; Florence (1346), Mansi XXVI, cc. 38–9.
20. e.g. Meaux (1245), cap. vi; Mansi XXIII, c. 686; Milan (1311), rubric v, Mansi XXV, c. 482; Ravenna IV (1317), rubric iv, Ibid., cc. 603–5; Paris (1346), cap. 2, Mansi XXVI, c. 19.
21. e.g. Tarragona (1329), cap. xxx; Mansi XXV, c. 849; Trier (1337) cap. 6, Ibid., c. 1084.
22. Toledo (1339), cap. iii, Mansi XXV, cc. 1145–6.
23. Gubbio (1303), Mansi XXV, c. 121.
24. Ravenna III (1314), rubric i; Mansi XXV, c. 537.
25. Liège (1287), tit. xii, no. v; Mansi XXIV, c. 910; Gubbio (1303), Mansi XXV, cc. 121–2; Mainz (1310), Ibid., c. 311; Avignon (1337), cap. 38; Ibid., c. 1097.
26. Liège (1287), tit. IX, cap. 18; Mansi XXIV, c. 908.
27. Decreta Hungarorum (1268), no. xi, xii; Mansi XXIII, cc. 1183–4; Concilium Budense (1279), canon xxvi; Mansi XXIV, c. 283.
28. S. Th., suppl. LX, i, respondeo. (see chapter 1 note 50 above)
29. See Gibbs, *Early Charters*, and Sparrow Simpson, *Registrum Statutorum*.
30. Gibbs, *Early Charters*, p. 10.
31. Sparrow Simpson, *Registrum*, pp. xxii-xliii.
32. Ibid., p. 173. The Mark is two thirds of a pound, or 13 shillings and 4 pence. Or 160 pence.
33. Sparow Simpson, *Registrum*, pp. 130, 173.
34. Sparrow Simpson, *Registrum*, pp. xxix-xxx, xl.
35. Bradshaw and Wordsworth, *Statutes of Lincoln Cathedral*, I, pp. 30–1.
36. Ibid., I, p. 35.
37. Ibid., II, pp. 8, 10.
38. Ibid., I, pp. 98 ff.
39. Ibid., II, pp. 96, 99.
40. Ibid., II, pp. 1–6.
41. Alexander II, Epistle 39; Mansi XIX, cc. 969–70.
42. Mansi XXII, cc. 612–3.

43. Bradshaw & Wordsworth, *Statutes of Lincoln Cathedral*, III, p. xlvii.
44. Ibid., I, pp. 308, 335–6.
45. Ibid., II, pp. 47–86.
46. Ibid., III, pp. 96–129.
47. Ibid., II, p. 151; III, p. 329.
48. AA.SS. June I, p. 764.
49. Published in Martène, *De Antiquis Ecclesiae Ritibus*, II, pp. 182 sq.
50. e.g. slab of Jean de Trélon, 1412; Adhémar and Dordor, *Tombeaux Gaignères*, no 1021.
51. The earliest canon of Paris shown in an almuce is Pierre Thomas, 1319, Adhémar and Dordor, *Tombeaux Gaignières*, no. 623.
52. Bradshaw & Wordsworth, *Statutes of Lincoln Cathedral*, I, p. 308.
53. Dugdale, *Monasticon*, VI, p. 1258. cf also Council of Utrecht (1209), Mansi XXII, cc. 805–9.
54. Gibbs, *Early Charters*, p. xx.
55. Sparrow Simpson, *Registrum*, pp xxix-xxxiii. (The same provision was made at York and Hereford, Bradshaw & Wordsworth, *Statutes of Lincoln Cathedral*, II, pp. 61, 107.)
56. Sparrow Simpson, *Registrum*, pp. 233 and 248.
57. Dugdale, *Monasticon* VI, pp. 1255–65.
58. Bradshaw & Wordsworth, *Statutes of Lincoln Cathedral*, II, pp. 47–52.
59. Ibid., II, pp. 108, 125.
60. Dugdale, *Monasticon*, VI, pp. 1255–61.
61. See especially Hall and Stocker, *Vicars Choral at English Cathedrals*.
62. See Harrison, *Life in a Medieval College*, and Richards, *The Vicars Choral of York Minster*.
63. Bradshaw & Wordsworth, *Statutes of Lincoln Cathedral*, I, pp. 307–410, II, pp. 136–51, III, pp. xlix-l.
64. Hall & Stocker, *Vicars Choral*, pp. 62–4.
65. Ibid., pp. 98–102.
66. Ibid., pp. 132–3.
67. See Julia Barrow, 'The Origins of Vicars Choral to 1300' in Hall & Stocker, *Vicars Choral*, pp. 11–16.
68. L. Altmann, *Stiftskirche St Johann* (Regensburg: Schnell & Steiner, 1997).
69. Betz, *The Collegiate Church of Our Lady at the Alte Kapelle*.

Chapter 9

Other Collegiate Churches in the High Middle Ages

Having looked at the great cathedral establishments, we can now turn to the bewildering variety of other collegiate communities which continued to multiply through the centuries between the Gregorian Reforms and the Wars of Religion. In dividing them into the broad categories of 'rural colleges, those attached to great households, hospital and educational colleges, and informal communities' (p. 141 above), we are not proposing to make any clear or rigid distinction between them, for no such distinctions can be made. Collegiate churches overlap all possible categories, and defy any simple system of analysis, so that the attempts which have been made in the past to divide them into clearly defined types are often more misleading than helpful. What all colleges have in common is that they are communities of secular clergy, including those in major and minor orders, living together in some sort of recognizable common life, and distinguished above all by their freedom from vows. Members can own their own property, and are free to leave the community at any time: that makes them quite different from monks, canons regular or friars. Most of the available information is about colleges in England, which have suddenly become the object of detailed study,[1] but it is clear that the same variety and types of college existed in all countries of Western Europe.

The way of life, on the other hand, could vary from something almost indistinguishable from a monastery, to what looks like a very leisurely country gentleman's residence. Extreme Augustinians might still rant against the seculars, as in the astonishing denunciation of the community at Wolverhampton by Peter of Blois in around 1200,[2] but communities could mutate in either direction. Many old collegiate establishments from before the Conquest survived, and new foundations were made, even during the second half of the eleventh century, such as St Chad's and St

Michael's in Shrewsbury, and the castle chapelries of Bridgnorth, Pontefract, and St George's College, Oxford. Many secular communities, including some very old ones, did become Augustinian during the late eleventh and early twelfth centuries, such as Dorchester, St Frideswide's and St George's in Oxford, Waltham in Essex, and St Oswald's, Gloucester, but new communities of secular canons continued to be founded, both in castles (like Windsor, Hastings and Exeter), and in market towns (like St Mary's, Warwick). Some Benedictine or Augustinian houses changed over to the secular life, like St John's, Regensburg, already mentioned. At Heytesbury, Wiltshire, a small monastic community was reconstructed in 1165 for four secular canons, to serve four dependent churches.[3]

By the thirteenth century, in some of the older colleges where the property was held as separate prebendaries, the common life had effectively died out, since each prebendary maintained his own house near the church as well as a house on his prebendal estate, much as some cathedral prebendaries did; he lived effectively as a master in his own household, surrounded possibly by junior or minor clerics who would have lived much like servants in any great house. The prebendal system, and its inequalities, was certainly seen by some as the cause of many of the problems, giving canons very unequal incomes, which militated against the very idea of the common life. For instance in Hastings in 1275 out of ten prebends the income varied between Wartling at fifty marks a year and Marlrepast at one mark. Since a vicar's income was fixed, at tuppence a day, adding up to three pounds, one shilling a year, the poorer prebendaries were considerably worse off than the vicars.[4] It appears that reforming bishops experimented with a variety of ways of correcting the system, either by equalizing the prebends, or by abolishing them altogether in favour of a single common fund; this helped add to the extraordinary variety of types of college and secular community that can be found in the remaining three centuries of the Middle Ages.

Many small colleges have been categorized as 'chantry foundations', because the stated aim of the foundation was to pray for the souls of the founder and her kin. This can be more than a little misleading, for every college, like every monastery, had an obligation to pray for the dead – indeed Edward VI's government took advantage of this factor to suppress them all, deliberately misrepresenting them as having no other purpose. As we have seen, Charlemagne's original college of priests in Aachen was founded explicitly to pray for the souls of deceased members of the Imperial family, and all surviving founders' statutes express the same sort of concern, an obligation to pray for founders and benefactors, and usually for 'all Christian souls' as well as the good estate of the realm. It might be better to preserve the term 'chantry' for its original purpose: the endowment of a permanent income to subsidize a priest to celebrate Mass for the repose of the soul of a particular person, on a particular occasion (which might be once a year or every day). Most colleges contained chantries within them, but they had a much wider purpose and a wider field of activity.

During the thirteenth century there was an increasing tendency for the superior to be called dean, rather than provost, after a period when the two officials struggled for supremacy. The office of provost eventually settled down to be effectively that of bursar of the community, leaving the role of superior to the dean. The small college of St Nicolas in Provins began in 1218 with provosts, but after 1262 was governed by deans. At St Quiriace in the same town the dean, chosen by the canons, was the overall superior, the provost responsible for the finances, the treasurer only for lights, the cantor and succentor over the schools. Dean Etienne de Cucharmoy (1135–7) was born a serf, illustrating the social mobility that these communities could facilitate in the High Middle Ages. There was also a curé with pastoral responsibility, answerable directly to the bishop, but still a member of the chapter.[5]

Many large houses had a cantor or precentor, who was responsible for schools as well as the singers, and often a chancellor as well, assimilating them to the 'four-square' cathedral model. Other officials could include the cellerar, as in the earliest canonical rules, the almoner, and also a custos or warden to look after the church building. In small houses the title of the superior was commonly warden. The early medieval custom of calling the superiors of secular communities 'abbots' became obsolete. All officials could have deputies, but in some cases the nominal superior was a bishop or other prelate, and so the sub-dean or sub-warden was the real superior of the community (as at All Saints College, Derby). Members of the community could still be called 'canons', though this title tended to be restricted to the senior members of the larger communities. Their juniors were usually called 'vicars', because they substituted for the canons if absent. In small colleges the priests were commonly termed chaplains, as were those in receipt of chantry endowments within larger colleges. However the variety of college constitution encouraged variety of nomenclature, and it is impossible to force them into a standard pattern. Even the minor clerics might acquire special titles in particular colleges. In every college there was some educational function, even if it was only the training of their own minor clerics; in every college there was some charitable almsgiving for the poor. Certain colleges were founded with a more specific role in education or almsgiving, which could be on a very large scale indeed.

Rural Colleges, Founded by Bishops

The term 'rural college' is perhaps misleading: many of them are in great cities, or just outside, but they were always quite separate from the cathedrals and their associated minor corporations. Colleges continued to be founded outside the walls of German cities throughout the eleventh century. The oldest surviving collegiate buildings are probably those of St Simeon in Trier, adjacent to the famous Black Gate which formed the framework of the church. A courtyard surrounded by two-storey eleventh-century buildings, with connecting walkways, is now used as a museum. Large chambers in the north range were presumably the refectory and dormitory; the west range has smaller rooms and a domestic chapel.[6]

Many colleges were founded, or refounded, by bishops, anxious to ensure proper pastoral care for the outlying parishes of the diocese. In the late eleventh century, Pope Alexander II wrote to the Archbishop of Passau confirming his establishment of a collegiate church, where the canons are to live the common life. He affirms that they are not to appropriate any of the church's property to themselves, which clearly implies that they could own property from other sources.[7]

Some of these colleges were in the city centres, and although not intended to be part of the cathedral establishment, came to play a role in the life of the cathedral, at least on certain occasions, on the model of the Continental urban colleges already mentioned. (pp. 159–60 above). The corporation of vicars, for instance, was not the only minor college associated with York. In 1258, the Chapel of St Mary was founded for thirteen additional clerics, adjacent to the archiepiscopal palace.[8] The chapel building was constructed 'near the Mother Church', and in it the thirteen clerics of various orders were to live together permanently, serving the Divine Office just as is done in the cathedral. The college is to consist of four priests, four deacons, four subdeacons and one sacristan, and are directly under the archbishop, without, it seems, a local superior of their own. None of the clergy are to stay outside the city, but each is to receive a stipend, ten marks a year for a priest, one hundred shillings (seven and a half marks) for a deacon, and six marks for a subdeacon, all to be administered by the sacristan, who has the use of whatever remains of the income from the parishes assigned to the foundation. On Maundy Thursday the said sacristan is to provide for the canons of the cathedral their *velulae*, wine and beer, with vessels and water in which to wash their feet, as well as ten shillings for the poor and to provide for the necessities of sixty poor folk, 'so that in all things unity and brotherhood be preserved in the church'. Similar colleges associated closely with cathedrals were Cantilupe College in Lincoln, Holmes' and Lancaster Colleges, London, and St Sepulchre's, also in York.[9]

Bishops of monastic cathedrals in particular seem to have favoured the foundation of secular colleges as a counterbalance to their monastic chapters. Indeed in the late twelfth century, after a dispute with the Benedictines, Archbishop Baldwin of Canterbury made a determined effort to found a rival secular establishment at Hackington, which would make Canterbury a double diocese like Lichfield and Coventry. It came to nothing, though a later attempt at a duplicate cathedral, at Westbury to rival Worcester, very nearly succeeded.[10]

Many colleges were founded in existing parish churches, which were newly endowed, and extended to provide accommodation for large numbers. At Wingham in Kent in 1287 the Archbishop of Canterbury provided for a provost and ten secular canons, each to maintain a vicar, to serve the existing parish church of Wingham and three neighbouring chapelries. He required strict residence of at least four months in the year, on pain of losing the share of the revenue: the vicars were expected to reside continually and keep the Divine Office going day and night. No one was to be admitted as a vicar unless they he was 'a good singer, of respectable behaviour, and sufficiently well educated, and if any of them are discovered to be immoral, they must be expelled at once with no excuses accepted'.[11]

Some mid thirteenth-century English bishops retained the structure by which a particular cleric would draw his revenue from a particular prebend, but without allowing them the possibilities of non-residence or plurality. At Lanchester in 1273 Bishop Anthony Bek of Durham made the church collegiate for a dean and seven prebends, to support two chaplains (who must dress like the vicars of the cathedral canons) and five vicars, all of whom are to keep residence, celebrate divine worship in the collegiate church at Lanchester and also ensure that the chapels of Essche, Medmesley and Helay are adequately served. At the same time the same bishop established colleges in Bishop Auckland and Chester le Street, on much the same lines. At Auckland he admits that hitherto the canons' excuse for non-residence has been the absence of anywhere to reside, and he therefore grants them land on which to build.[12] His brother, Bishop Thomas Bek of St Davids, established a college in Carmarthenshire, at Abergwili, in 1287. This was one of the largest, with a precentor, seven priests, seven deacons, and seven sub-deacons, all holding prebends, and each supporting a vicar of the same order, as well as clerks and choristers.[13] Another foundation by the bishop of a monastic cathedral was Carnary College in Norwich, established in 1316 by Bishop Salmon, though only for four priests. The chapel survives in good condition, and like many other college chapels is of two storeys, with a tall vaulted undercroft.

The much more ambitious foundation at Ottery St Mary in Devon, enshrined in a fine surviving church, provided for an establishment of a warden, eight prebendaries, ten vicars, two masters, two other priests, eight 'secondaries', eight choristers and two clerks. The property had formerly belonged to the collegiate chapter of Rouen Cathedral, who sold it to Bishop Grandisson in order that he might make his foundation in 1337. Unfortunately no statutes survive, but this new college has been seen as in some way the inspiration behind Edward III's two major foundations, St Stephen's, Westminster, and St George's, Windsor.

These foundations by bishops set the tone for a considerable number of parish-based colleges founded by local clergy or laymen, either taking over the whole of an existing church (and rebuilding it on a larger scale) or operating in one portion of the church. An example of the first is Cotterstock, Northamptonshire, founded by a former rector in 1339 for a provost, twelve canons and a clerk, to keep the full common life. He enjoined silent meals with reading, a common dormitory, daily chapter meetings, and a very restricted holiday allowance. Here only the chancel was rebuilt to house the college, and makes a startling contrast with the remainder of the church.[14] At Sibthorpe in Nottinghamshire, after several false starts, a college was endowed for a warden, nine chaplains and two clerks. Here the statutes survive in full, and are strict in laying down the requirements of community life, including the anachronistic requirement of a common dormitory.[15]

In other parishes, private benefactors established sufficient endowment for a small group of priests, usually referred to as 'chaplains', who might treat one aisle or one chapel of the church as their community chapel, while an independent rector ministered in the chancel. Typical smaller ones are Shottesbrooke in Berkshire, founded in 1337, for a warden, five chaplains and two clerks, and Tormarton in Gloucestershire, 1344, for a warden with four chaplains, two clerks and a chorister. In neither case does the architecture immediately indicate a collegiate church. In contrast, the splendid chancel of Norbury, Derbyshire, built in the early 1340s, cries out for a collegiate foundation, especially when we observe what looks suspiciously like the remains of a community house just southwest of the church, but none of the usual sources indicate that the church was ever collegiate.

Material on English colleges has been made readily available, but exactly the same pattern is observable on the Continent. The ancient college of St Mary at Erfurt had existed since the eighth century, but it is only in the thirteenth century that we begin to hear much about it. In 1261 a dispute arise over whether the Archbishop of Mainz had the appointment of the provost, or whether he should be elected by the canons. In effect provosts were nearly always chosen from among the canons of Mainz, and appointed by the archbishop as were the provosts of other collegiate churches in the province, such as Mockstadt, Bingen, Aschaffenburg and Geismar. The provost, although not himself much involved in the college, had great patronage over it. The dean was elected by the chapter, and was responsible for the cure of souls, outside as well as inside the community. He was always chosen from among the existing canons. The scholaster, assisted by the *magister puerorum*, was responsible for the schooling both of the internal students, and those outside. The internal students, or *domicellen*, were boy-canons, living the common life, and aspiring to full status in the college, 'emancipation', probably at the age of twenty-one. The external students were those not destined for a place in the college, but for pastoral work in the archdeaconry. All students of both classes were tonsured and admitted to minor orders.[16]

The canons of Erfurt, for whom fifteen prebends were available by 1158, were bound to residence, and to celebrate Mass and the Divine Office, though only a small proportion were actually ordained priest (of 303 canons between 1117 and 1400 only twenty-nine were priests, the others deacons or subdeacons). Minor clerics waiting for a place on the chapter were known as *canonici expectantes*, or *in herbis*, whereas the boy scholars were *canonici domicellares*, or *in pulvere*. By the early fourteenth century most canons had separate houses, *kurien*, whereas the boys continued to live together in the dormitory. As well as food and clothing, a sum of money was paid to each grade of canon depending on their presence in choir: there was thus no incentive to plurality or absenteeism, and it seems that even the senior canons kept residence. The income from the prebend was on average eighteen marks, whereas attendance at Mass and choir would bring in another thirty pence a day, adding up over a year to sixty eight marks or so. As a result, out of the 303 known canons, only twenty-five had stalls in cathedrals elsewhere, and thirty-nine were also members of other colleges, so that 239 of the canons had no responsibilities outside Erfurt, though eighteen had associate membership of the other Erfurt college, St Severin (which is adjacent on the same hill), and some had cures in the city. Pluralism was by no means as widespread as generally believed. Most of them remained in the community until death.

Erfurt is a remarkable survival, but there are other early medieval communities in the German lands which were given new constitutions in the thirteenth or fourteenth centuries, and survived at least until the Revolution, in a few cases to the present day. As well as the two collegiate churches in Regensburg, already mentioned, we hear of new statutes for the college of Mattsee in 1321, and a new foundation at Eisgarn, in 1330, both still functioning in present-day Austria. Other medieval colleges, like Tittmoning, were to play a more significant role later.

Foundations by Laymen

Laypeople still continued to support the idea of the collegiate life with undiminished fervour, and the majority of the new foundations after the Gregorian reforms were endowed by secular lords and ladies. New foundations were made continuously in the later eleventh century, and throughout the twelfth and thirteenth, increasing after the Fourth Lateran Council. These included some of great size and importance. Obviously lay benefactors valued the contribution of communities of priests, and it can be assumed that the common people were also contented with the system. We hear of few complaints against collegiate clerics, in contrast to the often-quoted grumblings against monks, friars and canons regular. Since these colleges were under lay patronage, the patrons might demand the right to appoint the canons and the superiors. In practice a compromise was reached by which the patron would nominate his candidate, and the bishop would make the appointment. Occasionally the members of a college, or at least the senior ones, were given the right to propose names to the lay patron. However the statutes usually include a default clause, giving the bishop the right to fill vacancies if the patron had failed to act. The system was certainly open to abuse, and patrons might well nominate unsuitable laymen for profitable prebends, but any appointment would still have always carried the obligation of proceeding to ordination, at least to minor orders.

Many of these foundations were made in rural parishes, from the late thirteenth century onwards, where the chaplains served a public church, with responsibility for the souls of the local population, as well as the daily round of prayer. One of the earliest was St Mary's, Warwick, founded in 1123 by Earl Roger, for a dean, five canons, ten vicars and six choristers. The statutes insist on residence, for hitherto some canons have been finding excuses to disperse and lie on their prebends.[17] In other cases a miniature college of secular priests could even be established within a church belonging to a religious order, as in the case of the Montacute Chantry in Oxford. Elizabeth Montacute, in 1346, gave an endowment to the prior and community of St Frideswide's, (now an Augustinian house, though long before it had been a house of secular canons). From this endowment two secular priests were to be paid ten marks a year, divided unequally, and provided with the necessities for Mass. They were each to celebrate Mass daily for the Montacute family, and to stand by the founder's tomb to recite the Placebo and Dirge, clad in grey almuces with badges of the Montacute arms. For their lodging together they were given a house on the north side of the church; the implication is that they ate there rather than sharing in the community refectory. This curious arrangement did not last very long in the event, and after the Black Death the Augustinians themselves undertook the chantry obligations.[18] (The endowment continues to be enjoyed by the canons of Christ Church, who do not, however, either wear grey almuces or recite the Placebo and Dirge.)

An important and well-documented example of a lay foundation is Astley College in Warwickshire.[19] It had originally been founded by Sir Thomas Astley as a small college with a warden and three other priests, soon afterwards augmented with three further priests, one to be subwarden. In 1343 the knight changed his mind again, and procured a licence from Roger, Bishop of Lichfield, to transform it into a full-scale college, for which he built a suitably impressive church. The chapter is to be formed of a dean and two canons prebendary. The dean is to reside continuously in person, and is to have the rectory of Astley and its revenue, out of which he is to distribute ten shillings a year to the poor, in two instalments. At first these are to be paid on Assumption Day in Astley, and the first Friday in Lent at Withybrook, but after the death of the founder the Astley payment is to be made on his anniversary. The dean has a further income from Wolvey, out of which he is to distribute twenty-seven shillings in bread and cash, on Easter Eve and the Assumption until the death of Sir Thomas and his mother, after which it will be on their anniversaries.

The two canons are allotted prebends, one based at Milverton, the other at Wolvey, 'because you cannot have canons without prebends', to which is added most of the revenue from Hullmartin parish. For the proper performance of divine worship, the Dean must find a perpetual vicar, at five marks per year, plus a parochial chaplain, and a suitable cleric: he must celebrate in person at all major feasts of the year. The canons must each find a priest vicar, and a 'perpetual priest' at five marks each: they are to present these to the bishop for institution, and to the chapter for admission, whereupon they take an oath to observe the statutes, and keep the secrets of the house. Moreover, if the canon does not intend to reside, he must find and pay yet another priest, and give the dean one mark a year towards the support of the minor cleric. If a canon is not resident, his vicar takes his place at chapter. The vicars and perpetual priests are allotted a house near the churchyard for their residence, if they choose, or can find their own accommodation. If the canons or dean neglect to fill any vacancies within two months, the bishop can appoint.

All the clergy, amounting to nine priests and a minor cleric, must behave themselves well and honourably, and wear the tonsure and appropriate dress. Their principal obligation is the sung celebration of the entire Divine Office, and a complicated pattern of said and sung Masses every day, with the Placebo and Dirge every afternoon, for the founder, his family, friends and benefactors, whose names are to be clearly inscribed on a schedule, table or *matricula*. In choir, the dean and canons are to wear surplices, almuces of grey minever (*de griso et hamero*), and black hooded cappas, lined with muslin or silk (*de sindone vel taffeta*), from Michaelmas to Easter. The vicars and perpetual priests wear black cloth almuces, lined with fur in winter, and with muslin or silk in summer, with cappas like the canons. The remaining priests wear the same, except for the linings, and should be given these vestments by their patrons, whereas all the others have to supply their own. The dean's vicar is to rule the choir.

There is to be a common seal, kept in a chest of four locks by the dean and three vicars; bells are to be rung for Matins and Curfew; any revenue during a vacancy is to be used 'as is commonly observed in other collegiate churches'. All the vicars and priests without exception must be present for all the canonical Hours, on pain of a halfpenny fine for each Office missed, to the common fund. The Bishop of Lichfield undertakes to ensure that salaries are paid as well as the cathedral dues from Hulmartin parish.

In the absence of information as to the value of the Astley prebends, it is unclear how much of a canon's income would be left over after paying the salaries of his vicar and perpetual priest, and whether there would be anything left if a non-resident also had to pay his third priest. The implication is that there would not be much: it would be hardly worth-while accepting a prebend at Astley unless one was prepared to be resident and play a full part in the liturgical round. Clearly the intention is that there should be a sufficient body of clergy in attendance at all times to ensure that the Office could be sung properly, and the required number of said or sung Masses celebrated. In this case, the college has no other function than to pray for the souls of the benefactors: there is no mention of 'all Christian souls' as in other cases. Only the dean's second priest has any parochial responsibility. There is no mention of a common table, which was formerly considered essential to the common life, and the fact that the clergy can choose whether to take advantage of the house provided implies that they are at perfect liberty to set up their own households, as far as they can on five marks a year. There is, therefore, only a limited degree of the common life, but a great insistence on common worship.

In France, or rather in Champagne, collegiate life continued to flourish at Provins. The canons of Saint Quiriace were usually chosen from local families, and forty-four prebends were available for them. They were responsible for supporting the poor vicars, including deacons, various lay members of the community, the *marguilliers*, sacristans, servants and (after 1283) child canons. There is no evidence for a school or a hospital within the enclosure, but the cantor was responsible for all schools in the town, and the treasurer supervised the *maison-Dieu* for the poor, to which the college contributed fifty-two pounds a year. Curious glimpses of community life at St Quiriace are granted by the information that Canon Hugues de Brète attempted to kill the provost in front of the church, for which he was exiled for five years, and condemned to teach schools in Orleans or Angers. (A worse fate befell two canons who murdered the precentor of Chartres in 1256 – they were sent to Oxford for five years.) After 1284 Champagne came under the throne of France, and Canon Veissière loses interest.[20]

Colleges attached to Great Households

A common feature of eleventh- and twelfth-century courts was the foundation of colleges associated with royal, noble, or episcopal households. Some were mobile communities, minor clerics and priests who followed the court from place to place, and provided not only regular divine worship but also secretarial 'clerical' services. Others were based permanently in palaces or castles, such as Bosham, Dover, Hastings, and most notably the Tower of London where the chapel survives as the earliest of many two-storey structures, the upper floor for public worship in the presence of the Court, the lower for the clergy alone. Another two-storey chapel was in the private palace college at Provins, founded by Henri the Liberal before 1179 for four canons and one chaplain. In 1268 Thibaut V changed the four non-resident canons into six resident chaplains, though he took little interest in the elder college of St Quiriace, and applied himself more to crusading.[21] In the late twelfth century there was a general tidying up of these communities, and some sort of genuine collegiate life certainly existed in them. In that capacity they could survive for centuries, assuming the dynasty or household itself survived.

An important domestic college in England, the first for which detailed statutes survive, is that founded by John de Pontoise, Bishop of Winchester in 1301, dedicated to Saint Elizabeth.[22] It is described as a 'chapel' attached to the palace of Wolveseye in Winchester, served by seven 'chaplains', one of whom is to be provost, with three deacons, three subdeacons, and six choristers. The statutes give much more detail about daily life than most others, and reveal a concern to restore the true common life. The provost was to be appointed directly by the bishop, and to command the obedience of the other members. He was expected to reside continuously at the chapel, except for necessary business for the good of the chapel or house. In case of the unavoidable absence of any of the chaplains or clerics, the bishop was to appoint a substitute; on the death of a cleric, the available income was to accrue to the chapel.

The food ration was to be a single *ferculum* with a pittance each day, except on Sundays and double feasts when a second *ferculum* and pittance were allowed. The clergy were always to be obedient, and modest, decently dressed and well behaved, sober and of good conduct, 'and their life and bearing should be quite distinct from that of the laity'. All of them were to wear the surplice with a black cappa when in chapel, and outside to wear simple garments of a single colour, *utpote de persio vel nigrâ burnetâ, aut etiam de russeto*. The clothing allowance was to be six marks annually for the provost, forty shillings (three marks) twice a year for the chaplains, and twenty shillings twice a year for the minor clerics. They were all to drink and eat together in one house, the provost and chaplains at one table, the junior clerics at another. All must sleep together in the house, unless they be ill or validly excused. Each chaplain was to have a minor cleric as a servant, aged between ten and eighteen, who could sing and read in church and serve him in his chamber: the provost was to provide food and clothing for these young clerics, who were to eat together in a separate room.

The statutes then proceed to detail arrangements for divine worship. Matins of Our Lady is followed by Matins of the day, sung carefully without one side of the choir overlapping the end of the other choir's verses, and with a pause in the middle of each verse. Every day there are to be sung Masses of the Blessed Virgin and St Elizabeth, two said Masses for the dead and one of the Holy Spirit, followed by the High Mass, interspersed with the rest of the Divine Office of the day and of Our Lady. Before Vespers they were to celebrate the Placebo and Dirge, the Office of the Dead. All is to be done according to the use of Sarum, and all are to be present at every Office. The provost is to appoint a precentor, who will oversee the liturgy and compose the *tabula* appointing the priests for each Mass week by week. The provost, or his deputy, must present accounts every year at Michaelmas in the presence of the chaplains and the diocesan treasurer. A new chaplain or cleric is not to be admitted until he has been examined, proving he can read, sing, and understand the Office. No woman is to enter the house, save for the chapel and hall. New members must swear to observe the statutes, and keep residence in person, from which there can be no dispensation. The statutes conclude with a record of the lands with which the new foundation is endowed.

Here there has been a distinctive reform. St Elizabeth's marks a return to a more religious life: the chaplains and junior clerics evidently have their own rooms, rather than sleeping in a dormitory, but they do always eat together, and they do spend most of their waking hours in the chapel celebrating the Mass and Office. They differ from monks only in that they are all in Holy Orders, that they are not committed to the college for life, and that they can evidently own their own property, their clothing, and presumably books and portable effects. The only significant difference, therefore, from the Chrodegangian canons of five centuries before, lies in the substitution of private rooms for the common dormitory, reflecting a change in the way of life in general. Notable is the disappearance of the prebendal system altogether: the entire revenue of the college is treated as a single unit, to be distributed according to the needs of each member.

St Elizabeth's was not the first of these colleges to be founded in association with episcopal households. In 1226 the Bishop of Winchester had founded a college in his manor at Merewell in Hampshire for four honest chaplains with a single deacon, who were 'to live together, sleep together and eat together in the buildings which we have had constructed for them within the enclosure'. They could choose their own prior, to hold office for a year, and were allowed no more than eight days' absence a year. The stipend for each chaplain was to be twelve pounds a year, with fifty quarters of grain and four loads of hay for common use.[23] Another episcopal domestic chapel is the one built just before 1300 at the London house of the Bishops of Ely, now St Etheldreda's, Ely Place. Although there is no record of a collegiate foundation, there must have been a household community to serve the typical two-storey chapel.

These communities of priests within episcopal households mark an obvious return to the idea of St Chrodegang and the earlier ideal life of the clergy around St Eusebius or St Ratherius, though it does not seem that the bishop himself ever envisaged sharing in the common life. However the real boost to the new type of college within a great household came with the prestigious royal foundations in Paris and Westminster.

The most important collegiate foundation of the High Middle Ages is the Sainte Chapelle Royale du Palais.[24] There had been a chapel in the palace, dedicated to St Nicholas, since the time of Louis the Fat, in 1090, and Louis the Young had endowed a perpetual chaplain of St Mary there in 1154. It was the existence of these two endowed chapels that resulted in the famous two-storey Sainte Chapelle founded by St Louis in 1245–8.

Louis issued a foundation charter in 1245 for a college in honour of God and the Crown of Thorns, the major relic which had had brought back from the Crusades. The stated purpose of the college was the repose of his own soul, for those of his father King Louis and his mother Queen Blanche, for the honour of the relics, and for the greater worship of God. There were to be five principal priests or *maîtres chapelains*, and two *marguilliers*, either deacons or subdeacons. Each principal chaplain was to have an assistant priest, and a deacon or subdeacon, supported by a prebend of twenty pounds, and also given a daily stipend of twelve pence for a master, fourpence for an assistant or *marguillier*, and threepence for minor clerics, paid only if they attended Matins, High Mass and Vespers (unless they were ill). There would thus be very little financial incentive for a principal chaplain to be non-resident, since most of his prebend would be used up in supporting the assistants and deacons, as well as their obligations to maintain the lights and the windows (no easy task in the Sainte Chapelle). Mass was to be celebrated in the lower chapel every day, and the entire Office sung in the upper chapel, which contained the royal box. In August 1245 the King added a third marguillier, a priest, and provided the marguilliers with a prebend sufficient for them also to maintain an assistant priest and a cleric. He also appointed a *chef*, to be the religious superior, with an increased prebend. This caused some tension with the other principal chaplains.[25]

Subsequent kings added to the foundation, and increased the numbers and the revenue. By 1263 the *maîtres chapelains* and *marguilliers* were being called canons. In 1275 King Philip le Hardi increased the commons of bread and army-standard wine: the latter now to be a *sextier* (six pints) per day, *de vino quod militibus liberatur*. Here is a return to the standard of Aachen, which so scandalized Peter Damian. Four perpetual chapels, chantries, were endowed by Philip le Hardi and Philip le Bel, and the latter incorporated the choirboys into the foundation as *enfans de choeur*. The treasurer was given the pastoral responsibility for all residents in the palace, although the King himself now moved out to the Louvre, leaving the old palace to become exclusively a collegiate building, enclosed and guarded by a porter. The enclosure included substantial houses for the principal chaplains, in which they were presumably expected to house their assistants and clerics, and from which women were totally excluded.[26]

Such a prominent collegiate church, in the very heart of the royal capital, naturally inspired imitation, not only in France but throughout Europe. Although with the passage of time the emoluments were increased beyond St Louis' intentions, they remained equal, and the statutes continued to insist on the strong obligation of residence. There is no mention of a common refectory, but we can assume the household of each *maître chapelain* ate together. Certainly the Divine Office was celebrated in common, as the main object of the establishment, and residence within the enclosure naturally generated a community spirit. We cannot say that this sort of late-medieval college was a mere fiction of common life, designed only to provide an income for favoured clergy, as has so often been stated.

Inspired by St Louis, royal or princely patrons in France founded other *Saintes-Chapelles*, including Bourbon-l'Archambault, founded in 1314 or 1315 by Louis, Duke of Bourbon, a grandson of St Louis, and Gue-de-Maulny, near Le Mans, founded in 1329 by Philip VI.[27] Both were on a smaller scale than Paris, but included the same sort of collegiate community. Others were to be founded in the later Middle Ages, as were the two greatest English royal colleges, St Stephen's at Westminster, and St George's at Windsor, which really belong in the next chapter.

The royal precedent inspired an increasing number of imitators. Small colleges were set up in the households of secular lords more often than of bishops, whether in great castles or in domestic manor houses. For England, the later editions of the *Monasticon* mention such colleges in the episcopal castles of Bishop's Stortford and Gnosall, and the lay establishments at Exeter, Leicester, Nottingham, Oxford, Bridgenorth, Stoke sub Hampden, Mettingham, Hastings, Warwick, Elmley, Pontefract, and Tickhill.[28] However in the late twelfth century, many of these castle colleges were opened up by being transferred into town churches, like St Mary's, Dover, thus bridging the distinction between domestic and public colleges.

Hospital and Educational Colleges

The borderline between secular and Augustinian houses is particularly obscure when it comes to hospitals, most of which expected the inmates to join in the common life of prayer, but sometimes had vowed religious as well.[29] The small hospital at North Creake in Norfolk certainly began as a secular foundation in 1206, with a master, four chaplains and thirteen poor lay brethren, but by 1226 had become formally Augustinian. Yet the original charter had charged the master with providing for the brethren on the grounds that no brother or layman should have anything of his own, implying that the ideal had been abdication of private property from the very beginning.[30] Later historians often refer to hospital communities as 'Augustinian' through ignorance of the existence of secular colleges, and Dugdale lists them all under

Augustinian houses, even though it is obvious from his own pages that many of them were true communities of secular clergy.[31]

A great many hospitals were founded in medieval England, often growing out of comparatively informal infirmaries dependent on monasteries or older colleges. Hospitality had always been a feature both of Benedictine and secular communities, and provision for travellers, the poor and aged was a regular part of community life. In the twelfth century some new hospital foundations certainly did adopt the Rule of St Augustine, while others developed as sub-sets of existing colleges, such as those in Beverley and Ripon. Often there was only one priest, the master, but a number of sound lay brothers or sisters with responsibility for the care of the infirm members. St Julian's Hospital in St Albans was established in 1344 by Abbot Michael specifically for lepers, who were to make a promise of obedience, wear a habit, attend Office daily, preserve mutual charity among each other and exclude all company of women (save for a washerwoman of mature age). They were specifically permitted to own portable goods and whatever might be honestly acquired to supplement their needs and mitigate their condition, though they could not bequeath this away from the house. The numbers of infirm could vary considerably: Elsing Spital in London started with a hundred blind men, though thirteen poor men seems to have been more usual. St Giles outside London (1299) housed forty lepers; St James, Westminster (mid thirteenth century) had fourteen lepresses, St Bartlemas, Oxford (early twelfth century) just a master, two healthful brethren, six infirm or leprous, and one clerk. Most had only a single priest, the master, though often with a cleric or two, but since the patients were expected to live a religious life, they were in effect small religious communities without vows. In some cases the Rule of St Augustine was subsequently adopted, as for instance at Elsing Spital in 1340, because 'experience had shown that the more relaxed life of secular priests had tended to deprave and dissipate the divine worship in the said hospital'.[32]

One of the largest of all was the great Hospital of St Leonard at York, founded under William I, and confirmed by Stephen as a community of a warden, thirteen brethren, four secular priests, eight sisters, thirty choristers, two schoolmasters, two hundred and six bedesmen and six servitors. This huge establishment served not only to care for the needs of the poor (the bedesmen), but also to maintain the daily round of prayer, in which all were to join according to their status; it was only one of many such houses of prayer and social welfare combined.[33] Another large and important establishment, destined to grow greater yet, was St Mary's (the 'New Work') at Leicester, founded as a hospital in 1330–1 by Henry, Earl of Lancaster and Leicestershire. To begin with it was to house a master and four chaplains, fifty paupers, and three serving women. The master and chaplains were obliged to perpetual residence, sleeping in the dormitory and eating in the refectory. They were paid a stipend, but were obliged to bequeath all their property to the college. The poor inmates, and the out patients, were to be paid a penny a day. Any of the women who became too frail to work were guaranteed a place for life as one of the paupers. The master and chaplains kept up the full round of prayer, though in this case the paupers do not seem to have been obliged to more than daily Mass.[34]

Collegiate churches also came to be established in university cities, to provide a home for a number of clergy who could be studying or teaching at the university, as well as for the usual purposes of prayer for the living and the dead. The earliest appears to be Bishop Merton's innovative establishment. It was chartered in 1264, and at first was to be a fairly conventional college at Maldon in Surrey, except that a house was to be provided in Oxford in case any of them should want to study there. Very shortly afterwards however the entire establishment was transferred to Oxford, where like many secular colleges they took over an existing parish church and began to rebuild it on a grand scale. The stated purpose of the college was 'for the profit of the holy Church of God, and for the health of the souls of our lord the King', of named benefactors, 'and all my relations and benefactors', like most collegiate foundations. The warden and twenty scholars of the college were to be in holy orders, celebrate the Mass, and attend the Divine Office like members of any other college. Additional priests, 'chaplains', were included to ensure the proper celebration of the Hours. All were to eat together at a common table, with readings, and wear a common livery. Members slept in a number of separate rooms, in each of which one 'fellow more distinguished for his maturity and common sense' was to keep order. The difference from preceding colleges was that the 'scholars assigned to the liberal arts were obliged to devote themselves to the study of arts or philosophy, canons or theology', and one was to be a teacher of grammar. Moreover thirteen small boys, all related to the founder, should be educated by the Warden.[35]

After this precedent, other colleges rapidly followed, with very similar statutes. Two existing associations of scholars, the 'Great Hall of the University' and another place in the northern suburbs, were reconstituted as colleges, and new foundations included Exeter College (1314), Oriel College (1326), and the Queen's College (1348). The intended Lacy College (1304) was a failure, planned for thirteen students, but never incorporated. To begin with the definition of college was as fluid as ever. Exeter was usually known as a 'hall', like the older houses for academic students, but it did have a community of a rector and twelve fellows who lived and studied just like the members of the incorporated colleges. At Oriel, the ten fellows were all to be theologians. Like all collegiate churches, some part of the function of these colleges was to educate younger students, but it was the Queen's college that established a new principle by including poor young scholars as an integral part of the community, to the number of twice that of the fellows. They were still tonsured minor clerics, however, destined for advancement in holy orders as well as learning. They were strictly enclosed at night, and forbidden to keep horse, hound or hawk, to play musical instruments or games of chance. All were to attend at least daily Mass and evening devotions, and the chaplains were to maintain the entire Divine Office. At Queen's the intention was, 'The honour of Our Lord Jesus Christ, of his blessed Mother and the whole heavenly host, for the advancement of the Church universally, and particularly in England, for the happy estate of my Lord the King, and of the Queen, and their children, for the salvation of the souls of their ancestors and descendents, of my father and mother and their children, of my ancestors, benefactors and friends, of all the living and of all the dead.' In addition, each college maintained an obligation of feeding the poor, who have always been abundant in Oxford.[36] At Cambridge also, colleges began to form in the late thirteenth century, beginning with Peterhouse (1284), and with several colleges and halls in the first half of the fourteenth century.

Collegiate Hermitages

At the other end of the spectrum from these huge prominent educational colleges, were a number of humble foundations about which very little is known, unstructured, and apparently informal. Although the idea of a hermitage would seem to be the exact contrary to that of the common life, certain small groups of men or women appear to have lived in fairly rustic buildings dignified with the name of 'hermitages'. One such was excavated at Grafton Regis in Northamptonshire; another operated at 'Felelia' near

Bloxham in the twelfth and thirteenth centuries. Clusters of simple buildings grouped around a chapel, with some sort of agreed brotherhood structure to hold them together, these institutions left tantalizingly little trace. A congregation of hermits at Monte Luco in Italy had a form of common life, meeting regularly for prayer and spiritual direction. They took no vows but lived under the direction of a superior.[37]

Notes
1. See in particular, Burgess and Heale, *English College*, and Jeffery, *Collegiate Churches*.
2. Quoted in Burgess and Heale, *English College*, p. 68, and Blair, *Church in Anglo-Saxon Society*, p. 509.
3. Page, 'Domesday Survey', p. 101.
4. Jeffery, *Collegiate Churches*, p. 18.
5. Veissière, *Saint-Quiriace*, pp. 111–45, 147.
6. Heyen, *Stift St Simeon in Trier*, pp. 165–83.
7. Alexander II, Epistle 45; Mansi XIX, c. 976.
8. Dugdale, *Monasticon*, VI, pp. 1181–3.
9. Ibid., VI, pp. 1456–7, 1475.
10. Jeffery, *Collegiate Churches*, pp. 176, 445.
11. Dugdale, *Monasticon*, VI, pp. 1341–3.
12. Ibid., VI, pp. 1333–9.
13. Jeffery, *Collegiate Churches*, p. 418.
14. Ibid., pp. 244–5.
15. Printed in full in Hamilton Thompson, *English Clergy*, pp. 247–91.
16. Sonntag, *Kollegiatstift St Marien zu Erfurt*, pp. 11–37.
17. Dugdale, *Monasticon*, VI, pp. 1325–30.
18. A. Wood, *City of Oxford*, ed. A. Clark, (Oxford Historical Society, 1890) II, p. 171.
19. Statutes in Dugdale, *Monasticon*, VI, pp. 1372–4.
20. Veissière, *Saint-Quiriace*, pp. 195–206.
21. Ibid., pp. 93–8, 190.
22. Statutes in Dugdale, *Monasticon*, VI, pp. 1339–41.
23. Ibid., VI, p. 1343.
24. See Morand, *Histoire de la Ste Chapelle*.
25. Ibid., pp. 65–70.
26. Ibid., pp. 73–102.
27. Billot, *Les Saintes Chapelles*, pp. 51–4, 43.
28. Dugdale, *Monasticon*, VI, pp. 1451–74.
29. See on this P. H. Cullum, 'Medieval Colleges and Charity', in Burgess and Heale, *English College*, pp. 140–53.
30. Dugdale, *Monasticon*, VI, pp. 486–8.
31. See ibid., VI, pp. 607–812, for the full list.

32. Ibid., VI, p. 642 (Bartlemas), pp. 618–20 (St Albans), pp. 703–8 (Elsing).
33. Ibid., VI, p. 607.
34. Hamilton Thompson, *Newarke, Leicester*, pp. 1–27.
35. Statutes in *Statutes of the Colleges of Oxford*, vol. I.
36. J. R. L. Highfield, in J.I. Catto (ed.), *The Early Oxford Schools* (1984), pp. 244–52. Statutes of Oriel and Queen's are also in *Statutes of the Colleges of Oxford*, vol. I.
37. Helyot, *Ordres Religieux*, VIII, p. 117.

Chapter 10

After the Black Death: the Heyday of late Medieval Colleges

The great plagues that swept Europe in the middle years of the fourteenth century provide a convenient marker to divide off the 'later Middle Ages' from the 'High Middle Ages', although of course no such division can ever be more than an artificial convention. Things were certainly different afterwards. The number of new collegiate foundations increased dramatically after 1350, and at the same time the older colleges and chapters were systematically given new statutes. There is no specific papal or conciliar document to account for this development. It coincides with a marked decline in the number of new monastic foundations, and it is obvious that patrons, both ecclesiastical and lay, were much more likely to commit new resources to secular communities during the two centuries between the plague and the wars of religion.

Whether all this really has anything to do with the plague is doubtful. What had changed was that the papacy was divided and weakened, and the 'nation state' began to appear. This may be the principal reason why international organizations like religious orders were less popular, while locally based communities prospered. The trend towards nationalism was already noticeable at the beginning of the fourteenth century, when Edward I and Philip IV began the long and disastrous conflict between England and France, but it became more and more dominant in European politics until the sixteenth century inaugurated the 'age of absolutism'. By the nineteenth century people had largely forgotten that Christendom had ever existed, and took it for granted that the world is intended to be divided into separate units called 'nations', and that each nation has the right to conduct its own affairs in total isolation from any other. The history of the twentieth century consisted largely in redefining what the limits of these 'nations' should be.

The plague did of course have a devastating effect on all religious communities. It is possible that the very high mortality observed in traditional monasteries and friaries recommended secular communities where members did not live quite so close together, but in fact the open dormitory was already something of an anachronism before 1349, and most monasteries provided separate cubicles for their members. Secular canons might live in separate houses, but they shared them with their vicars and clerics, so there was no less proximity than in monastic communities, no obvious advantage in the secular model. Secular clergy died just as much as monks: of the thirteen prebendaries of Newarke College no less than eight died in the autumn of 1361, as another wave of plague swept across Leicestershire.[1]

We need not imagine that monasticism had fallen out of favour. There may not have been many new foundations, but virtually all the existing communities continued in existence, their ancient endowments remained, and new sources of revenue, particularly advowsons, continued to be added. Wills demonstrate that bequests were being made to colleges, monasteries and friaries by the same testators. The occasional late fourteenth-century satire against worldly friars should not be interpreted as widespread disillusion with the system as such, and the great fifteenth-century reform movements associated with saints such as St Antoninus of Florence, St Bernadine of Siena or St John of Capistrano shows the vigour and authenticity of the late medieval friars. Monastic reforms came slightly later, but the very fact that movements such as the Cassinese Benedictine reform in Italy were possible shows that the monastic ideal was very far from dead. Every institution needs reform from time to time: it is only when the institution itself has fallen out of favour that no one bothers to reform it. Secular colleges themselves were reformed at intervals, showing that they were not being adopted as the solution to a failed monastic system, but existed side by side with monastic orders as institutions within a church that continually renewed herself.

Perhaps we can conclude that the increase in secular communities was partly because every form of vowed religious life was now adequately catered for, so that those who wanted to make new foundations turned their attention to colleges instead, and partly because the centuries after the Black Death were the age of a greatly increased lay spirituality. Secular colleges, directly involved with the laity, were better placed to direct the piety of lay men and women who developed an increasingly vigorous sense of devotion. Conversely, secular colleges were more directly under the control of the laity, as founders and their descendents exercised patronage over the community, often with the right to nominate the superiors and the individual members. As Scarisbrick comments, 'Had clerks ever been more completely and clearly subject to laymen?'[2] Unlike monastic houses, a secular college was entirely under local control, with no international connections. As the nations of Europe grew more separate and nationalistic, suspicious monarchs might well prefer an institute they could control without interference from General Chapters overseas. A consequence can be seen in the way in which lands and houses of 'alien priories' were often made over to secular colleges in fourteenth- and fifteenth-century England, as at Arundel and Stoke by Clare, while decayed houses, or those wiped out by the plague, might be refounded as colleges.

Further advantages of the college system over religious orders could be expressed in regulations such as those limiting the power of the superior, who might be genuinely elected from among the brethren, and hold office for only a limited term, unable to make major decisions without the consent of the chapter. This contrasted with the almost limitless powers of the great Benedictine abbots, who were increasingly becoming royal or noble appointments. Colleges also often had limits set on the hospitality they could offer, to avoid the practice of great households on the move suddenly battening themselves on the community, and they were usually forbidden to accept *corrodies*, lay pensioners establishing themselves for life within the enclosure. In these ways the secular colleges provided example and inspiration for the growing reform movements among older religious orders during the fifteenth century.

However there is little evidence for any hostility between the two ways of life, and benefactors were often happy to support both types of institution. Nicholas de Cantilupe founded both a charterhouse and a college; the Poles who founded colleges at Wingfield and Ewelme were buried in the Hull Charterhouse; a canon of Erfurt founded and was buried in a charterhouse in 1376.[3] In many cases colleges and religious communities cooperated happily. A convent of vowed nuns could be served by a college of secular priests, as at Tuxford, Nottinghamshire, or a college could be wholly owned by a religious house, like Hemingborough College, founded and owned by Durham cathedral priory, or St Martin le Grand, London, which was granted to Westminster

Abbey by Henry VII. Small secular communities could exist actually inside monastic houses.

Communities could still be transferred from one type of life to another. At Marstoke, Warwickshire, Kirkby Beler, Leicestershire, and Edington, Wiltshire, small colleges of seculars became Augustinian as late as the mid fourteenth century, and at Ingham in 1361 a planned secular college was in the event founded as a Trinitarian friary.[4] In contrast, in 1494 Henry VII procured a bull from Alexander VI to suppress the decayed Augustinian house of Mottisfont, Hampshire, and replace it with a collegiate church for a dean and prebendaries. The Pope declared that the prior and three canons scarcely kept residence, and there was no prospect of any more canons regular being recruited, so that it was better for it to be a collegiate church *cum communi mensa, archa, bursa, capitulo et aliis collegialibus insignias*. In the event, although the king twice changed his mind about it, nothing was actually done.[5] Nevertheless this did provide Cardinal Wolsey with a dangerous precedent, which he was to use in suppressing a small priory in Ipswich in favour of a college for a dean and twelve secular canons, with eight clerks and as many choristers, to run a grammar school as a feeder for his monstrous new college in Oxford, which was fed by a large collection of suppressed houses, both religious and secular.[6]

Colleges in Germany, and their life, can be observed from the record left by tombstones and other inscriptions, collected in the great *Deutsche Inschriften* series. For instance at Bleidenstadt in the Rhine valley we find a late eighth-century secular foundation, which became Benedictine during the Gorze reform in the late ninth century, but had dwindled to the point that in 1495 it was suppressed by licence of Alexander VI and refounded as a secular college. The last abbot, Eckhard Klüppel, became the first provost, and appears on his incised slab in cappa and biretta, though with no almuce.[7] After 1538 the office of provost was abolished and replaced by a dean. The series of inscriptions to canons, including deans, scholastics, and cantors, continues to the suppression of the college in 1802–3. However it does betray the fact that canons tended to be drawn from a fairly small number of wealthy families.

Conciliar Documents

Late medieval councils continue to legislate for collegiate life, tightening up on abuses, but evidently still wholeheartedly in favour of the institution as such. At Angers in 1365, canons were requested to be present for the whole of Mass and Office, or lose their distribution.[8] The Council of Narbonne in 1368 decreed that the canons and all members of collegiate churches must wear the *cappa nigra* from All Saints Day till Easter, except on great feasts when they wear silk copes; canons are to take turns as hebdomadaries; at least two from each college must be sent to study theology or canon law.[9] At Palermo in 1388 absent canons are ordered to lose their revenues completely in favour of residents.[10] The Council of London, 1399, required secular clerics to be sent into confiscated alien priories in order to maintain the round of the Office.[11]

The major reforming Council of Konstanz in 1415 made several important regulations to improve the life of secular canons. Noticing that there were too many ill-educated members of the upper class in colleges, it restricted the amount of entrance dues, deplored any insistence on noble or gentry birth for canonries and insisted that vicars should be 'literate', meaning able to read Latin. Chapters were not to impose an oath on new members.[12] Canons were to live more regularly and devoutly than others, must attend choir properly dressed and behave decently. Prelates must keep residence; subdeacons who are away studying may defer priestly orders for up to seven years, but must ensure that their titles were properly served. Every college must have at least four graduate theologians. No one under eighteen may attend chapter, but they can be ordained subdeacon at eighteen, after which they will attend and have a voice. The prebends of absent canons are to be confiscated and distributed among the residents, and all prebends must be equal. Prebends that are occupied may not be granted away, and the majority voice is to prevail in chapter.[13] The fact that such regulations were necessary shows that they were not already being observed, but the intention is clear that secular colleges should be genuine communities of clergy, well educated and diligent in keeping the round of daily prayer.

The council itself may have been in favour of secular communities, but there were not lacking those who deplored them in the spirit of Peter Damian. A Dominican friar, Matthew Grabon, launched an intemperate attack on any sort of community life without vows. 'It is not lawful', he declared, 'for priests and clerics to live the common life except in an approved religious order, under pain of mortal sin.' Like Damian, he seems to consider that priests may live alone, enjoying their property, but must not dare to live together except as vowed religious. In reality he was more opposed to new movements like the Béguines and the Brethren of the Common Life than to ancient collegiate churches. This illogical position was ably attacked by Jean Gerson, and many doctors, and Grabon retracted his position.[14]

Subsequent councils took it for granted that the collegiate life should continue and flourish. The Council of Paris in 1429 noted that canons had been seen running from one collegiate church to another, in their choir vestments, in order to attend Divine Office twice and so collect a double stipend.[15] The murder in that year of the Dean of Reval and his colleagues from Riga and Dorpat colleges by the Teutonic Knights was noticed and deplored, showing that colleges already existed on the very fringes of Latin Christendom.[16] In 1438 the Synod of Venice repeated the same regulations as previous councils on the provision of proper accommodation for clergy, the need to attend Divine Office together in choir, and to divide the offerings among the residents.[17] A summary of previous conciliar legislation known as the *Provinciale Anglicanum*, printed in 1509, reminds us that those who wish to found 'a house, hospital or zenodochium' must get a rule and institute from the local Ordinary 'so that they may live regularly and religiously'. Poor clerics are to be given their own benefices, 'of holy water', so that they can be trained up as the clergy of the future.[18]

With this, the great series of volumes edited by Mansi comes to an end: for fifteen hundred years it had been the greatest source for papal, conciliar and synodal legislation all over Europe, and a steady witness to the continuity of the ideal of the common life for secular clergy.

Cathedrals and their Minor Corporations

By and large it appears that the ideal of the common life did survive right to the end of the Middle Ages, even among the senior cathedral clergy, to a much greater extent than normally thought. Abuses undoubtedly existed, and there must have been unworthy canons, vicars and minor clerics who found ways to evade their responsibilities, but at no period is there any evidence of official connivance. Statutes and episcopal visitations continue to insist on the duty of residence, and attendance at the Hours of the Divine Office, with Mass and chapter, and if anything these requirements become stricter as the centuries pass. The sweeping judgement of Margaret Bowker that the collegiate clergy of Lincoln had lost all sense of purpose, and were no more than an 'acrimonious country club',[19] cannot be maintained, and is more due to reading Barchester back into the Middle Ages than to the evidence of the time.

The number of clergy increased steadily, as newly endowed chantry priests and others were added to the original communities of canons and vicars. By 1390, for instance, there were 130 priests at Salisbury, 89 at Exeter. The canons lived in separate residences, but sharing them with vicars and minor clerics, until the practice of establishing lodgings specifically for the vicars became general. The gathered vicars were expected to eat together and recreate together as well as assembling regularly for divine worship. Later, similar colleges were established for chantry priests, also with a common life.

Customs and statutes continued to accumulate until they were codified into new statutes. In the case of Lincoln, always the best documented, this was in the massive 'Black Book' of Bishop Alnwick in 1440, into which later statutes and additions were afterwards written. The canonical buildings were restored at the same time. By now there were fifty-six canons, to wear the grey almuce and black cappa. In the following year, 1441, the same number of vicars were incorporated into a separate college, for each of whom the canons were obliged to pay forty shillings per year. The statutes also speak of the 'poor clerics', evidently boys in minor orders, who are appointed by the dean, and look after the altars, maintaining the candles there (hence they are sometimes called *altaristae*). They are to be able to read and sing, and will serve Mass in choir dress, each at his own altar. They are to live together and be well guarded, especially when they go out for walk or play, *ad spaciatum vel solacium*. When one of them is ordained priest, another must be recruited to take his place. They may have been supposed to be well looked after, but we do hear of them complaining to Bishop Gray (1437–44) about the food and the cold.[20] Later, around 1525, we hear that there should be twelve boys, two of them being thurifers, 'and that they should live together in one building, living in common under a single master, who will provide a stipend for them and pocket money'.[21] Within Lincoln Cathedral, there were also the Burghersh and Cantelupe collegiate chantries.[22] This means that with the canons, vicars, poor clerics and two chantries there were five collegiate bodies serving a single cathedral. The same sort of pattern emerged in other cathedrals, though usually with fewer corporations, depending on the size and revenue of the see. Statutes at Lichfield collected under Bishop Blithe (1503–34) expect both canons and vicars to keep the close in good order, and to attend choir properly vested, vicars at least are never to be absent.[23]

A set of statutes for the canons of Tours, probably dating from the late fourteenth century, is printed by Martène.[24] A new canon was obliged to swear to renounce simony, to obey and preserve the rights of the Church, to give honest advice in chapter, to keep the secrets of the house, not to admit a serf or a bastard to a canonry (unless he be a bishop), and to keep the constitutions. On admission he paid fifteen pounds to the Church, and thirty pounds *ad opus bursae panis*, out of his future dividends. Similar procedures are demanded in a contemporary document from Boulogne, and the Lincoln constitutions of 1412.[25] A new canon usually had to subsist on his existing savings, contented with his ration of wine and nothing else, until the bishop could find him a prebend. Normally the revenues of a deceased canon belonged to his estate for one year, but the house had to be left furnished for his successor. It appears therefore that it was normal for a new canon to be appointed, to pay his entrance fee, and to pass a probationary year without lodging or prebend during his predecessor's year of grace. Only after that would he succeed to all the emoluments of the position. These circumstances naturally made the position of canon unattractive to idlers looking for an easy life, though obviously the idle rich could be supported by their parents during the probationary year.

In a number of English cathedral cities, notably at Chichester, Wells and Hereford, significant architectural remains testify to the renewed corporate life of the vicars from the fourteenth century onwards. At Chichester and Hereford the vicars' closes connect directly with the cathedral cloisters, whereas at Wells the famous Vicars' Close was reached by a bridge from the chapterhouse stairs. At York, Beverley, and Ripon the enclosure for the vicars was called the *Bedern*, a word of uncertain derivation. Nothing remains to be seen at Beverley or Ripon. The Bedern in York has been described in detail by Canon Harrison, though not much of the buildings survives in a recognizable condition.[26] It was not actually within the cathedral close, and the vicars had to cross a public thoroughfare to attend the Night Offices. The inconvenience of this led them in 1394 to construct a covered bridge so that they could safely enter the close. The Bedern was remodelled in the late fourteenth century, and the Church of St Sampson was granted as a source of revenue for the common hall, which was rebuilt at the time. New statutes were issued, enforcing the common life. Nevertheless numbers were apparently falling in the mid fifteenth century, and continued to dwindle until the 1520s.[27]

At London the statutes for the college of 'Petty Canons' issued in 1396 provided for 'a hall and dwelling place for a society or company of equal power and authority, which hall and edifices we term a College ... The said Peticanons do come together every day in the year to dinner in the common hall', they are to sit in random order as they come in, except for the warden, and to hear grace before and after, though they may converse during the meal 'once one lesson of the Holy Bible has been read distinctly'. The gates are to be kept shut, and 'every man to be come in by nine of the clock at night'. Moreover, 'None of the said Peticanons shall presume to detect or disclose the aforesaid secrets of the college in the houses of their masters the greater Canons.'[28] Discretion in keeping quiet about the internal affairs, the *secretum domus*, is characteristic of many religious communities.

The incorporation of the vicars could leave the remaining junior clergy of the cathedral without a structured community life. In most cases, minor clerics apparently still lived in the canons' residences, probably acting to some degree as domestic servants during what was in effect a residential apprenticeship. The remaining chantry priests, however, an increasing body as chantry foundations continued to be made, were often living scattered around in the city until the fifteenth century, when efforts were made to incorporate them into the common life as well.

In 1455 a royal licence was granted to create a new foundation at York, St William's College, for the chantry priests. The motive is clearly stated: 'Because there are many priests serving chantries who have no homes of their own, in which they may live either alone or with others, and since they have no means to support themselves, many of them are lodging in the houses of laymen, living together with laymen who have wives, contrary to the dignity of the church and what is fitting for the clerical order.' The members of the new college are to choose from among themselves a supervisor, to serve for one year, and the clerics and their supervisor are to form a perpetual corporate body, capable of holding property and acting in law. Statutes to be administered by this new foundation are to be drawn up by the Dean and Chapter. The foundation was confirmed by Edward IV in almost the same words in 1461, but now the superior is called a provost, who is to be appointed for life by the bishop and the Earl of Warwick.[29] The buildings remain, in working order.

Similar colleges of chantry priests existed in London and

Wells.[30] The chantry priests at St Paul's London were gathered into a common dwelling in 1395, and were expected to attend choir and receive their pittance as well as celebrating their specific chantry Masses. Innumerable other grades of minor officials collected around the cathedral, vergers, librarians, bookbinders, the *tractator cervisiae* and two *garciones*, many of whom were married laymen towards the end, but all had to be regulated as part of the cathedral establishment. In 1506 the great reformer Dean Colet issued new statutes.[31] His intention was to recast all the statutes into a more observant form, but this task was never completed. Even for the senior canons, he envisaged a return to a more regular life, specifically citing St Augustine and lamenting the growth of 'secular' canons. He demanded that the canons keep continuous residence in the building near the church, and attendance at the Hours, both day and night. The vicars are to live in a single building, the 'presteshaus', where they could maintain a common table, and they are to attend choir regularly. Minor canons and chaplains likewise are to live together in St Peter's College, and attend the Office.[32]

Colet's reforms were in accordance with the spirit of the age, but the old corruptions ran deep: within a few years his statutes were set aside in favour of statutes from Cardinal Wolsey, which while paying lip service to the ideal of residence, permitted absence for up to nine months of the year.[33] While continental Europe, and intelligent men like Colet who knew what was stirring there, moved steadily towards a real reform of clerical life, the increasing power of the monarchy and its minions in England were to stifle reform at its roots.

Rural Colleges: Ecclesiastical Foundations

During the next two centuries colleges continued to be founded or reformed all over Europe. Problems of non-residence and inequalities of income were met by redistributing prebends, and enforcing the statutes about periods of absence. The simplest method of returning to the more equable type of community was to abolish separate prebends altogether, and treat the college revenue as a single fund to be distributed according to grade and attendance. Most new colleges from the beginning of the thirteenth century onwards provided for a number of members all supported at an equal rate on the common fund, and all paid an equal stipend for their services. Residence was insisted on as a prerequisite for receiving any share in the income, and a full community of life was restored, occasionally extending even to the use of a single dormitory. There was no standard pattern or common rule, but a number of types emerge. The numbers of canons or chaplains could vary from three to twenty-four, with varying numbers of junior members. Irthlingborough, founded in 1379, still had individual prebends for a dean, five canons and four clerks; Maidstone was founded in 1395 for a Master and twenty-four canons; Tong in 1410 for five priests to live in one house and dine together. Hemingborough, founded in 1426, consisted of a provost, three prebendaries, six vicars and six clerics to live together in a Bedern (cf. p. 191). In some cases the foundation actually incorporated the poor, as at Newarke, Wenslow and Ewelme, or even schoolboys, as at Winchester and Eton. In other cases the poor and the boys remained external to the foundation, but were recommended to the members as objects of charity.[34]

Like the cathedrals, the long-established greater colleges were reformed during the later Middle Ages, with new statutes. At Bishop Auckland the 1428 reform statutes redistribute the prebends, encourage the personal residence of the prebendaries, and increase the vicars' salaries from five marks to ten marks. The new prebends are worth ten pounds per annum, so a non-resident who pays his vicar at the new rate only retains the difference of five marks.[35] This seems to have become the standard, that a vicar was paid one mark for every pound of the canon's income. Non-residence became increasingly unattractive.

For a reformed prebendal college on the really grand scale, we must look at the revised statutes for Beverley, issued in 1391.[36] Thomas, Archbishop of York, wrote to the entire community of Beverley, introducing the new statutes by explaining the need for reform, and a more equitable distribution of the revenue, and states that the following decrees have been agreed in chapter by four of the canons and the proxies of the four others. He describes the existing community: there are in fact nine canonries, each with a prebend, the Archbishop himself holding one. The precentor, chancellor and sacrist are additional to these nine; there follow seven parsons 'who were formerly called *berefellarii*', nine vicars, and seven chantry chaplains, making thirty-four clergy in major orders not counting the Archbishop; then there are nine clerics belonging to the canons, one each for the precentor and chancellor, two for the sacrist, and seven for the beerfellows, making twenty youths in minor orders, with two thurifers, and eight boy choristers, and two virgers or bellringers, who might be quite young and probably not yet tonsured. There are, therefore, sixty-six members of the foundation, not counting the lay servants, such as the receiver, auditor and janitor of the Bedern, and the vicar of St Mary's with his four clerics, the submaster of the schools, the chaplain of St Martin's altar (possibly in St Mary's), chaplains to the outlying chapels of Ulbrigg and Mollescrofte and to St Nicholas' Hospital.

Among the reforms, the Archbishop insists that the 'disgraceful term *beerfellow*, which only causes ridicule', be scrapped. (It has been suggested that they were originally poor recipients of charity rather than junior clergy as they were by now.[37] The name must derive from *beer vel*, 'bear skin', and refer to the trimmings on their almuces.) The provost is given enormous responsibilities, although he was not mentioned in the aforegoing list at all, nor in the list of those who attended the chapter which approved the reform. He can appoint the canons and parsons, whereas they in turn appoint their vicars and clerics, but the right of appointment lapses to the Archbishop if a vacancy remains for more than forty days. All newly appointed members must swear to obey the statutes. On no account is anyone to hold more than one position, but everyone is entitled to their proper stipend, as long as they are personally resident and attend each and every one of the canonical Hours. The only exceptions seem to be the eight prebendaries, who are excluded from the otherwise complete list of those obliged to reside. Every one appointed to a major clerical post, parson or vicar, must be ordained subdeacon at the next Ember Days, and priest within the year. There are fines for absences from choir, depending on the occasion and the rank of the offender. For example, those who miss the anniversary of King Athelstan, considered the founder, must pay twelvepence for a canon, fourpence for a vicar, tuppence for the chantry priests, and a penny for minor clerics, the proceeds to go to the thurifers and choristers.

The provost is responsible for most of the salaries. For each of the nine canons (including therefore the archbishop himself) he must pay the chapter ten pounds (fifteen marks) a year. The same sum is to be given to the precentor, chancellor and sacrist. The parsons get six pounds, thirteen shillings and fourpence (ten marks) each, the vicars eight pounds (twelve marks) each, the minor clerics six shillings and eightpence (half a mark). Fifty quarters of oats a year must be found for the canons, precentor and chancellor, and four bushels of wheat a week to the Bedern, 'the houses where the vicars live'. He must also allow them two peat bogs, and somewhere to dry their peat, and be responsible for the repair of the Bedern, and supplying tablecloths, floor-rushes and firewood. He must give a party for the boys on the three days following Christmas, and one for the youths on the Christmas Octave, but is not to permit the 'Feast of Fools' to continue. Distributions to the poor and to servants are to be made in the Bedern. In case the provost's revenue is stretched by this, the archbishop suggests he need not replace his personal goldsmith, stone mason and scullion when they retire. If he should be late in paying the salaries, he is to be fined five marks for each offence, to the archbishop, or the fabric of either York or Beverley. The archbishop undertakes to pay his personal cleric forty shillings (three marks), as must each of the eight other canons, and the precentor; the parsons should pay theirs thirty shillings, and the boys should each get twenty shillings from the canons. There is a further distribution of pence on certain anniversaries.

The concluding paragraph urges all members of the establishment to 'Come together eagerly, without delay, and devoutly, to sing the canonical hours together; not running, or skipping (*enicopando*), with no chattering about extraneous or frivolous things; to perform the Divine Office, to which you are bound, as devoutly as you ought, with all fervour of spirit and a good will, with no one leaving before the end.'

We do not hear much about the actual common life, but much can be inferred. It seems that the actual canon prebendaries themselves are hardly expected to appear, though it is they or their proxies who form the governing chapter. Of the remainder of this enormous foundation, those who lived in the bedern obviously had a common table, in a hall or refectory, with a log fire and plenty of oatmeal porridge. The peat was presumably either for cooking, or for heating individual rooms or lodgings. The boys and youths were obviously expected to live in or near the bedern, and were in residence over Christmas, so they had effectively left home on being admitted to the foundation. Attendance at choir would have occupied the most significant part of the day, leaving parish work to the vicar of St Mary's and the chaplains of the outlying chapels. The implication is that the choir boys and thurifers would naturally consider moving on to become minor clerics, gaining an education useful whether they intended to progress to major orders or not. A number of contemporary references to unmarried minor clerics implies that a proportion of the youths would in the event have married and found gainful employment as 'clerks' in the town, while others of their contemporaries would proceed to the subdiaconate as soon as a suitable vacancy occurred. To the end of the Catholic Middle Ages there is no evidence that the term *clericus* was ever used other than for someone actually in minor orders. The phrase 'lay clerks' refers to those in minor orders who had no intention of proceeding to the subdiaconate, were usually married, but still very much functioned as members of the clergy, as singers, porters, almoners and the like.

Southwell and Ripon, the other two great collegiate churches in the Diocese of York, were comparable in establishment. At Southwell, a charter of 1379 provides for a new residence for the vicars, with dormitory and refectory, because the existing residence 'is situated far from the church, and the street in between is muddy and deeply rutted, moreover the building is greatly dilapidated, so that the vicars cannot conveniently live there, but are settled in the town in different houses'. Since there was ample space in the graveyard, a new house was constructed there, east of the church. A charter of Henry VI tells us that there should be sixty members of the college, including canons, vicars, chaplains, cantarists, deacons, subdeacons, choristers, and others.[38] At Ripon a reform made rather earlier, in 1331, notes, though in much less detail than at Beverley, that the prebendaries have not been sufficiently resident, and so redistributes the revenues more equably, as well as ensuring that salaries for the vicars and other ministers should be paid from the common fund. A charter of Henry V notes that the canons should present vicars according to the ancient statutes, and that the vicars should be diligent in observing the customs, ordinances and statutes.[39] The three York colleges were on a larger scale than most, but after these fourteenth-century reforms were not substantially different in structure. Prebends everywhere became much more equable, and non-residence much less attractive, as the older colleges were to some extent assimilated to the newly founded colleges, without individual prebends, which were to become so popular from the late thirteenth century onwards.

The process of issuing new statutes for old colleges is also noticed on the Continent. The ancient college of St John in Regensburg received new statutes in 1493, and again in 1511, so the tide of reform ran strong, and the community was well able to withstand the turmoils of the Lutheran rebellion. Canons were to be of respectable origin, and had to wait two years before receiving their prebends. They were obliged to reside in the city, and could receive a voice in chapter after ordination to the subdiaconate.

Holidays were few, and provision was made for the sick. As elsewhere, the revenue of a deceased canon was applied to his estate for one year. The vicars were to receive a pittance on attending Day and Night Offices.[40]

Likewise at Trier, the foundation of St Simeon, built in and around the ancient Black Gate, received new statutes in 1443, following a visitation of 'reform in head and members' conducted by the archbishop who was accompanied by Nicholas of Cusa. The structure now comprised a dean, *scholasticus, custos,* thirteen canons and eight others. The prebends were all equalized, and discipline in choir enforced. All were expected to attend, and detailed instructions were given on such things as posture. However there is no mention of a common table, and it seems that the canons each maintained their own households.[41]

As well as reforming and restoring the manner of life within colleges, the period witnessed much rebuilding, extending and improving of the buildings. Substantial building works continued at Beverley and Ripon through the fifteenth century, leaving them among the most spectacular churches in England. Many of the other large collegiate churches were rebuilt on the grand scale, though some of the finest have disappeared. An impressive example from the late fifteenth century is Manchester, where both the collegiate church and the college accommodation remain entire and have never gone out of use. The church is now used as an Anglican cathedral, the college houses the Chetham library and Chetham's School of Music. This college was founded by the last rector of the parish church, Thomas de la Warre, in 1421, and had a complement of a warden, eight fellows, four clerics, and six choristers. In 1501 Robert Cheetham established a chantry within the college, to be served by the warden and fellows, so this did not increase the number of clergy.[42] The building, arranged around a quadrangle, has galleries on two floors connecting the individual rooms, and a substantial dining hall. It stands a hundred metres or so away from the church, which was rebuilt on a grand scale.

In the case of many of the smaller colleges as well, the buildings stood separate from the church, rather than invariably being joined on as they would be in a monastery. At Cobham there is a gap no wider than a processional way between church and college, but at Higham Ferrers, Maidstone, and Westbury on Trym the college buildings are some distance away from the church. This must have been very inconvenient for the Night Offices in winter, and can only be explained by the fact that the existing parish churches were already surrounded by their burial grounds, and founders were reluctant to build domestic accommodation over the graves of the Christian dead. At Tattershall there are remains of a brick cloister on the north side of the choir, so that the buildings were at least accessible under cover, though there too they must have stood at a distance. At Ewelme a short covered passage links the church with the Godshouse, with precipitous steps ill-suited to the elderly bedesmen. It was considered a privilege to be buried in a cloister walk, still more so in a church, so that extending church or cloister over a graveyard would cause no offence, but rather the opposite. On the other hand to build a kitchen or a dining hall over a graveyard might well be thought unacceptable.

Where buildings survive, the most common plan is a courtyard or quadrangle, occasionally with an arcaded walk. Instead of a large dormitory, there are usually individual doorways opening into self-contained dwellings, often with an upper floor. In some cases there is a large kitchen and a vast communal dining hall, and it is obvious that the community were intended to dine together regularly. In other cases there is no such provision, and it appears that each household catered for itself. If the household comprised a canon, his vicar, and some minor clerics, they presumably kept common table together, and it would not have been impossible to preserve the formality of grace and reading at meals. The degree of 'community' life therefore varied. Where each one had his own household, or where the canons' residences were freestanding buildings arranged around a large open space, there was obviously less day-to-day contact than where all dined together every day. What all colleges had in common, however, was prayer together, at least Mass and the Divine Office, and often extra devotions decreed by the founder. This could include a daily Requiem Mass, the Office of the Dead, the Rosary, the Seven Penitential Psalms, or specially composed collects and antiphons. At Windsor the text of one such collect is inscribed on the walls of the Urswick chantry chapel.

Many small colleges existed inside parish churches, without themselves owning the church or providing the cure of souls. The parish itself remained independent under its rector, or a vicar who acted for a monastery or other impropriator. At Cirencester the secular chantry priests were not under the control of the vicar but formed a self-governing corporation, within the large parish church at the very gate of the Augustinian Abbey. At Higham Ferrers the church was appropriated to Newarke College, but a new foundation by Archbishop Chichele provided for eight priests with their clerics, and six choristers, including a grammar master and choirmaster. They were to live in a new college some distance away from the church, but also to be responsible for bedesmen who lived in a building on the south side of the churchyard. At Rotherham, although the church belonged to Rufford Abbey, Archbishop Rotherham was able to establish the substantial Jesus College for all the existing chantry priests, with a provost and two fellows, to live in a sumptuous new building east of the church, with its own chapel and schools.[43] Other colleges were entirely extra-parochial, such as the chapel at Kingston on Thames, which eventually grew into a grammar school; Bablake in Coventry, which developed from merchant guilds with nine endowed priests, and Guildhall College, London, beginning as a chantry of five priests with bedesmen. An impressive surviving church is Battlefield in Shropshire, built on the site of the mass grave of the fallen at Shrewsbury Field (1403), founded for a master and five chaplains to live in accommodation which joined onto the south side of the chancel.

Not all collegiate churches seem to have had foundation charters, as there is evidence for some form of small-scale collegiate life in many of the greater parish churches without any record of a chartered incorporation. At Bampton in Oxfordshire the advowson had belonged to Exeter Cathedral since the time of St Leofric, and provided a prebend for one of the canons. This involved the setting up of a vicarage to serve the parish, which in the case of Bampton was divided into three parts or portions. The brasses of two of the vicars show them in canonical garb, the almuce and cappa nigra, and the surviving place name of 'The Deanery' suggests that by at least the late fourteenth century the three portionist vicars had begun to live as if they were a college under a dean. Late fifteenth-century choir-stalls survive in the church, providing four places with tip-up misericordes, as well as simpler benches, presumably for chantry chaplains, minor clerics or choristers. Yet there is no evidence for incorporation as a college, and while any chantries were duly suppressed, the arrangement of three vicars survived for centuries, although the three married Protestant vicars lived separately in three splendid vicarages arranged around the churchyard, the western one still being called the 'Deanery'. An inscription of 1546 on the wall of the south vicarage may indicate the date that community life ended. This is one example out of several 'portionist' parishes around the country, others of which may also have imitated the collegiate life on the small scale.

Foundations by Lay Patrons

Although some new colleges were established by bishops or other clergy, most of the new foundations after 1350 were the initiative of laymen. The greatest collegiate foundations after the Black Death were those attached to great households, from the Emperor upwards. King Edward III's prestigious foundations at Westminster and Windsor inspired imitators at every level. The York dynastic college at Fotheringay made a counterbalance to the Lancastrian hospital foundation of Newarke, Leicester. The Earls of Arundel transformed the tiny college of St Martin in the Castle into the college of St Nicholas attached to the parish church. In France, the example of St Louis in establishing the Sainte Chapelle du Palais was imitated in a dozen smaller Saintes-Chapelles, such as Bourges, Châteaudun and Brou. Similarly at Mettingham, Suffolk, the now old-fashioned castle buildings were turned over to a college in 1392. This was after the Norwich family had made several false starts in the attempt to establish a dynastic college, which involved moving all the family tombs from Raveningham to Norton Subcourse in 1362, and on to Mettingham in 1373.[44] In Scotland most late-medieval collegiate foundations were made by great families, although some, unusually, were made by burgh councils, including many as late as the 1540s.[45] Most great households maintained teams of clergy, priests, minor clerics and boys, to provide daily worship and pray for the good estate of the family, and although these were not usually incorporated, the life therein must have been indistinguishable from that of a formal college.

The founders usually laid down detailed statutes for their colleges, often reserving to themselves the right to nominate the master or warden, at least during their own lifetime. With the extinction of most of the older families by the end of the fifteenth century, the patronage usually lapsed to the diocesan bishop. Patronage of any sort was of course a danger, with the risk that lay patrons could commend unsuitable youths to positions as canons or superiors – but then bishops could be just as irresponsible. However in most of the new or reformed colleges, there was little attraction for such youths in an institution which required them to attend Matins in the middle of the night as well as daily Mass and the other Hours if they wanted to collect their stipend. As a result, abuses were concentrated in the older cathedral chapters. Even there we should not be too quick to observe abuse, for sometimes the granting of a prebend to a youth, with a dispensation from taking major orders at once, enabled him to study for the priesthood at a university, and eventually become a much better educated priest than he could otherwise have been. Appointments or commendations were a means of educating poor scholars to serve both Church and State, though the increasing insistence on residence for canons meant that civil servants were increasingly drawn from the laity rather than the clergy, in itself no bad development.[46] Nevertheless no statutes or regulations could guard against the abuse of power, as is seen in the scandalous way in which Henry VIII rode roughshod over the statutes in appointing an unsuitable sprig of nobility, Lord George Grey, as Dean of Newarke. The inevitable result was corruption on the large scale, and a serious breakdown of relationships betweeen dean and canons.[47]

Above all, these dynastic or family colleges provided settings for the family tombs. Important collections of such tombs survive at Arundel, Berkeley, Cobham, Lingfield, Staindrop, Tattershall, Warwick, and elsewhere. Demolished colleges such as Fotheringay and Newarke also contained tombs of significant royal ancestors, so that even Queen Elizabeth was shocked to hear of their destruction during the terrible years under the regime of her brother.

In Paris, the Sainte-Chapelle du Palais itself continued to grow and attract new endowments, in the shape of chantry foundations. In 1369 Philippe le Long founded five new prebends, each for a principal chaplain, sub-chaplain and clerk, and an extra sub-chaplain for each of the three marguilliers, at a total rent roll of £1,752 9s 3d. The choir boys, *enfans de choeur*, became part of the foundation, and Francis I allocated them two scholarships to the College de Navarre in 1520. In 1401 Charles VI issued reforming measures to ensure that chaplains and clerks attended all the Little Hours, remained continually in residence, and wore the canonical habit at all times. There was some debate at this time over whether the Sainte-Chapelle was legally a college with a chapter, a status resisted by the king, in order to keep it more firmly under his control.

In 1379 Charles V established a second royal Sainte-Chapelle at Vincennes, handing over to the canons the existing royal hunting lodge, and beginning the construction of the impressive chapel. The lodge was extended into a quadrangle, with a fountain in the centre, but the excavators found that the wine cellar, which had been built as a single unit for the royal bins, was divided up into compartments, each with a locked door, for the individual canons. The daily allowance of one *muid* of wine evidently needed protection. The treasurer of the Sainte-Chapelle du Palais was made the visitator of the new college.[48]

Where France led, England was not far behind. Edward III established two major colleges in royal residences, at Westminster and Windsor. In both cases existing small communities of household clergy were replaced by large communities with buildings to match. St Stephen's, Westminster, was reconstituted in 1348 as a college with a dean, twelve secular canons, as many vicars, and other sufficient ministers. The King took several years over remodelling the buildings and establishing the endowment. Accommodation was provided, at first in a little cloister, and later in rather grander houses. Their function was explicitly liturgical, 'to celebrate the Divine Office daily for the royal family, their ancestors and descendents, ... to perform the Hours, both by night and by day, with singing, every day in common according to the form which we shall establish hereafter in greater detail'. They were to be paid regularly out of the Treasury, as well as having an endowment in land and advowsens settled on them.[49] The chapel was a tall edifice in two storeys, looking very like the Sainte-Chapelle. (The lower storey survives as the chapel to the House of Commons.) Such two-storey chapels, found as early as the eleventh century in the Tower of London, and made famous by the Sainte-Chapelle, were often imitated on a smaller scale.

A few years later the same king refounded the castle chapel at Windsor on an even more ambitious scale, with a warden, twelve secular canons, thirteen vicars, four clerics, six choristers and twenty-six poor knights. Ample accommodation was provided for the collegiate staff, and again their primary obligation was to pray for the royal family. Here, unusually, the institution itself survives, though on a reduced scale. The collegiate church, rebuilt by Edward IV, is the impressive St George's Chapel, behind which is the college cloister with an arcaded passage fronting the entrances to individual houses. Further down the hill is the vast communal dining hall of the vicars, and the 'Horseshoe Cloister' for the poor knights.[50] A third foundation by Edward III, on a much smaller scale, was that in the Tower of London, with four chaplains under a rector, which Edward IV later intended to transform into a dean with three canons.[51]

As well as kings, wealthy noble patrons were able to provide foundations sufficient to keep large communities of secular priests, in buildings appropriate to their status. Fotheringay was the princely foundation of the House of York, founded in 1411 for a master with twelve chaplains or fellows, eight minor clerics and thirteen choristers to pray for the souls of that branch of the royal family, 'and for the souls of all the faithful departed'. The original charter refers to 'houses and other buildings that are necessary for the accommodation of the said master and all other persons'. That these buildings comprised a courtyard structure rather than a scatter of separate houses is implied by the reference in the contract for building the nave of the church, which includes 'in the south side to the cloystre-ward another porche joyning to the dore of the said cloystre'.[52] The church was built on the grand scale, and part of it survives, although the community buildings have completely disappeared, as have nearly all those attached to the greater foundations.

Detailed statutes survive for some of these foundations by influential laymen. At Stoke-by-Clare in Suffolk, Edward Mortimer, Earl of March, made a new foundation in 1415, in the place of a suppressed 'alien priory'. The statutes lay down strict conditions for the prebendaries, granting them a handsome income only on condition of residence, and cutting them off with forty shillings if they fail to reside. There is to be a dean, with six prebendaries, who have prebends of surprisingly differing values: the second stall, for instance, gets fourteen pounds, seven shillings and fourpence, whereas the fourth stall has only two pounds. However the canons are not here responsible for paying the eight vicars, who have a collective endowment, to be divided equally. The canons are to be resident for thirty-two weeks of the year, with no excuses accepted for longer absence, whereas the vicars get six weeks' holiday, specifically 'to recreate themselves, and to visit their friends'. No holidays are envisaged for the minor clerics and the boys.

Canons in residence have their own houses, either inside the close or outside, whereas the vicars must live in the lodgings appointed to them, maintain their share of the garden, and eat together in Hall. The minor clerics and boys also eat in Hall, but at separate tables. Disciplinary statutes are strict: all must be within the enclosure after curfew, and in the daytime they are never to go out alone. Hunting is prohibited, as is keeping hounds except for the dean who may keep two couples. No one may carry a weapon, and fist fighting among the canons is punished by five years' suspension. Any member who is intolerable to live with may be expelled after three warnings, though for certain heinous crimes expulsion is immediate.[53]

Similar statutes survive for the little college at Tong in Shropshire, founded by the Pembrugge family. As usual, the intention was to pray for the founders and their ancestors, as well as all the faithful departed, particularly the benefactors of the college. There was to be a warden and five other priests, with two clerics, choristers, and thirteen paupers 'of whom seven shall be so feeble and weakened that they are rarely or never able to stand by themselves without assistance'. The complete Divine Office is to be celebrated in church, and there is to be Mass in the almshouse for those paupers who cannot get to church. One chaplain is to teach grammar to the choristers, as well as the poor children of the neighbourhood. The paupers are to attend Mass and Office as far as they are able, and to pray daily for 'his own salvation and for that of the souls for which he is bound to pray'. The customary canonical dress of surplice, black almuce and black cappa is to be worn. The clergy are to live in separate chambers within one building and to eat together within the house.[54] These exceptionally detailed statutes demonstrate how difficult it is to divide collegiate establishments into neat categories: Tong might be classified as a chantry college, a hospital, or an educational college depending on where the emphasis lies. In reality almost all colleges performed all three functions. None was without its purpose of prayer for the souls of the departed, none was permitted to neglect the poor, or the education of the youths who lived in and around it. Our treatment of different categories of college is purely for the sake of convenience, not because founders or contemporaries thought of them as essentially different.

One small college omitted in all the standard sources is the well-documented college at Stonor in Oxfordshire. Here in 1349 Sir John Stonor established a community of six chaplains, who were given the earlier Great Hall and Solar of Stonor as their refectory and recreation room, with a range of rooms connecting these old buildings to the existing chapel. They were given a permanent endowment, rather than depending on day-to-day maintenance by the family, drawing part of their revenue from the woodland immediately above the house. The function of the chaplains, apart from incidentally serving the sacramental needs of the household, was to 'celebrate the Divine Office for ever ... for the good estate of the King and himself [Sir John Stonor], for their souls when they are dead, and for the souls of the progenitors and successors of the King and his ancestors, and for the heirs of John'.[55] Such a clearly organized college of priests was doubtless not unique to Stonor, and the fact that Cook, Jeffray, Tanner and all editions of Dugdale were unaware of it suggests that there may have been a great many more such small private colleges in households around the country. Certainly Wolsey had a collegiate establishment of chaplains in Hampton Court, which continued to exist after the palace was confiscated by the Tudor tyrant.

Colleges attached to Almshouses or Hospitals

While all colleges exercised at least some charitable work towards the indigent and the frail, many were specifically founded for that purpose, and the community of priests was set up to pray in particular for the inmates of the hospital or almshouse. Moreover the poor bedesmen themselves were not passive recipients of alms, but were expected to pray and maintain a religious manner of life to the best of their ability.

St Leonard's, York, has already been mentioned as one of the largest foundations of the earlier period. The largest of the late medieval hospitals was the refounded college of Newarke in Leicester.[56] In 1355–6 Henry, Duke of Lancaster, brought home a thorn from the Crown of Thorns in the Sainte Chapelle, and reconstructed the Newarke as a family dynastic chapel, now with a dean, twelve canons, thirteen vicars, three clerks, six choristers, fifty poor men and fifty poor women, with ten women to look after them. The dean and canons were all to be priests, and were obliged to reside for at least ten months of the year; they were to have a suitable dwelling place, apart and separate. For the vicars there was to be a dwelling house with a hall and great chamber, and the choristers were to have a house to live and eat together. All, therefore, were to live in common, but in separate communities depending on grade. The revised statutes of 1490–1 changed this arrangement to the extent that the choristers must now live with the canons who pay their board. In the bishop's visitation of 1525 it is mentioned that the porter is to be a 'layman or married cleric', so there was a job available for at least one of the junior members who had chosen not to proceed to major orders. When the House of Lancaster succeeded to the Crown, the hospital enjoyed even greater status as the dynastic chapel, though it was not used for major royal burials.

The detailed statutes give an idea of community life within the college, and to a lesser extent within the almshouse, which was a separate building. More can be gathered from the extensive records of Bishop Longland's visitation in 1525, following the breakdown of relationships between the intruded dean and the canons.[57] For instance we gather that Matins was supposed to start at six in the morning. It was quite normal for laypeople, both men and women, to come into the porch or nave of the church during the singing of the Divine Office, there to make their own devotions, either following the psalms in their Books of Hours, or using other prayers against the background of the chanting.

Thomas Cawardyn and others were standing about the door of the choir screen during the Magnificat ... He found Cawardyn leaning on the porch-side, saying his evensong ... Haryngton standing with a book in his hand, apparently saying his prayers: there were several others standing there, as was usual. William Gillot said that it was the custom for lay-folk and serving men to stand in the porch during service.[58]

However we also hear that illicit doorways had been opened in the enclosure wall by which the clergy could go out into the town without passing through the great gate: the bishop ordered all such doors to be stopped up, and for the gate to be locked at night.[59] As late as the second quarter of the sixteenth century, therefore, there was a reasonable expectation that collegiate life would be maintained as a genuine round of prayer under real discipline, and that ordinary lay folk would be able to attend and profit from the sung Offices. Most significantly, the bishop declared that prayer was the real reason for their existence: 'All of you, the canons and vicars of this college, are clerks, chosen into the lot of the Lord, received into the number of this college for this purpose chiefly, that you may undergo and fulfil the task and burthen of divine service day by day to the praise and honour of God.'[60] Anything else the canons and vicars might do was for their spare time: their work was the 'Work of God', the *Opus Dei*. One of them certainly would celebrate Mass for the poor bedesmen who were unable to come to church, and a priest would undoubtedly hear confessions and anoint the sick, but the regular nursing care of the bedesmen fell to the ten serving-women. The church was not a parish, so none of the priests had parochial duties: their task was to pray. In a world where everyone believed in the power of prayer, for the wellbeing of the living and of the dead, benefactors were happy to endow these colleges, but expected to get their money's worth of intercession.

If this is true of the Newarke, it is equally true of the small chantry communities which incorporated a number of poor folk, to share in the benefaction, and to pray for the donors. At Thame, for example, the powerful Quartermayne family established 'a Chauntrie, vi pore men and a fraternitie in the worshipp of Seynt Christophere to be relived in perpetuyte', as the inscription says on the brass of the founder in Thame church. In a similar foundation at Banbury, the Guild maintained three chaplains and eight poor men. On a larger scale, Tattershall College housed six priests, six clerks, six choristers and thirteen poor, as well as serving a school in the village. (The almshouse for the poor alone survives: the school is a roofless ruin to testify to the real effect of the policies of Edward VI.) These and innumerable other hospitals throughout the country did not only provide housing and support for the elderly and infirm, but ensured a ceaseless round of prayer and praise for the founders, their kin, and all Christian souls.

The best researched of these hospital foundations is Ewelme in Oxfordshire, founded in 1437, where there were only two priests and thirteen poor, but the statutes are specific about the obligations they had in common. Not only were the priests to celebrate Mass daily and recite the entire Divine Office in church along with the rector, but the poor men were to attend all these Offices, following them in their primers if they could read. In addition, they were to gather round the founders' tomb and recite prayers for the dead, as well as the entire Rosary daily. This will not have left much time over for other occupations: it is clear that accepting a place in Dame Alice's foundation effectively meant adopting the religious life in everything except the vow of poverty: and naturally places were only offered to those with no other means of support.[61]

Another very important Hospital foundation was Sir Richard Whittington's College in London. This was established in 1424 in the existing parish church of St Michael, Paternoster Royal, and provided for a master, four secular priests as fellows, clerks, choristers, and thirteen poor, one of whom was to be tutor. All the clergy are to celebrate the entire Office together, and also attend sermons at St Paul's on Sundays. They are to live together in a house provided at the east end of the church, and to eat together in the hall. They wear the common habit, which is not to be luxurious or splendid, and meet regularly for chapter. They may be absent for no more than twenty days a year, and must not frequent local taverns. The stipend for the master is to be ten marks, over and above his income as rector of the parish, for the chaplains eleven marks each *pro victu et vestitu,* for the first cleric eight marks, the second a hundred shillings (seven and a half marks), the choristers five marks each. A newly appointed master is to take an oath of office, whereas the chaplains only make a promise of obedience, as the clerics are also to do when they are old enough. Chaplains are appointed for life, and must give four months' notice if they propose to resign and accept a benefice elsewhere. To ensure that all remember their obligations, the statutes are to be read out four times a year, like the Rules of St Benedict and St Chrodegang.[62] (Sadly, unlike the *Ancrene Rewle,* the statutes of Dick Whittington College make no mention of the community cat.)

The distinction between hospital and chantry is not always easy to make, though many have tried. The foundation at Thame, for instance, as mentioned above was explicitly called a 'Chantrie'. By the end of the Middle Ages there were enormous numbers of foundations all over Europe that combined the functions of prayer for the souls of the founders and benefactors with practical care for the sick, poor, travellers and pilgrims. The two English Hospices at Rome provided a common life for the resident fellows, as well as entertainment for poor pilgrims from England visiting the Holy City. They depended on benefactions from England for their foundation and maintenance, and interceded daily for the king and realm. Poor visitors could stay freely for three days; rich pilgrims were invited to become benefactors, and enrol as *confratres*.[63] At all colleges, suffrages for the local sick and dead were celebrated, often publicly. At Oxford, bellmen were sent around the streets to invite the citizens to attend the anniversary Masses. The number of foundations for such anniversaries, 'obits', naturally increased year by year, and the offerings made in connection with them made up a significant part of the running costs of the colleges. Local boys or lay singers might be employed to augment the singing, for which they would be educated free of charge, and even those colleges with no direct parochial responsibilities became an integral part of the local community.[64]

Educational Colleges

A few colleges, in addition to providing for the elderly poor, included on the foundation a significant number of boys for education, besides the handful of choristers provided in most cases for the sake of the liturgy. In 1387, the Bishop of Winchester, for instance, one William of Wykeham, created a huge college just outside the city walls for a warden, ten perpetual chaplains, three transitory (*conductitiorum*) chaplains, three clerics and seventy poor scholars learning grammar. The stated purpose was 'the increase of divine worship and the Catholic faith, and to the benefit of the commonwealth and of the individual, ... to the praise of God and of his glorious Virgin Mother'.[65] There was something similar at Eton, on a smaller scale. Whereas in most colleges a small number of boys and youths were educated with the reasonable expectation that if they decided to follow an ecclesiastical career it would be within the college in question, in these two larger foundations they were obviously expected to move on to some other sphere of education, in one of the two universities.

At Oxford the first collegiate bodies had been established to provide community accommodation for priests who might be studying or teaching in the established schools. They remained small, until the end of the fourteenth century when the same Bishop William of Wykeham founded a new college on a new model, to complement his junior foundation in Winchester. This 'New College' was founded 'for the praise and glory of the Crucified, and of his mother, for the support and exaltation of the Christian faith, the advantage of Holy Church, divine worship and the liberal arts'. Here too there were to be seventy 'poor and indigent clerical scholars, attentive to their studies' as well as the warden, ten priest fellows, three chaplains, three clerks and 'sixteen boys who are competent at reading and singing'. As in any college, the daily round of seven Masses and the Divine Office was to be kept up ceaselessly, by the chaplains and clerics. The intention was 'for the good estate of our lord the King and his consort, and of our own, and for the souls of my father and mother, and all the departed, those mentioned above and the benefactors'. The entire college was expected to attend at least one Mass daily, as well as the evening devotion concluding with the Antiphon of the Virgin, but, to leave time for study, the warden and scholars seem to have been obliged to attend the entire Office only on Sundays and feastdays. All dined together in Hall, with readings during the meal. In each room there was to be a senior fellow to keep order, and every boy was to have his own separate bed.[66]

This seems to have been the first instance of a college conceived as a large body of university-level students with their own internal teachers. Although 'education was important to Wykeham, the fundamental purpose of the college was to make intercession for the repose of his soul'. However despite the lengthy and detailed instructions for maintenance of the daily round of prayer, 'The century-by-century torrent of prayers has dwindled to a trickle of two prayers per year.'[67] Later bishops of Winchester, William Waynefleet, and Thomas Wolsey, established two more enormous colleges, Magdalen in 1457 and Cardinal College in 1525. Henry VI, as well as founding the junior college at Eton in 1440, established King's College in Cambridge in 1441, consciously modelling both foundations on Wykeham's colleges. The model was widely copied, and the older secular colleges largely assimilated, until by the end of the Middle Ages both Oxford and Cambridge had significant numbers of secular colleges to set against the religious houses that had formed the majority of the teaching establishments in both towns. (Confusingly, many of these religious houses were called 'colleges', such as Durham, Canterbury, London, Gloucester, St Mary's and St Bernard's Colleges, Oxford, though they were explicitly for vowed monks or canons regular.) Archbishop Chichele's foundation of 1438, All Souls, was on a more conventional model; never intended to be a teaching body, it provided mainly for priests to pray for the souls of those killed in the current wars, with only a few junior clerics to assist at Mass and the Office.

On the Continent the first specifically university college was All Saints, Prague, founded in 1366, though other ancient collegiate churches had schools which could develop. In Paris there were a large number of colleges associated with the university. At Erfurt the external school attached to St Marien acquired a widespread reputation for philosophy, and developed until by the late fourteenth century it was already being styled a university, which it became formally in 1392. Twelve of the canons joined the new university, and individual canons could give patronage to poor students, using vicariate foundations. As a university, Erfurt continues to flourish, although at least in the period of Communist rule (1945–89) is unlikely to have remembered its origin in a collegiate church. A strong link evolved between German colleges and universities, and the number of graduates in the communities steadily increased. In the fourteenth century 57 per cent of canons at Bamberg were graduates, in the fifteenth century 75 per cent, in the sixteenth, 90 per cent. Canons of colleges formed a significant proportion of university members, 3 per cent at Cologne, 209 out of 3563 at Prague. Pope John XXII promoted similar ideas in France.[68]

Educational colleges more than most are marked by large numbers of tombstones commemorating their members, from which much can be perceived of the ways in which they wished to be remembered. They tend to be of the simpler type, brasses and incised slabs, commemorating the canons or fellows, and occasionally the junior clergy and scholars. Many in Germany mark their academic distinction by showing the deceased with his head pillowed on a book, or, as at Ingolstadt, lying on a bed of books. Brasses in colleges at Oxford and Cambridge are more likely to display academic dress, except for the heads of houses who are often seen in almuces and silk copes. The inscriptions invariably draw attention to their degrees. At the University of St Andrews, incised slabs both at St Leonard's and St Salvator's colleges show the fellows in canonical dress, with the almuce worn over the head. Flat tombs were common, because canons or fellows were allowed to own property sufficient to pay for such memorials, but not enough for the expensive high tombs of the gentry and nobility. Few high tombs are to be found in university college chapels: there is one at St Salvator's, to the founder Bishop Kennedy; another for the royal favourite, Hugh Ashton, at St John's, Cambridge.

Informal Communities or Hermitages

These tantalizingly elusive institutions seem to have continued and even increased during the later Middle Ages. There were three or four of them in Oxford, described by Wood as 'houses containing divers men (and women sometimes) gathered into one combination, supporting their common charge by a mutuall contribution and spending their times in continuall devotion. They belonged for the most part to some parish church, and consisted of poore preists, lay brothers, and others.' Of these, the community of St Catherine was sufficiently organized to be able to hold property, for it was bequeathed a sum of money in a will of 1430.[69]

These last, informal or unstructured, communities were probably the English equivalent of the Béguinage or Gods Huis which was so prominent a feature of late medieval Catholicism in the Low Countries. At the end of the thirteenth century we begin to find conciliar warnings against the married minor clerics becoming goliards or beghards,[70] and in the fourteenth century such warnings continue. By a decree of the Council of Mainz in 1310, no one is to begin as a béguine before the age of forty, and beghards and beguttae are to be suppressed altogether. They wander the streets, pretending to be religious, and calling out *brot durch Got*, 'bread, for God's sake!' At Tarragona in 1317 béguines are forbidden to live in communities, to wear mantles, or to read theological books in the vulgar tongue.[71] Nevertheless the béguine movement eventually became very respectable, and remains a well-known feature of the Low Countries, even though its origin lay in undisciplined informal mendicant life. As communities of ladies living together, without vows but following a disciplined pattern of religious life, they are the female equivalent of communities of secular clegy. One such establishment at Lecce in Puglia is noted as providing a safe refuge for 'virgins, widows and the unhappily married (*malmaritate*)'. Wandering beghards, on the other hand, have never been absent, but the Western Church has never accepted this as a valid form of religious life.

Notes

1. Hamilton Thompson, *Newarke, Leicester*, pp. 231-51.
2. Scarisbrick, 'Henry VIII and the Dissolution of the Secular Colleges', p. 57.
3. Burgess and Heale, *English College*, pp. 79-80; see also Sonntag, *Kollegiatstift zu Erfurt*, biographical catalogue, entry for Johann Orton.
4. Dugdale, *Monasticon*, VI, pp. 511-14 (Kirkby Beler); VI, p. 536 (Edington); S. Badham, 'Beautiful remains of antiquity' in *Church Monuments* XXI (2006), pp. 10-14 (Ingham).
5. Dugdale, *Monasticon*, VI, p. 483.
6. Ibid., VI, p. 599.
7. D.I. 43, Rheingau-Taunus Kreis, no. 334.
8. Angers (1365), canon xviii; Mansi XXVI, cc. 433-4.
9. Narbonne (*Vausense* 1368), canons xlvi, l and cxi; Mansi XXVI, cc. 507-8, 535.
10. Palermo (1388); Mansi XXVI, cc. 745-6.
11. London (1399), canon liv; Mansi XXVI, c. 933.
12. Konstanz (1415) *Avisamenta ... in loco Reformatorii*, caps. xxvii, xxxvii; Mansi XXVIII, cc. 292-3, 299.
13. Konstanz (1415) *Avisamenta pro Reformatione congrua facienda*, Liber III, tituli i-v; Mansi XXVIII, cc. 316-22.
14. Konstanz (1415), *De Rebus Mattheæ Grabon*, Mansi XXVIII, cc. 386-94.
15. Paris (1429), cap. v; Mansi XXVIII, c. 1099.
16. Riga (*c.* 1429), Mansi XXVIII, cc. 1115-8.
17. Venice (1438), canons xiv-xvii; Mansi XXXI, cc. 311-332.
18. Provinciale Anglicanum (1509) Liber III, *De vita et Honestate Clericorum*; Mansi XXXI, cc. 390-431.
19. Bowker, *Secular Clergy of the Diocese of Lincoln*, p. 176.
20. Bradshaw & Wordsworth, *Statutes of Lincoln Cathedral* III, pp. 361, 414-5.
21. Ibid., I, p. 410; III, p. 160.
22. Hamilton Thompson, *Cathedral Churches*, chapter V.
23. Dugdale, *Monasticon*, VI, pp. 1255-65.
24. Martène, *De Antiquis Ecclesiæ Ritibus*, II, pp. 183-4.
25. Ibid., II, 184-5 (Boulogne); Bradshaw and Wordsworth *Statutes of Lincoln Cathedral* I, p. 98 (Lincoln).
26. Harrison, *Life in a Medieval College*.
27. Richards, *The Vicars Choral of York Minster*.
28. Sparrow Simpson, *Registrum*, pp. 330-39, also in *Archaeologia* XL (1866), pp. 165-200.
29. Dugdale, *Monasticon*, VI, pp. 1183-4.
30. Ibid., VI, pp. 1457, 1465-6.
31. Sparrow Simpson, in *Archaeologia* LII p. 145.
32. Sparrow Simpson, *Registrum*, xxxix-xlv, pp. 217-36.
33. Ibid., p. 248 sq.
34. See Cook, *English Collegiate Churches*, chapter 5, and P. H. Cullum, 'Medieval Colleges and Charity' in Burgess and Heale, *English College*, pp. 140-53.
35. Dugdale, *Monasticon*, VI, pp. 1334-7.
36. Ibid., VI, pp. 1308-12.
37. Burgess and Heale, *English College*, pp. 144.

38. Dugdale, *Monasticon*, VI, pp. 1315–16.
39. Ibid., VI, pp. 1368–9.
40. Mai, *850–Jahre Kollegiatstift zu Regensburg*, pp. 67–97.
41. Heyen, *Das Stift St Simeon in Trier*, p. 302 sq.
42. Raines, *The Rectors of Manchester*.
43. Cook, *Collegiate Churches*, chapter 8.
44. Burgess and Heale, *English College*, p. 117.
45. See H. Brown, 'Secular Colleges in Late Medieval Scotland', in Burgess and Heale, *English College*, pp. 44–66.
46. Ibid., pp. 107–9.
47. Hamilton Thompson, *Hospital of the Newarke*, pp. 139–40, and 143–96 (bishop Longland's Visitation of 1525).
48. B Bioul (ed.), 'Vincennes', *Dossiers d'Archéologie* no. 289 (2003–4), pp. 16–17.
49. Dugdale, *Monasticon*, VI, pp. 1349–51.
50. Saul, *St George's Chapel Windsor*; see also Dugdale, *Monasticon*, VI, pp. 1353–6.
51. Ibid., VI, p. 1458.
52. Ibid., VI, pp. 1411–15.
53. Ibid., VI, pp. 1417–23.
54. Ibid., VI, pp. 1401–11, translation in Boden, *The History of Tong Church, College, and Castle*.
55. R. J. Stonor, *Stonor*, Newport 1951, p. 88.
56. Hamilton Thompson, *St Mary in the Newarke, Leicester*.
57. Ibid., pp. 143–96.
58. Ibid., pp. 151–2.
59. Ibid., pp. 187–8.
60. Ibid., p. 190.
61. Goodall, *God's House at Ewelme*.
62. Statutes in Dugdale, *Monasticon*, VI, pp. 738–47.
63. A. Kenny, *The English Hospice in Rome*, Venerabile Sexcentenary Issue, 1962.
64. M. Williamson, 'Musicians within Collegiate and Parochial Communities', in Burgess and Heale, *English College*, pp. 180–95.
65. Dugdale, *Monasticon*, VI, pp. 1380–81.
66. Lengthy statutes in *Statutes of the Colleges of Oxford*, vol. I.
67. Richard Dawkins, *The God Delusion*, 2006, p. 402. The author concludes, 'Even I feel a twinge of guilt, as a member of that Fellowship, for a trust betrayed.'
68. Moraw, in Crusius, *Weltlichen Kollegiatstift*, pp. 270–97.
69. A. Wood, *City of Oxford*, II, pp. 503–4.
70. Liège (1287), tit. XII, cap. 5; Mansi XXIV, c. 935.
71. Mainz (1310), Mansi XXV, c. 325; Tarragona (1317), I and II, Mansi XXV, cc. 627–8.

Chapter 11

The Age of Reform, and the Wars of Religion

From the early fifteenth century to the mid seventeenth the Catholic Church experienced an unprecedented period of reform, which concentrated on the renewal of the older religious orders, the appearance of new ones, of new types, and the development of a strong lay spirituality. The Church set herself against the influence of the rich and powerful, and against the growing capitalist system of an economy based on usury. As a result the rich and powerful banded together with the capitalists to oppose these reforms, and eventually tore away half of Europe from the unity of the Church, while institutionalizing the abuses. Against the background of the wars of religion released by this situation, we can see the emergence of powerful new forms of the common life, which provided a basis for the successful consolidation of the reforms in Catholic countries, and the extension of the Church to new continents.

In Catholic countries the concept of the collegiate church remained unassailed as a useful element in the commonwealth. Necessary reforms were carried out in order to ensure that they remained so, but the increasing trend towards royal absolutism and national centralization meant that they were liable to be completely under the control of the secular patrons. This was not always detrimental: sometimes lay patrons were vigorous in promoting reforms which the clergy, left to themselves, might have resisted. For example, Francis I made a *Réformation* of the Sainte Chapelle in 1520, imposing a new set of statutes, and deploring the lack of charity among the members. Now every canon was to live in community with his chaplain and clerk, whom they could choose and present to the treasurer for appointment. Thus a number of small communities was formed within the greater whole. To qualify for their daily stipend, each had to be in choir before the Epistle of High Mass, and by the *Gloria Patri* of the first psalm of each Office. Three bedells or *huissiers* were appointed, presumably to supervise this attendance. The two best choristers each year were granted scholarships to Navarre College. All were to keep perpetual residence within the enclosure, and could not leave Paris for more than three days without permission.[1]

Fifteenth-Century Congregations

A new development was the notion of 'congregations' of communities. Hitherto each community or college had been completely autonomous, though subject to the authority of the local bishop. Different colleges could have ties of friendship or mutual support, but there were no juridical structures to link them together. During the thirteenth century first monks and then Augustinian canons were grouped into national or regional 'congregations' with a degree of independence from episcopal control and a central structure adequate to supervise the different separate houses. This idea was eventually extended to secular communities. Existing colleges were never federated into such congregations, but new reform movements were characterized by forming congregations from the start. This meant that each house within the congregation followed the same rule of life, and that through periodical meetings of some sort their affairs could be directed and their fidelity to the rule ensured.

The first reformed congregation of secular priests seems to have been that of San Giorgio in Alga. A group of Venetian clergy, including Antonio Correr and Gabriele Condulmar (Gondelmaire), resolved to dedicate themselves to God and live in community. They began meeting in the Palazzo Correr, before moving to the Lido, then a quiet and unfrequented island, suitable for prayer and meditation. They were subsequently offered a decayed Augustinian priory, San Giorgio in Alga, and in 1404 Boniface IX had it changed from a monastery into a collegiate church. There was a community of seventeen members, including priests, deacons and sub-deacons. When Antonio Correr's uncle became pope, as Gregory XII, one of the number, Lorenzo Giustiniani, became Patriarch of Venice, and both Correr and Condulmar were created cardinals. Despite this, community life continued to be marked by great simplicity and charity, combining a deep spirituality similar to that of the *Devotio Moderna* with a life of voluntary poverty. Several other collegiate churches in Italy were associated with it to form the Congregation of San Giorgio, including one in Rome (San Salvatore in Lauro). The habit was a white cassock, and a blue gown with wide sleeves. At the first general chapter, in 1424, St Lorenzo Giustiniani was elected superior general. He added to the constitutions, and made various regulations, which led to him being thought of afterwards as the real founder of the Congregation. Condulmar afterwards became pope, as Eugenius IV, while Correr died and was buried at San Giorgio in 1445. It appears that the congregation did not remain long in its strict and reformed state, but since many of the members were Venetian nobles they took to living quite independently, 'walking through the city accompanied by various bandits and cut-purses', till in 1568 St Pius V effectively put an end to the congregation as an institute of seculars by making them take vows of poverty, under the Rule of St Augustine. Even so, they did not reform, and they were eventually suppressed by Clement IX in 1668.[2] An offshoot was formed in Sicily, founded by Enrique di Simeone at Palermo in 1433. They had several communities, and lived in great austerity, walking barefoot or in wooden sandals. Another similar congregation arose in the territory of Genoa, in Parma, and there was possibly also one in the Low Countries.[3]

A more successful and lasting reform inspired by that of San Giorgio was the Congregation of St John the Evangelist in Portugal, founded by John of Vicenza in the reign of King John I. After false starts in Lisbon and Porto, John of Vicenza and a few companions were offered a decayed monastery near Braga, where they began the Common Life in 1425. They adopted the way of life of the Secular Canons of San Giorgio in Algha, with their blue and white habit. The congregation was given papal recognition by Martin V, under the title of 'Good Men of Villar de Frades', but after they took responsibility for the monastery of St John the Evangelist near Lisbon, Eugenius IV renamed them after that Apostle. The congregation grew rapidly and spread throughout Portugal, until by the early eighteenth century they had fourteen communities, and were still marked by their strict austerity, continuing to thrive long after the San Giorgio group had been disbanded. There were also canonesses associated with the congregation, who like the men did not take solemn vows, but only a promise to observe the rule, and a vow of poverty, chastity and obedience for only as long as they remained in the institute, which they were free to leave at their own choice.[4]

These congregations of secular canons mark something new in

the story of the common life of the secular clergy. Congregations comprising a number of different houses, in more than one diocese, inevitably took on something of the nature of a religious order, but as long as they refrained from taking solemn vows, they remained technically seculars. The papal recognition extended to them meant that they had a valuable degree of independence from the local bishops and even the local kings, unlike the older type of collegiate church. The very different fates of the two congregations discussed illustrates the opposite extremes to which all religious institutes are prone: those of San Giorgio rapidly became decadent and had to be suppressed, those of St John kept up their first fervour to a remarkable extent, praised for their austerity more than three centuries after their foundation. As 'Congregations of Canons Secular' they seem to be something of an anomaly, and no further such congregations were founded, but they were the forerunners of the Clerks Regular which were to become such a feature of the sixteenth century, as well as of the various institutes of secular clergy which flourished in the seventeenth century and beyond.

Brethren of the Common Life

An important reform movement, which does not seem to have affected England directly, was the Brethren of the Common Life, which thrived in the Low Countries and neighbouring states.[5] It originated in the *Devotio Moderna* of Gerard Groote, a prebendary of Paris and Aachen, who experienced a conversion in 1374, and came under the influence of Jan Ruysbroeck, the mystical prior of the Augustinian house of Groenendaal. Ordained deacon in 1380, Groote began to preach a lay spirituality, of strongly Augustinian character, and gathered disciples around him. There emerged three classes of followers: the devout laity who came under Groote's direction, the brothers and sisters of the common life, and the fully vowed Augustinian canons and canonesses, members of the Congregation of Windesheim. As Groote died, in 1384, he recommended the Augustinian life for those called to it, though without cancelling the existing forms of unvowed Common Life. Regular life at Windesheim and its filiations was not dissimilar to that in the houses of the Common Life, but canons or canonesses took proper religious vows. There was a strong tendency for brethren or sisters of the Common Life to move on to join an Augustinian house, and many of the secular community houses did eventually become Augustininan priories.

The secular clergy and laity of the Common Life began to form communities in around 1382, earning their living by copying and binding books, and teaching children. They did not maintain their own churches, but attended Mass and the Office in their local parishes or in monasteries, so in this sense they differ greatly from secular colleges. By 1396 the norm had emerged that each community should contain at least four priests and eight clerics, with an unspecified number of laymen or women. Obedience was due to the community as a whole, and there was a common purse, although individuals did not take vows. They practised discursive meditation as well as attending the liturgy, and ate together, either with readings, or the discussion of questions of theology or morals over the table. Preaching, in the vernacular, was in the form of familiar discourse on the Word of God, and lay members were encouraged to give exhortations.

During the fifteenth century a great many more such houses were founded for secular clergy and layfolk. They called themselves by a bewildering number of names, testified by their common seals, but it is clear that they thought of themselves as simply a particular form of secular college. That of Herrenberg, founded in 1481, for example, describes itself as *Capitulum canonicorum, presbyterorum et clericorum secularium in commune viventium sub uno dormitorio et refectorio in obedientia unius prepositi.* the 'Chapter of secular canons, priests and clerics living in common in a single dormitory and refectory in obedience to a single provost'. The name of chapter, college or collegiate church is often used, as at Marienthal the *Collegiata ecclesia presbyterorum et clericorum communiter viventium beatae Mariae virginis prope Gysenheim,* the 'Collegiate church of priests and clerics living in common, of the Blessed Virgin Mary near Geisenheim'. Others used Low German names, like *Kappenherren* (the gentlemen who wear the cappa) *Kogelherren* (hoods) *Der clercken hus* (clerics' house), *Kappenhuis* (cappa house) etc. At Kulm they were known as the *Haus der Lolharder,* which raises the spectre of possible links with heretical groups. In fact the movement seems to have been scrupulously orthodox, but it did arouse suspicions from bishops and from members of established religious orders.[6]

Members of existing collegiate churches took up the *Devotio Moderna* with enthusiasm, such as Gabriel Biel from Erfurt who joined a contemplative house in the Groote tradition in 1470 and wrote in praise of the Common Life.[7] From the vowed Augustinian community at Windesheim came the *Imitation of Christ,* the best-known exemplar of the *Devotio Moderna*; from the houses of the

Common Life came influences that helped to shape sixteenth-century Europe, for good or for ill.

Confraternities and Archconfraternities

Meanwhile throughout Europe there grew a widespread movement which was to result in some very important developments in the story of the common life of the secular clergy, though it was not in itself a clerical movement. This was the multiplication of fraternities or associations of lay men and women, together with some ecclesiastics, banded together in a fellowship of prayer, and with some particular work of mercy. They are particularly noted in Italy, where large numbers of these fraternities were founded.[8] Some of them were specifically penitential, some more practically involved in hospital work. In a number of cases they developed common residences, at least for the unmarried members and the clerics, though without formal establishment as colleges. Often little record survives, since they were not always legally incorporated, but all of them were to some extent capable of owning property in common. One is left with the impression that late medieval Catholicism laid a very strong emphasis on the sanctification of the laity, and that between guilds, fraternities and other associations, opportunities for collective prayer and charity were far more accessible than they are today.

Of the many Italian fraternities, two in particular demand attention: the Oratory of Divine Love, and the Archconfraternity of Charity. The former originated in Genoa, among the circle of that astonishing woman St Catherine of Genoa, and was introduced to Rome in 1517 by her kinsman Ettore Vernaccia. The brothers were drawn from a wide social circle, but stood on conditions of absolute equality within the circle. They met regularly for prayer, including a weekly chapter of faults and penitential exercises with 'no other end than to root and plant in our own hearts divine love, that is to say charity'.[9] The practical expression of this charity was their ministry in the hospital of San Giacomo 'degli Incurabili'. Part of their rule was secrecy about membership and work, so they also joined an existing fraternity, that of Santa Maria del Popolo and San Giacomo, in order to conceal their identity.[10] Presumably, like many fraternity members, they wore hoods over their faces. The Oratory of Divine Love was not to have any long existence in Rome: it was dispersed in the sack of 1527, but it left a permanent legacy in the new society founded by two of its clerical members,

Gaetano da Thiene and Pietro Carafa. They set out to reform the life of the secular clergy, by giving them an example of total dedication, austerity and poverty. What they founded was indeed a vowed religious order, the Order of Clerks Regular, popularly known as the Theatines, but the example they gave did have a great influence on the congregations of secular priests which were to emerge later in the century. The fraternity of San Giacomo survived the sack, and among its later members was enrolled one 'Philippo Neri da Santo Ludoico fiorentino' (Philip Neri, from the parish of St Louis, a Florentine) shortly before 1548.[11]

The Archconfraternity of Charity was another predominantly lay association, which also survived the sack, and incorporated a few survivors of the Divine Love. In 1524 they were granted the use of the tiny church built on the site of St Jerome's house, and known afterwards as San Girolamo della Carità. Here they installed a group of 'the best priests possible, for the service of the same', who were to live in community and serve the fraternity. They had no superior among themselves, other than seniority, but were governed by a *presidente* appointed by the Confraternity, assisted by four deputies entrusted by the Confraternity with temporal administration.[12] Only in 1558, after this curious arrangement of a community of priests being ruled by a lay external superior had proved impossible, was a clerical superior appointed, the first being the engaging retired bandit Buonsignore Cacciaguerra.

The Reaction against the Reforms

The widespread movement of reform which had made such progress through most of Europe by the end of the fifteenth century unfortunately failed to penetrate to Rome itself, and the papal court remained notoriously subordinate to the powerful noble, mercantile and banking families of Italy. Only one noble Spanish family managed to intrude itself into the papacy, the Borja, and they made common cause with the Medici, who tyrannized over Florence for so long, to act decisively against the great Dominican reformer Girolamo Savonarola. The legacy of Savonarola, and the Convento di San Marco in Florence where he had lived, was to bear great fruit in the next generation, but in the meantime the worldly court of Rome was so subject to the rivalries of the great families that it was utterly unable to act efficiently against the sudden revolt that sprang up in Germany and Switzerland. Here the independent-minded princes of Germany and the crafty bankers of Zürich supported a new religion that granted them the power they craved over the Church, and tore half of Europe away from Christendom. In the new sects that sprang up, all the abuses and corruptions that had marred the Church in the Middle Ages found themselves institutionalized. Usury, formerly condemned as a crime against God and man, became the mainspring of the new capitalist system, which enabled Dutch and Scots merchants to carve out vast mercantile empires for themselves in far-flung parts of the world. The tendency of kings, nobles and squires to impose their candidates on bishoprics, abbeys and parishes was enshrined in law, and unsuitable youths of noble or gentle birth were foisted into church positions, often held in plurality, simply as sources of revenue for the great families concerned. Clergy who had defied the age-old rule of continence were rewarded by permission to marry and start families, which rapidly became ecclesiastical dynasties.

The effect on all types of clerical community was devastating. Monasticism was destroyed by the new religion, partly because it represented a clear protest against a way of life dedicated to money and worldly power, and partly because its international organization was incompatible with the organization of sects on purely national lines. Excuses were put forward for the suppression of monastic orders, but they were transparently shallow, and can have deceived no one at the time, though they have certainly deceived many since. The common pretext is that it was a bad thing for much wealth to be held in the hands of religious orders, but this rings false when one remembers that all the confiscated wealth was concentrated into the hands of a few powerful families, who made no pretence of maintaining the charitable works for which the monasteries had held the wealth in the first place. Accusations of immorality against monks and nuns, whether justified or not, hardly excuse the confiscation of their property to enrich the corrupt and decadent aristocracy of Europe, whose morals were certainly worse than anything alleged against the monks.

The monasteries fell into the hands of the kings, and the kings squandered in a few years the revenues which had supported a third of the realm, and the kings looked elsewhere for more institutions to plunder. So the colleges were to fall. In Lutheran countries there does not seem to have been any systematic suppression of colleges, or for that matter monasteries. Some survived in a modified form for centuries. However the introduction of married clergy struck at the heart of community life: the canons, *Domherren*, of Lutheran cathedrals still appear on their tombstones in their square caps and ruffs, but if they occasionally dined together they returned after dinner to their families, and without the regular round of the Divine Office to keep them in residence, the practice of pluralism became institutionalized. Curiously in some cathedrals the canons agreed to divide into two chapters, Catholic and Protestant, and shared the building between them. At Halberstadt, for instance, the Lutherans retained the cathedral church, while the Catholics had the *Liebfrauenkirche* at the other end of the long open space, lined on both sides by the canons' houses, the *Kurien*.[13] Yet although the Catholic canons kept up their round of devotions until the Revolution, it seems unlikely that any real community life survived even among them.

In Calvinist countries the revolt was much more violent; cathedrals and collegiate churches were sacked, and usually demolished, and the revenues confiscated. With an utter abhorrence of intercessory prayer for the dead, and the repudiation of all charitable works (as 'works of supererogation'), there was no place at all for communities of clergy. Throughout the northern Low Countries, Switzerland, and Scotland most collegiate churches disappeared at once; in the Protestant states of Germany, and in the kingdoms of Denmark and Sweden, they faded away gracefully. An exception was made in Scotland for the colleges attached to the universities. Unlike in England, education was valued, and the *First Book of Discipline* explicitly maintained the universities and their colleges. In the final 'reformation' of 1579, the faculties were divided among the colleges, thus bringing about the modern understanding of the word 'college'. At St Andrews, for instance, St Salvator's was to teach Arts and Medicine, St Leonard's taught Philosophy and Law, and St Mary's became (and remains) the school of Divinity.[14] Colleges thus survived as institutions, but they ceased to be communities of clergy with an intercessory purpose.

Suppression in England

The story is more familiar in England. Henry VIII, after a campaign of trickery, torture, and propaganda, had seized the monastic properties, and squandered the lot within ten years. All that remained in England were the innumerable types of secular corporations: the colleges, chantries, schools, hospitals, almshouses, hermitages and oratories. No one had hitherto raised any complaints against colleges as an institution: for centuries occasional satirists and grumblers had murmured against monks and friars and mocked them, but neither Lollards not Humanists had ever thought of attacking colleges as such, which so obviously performed useful functions for both Church and State. The colleges themselves sat secure in the knowledge that they were favoured by the people and (so they thought) the government as well.

Despite this, Henry VIII began the process of dismantling colleges and chantries, as well as pruning the revenues of cathedrals, including the ones he himself had just endowed. With few exceptions, the collegiate clergy had all meekly signed the Act of Supremacy, so in effect recognizing the absolute authority of the monarch over their religion, though it can hardly have occurred to any of them how he was about to use that supremacy. Scarisbrick estimates that even before the 1545 Chantries Act Henry had already 'shaken off a quarter of the crop'.[15] Some of the greatest colleges, such as St Martin le Grand, Westbury on Trym, Tattershall and Ottery St Mary, fell by 'voluntary' surrender of their property and rights to the Crown, in exactly the same way as the greater monasteries. However the Act of 1545 was intended to put an end to every one of them, not excepting the colleges of Oxford and Cambridge. All were declared forfeit to the Crown, but there was time for very few more to go before the old tyrant himself was dead. Had he survived a few months more, England would have had no universities, no schools, no hospitals and no almshouses.

No one could believe such a thing was about to happen, and colleges continued to operate as if nothing was wrong. At Fotheringay for instance, up to the very end new members were being recruited, both clergy and boys; new music was still being commissioned in August 1547, and a glazier was hard at work on new windows while the king's visitors were actually on the premises.[16] At Newarke, Leicester, a new prebendary was appointed in March 1546–7, even though the first Chantries Act had already prompted Edward Seymour, Earl of Hertford, to make representations to the Crown for the property. The second Act, passed at Christmas 1547 by the same Seymour, now Duke of Somerset and Lord Protector, decreed that all chantries and colleges were to be abolished by Easter 1548, though in the event Newarke was given to the Marquess of Dorset, not to Seymour himself.[17]

Henry's death meant that a new Act was necessary, and this time there was sufficient interest to rescue the colleges of Windsor, Eton, Westminster, and those in Oxford and Cambridge, which were specifically excluded from the Act of 1547. But by now some powerful landlords had begun taking the law into their own hands and simply seizing colleges, chantries and their endowments on the grounds that their ancestors (whether by birth or purchase) had granted these endowments in the first place. That seems to be how the Earls of Arundel regained possession of Arundel College.

Little attempt was ever made to justify the seizure, by peer or king, other than the king's pressing need for money. The official excuse was that in every case the founders of colleges and chantries had requested prayers for the repose of their souls, before going on to detail duties of public worship, education, provision of hospital or almshouse. Since prayer for the dead was now illegal, that was sufficient to condemn all the institutions unheard. There was no propaganda exercise to blacken the reputations of collegiate clergy as there had been against the monks and nuns. Indeed even the proponents of the new religion had thought collegiate churches a good thing, and a few new ones had been founded out of the wreckage of the monasteries. The two large new colleges founded by Henry VIII out of despoiled monasteries, Burton and Thornton, both went very quickly. He had promised that many of the larger monasteries would be preserved as colleges, to continue their works of charity (firmly under the king's thumb), but Henry's promises to his people were as short-lived as his marriage vows. Matthew Parker, Master of Stoke-by-Clare College, wrote to Queen Katherine Parr with a glowing recommendation of the College at Fotheringay, praising the work it did in educating the poor and caring for the sick and for pilgrims. He also reminded her that, as it was within her patronage, she was entitled to free accommodation there. Of Stoke College itself he wrote that they 'distributed alms and hospitality daily, instructed in the word of God and taught children grammar, singing and playing'.[18]

But all was of no avail. Everything was destroyed, and in the process every village school in England was closed. In a few cases local people banded together to buy the premises, and raise the money to start the schools and almshouses up again, which they were permitted to do if they bribed the Crown and named Edward VI as the founder. As Hamilton Thompson comments,

> The specious proposals of the act to augment the endowments of preachers and further education out of the revenues of the forfeited lands had no very far-reaching result; and the little that was done for education, apart from the gift of the royal name to schools which Edward VI can hardly be said to have founded, bears no comparison with the marketing of lands and rents with which the Crown met its

current expenses and founders of estates prepared their future fortunes.[19]

There were local protests, such as that delivered by the people of Oxfordshire in 1547, not only on behalf of their ancestors, but on the practical point that there were so many 'howseling people' that the parish priests alone would be unable to administer Communion to them without the assistance of the chantry priests.[20] Like the much more widespread protests and open rebellions of 1549, this attracted nothing but contempt and savage repression from the Government. Official propaganda, which can have deceived no one at the time, has stood the test of centuries.

There were curious consequences in some cases. At Stonor the little household college had been incorporated, and was therefore suppressed. As a result the 300 acres of beechwood which lies in Stonor Park directly behind the house, was seized because it had been made over for the support of the chaplains. It was eventually granted to the Dean and Canons of Windsor, one of those very few colleges that had been suffered to survive in the new religion, and the Stonors were obliged to buy them back, which they were finally able to do in 1794.[21]

Apart from the ones explicitly excluded from the Act, a very few escaped, apparently by accident or oversight. The great Welsh college of Abergwili was transferred to Brecon in 1541 and gradually mutated into a public school. Colleges at Heytesbury in Wiltshire, and Middleham in Yorkshire lingered on until the Cathedrals Act of 1840 put a stop to them. The one at St Endellion in Cornwall escaped even the nineteenth-century dissolution, and still exists in a nominal form. In other cases the bedesmen survived, on a fraction of the original income, as almoners, though forbidden to pray for the founders as they were originally intended to do. Some of the unincorporated communities of 'portioners' also survive in some form, though in all these cases all trace of community life for the clergy has long vanished.[22]

A number of the largest colleges were refounded, and in some cases continue to exist. At Manchester, the last Warden, George Collier, had courageously refused to acknowledge the royal supremacy, but was suffered to remain in post unmolested while the tyrant devoted his attention to the monasteries. When suppression eventually came in 1547, Collier was duly deprived of his orders for refusing the supremacy, but still gained a pension of thirty-four pounds, five shillings. He lived quietly in retirement until Queen Mary refounded the college and recalled him as warden, in which post he had the good fortune to die before the Queen. His successor, Lawrence Vaux, refused to acknowledge Queen Elizabeth as head of the Church, and was duly deprived in 1558; after some time in exile he returned to England to work in secret among the recusants, but was caught and died in prison in 1583. (He wrote a catechism of great educational value, and a chasuble which he owned is now in the possession of Liverpool metropolitan Cathedral.) The college was not again suppressed, but became one of the few non-cathedral colleges in Protestant England.[23]

Wolverhampton, Southwell and Whittington Colleges were also refounded by Queen Mary, and the first two continued to exist as collegiate churches, joined in 1604 by Ripon. However since the fellows were now permitted to marry, the common life rapidly disappeared; the college buildings were sold, and fellowships became unashamed sinecures. Eventually Ripon and Manchester became cathedrals in 1836 and 1847 respectively, whereas Southwell was dissolved in 1841 and only restored as a cathedral in 1884. Wolverhampton was suppressed in 1848; Whittington College was the only one to be suppressed by Elizabeth I. In return, Westminster Abbey, after the brief revival of monastic life in 1556, was re-converted into a collegiate church by the same queen, in 1560.

In the cathedrals the corporate bodies mostly survived the turmoil, though with drastically reduced revenues. The corporations of vicars lingered on. At York Edward VI sold away their home, the Bedern, but they bought it back, and until 1574 continued to dine together in the old hall. Chapters of canons remained in possession of much of their original endowments, though residence requirements were effectively abolished, and many canons were permanent absentees, pluralists, doing no duty whatever, but living in comfort on the revenues originally provided to support daily worship. Yet another crying abuse, which medieval popes and councils had so often protested against, became an institution. It was only in the nineteenth century that the Cathedrals Act of 1840 abolished prebends and dissolved most of the remaining colleges, and, after Trollope's satires on cathedral sinecures, reformers abolished these sinecures, reducing the title of 'canon' to a purely honorary distinction, save for a very few in each cathedral who survived as the governing body, and did, indeed, reside in the close. Yet at the same time genuine reformers like John Henry Newman and Richard Hurrell Froude corresponded on the idea of reviving colleges of unmarried priests to serve in cities.[24]

The colleges of Oxford and Cambridge were the last to retain a real community life. Escaping suppression by the skin of their teeth, they were given encouragement by Queen Mary, who endowed new lectureships and built new lecture halls to replace those burnt by the Edwardian Taliban. During her reign benefactors founded two new Oxford colleges, Trinity and St John's. The statutes of the latter, extending to over a hunded pages of closely printed Latin, make it clear that the founder had every intention of creating something in full continuity with the medieval model.

The purpose of the college was 'to the honour of the most holy and individual Trinity, and the glory of the whole court of heaven, and for the increase of the Christian religion'. There was to be a president, wearing surplice and grey almuce, fifty scholars or fellows divided into three grades by seniority, three priest chaplains, three unmarried minor clerics, and six choristers. The scholars were to have a three-year probation, and to be chosen from 'poor and needy students, clerics, already given the first clerical tonsure, able to sing, no less than fourteen nor more than nineteen years old'. After studying the arts, a quarter of them were to take to the Law, and one might study medicine: he alone was exempted from the obligation of being ordained priest within three years of taking the MA. All were to dress and live as clerics, to attend Mass and the evening Antiphon every day, and to celebrate the entire Divine Office in chapel on Sundays and many feastdays. On weekdays when the scholars were studying, the Divine Office was kept up by the chaplains, minor clerics and choristers. The intentions were to pray for the Founder, Sir Thomas White, and his two wives, all relations and benefactors, and for all the faithful departed.

Members of the college slept together in chambers, each of which had a senior fellow as monitor, 'so that the seniors may keep a good eye on their chambermates, and give them good advice'. (Here we find the last echo of Chrodegang's similar requirement for the seniors and juniors to be accommodated together.) In order to maintain the proper clerical demeanour, members of the college are strictly prohibited from keeping dogs of any sort, or ferrets, or any species of hunting bird, or song bird (they are listed at length), nor may they play games of chance, cards, tennis or football, 'or any other sort of game which is illegal and prohibited by canon or civil law'.[25] (The author has done his best to abide by these obligations, was ordained priest within three years of taking his MA, and has never kept a ferret.)

St John's College was founded in 1556. Two years later all the liturgical commemorations the founder had hoped for came to an end, and, like all the other university colleges, St John's had to conform to the new religion. However the obligation of celibacy was not lifted, so that fellows and scholars of all the colleges were able to maintain much more of a community life than would have otherwise been possible. All were expected to attend the new forms of common prayer, morning and evening, and all continued to dine together in Hall. Studying at Oxford or Cambridge was still seen as the obvious preparation for church ministry, and any fellow could be ordained with no further qualification. Nearly all of them, therefore, were clergymen, praying, eating, and living in common. They took an oath to observe the statutes as long as they remained members of their colleges, but since, as ever, there was no obligation to remain for life, it became common for them to resign their fellowships on marriage, and to expect the college to present them to a suitable 'college living', a country parsonage where they could bring up their families in an appropriate style.

As the centuries passed rising standards meant that the senior members, the fellows, tended to have bedrooms to themselves, and extra accommodation was built as increasingly colleges filled up with rich young men who paid their own way as 'commoners', and were not very inclined to take orders. The poor scholars were seen as inferior, lower class youths who were glad of a free education but had to behave almost like servants, while the commoners, 'gentleman commoners', and nobles dined on high table and treated the university as a country club.

Nineteenth-century radicals like Froude and Newman set themselves against the gentleman commoners, and encouraged the scholars. More demanding examinations improved standards all round, and a considerable degree of the clerical common life remained in force. However after Newman left Oxford, the Royal Commissioners descended on both universities, determined to drag them into the nineteenth century. During the third quarter of the century the colleges were secularized, the number of clergymen drastically reduced, and most significantly the fellows were permitted to marry. Tradition and inertia meant that for decades fellows continued to attend chapel, and to dine together in Hall, leaving their wives to eat cold shape[26] alone in North Oxford, but gradually the fashions of the modern world intruded until by the early twenty-first century very little indeed remained of the forms of clerical common life even in the home of impossible loyalties and lost causes.

Notes
1. Morand, *Ste-Chapelle*, pp. 90, 109, 159, 184.
2. S. Tramontin, 'Canonici Secolari di San Giorgio in Alga', in G. Pellicia and G. Rocca, *Dizionario degli Istituti di Perfezione*, Rome 1975, II, cc. 154–8, and Helyot, *Histoire des Ordres*, Vol 2, pp. 363–69.
3. Ibid., 2, pp. 370–1.
4. Ibid., 2, pp. 371–6.
5. See Hyma, *The Christian Renaissance*.
6. Leesch, Persoon and Weiler, *Monasticon Fratrum Vitae Communis*.
7. Crusius, *Weltlichen Kollegiatstift*, pp. 298–322.
8. See S. Ditchfield, *Liturgy, Sanctity and History in Tridentine Italy* (Cambridge University Press, 1995).
9. Ponelle & Bordet, *St Philip Neri*, p. 74.
10. Cistellini, *San Filippo Neri*, I, pp. 27–8.
11. Ibid., I, p. 28.
12. Ponelle & Bordet, *St Philip Neri*, pp. 169, 184.
13. P. Findeisen, *Halberstadt, Dom, Liebfrauenkirche, Domplatz* (Königstein, 1995), p. 12.
14. R. G. Cant, *The University of St Andrews* (St Andrews, 1992), pp. 51–60.
15. Scarisbrick, 'Henry VIII and the Dissolution of the Secular Colleges', p. 52.
16. Burgess and Heale, *English College*, p. 264.
17. HamiltonThompson, *Newarke, Leicester*, pp. 208–9.
18. Scarisbrick, 'Henry VIII and the Dissolution', p. 57.
19. Hamilton Thompson, *Newarke, Leicester*, p. 209.
20. J. Stonor, *Stonor*, Newport, 1951, p. 230.
21. Ibid., p. 263.
22. Jeffery, *Collegiate Churches*, p. 456.
23. Raines, *The Rectors of Manchester*, pp. 55–75.
24. J. H. Newman, *Letters & Diaries* IV, ed. I. Ker and T. Gornall (Oxford University Press, 1980), pp. 38, 40.
25. Statutes in vol. 3 of *Statutes of the Colleges of Oxford*.
26. 'How curious it would be if the Day of Judgment came at a quarter to eight on a Sunday evening, to find all the dons carousing in Hall, and all their wives eating cold shape at home.' Ronald Knox, *Let Dons Delight* (London, Sheed and Ward, 1939), p. 1. 'Cold shape' meaning blancmange.

Chapter 12

The Glorious Catholic Reformation

While northern Europe was in turmoil, and community life for the clergy had been largely abolished along with much of Catholic doctrine and practice, the Council of Trent marked a significant moment in the never-ending process of reform, which not only answered the quibbles of the northern European rebels, but more importantly set the course for a remarkable expansion of the Church through the Americas, Africa and Asia. Among many topics treated, the council did not neglect the perennial theme of the life and manners of the clergy. At the end of each session, after the great doctrinal decrees, there were discipliniary measures, classed as 'reform decrees', many of which deal directly with the way the clergy should behave and live.

Decrees of the Council of Trent

The decree most immediately relevant to our subject is that of the twenty-third session, on the sacrament of order. Interestingly it still provides for married minor clerics, repeating the existing legislation that to benefit from their status they must continue to wear the tonsure and clerical dress, and that they may perform the functions of their order if no celibate minor clerics are available.[1] On the other hand no one is in future to be ordained to the minor orders unless they show aptitude for proceeding in due course to major, so in effect married minor clergy must have died out very rapidly. Although the council stated its intention to revive the functions of the minor orders, in practice the institution of seminaries meant that minor orders were only conferred on young students on their way to the priesthood, and they were never seen to exercise any ministry outside the confines of the seminary. For the seminary was Trent's greatest innovation: in every diocese one or more seminaries were to be provided for the training of youths and their preparation for the priesthood. This was to become the normal path to holy orders, so that except for members of religious orders, clergy could no longer be trained in the communities in which they would subsequently serve. The council does not actually state that collegiate churches could no longer recruit boys and train them up for their own communities, but that in effect is what happened.

Several disciplinary decrees of earlier sessions refer to colleges of secular clergy, which continued to exist in most European countries, and were being founded in the Americas as the young churches there began to take on the forms of settled life. There were strong prohibitions on pluralism, and on non-residence,[2] and instructions that canons and other beneficiaries must perform their liturgical duties in person, and so collect their daily distribution.[3] The most significant chapter prohibits dignities or canonries to which the care of souls is attached being conferred on anyone under the age of twenty-four, and insists that those on whom they are conferred are to be ordained immediately if not already in major orders. Positions without the cure of souls are not to be granted to those under twenty-two.[4] This eliminated the boy canons in minor orders who had formed a significant part of college life, and eventually led to the conclusion that positions in cathedral chapters or in collegiate churches became senior appointments for long-experienced priests. Earlier specific legislation for collegiate churches includes the provision that at least one member was to be qualified to lecture in Sacred Scripture, that at least a third of the revenues should be reserved for daily distribution to those who were actually present in choir, and that diocesan bishops should have the right and duty to conduct canonical visitations of all colleges and fraternities, except royal free chapels.[5]

While the council legislated in the usual terms for the reform of the life of the clergy, it did not repeat the recommendations of earlier councils for community life, and as a result, after leaving the seminary most diocesan priests from now on lived in ordinary presbyteries. If there were several priests in the parish, the model increasingly became that of master and servants rather than religious superior and brethren. The 'pale young curate' was expected to live and work under the direction of the parish priest, who alone had any rights and responsibilities. The curate counted the days until his seniority entitled him in turn to become a parish priest, and so the system was perpetuated. In country districts priests often lived alone, accompanied only by domestic servants. Those privileged to become members of collegiate churches still shared a common life to some extent, but these were a minority.

Surviving Colleges and New Institutes

Until the Revolution, colleges continued to exist, and new ones continued to be founded, in all the countries of Catholic Europe and America, and it is not to be supposed that they were all purely nominal in their pattern of community life. The ceaseless process of reform and revision of statutes also continued. At the Sainte-Chapelle in Paris, new regulations issued in 1681 were confirmed in 1720. The corporation now comprised thirteen canons, with the treasurer as the sole dignitary, who also served as the parish priest; in addition there was a chanter, six perpetual chaplains, twenty clerics (three of them still styled *marguilliers*), a ringer, eight choirboys, a music master, a grammar master (appointed by the treasurer) and four ushers. The distribution had by now increased to eighteempence for a canon, and twelvepence for a chaplain at the Little Hours, and the holding of a benefice elsewhere was declared incompatible with a position in the Sainte-Chapelle.[6] In Spain a new collegiate church was founded by Francis V in the mid eighteenth century to go with his grim new palace of la Granja, just south of Segovia. At Pastrana the dean moved out into a palace of his own, nearly a kilometre from the collegiate church, but the college of thirty *clericos* continued to reside across the road from the church.

In Germany, tombstone epitaphs continue to testify to active membership of collegiate churches. At Bleidenstadt, for example, they include Johann Wolfgang von der Leyen, 'of noble birth', who died in 1579 'in his youth', Gerhard Koeth von Warscheid, a canon for thirty-four years to his death in 1599, and Emich Philipp Zum Jungen, canon for twenty years, to his death aged forty-five in 1611. The implication is that one could still join a college comparatively young, and remain there for life.[7] The troubles of the seventeenth century could mean dispersal and plunder of communities, but when peace returned they could be refounded, as happened in Bleidenstadt in 1685, when the church was rebuilt in the Baroque style. After the Church of St Rupert in Seekirchen, Salzburgland, burnt down on 1679, the Prince-Archbishop took the opportunity to rebuild it and found a new collegiate church there, for a dean and six secular priests. They were to celebrate the entire Divine Office, and provide pastoral care for the surrounding parish. The community expanded to include a schoolmaster, a cantor, an organist and four choirboys. It remains today as one of the handful of colleges that escaped secularization. Maybe in the seventeenth and eighteenth centuries the first fervour had gone out of the ideal of the collegiate church, but the institution was by no means dead, and was still capable of useful work.

Nevertheless, in lands where the decrees of Trent had been accepted, a number of new institutes appeared that provided an alternative structure for the common life of secular clergy. Some were successful and long lasting, though many either faded away and came to nothing, or adopted vows and joined the everlengthening list of religious orders. Amort refers to a number of institutes of secular clergy that existed in his time, the 'Berullian Oratorians, the Philippini or Neriani ... those called simply Petrini, as they are styled in Germany, the ones called Bartholomaei after Bartholomaus Holzhauser, those named after St Tiburius, and the Mission fathers etc'.[8] Of all these institutes the most significant and widespread were the Oratory of St Philip Neri in Italy, and the Bartolomeans in Bavaria, though a great many smaller ones appeared in Italy and France.

The Oratory of St Philip Neri

Philip Neri (1515–1595), a young Florentine who came to Rome as a troubled teenager, was ordained priest in 1551, under the direction of Persiano Rosa, a priest of the Archconfraternity of Charity, the community that lived in San Girolamo della Carità. Philip himself joined the community, and was to live there for many years. As we have seen, the priests lived together with no internal superior, but under the direction of a layman, Vicenzo Teccosi, as *presidente*. The unsatisfactory nature of this was amply demonstrated when two of the priests, with the encouragement of Teccosi, began to persecute the new arrival, ridiculing his resolve to live a more apostolic life, and putting every obstacle in his way when he tried to celebrate Mass daily. Their persecution was equally directed against Buonsignore Cacciaguerra, who had been encouraging lay people to receive Communion more frequently than hitherto.[9] The eventual outcome was that Teccosi and one of the persecuting priests were won over, and a change was made in the constitutions of the community, so that Cacciaguerra became a true religious superior. Nevertheless the priests at San Girolamo did not ever live a full common life, but continued to eat separately and run their lives very much in their own way.

This suited St Philip, who used San Girolamo as a base from which to extend his work among young laymen, gathering them for informal instruction, prayer, music and recreation, in what became known as the Exercises of the Oratory. As the numbers attending these exercises increased, they outgrew the tiny church of San Girolamo, and were offered a new home in the Florentine national church of San Giovanni in 1564. A few of Philip's disciples were ordained priest, and sent by him to live at San Giovanni, although he himself had no intention of leaving his old room. It was for these young priests that St Philip composed a brief rule of life. This takes its place in continuity with the long-established tradition. They were to regard him in every way as their superior 'offering themselves ready for every act of obedience', and observing absolute equality among themselves. St Philip, as 'The Father', would choose a local superior to 'undertake the care of the government and observe with all diligence that the orders are kept'. All were obliged to certain specific prayers and a time of mental prayer every morning (as well as reciting the Divine Office which was an obligation on all priests). Twice a day they were to gather in the refectory; during the first third of the meal a book would be read to them, after which the local superior 'shall propose or request another to propose a doubt', a question on which each was invited to contribute his opinion, 'in very few and simple words'. After meals there was to be half an hour of recreation, 'in pleasant conversation'. Each week one of the community took his turn at serving at table, as also to read while the others ate. All were to 'contribute equally to the expenses incurred, both for food and rents', and the local superior was to distribute temporal and spiritual responsibilities as appropriate.[10] We hear that Baronio grumbled that it always seemed to be his turn to cook, while the reading at meals always fell to one of the young Fedeli brothers, but the system seems to have worked well enough until the community left San Giovanni in 1575 for their permanent home in Santa Maria in Vallicella, the 'Chiesa Nuova'. The move was prompted by difficulties with the Florentine national guild, who wanted to control the community of priests themselves, but after all it was they who paid the salaries out of which the priests contributed to the common expenses.

In the Chiesa Nuova, the community was in its own home, and could run its own affairs without interference. When the old church of Santa Maria in Vallicella was handed over to them in 1575, Pope Gregory XIII established 'a congregation of secular priests and clerics known as the Oratory', thus giving canonical status to the group. Although the word 'college' was not used, the model of life was essentially that of a collegiate church, with permanent membership but without vows. Further draft constitutions were drawn up by St Philip, and adapted over the years, giving greater detail. For instance in the refectory, 'let no one throw on the ground bones, fish-bones or other things', and in the sacristy, 'long conversations are to be avoided'. They concentrate most on the 'Exercises of the Oratory', the particular function for which the community existed.[11] When the young priests repeatedly urged him to introduce a vow of poverty, he refused absolutely, saying *habeant, possideant*, and pointing out that there were already plenty of religious orders to join if they wanted vows of poverty. Nevertheless he did expect all to contribute what they could to the common fund, so that the principle of religious poverty was amply sustained. Some had a personal endowment, in effect a prebend, while others supported themselves on family money. Only the poor could be supported entirely by the congregation.[12]

The entire congregation met to decide matters of importance, while a number of deputies were chosen to supervise the day to day running of the community. These went to San Girolamo every Tuesday to report back to St Philip, until he was finally persuaded to move into the Vallicella and join them. Even there he did not often attend meetings of the deputies, although he did 'have a voice in everything, and it was usually his word that settled each point without dispute'. The agenda for the 'General Congregation' was set by the senior deputy (*il rettore*) but St Philip insisted all should be at liberty to express their views.[13]

Towards the end of the century, the Congregation of the Oratory at the Vallicella began to experiment with new foundations. For a time they resumed responsibility for San Giovanni, and a new rule of life was drawn up for the priests stationed there. A daughter house was successfully established at Naples, for which Talpa drew up a rule including a number of innovations of a monastic character.[14] A proposed foundation in Milan was withdrawn because the archbishop, St Charles Borromeo, demanded too much control over it. Eventually the fathers concluded that it was not advisable for the house in Rome to exercise authority over others, and it was suggested that new congregations be formed independently simply taking the Roman one as their model.

When the definitive statutes were drawn up in 1612, seventeen years after the death of St Philip, they were specifically for the Roman Oratory only. When other congregations were erected the form was that they should live 'according to the statutes of Santa

Maria in Vallicella in Rome', so that the way of life was duplicated, but each house remained totally autonomous. In this way they reversed the trend towards linking communities into 'congregations' to give them a collective identity and a degree of independence. In the Oratory, uniquely, each separate house was a congregation of its own, erected by act of the pope, and therefore enjoying individually the freedom from local episcopal control which other institutes gained by international structures. Such institutes were controlled by international 'general' superiors, or representative assemblies. Medieval collegiate churches were answerable to the local bishop, and usually to a lay patron as well. Congregations of the Oratory were answerable to the Holy See alone. The lack of regional or international structure meant that a failing house died alone, but it also meant that a successful house was not dragged down by failing neighbours, nor could an autocratic general superior damage the institute as a whole. Herein lies the strength of the Oratory idea, which has enabled it to survive and expand when almost every other form of common life has failed.

The 1612 Constitutions were largely drawn up by Father Consolini, who succeeded St Philip and Baronio as superior, and incorporates a number of decrees of the General Congregation at Rome.[15] They begin with a description of the exercises of the Oratory itself, meaning the prayers to be said with the people, as well as the requirement for each father to make mental prayer. No times are set for this mental prayer, but everyone is to meet in the evening at the public Oratory. The priests are expected to be busy in the church, especially on holy days, with long hours for hearing confessions, celebrating their own daily private Mass and attending the solemn Mass on Sundays and feasts. Vespers also are to be sung with solemnity on Sundays and feastdays, including a number of local festivities. Although the fathers do not celebrate the Office in choir apart from those Vespers, they do assemble there for certain important ceremonies, such as the giving of candles on Candlemas and ashes on Ash Wednesday, and Tenebrae in Holy Week. Also the Office of the Dead is celebrated in common when a priest dies.

Preaching being one of the principal purposes of the Oratory, every day there are to be four sermons, of half an hour each, regulated by an hourglass and a bell, after which there should be some music and short vocal prayers. In preaching they must 'fit their expressions to the capacity principally of the vulgar, and pretending to no pomp at all, or vain popularity, recreate the mind of their auditors with a very beneficial kind of discourse, confirming their matter especially with examples, and approved histories of the Saints' (chapter 3).

The chapter (no 4) on the government of the congregation 'that is never to be changed' cites two decrees of the Roman Congregation, one absolutely prohibiting the taking of vows, and the other insisting on the independence of every house modelled on the Roman Oratory. Each house is to be governed by a provost (translated by Woodhead as 'president'), and four deputies, elected by all priests who have spent more than ten years in the congregation, in an electoral process of amazing complexity. The term of office is three years, but the provost, though not the deputies, may be re-elected indefinitely. A very large number of officers, at least thirty-three, within the congregation are appointed by the provost and deputies, again for the three-year term.

New members are to be selected from those aged between eighteen and forty-five, who are 'as it were naturally disposed' (*quasi natus*) for the congregation. After they have been well examined, and have lived in the house as a guest for a month, they may be admitted to the congregation as probationers, and for three years live under the strict supervision of a novice-master. Then by a vote of the fathers of ten years' standing they can be aggregated to the congregation, and will attend meetings and may speak, but do not have a vote until their ten years have passed. Any decision that affects the entire community must be discussed among the fathers before they meet in a General Congregation, when all can speak, and all of ten years' standing can finally vote on it.

Particular customs of the house are described in three chapters (8–10), these include the regular chapter or 'Congregation for faults'. Members are to make a contribution to community funds out of private income, their style of dress is to be like that of secular clergy, the order of precedence is to be that of entering the community, and penances are to be performed in public for public offences. There are regulations on the ordering of the refectory, the readings during meals, and the discussion of 'doubts' during the second part of the meal. After dinner the community meets for an hour for recreation, but in general they are encouraged to keep to their rooms except when they have duties in the church or elsewhere. They are not to go out of the house without permission, and may not be absent for more than a month in the year except by a special vote of the provost and deputies.

The Constitutions end with an appendix describing the form of community prayer in greater detail, and the afternoon exercises of the Oratory with the laity. The laymen associated with the congregation came to be called the 'Little Oratory', even though they might greatly outnumber the priests; they have their own officers and regular duties. After receiving instruction from the fathers, and joining in prayer, the Brothers of the Little Oratory are expected to apply themselves to good works locally, especially in the hospitals. Thus just as every religious order has its penumbra of associated lay people, so too does the Oratory.

The major difference between earlier collegiate bodies and the Congregation of the Oratory is the fact that from the beginning Oratorians have not regularly recited the Divine Office in common, and are particularly responsible for the lengthy instruction and formation of lay people. The form of government is extremely democratic, given that even the youths of only three years' standing can speak and influence the General Congregation, and all of ten years' standing have an equal vote. In practice, in the days when when most joined as teenagers, everyone over thirty would have had the vote. The provost and deputies form a practical administration, but have no privileges in legislation, and the three-year terms of office prevent them from behaving like traditional religious superiors, effectively cut off for ever from the body of their brethren. The effectiveness of these rules is shown by the fact that they could remain unchanged for over three hundred years, not superseded until 1943.

By 1600, when Antonio Gallonio published his first Life of St Philip, Oratories modelled on the one in Rome had been set up in Lucca, Fermo, Palermo and Camerino, with others under construction in Fano, Padua, Vicenza and Ferrara, as well as Thonon and Fréjus across the Alps.[16] The house at Thonon did not last long, since its founder, St Francis de Sales, was taken away to be made a bishop, and nothing more is known of the house at Fréjus, but there is evidence for Oratories in Aix and Avignon in the early seventeenth century. In the event, the Oratory in France was to take a very different form, as we shall see. The Oratory of St Philip Neri spread most rapidly through the states of the Italian peninsula, until almost every town of any size had a community, some of them with very large numbers. Since each house was set up independently, no central register seems ever to have been kept, and to identify all those ever set up would involve a trawl through the entire archive of the relevant dicasteries of the Holy See. As a result we have no complete list of Oratories. Capecelatro lists 101 houses in Italy founded before 1774, and as many as he could identify in other countries. In Spain and her dominions the idea spread rapidly, and houses were founded in many provinces of Spain, and south America, likewise in Portugal, and her colonies in Brasil and Goa. Elsewhere in Europe Oratories were rare: a few in Bavaria and Austria, five in Flanders (which went backwards and forwards between the Roman and French styles), and four in the old kingdom of Poland.[17] Often the former existence of an Oratory can only be deduced from observing the Philippine symbols (an eight-pointed star, or a flaming heart) in a surviving church, or noting a street name, such as *Via dei Filippini*, or *Rue de l'Oratoire*.

Oratory Derivatives

The Oratory of St Philip Neri inspired many imitations and offshoots. The most significant was the Oblates of St Ambrose, founded by St Charles Borromeo (1538–1584) because he wanted more control over the priests than St Philip would have allowed him. St Charles had been given the Archbishopric of Milan at an unsuitably early age, but as a result had the energy to carry out the necessary reforms with vigour. He invited St Philip to send Oratorians to Milan, but after a brief experiment it became clear that the spirit of freedom so dear to St Philip was unsuited to the court of the great reformer. Instead in 1578 he instituted the Oblates to be a congregation of secular priests, under the direct authority of the archbishop, and whom he could deploy wherever he saw need. They were given the Church of San Sepolcro as their headquarters, in the very centre of the old city. They did make a simple vow of obedience to the Archbishop of Milan, undertaking to do whatever he decided for the good of souls. Daily 'exercises' modelled on those of the Roman Oratory were instituted at San Sepolcro. Some of the Oblates remained permanently at San Sepolcro, living in community, while others were dispersed throughout the diocese but grouped into small communities each with its local superior and spiritual director. Even those dispersed in the countryside were expected to return regularly to one of the small communities for an assembly and to strengthen the bonds of fraternity. St Charles himself was a frequent visitor to San Sepolcro and kept a room for himself there, joining in all the spiritual exercises of the Oblates. He also instituted a company of Ladies of the Oratory and encourged the association of laymen to the exercises. The constitutions of the Oblates were eventually printed in 1613.[18]

There were several other minor and little-known Oratory derivatives. For example, Matteo Guerra, a disciple of St Philip Neri, founded a Congregation of the Holy Nail in Siena on the model of the Oratory, but it does not seem to have lasted very long. St John Leonardi, another man influenced by the Oratory, founded an institution of Secular Clerks of the Blessed Virgin Mary, which became a religious order in 1609. Paolo Motta, yet another disciple of St Philip, founded a congregation of secular priests under the patronage of St Joseph in Rome in 1620, near the Church of San Lorenzo in Damaso. Their purpose was the formation of the clergy. Although at first they did not live in common, after 1646 they acquired the Church of San Pantaleone and began the true common life, very close to the Oratory itself. With advice from the Oratory, they drew up constitutions which were approved in 1684, and lived a life almost identical to that of the Oratorians. The difference was that they concentrated on the spiritual renewal of the clergy, whereas the purpose of the Oratory of St Philip was always the sanctification of the laity.[19] Another spin-off from the work of St Philip Neri was the Congregation of the Holy Trinity, established to give permanence to the work he had started in 1548 for pilgrims and convalescents. A community of twelve priests was endowed, and given approval by Innocent XI in 1677. They were subject to the *primicerio* of the Confraternity of the Holy Trinity, usually a ranking prelate, but they also chose a local superior of their own every three years.[20]

The Institute of Secular Clergy living the Common Life

Quite independently of the Oratory of St Philip, the Bavarian mystic Bartolomäus Holzhauser (1613–1658) established a similar institute, which was to have considerable influence in the German lands. While studying at Ingolstadt university, Holzhauser had a vision that he was to become a secular priest in order to reform the entire secular clergy, through community life and the establishment of seminaries. He also had a vision of the imminent conversion of England. After ordination he soon attracted followers, and was nominated canon of the existing college at Tittmoning, in Bavaria. Here he rapidly converted the other canons to share his vision of a renewed common life, and began to evangelize the surrounding countryside. The constitutions he drew up are in full continuity with the long tradition of collegiate life, and his priests were to retain their private property, while holding all ecclesiastical revenue in common. The breviary was to be recited in common (though not apparently sung), and there were to be periods of mental prayer together. The parishioners were to be regularly visited, and there was to be daily preaching and catechesis. The lay folk were to be encouraged to support the ministry of the priests, though there does not seem to have been a formal lay association.

With much encouragement from the Bishop of Chiemsee, and later the Archbishop of Salzburg, Holzhauser's institute spread rapidly, and the fathers began to establish seminaries to ensure the proper education of the next generation of priests. In contrast to the Oratory, the Institute operated on a hierarchical structure, from deanery to diocese to province. In each case the superiors were nominated by the superiors of the rank below, and appointed by the superior of the rank above, with the agreement of the relevant bishop; all were controlled ultimately by a superior general, elected for life by the superiors of each province, but assisted by a council, two assistants and two visitators. The seminaries in each diocese might be under the control of the local bishop, served by priests of the Institute, or might be wholly owned by the Institute. Each diocese was also to have a retreat house, where those called to contemplative life could retire, but they could also serve as reception centres for new members, and penitentiaries for erring clergy. When Holzhauser applied to Innocent X for ratification of his constitutions, he received the answer that no new approval was necessary, since everything he was doing was already highly commended, being the apostolic life according to the ancient canons. Innocent XI, more pragmatically, gave it full canonical recognition in 1680.[21]

In September 1655, Holzhauser met the exiled Charles II, and again confidently prophesied the imminent conversion of England. Later in the century, Cardinal Howard took an interest in Holzhauser and his Institute, and his secretary Thomas Codrington with another priest, John Morgan, returned to England in 1684 armed with letters from Hofer and Appelius, the superiors of the Institute, to Dr Perrot, the dean of the secular clergy. Appelius and Cardinal Howard promoted the Institute partly because 'the conversion of the Kingdom of England appears to be imminent'.[22] Several priests in London joined the Institute, and John Morgan extended it to Staffordshire; by 1701 there were seventeen English members. In 1697 the Constitutions were published in London, which triggered an arrest warrant for the publisher, Thomas Metcalf of Drury Lane. He was defended by John Dryden.

However not only the government but also the older Catholic

clergy opposed the institute, and John Sergeant wrote a twenty-two-page diatribe against them.[23] He complains that seventeen members of the Institute 'took upon them with an unheard of Insolancy to write a Circular Letter or Manifesto', and that they have a national superior, diocesan superiors, 'we know not how many', and stewards. His opposition was nominally because the common life was impracticable in times of persecution, not approved by the English vicars apostolic, and would weaken the authority of the chapter: in other words the main motives, as always, were jealousy of the power and influence that might be lost to any such communities. He resented the idea of a 'Reformation of our Clergy', who were he claims already exemplary, and calls the 'object of their vow a Chimaera or Impossibility'. Other documents on behalf of the chapter rehearse much the same arguments, calling the Institute 'impracticable and impossible' and 'inconsistent with the Common Interest of the Chapter', as well as making the telling point that it was divisive, 'breaking the Common bond of Unity in the Clergy by making a separate body'.[24] Disappointment after the brief moment of liberation under James II must have set in; Thomas Codrington left for Paris, and his will of 1688 makes no mention of the Institute.[25] Eventually Bishop Bonaventure Gifford, Vicar Apostolic of the London District, suppressed the Institute in 1703, and it was very soon quite forgotten.[26]

Despite the failure of Holzhauser's vision of the imminent conversion of England, the Institute continued to flourish in the German lands up to the secularizations at the beginning of the nineteenth century. The collegiate church of Tittmoning survives as a parish church, the Institute commemorated only by the inscription on the community burial vault. Behind the church stands Holzhauser's original community house, but in the market place is a later elegant Rococo residence for the Fathers of the Institute. Part is now a bank, part a private residence, after a period of use as a police station, in which capacity it was to play a very significant role in the twentieth-century Bavarian priesthood.[27]

New Congregations in France

Characteristic of the seventeenth century in France was the growth of several new congregations, all of which started as communities of secular priests, though many mutated into religious orders. The kings of France refused to permit the reforms of Trent to be applied in their realm, and the French Church continued to be marked by some of the worst of abuses. In the end these abuses could only be corrected after the removal of the head of the French king. A major problem was the practice of *commendam*, by which the king could nominate a useless youth to the position of abbot or prior of any monastery, to provide him with an unearned income which he might or might not use to enable him to study. (Hence arose the custom of referring to any junior French cleric of uncertain status as an *abbé*). Tridentine model seminaries could not be established, and most priests were ordained with virtually no preparation. Because of this, the principal aim of many of the new congregations was to establish seminaries for the secular clergy.

The most important and lasting of the new congregations was the Oratoire de Jésus or 'French Oratory'. Pierre, Cardinal de Bérulle (1575–1629) was one of the most influential men in the French Church of his time, involved in affairs of state as well as matters ecclesiastical, but described as 'too unworldly to be a second Richelieu'. Ordained in 1599, he resolved immediately to dedicate his life to the reform of Catholicism in France, and began by adopting the spirituality of St Ignatius, though with the intention of being not a Jesuit but a 'priest of Jesus'. He took a vow never to accept any benefice, thus distancing himself from the major cause of clerical corruption. Around him gathered a circle of mystic ladies who helped him in the work of bringing the reformed Carmel of St Teresa to France.

The turning point came in 1602 when he met St Francis de Sales, who had already founded an Oratory of St Philip Neri in Thonon, and who encouraged him to do something similar. De Bérulle wanted St Francis as superior of any new institute, but this was impossible because of the latter's promotion to the episcopate in the same year, quite apart from a fundamental difference in character and spirituality. Other Philippine Oratories already existed in France, notably one at Aix founded by Romillion, who had been associated with César de Bus in the foundation of the Congregation of Christian Doctrine or 'Doctrinaires', but who left them when they decided to take religious vows. De Bérulle studied what was happening at Aix and Thonon, and eventually gathered five companions to start a new congregation in the Faubourg St Jacques, in 1611. By 1613 the new congregation had acquired a Bull of Institution, in which were enshrined two principles radically different from those of the Oratory of St Philip Neri: firstly all power was concentrated in the hands of the Superior General, and secondly the institute was to be centralized, united throughout the realm. De Bérulle explained that the decentralized Oratory of St Philip Neri might be all very well in the scattered statelets of Italy, but France was a kingdom, and a French Oratory should reflect the strength of the nation state. Father Consolini, still Provost of the Roman Oratory, was very much opposed to this, but advised Romillion to submit to de Bérulle, and the house at Aix was affiliated to the French Oratory in 1619, as were a few other existing Oratories. Headquarters in Paris moved to the Rue St Honoré, and the new Oratory quickly attracted opposition from the university, and from the Jesuits, who were unable to check the increasing influence of de Bérulle over the royal family. In this capacity he visited England for the marriage of Henriette-Marie to Charles I, and left twelve of his French Oratorians to serve as her chaplains. In 1625 Urban VIII gave them faculties for working the English mission.[28]

The French Oratory grew very fast. The second Superior General, Charles de Condren, who joined in 1617, became well known as a writer and an influential spiritual director. By 1624 there were forty houses in nine provinces of France, and the Church of Saint-Louis-des-Français in Rome came under their control. The seminary of Saint-Magloire was taken over by the Oratorians, thus beginning their distinctive role in Christian education. De Bérulle was created cardinal in 1627. By the time he died in 1629, while saying Mass, there were four hundred priests in sixty houses. He was an austere man, without social graces, but considered a saint by both St Francis de Sales and St Vincent de Paul. In contrast with St Philip it was said that '*Philippe, veillard même, ne fut jamais vieux; Bérulle, lui, ne fut jamais jeune.*'[29]

The French Oratory eventually ran seminaries in Paris, Montpellier and Condom, and schools in at least half of their houses. They had little parish involvement, and retained the principle of never accepting benefices. The policy in the schools was increasingly to adopt a 'modern' curriculum, abandoning the use of Latin as a teaching medium, and encouraging new speculative sciences. In philosophy they adopted and developed Cartesianism, and are best remembered today for the writings of Nicolas de Malebranche (1638–1715). In theology they began the rationalist assault on the traditional interpretation of Scripture, notably in the writings of Richard Simon (1638–1712). During the eighteenth century they became increasingly tainted by Gallican and Jansenist tendencies. They led the resistance to Roman authority on the new devotions of the Sacred Heart, with its radically anti-Jansenist message of the love of God and the practice of frequent

Communion. The Bull *Unigenitus* of 1713, which condemned many Jansenist theses, is directed in particular against the Oratorian Quesnel. By the end of the eightenth century, the institute which was characterized from the first by French centralism came to be the greatest opponent of Roman centralism.[30] It thus represented the opposite extreme to the Roman Oratory, and all houses on the Roman model, as well as the traditions deriving from St Francis de Sales, in which the devotion to the Sacred Heart had developed.

An offspring of de Bérulle's Oratory was the Congregation of the Heart of Jesus and Mary, founded by St John Eudes (1601–1681). He withdrew from the French Oratory because he wanted to concentrate on the work of seminary formation, but retained the principle of making no more than a simple promise of stability and obedience, without religious vows. The name of the congregation implies that he also rejected any strain of Jansenism. As in the French and Roman Oratories, the only bond is the 'bond of charity'. Unlike the Roman Oratory, the Congregation has a Superior General, elected for life, assisted by elected Assistants: it is the General who appoints local superiors, retaining the centralized structure of the French Oratory.[31]

The other well-known congregation which still actively survives is that of Saint-Sulpice, founded by Jean-Jacques Olier (1608–1657). As a child he was blessed by St Francis de Sales; as he grew up he was influenced by the fathers of the French Oratory, particularly by de Condren, as well as by St Vincent de Paul. However this did not deter him from accepting the post of *commendam* abbot and prior of a few small monasteries, the revenue from which supported him for the rest of his life. Like Holzhauser, he made an unsuccessful attempt to convert the exiled Charles II of England. In 1641 he and a few companions began to live together at Vaugirard, where they began the work of a seminary. Within a few months there were twenty in the community, and a rule of life was drawn up, naming Olier as superior. Supported by Cardinal Richelieu, he was soon translated to the post of curé of the parish of Saint-Sulpice on the Left Bank in Paris. Here the community expanded their work of providing seminary education for those aspiring to the priesthood.

Olier was not the first to attempt this in the capital. Several years before Adrien Bourdoise had tried to found a seminary in his parish of Saint-Nicolas-du-Chardonnet, but for long had achieved no more than a community of priests (incorporated in 1631), which only became a seminary in 1644. The rule of life at Saint-Sulpice was in many ways similar to that of the French Oratory, under the guidance of de Condren, but they were governed solely by the will of the superior, appointed for life. They practised poverty and simplicity, kept the weekly chapter of faults like religious, but never instituted vows. Members of the congregation were given no choice in their employment, but were directed to dedicate themselve entirely to their charges. The seminary they established soon became well known, and continues to flourish, although in the early years the course for those seeking ordination might be only a few months long. When similar seminaries were wanted in other parts of France, Olier sent priests from Saint-Sulpice, but still regarded them as members of his own congregation on loan, rather than establishing separate or independent communities. Like the Oratorians, the Sulpicians strongly encouraged a lay spirituality, and supported groups of laymen attempting to live a more profound Christian life, such as the 'Brothers of Abstinence', a community of poor students.[32]

In their concern for seminaries, both the French Oratory and the Sulpicians were heavily influenced by the Congregation of the Priests of the Mission, or Lazarists, founded by St Vincent de Paul (1581–1660), who was himself for a time under the spiritual direction of de Bérulle. Like so many, St Vincent saw the need for seminaries to provide for others the training which he himself had never received. He, de Bérulle, Bourdaise and Olier all founded seminaries at the same time, to fill the gap left by the fact that the decrees of Trent had been completely ignored. St Vincent's principal work, however, was preaching missions to parishes throughout France, and the promotion of the practical acts of charity now most associated with his name. The group of companions who came together in 1625 met much opposition from the clergy and bishops, but received approval from Rome in 1633 as a company of secular priests without vows. However before long St Vincent decided that vows were actually necessary, and the Lazarists became, as they remain, a vowed society of clerks regular, though since their vows are 'private' they are now classed among the Societies of Apostolic Life.[33]

The first congregation of secular priests dedicated to overseas missions was the Society of the Foreign Mission of Paris, founded by François Pallu in 1654. A seminary was organized in France for their training, and the mission priests were deployed under a council of directors, organized by vicariates. Opposition came from the European powers more than from the indigineous peoples to whom they preached. Nevertheless from the beginning there were martyrdoms, and the society flourished in its difficulties.

Many smaller congregations came into being in France, but

either mutated into vowed religious orders, or faded away. At Paris in 1645 Henri-Michel Buch and others formed communities of apprentice boys, cobblers and tailors, who lived a true common religious life while practising their trades. A few years later, a married surgeon, M. de Cretenet, founded a congregation of Missionaries of St Joseph, in which clerics lived a common life and preached missions, under the direction of a layman. In 1703, Claude Poullart founded a Congregation of the Holy Ghost, at first to care for students in Paris, then to conduct a seminary, and eventually to work on the overseas mission. St Louis-Marie Grignon de Montfort began the Company of Mary as a home mission society of secular priests, but immediately after his death they took vows of religion.

Similar small and short-lived secular congregations existed in other countries. In Naples, Carlo Caraffa (1561–1633) founded a little congregation of frightening austerity to serve the poor, particularly fallen women. These 'Pious Workers' took no vows, but were governed by a general and four consultors. In Rome, St Joseph Calasancz founded the Piarists, or Clerks of Pious Schools, in 1597, with a group of companions who at first lived together without vows, but in 1617 they were established by the pope as a vowed order. In Bologna, a widower, Cesare Biancheti (1585–1655), formed a little Congregation of St Gabriel to educate the poor of the city in 1644. Those who shared the common life, known as *conviventi*, were supported by a lay association of *confluenti*. The superior and four councillors were elected annually. In Poland, Jan Papczyński founded a congregation of Missionaries of Mary in 1671, but within a few years they began to take regular vows.[34]

None of these obscure institutes now survive as congregations of secular clergy, though a number of existing religious orders derive from experiments in unvowed community life. To the very end of the Ancien Régime the age-old conflict of ideology was played out. Those whom we may class as 'Augustinians' still kept to the principles first stated by Peter Damian, and proclaimed that community life was impossible and undesirable without proper religious vows; those who, whether they were conscious of it or not, were in some sense 'Chrodegangians' still clung to the vision of reformed secular pastoral clergy living in community. So the debate continued until the tocsin rang.

Note

1. Session 23 (1565), reform decree, caps. 6 and 17; Schroeder, *Trent*, pp. 168, 174.
2. Session 6 (1547), reform decree, cap. 2; Session 7 (1547), reform decree caps. 2, 3, 4; Session 24 (1563), reform decree cap. 17; Schroeder, *Trent*, pp. 48, 55–7, and 206 respectively.
3. Session 22 (1562), reform decree cap. 3; Schroeder, *Trent*, p. 154.
4. Session 24 (1563), reform decree cap. 12; Schroeder, *Trent*, pp. 200–2.
5. Session 5 (1546), reform decree cap. 1; Session 21 (1562), reform decree cap. 3; Session 22 (1562), reform decree cap. 8; Session 24 (1563), reform decree cap. 9; Schroeder, *Trent*, pp. 24–5, 137, 157, 198 respectively.
6. Morand, *Sainte Chapelle*, pp. 225, 233.
7. D.I. 43, Rheingau-Taunus Kreis, nos. 492, 513, 560.
8. Amort, *Vetus disciplina canonicorum*, I, p. 73 b.
9. Ponelle & Bordet, *St Philip Neri*, pp. 184–5.
10. Interim Constitutions of 1565, in *Sapientia Majorum*, pp. 7–12.
11. Ponelle & Bordet, *St Philip Neri*, p. 261.
12. Ibid., p. 378.
13. Ibid., p. 365.
14. Ibid., pp. 468, 477–8.
15. English translation by Abraham Woodhead, Oxford 1687, reprinted in *Sapientia Majorum*, pp. 43–86.
16. Gallonio, *Life of St Philip*, pp. 150–1.
17. Capecelatro, *Life of Saint Philip Neri* II, pp. 534–5.
18. Helyot, *Ordres Religieux*, VIII, pp. 29–37.
19. Ibid., VIII, pp. 25–7.
20. Ibid., VIII, pp. 27–9.
21. See Gadiel, *Barthélemy Holzhauser*, which incorporates the full Statutes of the Institute.
22. Westminster Diocesan Archives, A series XXXIV, ff. 908, 909, 915.
23. 'A letter to our worthy Brethren of the New Institute', Westminster Diocesan Archives, Old Brotherhood Archives Book II part ii, no 139, ff. 303–13.
24. Westminster Diocesan Archives A series XXXIV, ff. 899–900; Old Brotherhood II, pt ii, ff. 314–17.
25. Westminster Diocesan Archives A Series XXXV, f. 459; XXXVI, ff. 79–80.
26. Birrell, 'Holzhauser and England'.
27. J. Kardinal Ratzinger, *Aus meinem Leben* (München 1997), pp. 11–14.
28. Westminster Diocesan Archives A Series XXXVII, ff. 163–5.
29. George, *L'Oratoire*, p. 35.
30. Boureau, *L'Oratoire en France*, pp. 58–62.
31. Pisani, *Congregations of Priests*, pp. 118–20.
32. Thompson, *Life of M. Olier*; Pisani, *Congregations of Priests*, pp. 94–104.
33. Pisani, *Congregations of Priests*, pp. 70–6; Bonfils, *Sociétés de Vie Apostolique*, pp. 55, 152–7.
34. For all these, see Helyot, *Histoire des Ordres*, vol. VIII; and Pisani, *Congregations of Priests*.

Chapter 13

The Revolution and After

The story of the common life of the secular clergy effectively comes to an end with the Great Revolution. The eighteenth century was marked by the growth of 'philosophical societies', groups of deist or atheist thinkers who vaunted themselves on being 'the Enlightenment'. They became more and more openly opposed to traditional religion, until they were strong enough to launch an open attack on the Catholic Church. They rejected belief in the possibility of any supernatural intervention in human affairs, and therefore saw no value in any type of prayer, neither private contemplation nor the regular chant of the Divine Office. If clergy and churches were to justify their existence at all, they had to be efficient, functional, 'useful to the Nation'. Their principal function must be to encourage the ignorant people to be good citizens. Public ceremonial might be useful to build up community and encourage a spirit of citizenship; private prayer and long clerical offices were utterly redundant.

Under the insane emperor Josef II, the 'enlightened despot', a radical change in the understanding of the priesthood was promulgated in Austria.[1] Hitherto manuals for priestly training had emphasized the role of prayer and study, with the daily Mass as the highlight of the day. A new approach pioneered by the *commendam* Abbot Franz Stefan Rautenstrauch saw the priest's role essentially as that of teacher, charged above all with 'the religious enlightenment of his congregation', in other words making them loyal subjects of the Empire.[2] Traditional images and 'devotions' were to be discouraged, and the public celebration of the Divine Office was actually banned by government decree. Even daily Mass was discouraged, it being considered more important for the priest to familiarize himself with the spirit of the age, and to hold his own in polite conversation. The discipline of 'pastoral theology', thus begun, has endured ever since, shorn of its more ludicrous aspects, and the function of the priest is still usually seen as primarily 'pastoral', doing good, rather than 'spiritual', being good.

Clearly in such a climate there was no room for communities of priests dedicated to prayer and the celebration of the Divine Office. All forms of religious community, whether vowed or not, came under the same condemnation, and were swept away under the inexorable glare of 'Enlightened' progress. All power was understood to derive from the people, or the 'nation', which meant that the nation felt entitled to claim back any concessions or grants it had once made to the clergy, if the nation felt the resources could be better used. This was the theory behind the wholesale confiscation of church buildings, lands and even furnishings, which were sold off as 'national property', or put to service for national objectives, particularly barracks and prisons.

A further feature of the 'Enlightenment' was the independence of each nation from any international obligation, particularly those revolving around the papacy. Hitherto the papacy had been accepted to some extent as the natural arbiter between Catholic nations, and there was at least some concept of international law and responsibility, based on the theology of papal primacy. This was to come to an end, and the idea of the 'independence' or 'sovereignty' of nations was used to absolve them from any consideration of responsibility to any other nation. England and other Protestant countries had already operated on this basis, and the rebel American colonies enshrined it in their constitution. Only in the mid twentieth century, with the appearance of the United Nations, was there a partial return to the idea of international law. In France, the Civil Constitution of the Clergy of 1790 was understood as marking an immediate and decisive break with the papacy, establishing a 'church' on a purely national and secular basis. Many churchmen agreed with this; they took the Oath to uphold the Civil Constitution, and collaborated cheerfully in the suppression of communities and even the sale of *biens nationaux*. This they saw as a means of throwing off the yoke of the international Catholic Church and establishing the Church as a truly national expression of enlightened thought. In this they were encouraged by the spectacle of the Anglican body across the Channel, conducted as a department of state and dedicated to maintaining the existing social order. The difference was that the new 'Constitutional Church' was to be dedicated to creating a revolutionary new and different social order. To be fair, at this stage they did not envisage the tumbrils.

In truth that unhappy century had better be called 'the

Obfuscation', for all that talk of humanity and progress led inevitably to the Terror. By affecting to despise reasonable theology, they cultivated ignorance and opened the path to superstition. Abolishing Catholic prayer and intercession, they prepared the way for exotic forms of pseudo-mysticism. For the next two hundred years, the history of France, and of western Europe in general, was to see a ceaseless alternation of tolerance and persecution of the Catholic Church. To begin with, twenty years of world war spread the ideas of the French Revolution through most of Europe. In Spain and Portugal, Italy, the Low Countries and most states of Germany, the march of the Revolution brought about the suppression of religious communities of all types, and the demolition of cathedrals, colleges and monasteries. The Restoration of 1815 brought hardly more than a brief lull in the process, for subsequent revolutions and anti-clerical governments continued the work of destruction at intervals until the mid twentieth century.

In England, 'enlightened' public opinion, drawing on well-established anti-Catholic prejudice, supported the most flagrant injustices, as it applauded the confiscation of religious property, which meant the closure of schools, orphanages and hospitals, and the casting out of busy nuns and clergy to become street vagrants wherever this was done by the anti-clerical governments that dominated most of Europe at intervals between 1789 and 1989.

Congregations of the Common Life in France

In France the various institutes of secular clergy had to confront the Revolution and the Terror in its birthplace. Some compromised badly, some resisted valiantly, but eventually all were suppressed, and only a few were able to regroup and form again afterwards. The first great order to fall was the Society of Jesus, destroyed by the 'enlightened' monarchs who thereby cleared the way for their own downfall. Other institutes profited gladly from the abolition of the Jesuits; their schools were taken over both by the vowed communities of Doctrinaires and the unvowed French Oratory. In order to staff them, both institutes had to recruit large numbers of auxiliaries, laymen who undertook no religious obligations, but wore the habit and appeared to be members of these institutes. It was possibly as a result of this that all the Doctrinaires, and a large proportion of the Oratorians, took the Oath to the Civil Constitution of the Clergy in 1790, and were briefly rewarded for it – before the Revolution began to devour its children. When many former canons of the collegiate churches of Angers died in the *noyades* at Nantes, one of the Oratorians jeered at them, 'they can't complain that they are being left to die of thirst'.[3] But their triumph was short lived. On 18 August 1792 the Assembly suppressed all the secular congregations, although friends and former pupils of the Oratory (such as Citoyen Robespierre) attempted to rescue them as true friends of the Revolution. There were in fact many French Oratorians who did retain their faith, and fifteen of them died during the Terror. The rest were scattered and never succeeded in regrouping, although projects of refoundation were floated under Napoleon and Louis XVIII.

In contrast, the Sulpicians all refused the Oath, under the guidance of their great superior, M. Emery. Many were martyred, others emigrated to Canada. Emery himself was imprisoned, but survived, and courted some controversy by intimating that the Oath of 1792, '*Liberté-Egalité*', could be taken with a clear conscience. In this he was supported by the pope, but the integrists were shocked. Nevertheless Emery survived to reconstitute the Sulpicians under the benevolent eye of Napoleon, to preserve them when that eye ceased to be benevolent, and to reconstitute them again after the Restoration.[4] After it was all over, many former seminarians remembered a famous remark of Emery's, which turned out to be a prophecy. The careless custom had grown up of leaving the refectory during the reading of the Martyrology, without waiting for the concluding formula, 'and elsewhere many other holy martyrs, confessors and virgins'. Emery scolded them, 'You can never expect that your name will one day be admitted to the martyrology, but you can very reasonably hope that one day you will be included in the "and elsewhere".'[5] (Actually, a fair number of his pupils, though not Emery himself, are included in the 2004 edition of the Roman Martyrology.)

Other congregations, such as the Eudists and the Mission Society, struggled through, with some apostates, many non-jurors, some martyrs, much confusion. Government approval came and went. At times these congregations were considered obviously beneficial because of their work in education, and were therefore tolerated; at times their resemblance to monasteries caused suppression or exile. In 1809 Napoleon suddenly decided to suppress all the missionary societies, but they came out into the open again in 1816. During the revolutionary period, most of the smaller institutes simply disappeared and were forgotten. The same pattern that was observed in France was repeated in Italy, and throughout Europe. The nineteenth century dawned with virtually no organized religious life in Europe.

The Fate of the Collegiate Churches in France

Collegiate churches had continued to exist throughout the eighteenth century, but increasingly canons tended to set up separate households, and abandon any pretence of living the common life. They did maintain the ceaseless round of prayer, and they did meet regularly in chapter for decisions to be made and business conducted, but the old rule of 'one refectory, one dormitory' was largely forgotten. Helyot, publishing in 1792, says that by his time the common life had been abolished in almost all cathedrals and colleges.[6]

At the Sainte-Chapelle in Paris, the greatest and most prestigious of all the high medieval foundations, the end came without ceremony. The statutes of 1681 had been confirmed in 1730, and the allowances increased, since revenue from rents was falling. In 1740 any alternative source of income from a benefice elsewhere was declared incompatible with possession of a canonry, in a belated attempt to reflect the reforms of Trent. However in 1787 the king declared that none of the Saintes-Chapelles were serving any useful purpose, and proposed to suppress them. He remarked ingenuously that in so doing he would acquire a considerable revenue for the Crown. By an *Arrêt du Conseil* on 11 March 1787, Louis XVI sequestrated the goods of the Sainte-Chapelle in Paris, and that in Vincennes, but ordered divine service to continue until further notice. Morand, writing in 1790, hopefully informs us that many nobles are petitioning the king to save the chapel from demolition, and have floated a scheme to set up a 'free chapel', staffed by clergy from different chapters.[7] In the event the king was prevented from demolishing the chapel, and it survives with most of its glass intact, and the incised slabs of canons and other clergy paving the lower storey; nothing remains of the canonical residences that once surrounded it.

A detailed study of the church in Angers on the brink of the Revolution, shows that there was a serious division between the collegiate clergy and the pastoral parish priests.[8] In 1789 there were seven collegiate churches in addition to the cathedral, and although two of them no longer had any members, there were still seventy-two resident canons. These canons had long since given up any practice of the true common life, for each one lived in his own house, surrounded by innumerable associates. They were well paid, and appointed from the very best families of the city and neighbourhood, often at an early age. What they did continue to do was keep residence and sing the Divine Office regularly in their churches. In contrast the pastoral clergy, the curés and their vicaires, were badly paid and overworked.[9] Those who served a parish attached to a collegiate church were not allowed to use the high altar in the choir but could only celebrate in the nave. Deep resentments between curés and canons surfaced in 1788, and culminated in the decisive move of the curés in March 1789 to associate themselves no longer with the aristocratic prelates and canons, but with the *Tiers Etat*. One of the very first consequences of the ensuing Civil Constitution of the Clergy (24 August 1790) was the abolition of all chapters.[10]

When the Assembly proceeded to demand an oath of allegiance to the Civil Constitution, on 27 November 1790, it is hardly surprising that the dispossessed canons refused it. In contrast, many of the curés and other clergy accepted it, with greater or lesser show of resistance.

A similar study of the cathedral clergy of Rouen shows the same division between beneficed senior canons and junior clergy.[11] By 1789 there were fifty-six members of chapter, including the Cardinal, de la Rochefoucauld, and the dignitaries. These comprised a dean, precentor, treasurer and chancellor, the familiar four-fold structure once common in Normandy and in England; there were also five archdeacons under a *grand-archidiacre*. Many of the canons were university doctors and teachers. However attendance was becoming slack. Prebends were very unequal, ranging from £40 to £4,900 per annum, balanced slightly by the daily distribution which could bring in an extra £2,400 per annum if one attended all Offices regularly. The poorer prebendaries did not resist the temptation to pluralism, which provoked the hostility of the pastoral clergy. Two of the canons were young boys, *in minoribus*; they had been admitted, tonsured and given minor orders, but were not permitted to take their place in the choir stalls, or to attend chapter. They stood among the choirboys for the Offices, and were effectively treated as choirboys until they should be of age for major orders. They were therefore the very last remnants of the ancient collegial structure in which boys of seven were regularly admitted to begin their career as canonical clergy, a custom abolished in the rest of Europe by the Council of Trent. An informant of Langlois recalled meeting a former boy-canon in 1844, M. Outrequin de Saint-Léger, found alive and well in a hotel dining room in Caen.[12]

Despite the Civil Constitution, the canons of Rouen managed to maintain divine service as usual for a while. They sang the Offices regularly until 28 December 1790, when after sext they were summoned to the chapter room to hear the decree of dissolution. The cathedral was immediately sealed against them. The last act of the chapter, a month before, had been to resolve that though all privileges might be revoked, the responsibilities of their office remained, and the canons undertook to continue to pray the breviary and celebrate Mass for the people of the diocese and past benefactors.[13] This demonstrates that they were not merely interested in their income, but had a genuine concern for prayer and the wellbeing of their people.

The day after the dismissal of the chapter, the minor clergy, petty-canons, chaplains and the like, were summoned to the chapterhouse and offered the right to take over the choir stalls and sing the Office in place of their *ci-devant* superiors. They began again with sext on 29 December, and continued to minister in the cathedral, mostly taking the Oath in January 1791. The deprived Cardinal Archbishop issued an *Instruction,* warning against accepting the ministry of the Constitutional clergy, and the persecution of non-jurors increased from the summer of 1791 onwards. Many fled to England: at one point there were over 8,000 French clergy in England, and up to 1,000 at a time lived some sort of common life in the King's House by Winchester Castle, forming incidentally the largest such community that ever existed. Their life was 'based on a strong community feeling', with meals in common, the regular round of liturgy, conferences on scripture, moral and dogmatic theology, and perpetual adoration of the Blessed Sacrament. In 1796 they were moved on to houses in Paddington, Reading and Thame, where these traditions continued until 1802.[14] However, many of these priests disliked the *atmosphère brumeuse de l'Angleterre,* and most moved on, either into Germany, or even back to Rouen in time to be incarcerated in the former seminary. On 6 *ventôse* II (28 February 1794) eighty priests from the seminary were deported to Rochefort, where most died on the prison hulks. Only three ever returned to Rouen.[15]

The confiscation and sale of church goods brought about economic hardship for the towns, in Rouen as in Angers. Local tradesmen quickly realized that the huge revenues of the collegiate chapters had been spent locally, boosting trade and providing employment, all of which disappeared once these revenues had fallen into the hands of the bourgeois purchasers. M. Papillant of the Rouen chapter had been accustomed to use his income of

£7,000 to relieve the needs of the poor in the inner city: the administration of the district recognized the distress caused by the loss of his income, and voted him a pension of £1,000 per annum for his needs and those of the poor around him – not that this pension was ever paid.[16] The end result of the closure of religious houses was inevitably the distress of considerable numbers of poor citizens who had been accustomed to rely on the Church to provide them with welfare care from cradle to grave. It was the same in France as it had been in England two and a half centuries before.

The attitude of Church and State to each other went through a bewildering succession of changes during the years after the Revolution. Priests might suddenly be recalled and reinstated, and then as suddenly dismissed and imprisoned. Loyal churchmen might accept one form of oath of allegiance and then turn against it; divisions appeared between those who could compromise with the regime to some extent, and those who remained implacably opposed. In an attempt to pacify the nation, in *floréal* of the year III (May 1795) all 'cults' were once again permitted, and non-juring priests invited to resume their duties subject only to a simple promise of fidelity. Many accepted this condition, but others, notably the exiled Archbishop of Rouen, and the Bishop of Séez, utterly rejected it. The Civil Constitution of the Clergy was finally abrogated in the year VIII, and the constitutional clergy mostly agreed to recognize Pope Pius VII. Rouen fell vacant with the death of Cardinal de la Rochefoucauld in the same year, and the chapter ventured to take control, appointing three *grands-vicaires* to administer the diocese. They did not venture as far as to elect a new archbishop. Under the lead of the former chapter most priests took the promise of loyalty, but the Bishop of Séez, as the senior surviving suffragan, tried to seize control of Rouen in *thermidor*, IX (July 1801), appointing M. Clément as his vicar general. The ensuing 'Clémentin' schism thus made a third party in the diocese. Pius VII did his best to reconcile all parties, and the Concordat of 5 *floréal* X (25 April 1802) officially marked the end of the irregular situation of the Church in France. The constitutional clergy were brought back into the fold, but the 'Clémentins' remained aloof, joining with the 'Blanchardistes' and other integrist groups to form the so-called 'Petite-Eglise', a schism which endured for decades.

As a result of the Concordat, the cathedral chapters were reconstituted in France, but on a much smaller scale than before the Revolution. At Rouen eight survivors of the old chapter were reinstated, but without prebends, and with a simplified choir dress. In token of *victum et vestitum* they received a pension of £1,000 a year. Collegiate churches were not restored. Cathedral canons resumed much of their liturgical function, and their role in governing the diocese, but the idea of the common life seems to have been utterly forgotten, despite, or perhaps because of, the manner of life the exiles had followed in England.

Collegiate Churches outside France

The same pattern is observable in all territories affected by the Revolution: collegiate churches continued to exist up to the last moment, but nearly all had gone by 1815. The Institute of Bartolomäus Holzhauser, being centrally organized, was centrally suppressed. Along with other communities of secular priests, the Bartholomeans had expected that the campaign against religious orders would not apply to them. Along with other communities of secular priests, they found that it did. Independent colleges fared slightly differently. New statutes for the collegiate church of St John in Regensburg were issued in 1785, mostly concerning new financial arrangements. The local duke made an attempt to suppress it in 1811, but it lingered on with only a few canons. At St Simeon, Trier, the *kurien* or canonries were still in use by the canons to the end of the eighteenth century; however these were houses near the ancient cloister building but not integrated into it, so that the canons were not even expected to share the Common Life. The college was finally extinguished in 1802, and the church, built into the third-century Black Gate, was demolished the following year.[17] The College of Bleidenstadt was also suppressed in 1802–3.[18] The Alte Kapelle in Regensburg survived only because most of its capital was invested in Viennese banks; the government of Bavaria realized that if they suppressed the college its assets would be lost to them, remaining in Austrian hands, and therefore decided they might as well allow it to continue. In 1830 King Ludwig I formally confirmed the foundation, which now claims unbroken continuity from Carolingian times.[19]

Elsewhere, in Germany, Austria-Hungary, Poland, Italy, Spain, Portugal and their overseas dominions, even where the actual Revolution did not reach, the spirit of the age dictated the suppression, dissolution and demolition of collegiate churches and their attendant buildings. Cathedrals usually survived in some form, and chapters were often revived on a small scale, but the great community buildings were either demolished or converted into comfortable private houses. For all practical purposes the history of collegiate churches comes to an end. Surviving church buildings are usually still known as *collègiales, Kollegiatkirchen, kolegiaty*, and the like, but with barely more than a memory of what the title had once meant.

Nineteenth-Century attempts at Revival

The restoration of the episcopate after the Revolution gave the bishops far more control over the junior clergy than ever before, a trend which was to continue, and the prospect of the clergy being at the mercy of the episcopal whim inspired several attempts at restoring a form of common life independent of bishops. At the same time, some of the more sensible bishops saw the value of community life among their clergy, and made attempts to revive old institutes or create new ones. Few were successful.

Despite its unfortunate record during the eighteenth century and the Revolution, and after several false starts, the French Oratory was successfully revived in the mid nineteenth century. France suffered from a shortage of priests, and few could be spared to teach in the institutes of higher education necessary for the training of future priests. The energetic Abbé Dupanloup saw the need for a congregation of studious teaching priests, and on becoming Bishop of Orleans recruited the Abbé Pierre Pététot (1801–1888) as the founder of a revived Bérullian Oratory. Pététot and Dupanloup had been together as teachers in the seminary at Saint-Nicolas-du-Chardonnet in Paris, and Pététot had already attempted to form a true community in the parish of St Roch. In 1852, Pététot and five companions began the common life in the rue de Calais, using the Constitutions of de Bérulle, but changing the name of the institute to the '*Oratoire de l'Immaculée Conception*', in an attempt to break with the Gallican and Jansenist past. The other leading member was Alphonse Gratry (1805–1872), a polymath and former teacher, who had hoped that the new Oratory would become a studious home for research. However by 1856 the community had taken on responsibility for running the minor seminary at St-Lô, and plunged into full-time teaching. Gratry, disillusioned, eventually left the Oratory. In 1864 the new Oratory gained papal approval, under the revised name of '*Oratoire de Jésus Christ notre Seigneur et de Marie Immaculée*'. By 1900 there were 113 members, running schools and seminaries throughout France. They survived the laws of 1903 by moving to Fribourg, and returned to France in the 1920s to expand their work. This time they refrained from becoming totally involved in teaching, and expanded into various other areas of ministry. However their most prominent member at the time was Laberthonnière, a leading Modernist philosopher, condemned by the Church. Following the 1917 Code of Canon Law, their new constitutions restored the original name of '*Oratoire de Jésus*', and after the Second World War they continued to flourish. Their most influential modern writer was the late Louis Bouyer.[20]

In the middle of the nineteenth century serious attempts were made to revive the Institute of Secular Priests living the Common Life, the Holzhauser foundation. Wilhelm Emmanuel Kettler (1811–1877), Bishop of Mainz, planned to revive the idea in 1850 in order to restore the spiritual life of his clergy. However, as so often happens, the clergy had no intention of being restored, and the vicar general led a determined opposition. As Professor Birrell concluded, 'The intense conservatism of his diocesan clergy was too much even for a man of Kettler's dominating personality.'

At the same time the great Archbishop of Orleans, Felix Dupanloup (1806–1878) returned to the theme of communities of the common life, perhaps disappointed that the French Oratory had become so closely associated with schoolteaching. He commented that '*Le clergé séculier est le clergé fondamental de l'Eglise ... les reguliers sont les auxiliaires des séculiers.*' His vicar general, Jean Gaduel (1811–1888), was much more co-operative than Kettler's: he published a pamphlet in 1843 recommending the common life for diocesan priests, and followed this with a definitive life of Barthélemy Holzhauser in 1868. (We have drawn extensively on this volume in our account of the Holzhauser institute above.) The book enjoys the unusual distinction of a preface by the reigning pontiff, as well as a long dedicatory epistle from the archbishop to the author, both strongly urging the establishment of communities on the Holzhauser lines. The pope pointed out that no special permission was necessary to live according to the rules of the institute, since they were simply the most ancient canons for clerical life. The archbishop, anxious about the loneliness of solitary clergy, hoped that the initiatives would come from the clergy themselves, and envisaged small local communities. The book was especially offered for consideration by seminarians. The idea was widely approved, and a speaker at the First Vatican Council of 1869–70, possibly Dupanloup himself, suggested promoting a common life for the clergy in general.[21] The events of 1870 put an end to all such hopes. Pio IX became a prisoner in the Vatican, estranged from Dupanloup by the latter's strong opposition to the definition of Papal Infallibility, and France was plunged into the chaos of the Franco-Prussian War and the Commune.[22]

A third attempt, on which a practical beginning was made, was that of William Bernard Ullathorne (1806–1889), Bishop of Birmingham. Despite being himself a Benedictine, Ullathorne valued the secular clergy as the 'Order of which Our Lord Himself was the Founder', but was under no illusions about their ever-present need for reform. Despairing of being able to reform the existing diocesan seminary at Oscott, he founded a new seminary in September 1873 at Olton, consciously modelled on Holzhauser's Institute as he found it in the pages of Gaduel. Seminarians were to be educated separately from the lay students who now dominated Oscott, and formed in such a way that they were prepared for life in small communities throughout the diocese. This project too came to nothing, extinguished by an unsympathetic successor before it had a chance to show its possibilities. The Olton seminary was closed within a month of Ullathorne's death, and the seminary buildings were transformed into a Franciscan friary. Nevertheless, the *Life of Holzhauser* by Gaduel was translated into English for public reading at Oscott, and the manuscript shows evidence of much handling.[23]

While Ullathorne was trying to revive the Holzhauser institute in Birmingham, Cardinal Manning was working in London, with much greater success, to reconstitute the Oblates founded by St Charles Borromeo. This was indeed an initiative of Cardinal Wiseman, who had seen the potential for a community of secular priests as missionaries in England. He was frustrated by the religious orders, who were disinclined to tear up their respective Rules in order to be at the whim of the local bishop, even in a work as important as the Conversion of England.

> Not one of them can – for it cannot be the want of will – undertake it. They are prevented by their Rule from helping ... at least in any but a particular and definite way ... I wish all to follow their Rules but they impress me strongly with the want of elasticity and power of adaptation in them.

Wiseman was familiar with the Oratory in Rome, but as soon as he had succeeded in bringing Oratorians to London realized that they were too independent for his taste. What he wanted was 'an Oratory with external action, and I do not think that dear San Filippo will be angry with me for trying to get it'.[24]

Henry Edward Manning (1802–1892) was an apt instrument to

Wiseman's hand. He was summoned back from his studies in Rome to begin a community based on Borromeo's Oblates of St Ambrose. Six original members of this congregation had survived the Revolutionary wars, and were reconstituted in 1853 by Archbishop Romilli of Milan. Within three years they had increased to sixty, and were directing four seminaries and a retreat house.[25] Manning visited them, and drew up a set of constitutions for a congregation of Oblates of St Charles, to be subject to the Archbishop of Westminster in exactly the same way that the Oblates of St Ambrose were subject to Milan. In 1857 the constitutions were approved, and community life began in Bayswater.[26] There they flourished until Manning was elevated to Westminster in 1865. Shortly before that one of their number, Herbert Vaughan, had founded a Missionary Society on similar principles, to be based in his huge new College at Mill Hill. Vaughan himself succeded Manning at Westminster, and supported both the Oblates and the Mill Hill Fathers, which continued to operate as societies of Apostolic Life within the Diocese of Westminster. The Mill Hill Fathers were advised and supported by the Milan Society for Foreign Missions, 'they, like us, sprang out of the Oblates of St Charles'.[27]

The Constitutions of the Oblates bear a similarity to those of collegiate churches and earlier congregations of secular clergy. The provost was to be appointed for a two-year term (later increased to three years) by the Archbishop of Westminster, who was invited to choose one of three names proposed by the priests meeting in chapter. The same chapter elected two consultors to assist the provost. All other offices were appointed by the provost. Later a vicar was introduced, to be chosen by the provost as his assistant. Members were to be either priests, or students on the way to the priesthood, and passed two years as novices, during which they were examined every six months. After this period, following a vote of two thirds of the assembled priests, they could be admitted to the 'Oblation', a solemn promise of obedience to the Archbishop of Westminster, 'for the glory of God and the salvation of souls, to assist and promote the Church of Westminster'. Although they took no vow of poverty, and continued to own their own property, all ecclesiastical revenue was to be held in common. Their daily spiritual exercises were like those of most communities; the Divine Office privately, except for Vespers on Sundays and great feasts, meditation, the rosary, spiritual reading, regular confession and days of recollection. For the people there were to be daily Mass at convenient times, regular preaching, and public lectures at least twice a week.

They lived in community at Bayswater, with a strict timetable, dining together, 'because the common table is the badge and pledge of fraternal charity'. If the archbishop required one of them to undertake a ministry elsewhere in the diocese he was obliged to consult the provost and consultors, who would nominate someone for the task. They could be summoned back to the house by the provost in consultation with the archbishop. A General Chapter of the Congregation was to meet once a year, or more often if necessary, but all decisions were to be referred to the archbishop.

A house of studies was maintained in Rome, so that new members could be prepared for the priesthood. Lay brothers were admitted as servants, who made the same Oblation after two years' novitiate, but were never admitted to chapter. They were to be shown 'a paternal charity in every matter, both bodily and spiritual'. In dress and ceremonial, the Roman style was always to be followed.[28]

The Oblates were not universally popular, and soon ran into difficulties with Wiseman's coadjutor, Archbishop Errington. He successfully had them removed from their influential position at the seminary, St Edmund's; they successfully had him removed from his right of succession to Westminster. Opposition came from the older diocesan clergy, who resented the rapid rise of Manning from new convert to provost to archbishop, and in general from those who saw the Oblates as an inner group in the archbishop's favour, with claims to be living a more spiritual life than the run of the clergy. As long as they were in that favour they flourished, but when a new archbishop came who knew not Manning, they shrank to become merely another little group of priests running a few parishes in their own peculiar way.

All these schemes for congregations of clergy within a diocese depended so much on the initiative of the individual bishops, and even if successful for a moment, often died with them. The Oblates, of whom eighteen survived in 1964, were eventually disbanded by Archbishop Heenan soon after that date, so that he could be free to move the priests around his diocese. The Mill Hill Fathers, like many 'missionary' societies, found that vocations no longer came from western Europe, but entirely from the indigenous peoples of the territories they went to evangelize, and that training them in Europe was therefore no longer appropriate.

Survivals and New Arrivals

A handful of ancient collegiate churches survived the Napoleonic wars and lingered into the twenty-first century. In Bavaria there remain two colleges in Regensburg, one in Landshut, and one in Altötting. St John's, Regensburg, received new statutes in 1861–4, which allowed the canons 100 florins a year, and insisted every prebendary must live in the city, except for ten weeks' holiday a year. The implication is that they now were expected to live in separate houses, although the obligation of attending choir remained paramount. By 1961 there were four canons and three vicars. In 1963 revised statutes gave the canons the right to live in a canonry house for DM 150 a year; new canons paid an entrance fee of DM 200. Their rights still included that of electing the dean. By 1970 only three canons were left, and the vicars were retroactively abolished in 1976.[29]

Four collegiate churches remain in Austria, mostly in Salzburgland. Mattsee is the largest and most famous of them. It was founded in the year 777 as a Benedictine house, and converted to a collegiate church in the eleventh century, for eleven canons under a provost. The oldest surviving statutes date from 1321. For four hundred years it was the seat of an archdeaconry of the Diocese of Passau. After great difficulties during the Thirty Years War, new statutes were issued. The only result of the revolutionary wars was to transfer the college from Passau diocese to Salzburg, and locate it in the new country of Austria. It acquired the title of '*Ecclesia Collegialis Insignis*', with new privileges from Leo XIII in 1881. After the turmoil of the twentieth-century wars and cultural revolution, new statutes were issued in 1986. Mattighofen was another very ancient foundation, which had survived the tenth-century Hungarian invasion and was endowed by Pope Leo XIII with the privilege of pontifical insignia. It is served by four priests, three of them Monsignors. Seekirchen, a seventeenth-century foundation, for six priests, was re-established in 1832. Eisgarn, the only college in Lower Austria, was founded around 1330, with the stated purpose of running a school as well as the liturgical cult: it remains the oldest school in Lower Austria. In 1997 the Bishop of St Pölten, Dr Kurt Krenn, increased the number of canons to eight, and issued new statutes. By these, the right of the bishop to appoint canons is modified by an undertaking to consult the chapter, who may propose a new member for his appointment. There is a provost, assisted by the senior canon, a canon penitentiary (*Bußcanonicus*), and some '*assistentes capituli*', junior clergy who should be considered in filling a vacant place in chapter. Honorary canons may also be appointed. The traditional choir dress is preserved, with a violet mozetta and biretta, and a silver medallion depicting the college seal. Chapter must meet at least twice a year. Choral Office is to be maintained, and a solemn liturgy on feast days. Their work is to be pastoral, theological or cultural, the provost is always the parish priest of Eisgarn. Canons are to be resident as far as possible, and in any case must come often for community prayer and 'brotherly table-fraternity together' (*zur brüderlichen Tischengemeinschaft zusammen*).

The well-established tradition of collegiate churches in the Alpine region gives hope that they will continue to exist. In other regions, where collegiate churches have long been forgotten, the prospects are less promising. Several short-lived schemes for new collegiate structures in the twentieth century vanished as soon as the initiating bishop was out of the way. For example, Blessed Marie-Léonie Paradis (d. 1912) founded an order of sisters in Quebec specifically to assist priests who lived in communities.[30] Cardinal Suhard of Paris set up a community of priests at Saint-Séverin in 1948, who were to live the common life and sing office together. In they event they were to become liturgical and cultural vandals.[31] Some communities that had somehow survived war and revolution came to an end under hostile bishops, such as the Congregation of San Girolamo in Pisa, suppressed in 1933.[32]

The Oratory of St Philip Neri

Of the survivals, the Oratory of St Philip Neri came through the revolutionary wars battered but alive. The majority of Italian houses were suppressed at intervals during the nineteenth century, as were those in the Portuguese dominions. However in Spain and Latin America they survived happily, and the entire institute was given a new lease of life by the work of Cardinal Newman.

On becoming a Catholic in 1845, John Henry Newman and the group who had lived together at Littlemore were offered a home by Bishop Wiseman at Old Oscott, the former seminary for the Central District, just north of Birmingham. Newman renamed it 'Maryvale', and envisaged some sort of adult educational establishment there. Soon afterwards, however, they were sent to Rome to begin formal ecclesiastical studies, and it did not take long for Newman to realize that the Oratory of St Philip was the ideal structure for a group of converts who had all been fellows of Oxford colleges. Common room life as they had known it in Oxford was, as we have seen, a remarkable survival of the old medieval collegiate life; the Oratory was the sole representative of that life in nineteenth-century Rome.

The Oxford converts underwent an Oratorian novitiate together in Rome, and returned to Maryvale in 1848, with clear ideas about how to adapt St Philip's Institute to modern industrial England. It was a curious plan, rather more like the French Oratory than the Roman, for Newman envisaged Maryvale as a common novitiate and retreat house, to be surrounded by satellite communities scattered throughout the industrial Midlands. Moreover he understood that the pope, in nominating him as superior, intended him to be superior for life, quite contrary to the constitutions of the Oratory. All this lasted for about two weeks, before the sudden influx of Faber and his 'Wilfridians' changed the nature of the community entirely. Instead of a small group of like-minded Oxford converts who had been trained together, they found themselves part of a large community, many of whom were farm boys from Huntingdonshire, who had been trained as lay brothers in a totally different form of religious life. The bewildering succession of changes of plan and location, which has been well chronicled elsewhere, resulted in the separation of the community into the two Oratories of Birmingham and London, and a firm resolve to preserve absolutely the ancient rule that every Oratory is completely separate and independent from every other.[33]

This resolve was to prove providential during the attempts to abolish this principle of autonomy in the twentieth century, the centralizing era of Italian history. Beginning in Sicily, and spreading through the new Kingdom of Italy, a movement arose to link the independent Oratory houses into ever closer union. The 1917 Code of Canon Law made it difficult to continue in the old decentralized manner, and there was pressure to transform the Oratory into an international body, subject to a Provost General in Rome. Largely owing to the efforts of the English Oratorians, this scheme was moderated, and the outcome was the appearance of the 'Institute of the Oratory', later the 'Confederation of the Oratory', as a grouping of autonomous houses, subject to regular inspection by a delegate appointed by the Holy See on the recommendation of a periodical congress of representatives from each Oratory.

Within each house, the old manner of community life without vows continues to survive. The autonomy of each house was preserved sufficient to ensure that a community could dwindle or disintegrate without affecting the stability of any other house, so that Oratories rose and fell without damaging each other, during the savage persecutions of the twentieth century. Houses in Spain and Mexico, that had escaped the Napoleonic suppressions, suffered greatly during the violently anti-clerical years, though curiously the houses in Poland and the DDR came through the communist period unscathed.

The 1917 Code of Canon Law

Attempts to revive the old form of collegiate church were effectively frustrated by the Code of Canon Law of 1917. The chapter *De Capitulis Canonicorum* (CIC 391–422) is primarily concerned with cathedral chapters, there being so few genuine other colleges surviving. They define the purpose of the chapter as firstly the choral worship of God, and secondly to advise the bishop. Many of the old legislative canons are preserved. The bishop is given the power to equalize prebends, or to combine them. Canons are to attend the Office, and a register of attendance is to be maintained. Every cathedral must have a Canon Theologian, to lecture regularly in the cathedral, and there should also be a Canon Penitentiary. Other colleges are to have the same if possible. The parish should be served by a vicar, and a clear division of responsibilities should be made between chapter and parish. Each chapter should have particular statutes, to regulate matters such as turns at celebrating at the High Altar. Titular canons, on the foundation, have a right to a stall and a vote in chapter – honorary canons do not.

All this is quite compatible with the ancient structure of the collegiate church. What really nullifies any restoration of it as a viable form of community life, however, is canon 403, which states that 'After conferring with the chapter, it pertains to the bishop to confer all and every benefice and canonry, whether in cathedral or other collegiate churches, repudiating all contrary customs, and repealing all contrary privileges.' The appointment to the posts of dignitaries is reserved to the Holy See (CIC 396). This means that the bishop has the right to select all members of chapters, and therefore also to depose them. Admittedly he is expected to consult the chapter before imposing a new member on them, but bishops have never felt bound to pay much attention to the results of consultation. Moreover he is expected to choose senior priests of proven worth, particularly those holding doctorates (CIC 404).

The position of being a cathedral canon thus becomes a privilege for those priests who are particularly in favour with the bishop. It carries with it the duty of celebrating the Office in the cathedral, as well as ministering in other parishes nearby, and the right to vote in chapter meetings which do still have a significant function in the administration of the diocese. However there is no mention of common life, and it seems to be taken for granted that canons will live in their own homes, either canonries around the cathedral, or the rectories of city parishes. For a community to have any genuine common life it is essential that the members of that community, or at the very least those who follow the same way of life in similar communities, should have the right to decide who shall be admitted as new members. If an outside person, whether bishop or landlord, has the right to impose a new member on the group, or to take him away, the group cannot be said to be living a community life in any meaningful way. It is obvious that those who compiled the 1917 Code of Canon Law did not think that collegiate bodies were or should be essentially communities of secular clergy.

However another title of the code does speak of 'societies, whether of men or of women, who live in common without vows' (CIC 673–81). Most of the legislation is in fact transferred from the relevant canons in the titles on religious orders. In rather nebulous terms, what was sometimes called a '*pia domus*' could be established by any bishop, under its own constitutions or statutes, and could not be suppressed except by the Holy See (CIC 492, 493). This means that in theory communities of secular clergy could be founded, of 'diocesan right', and could run their own affairs, including the recruitment and training of new members. The bishop would remain responsible for their general supervision, unless the institute progressed to become of 'pontifical right', in which case the Holy See would oversee it. This could have made it possible for priests to live in stable comunities without vows, and the ancient form of life we have been studying could exist, on condition they did not call themselves a 'collegiate church', still less 'canons secular'.

In practice, little advantage seems to have been taken of this possibility. In a few cases new communities aspiring to become Oratories of St Philip began life as *piae domus*, but the nearest most diocesan priests came to the common life was that of an elderly monsignor and his curates in a large rectory. Even where the parish priest was kindly and benevolent, the structures ensured that he was absolutely in charge, and the curates existed only on his good will. For this reason, many older priests are now very opposed to any idea of reviving community life, remembering the unsatisfactory state of affairs in their earlier years.

The Cultural Revolution

Despite this, the Second Vatican Council did offer some aspirations towards some sort of common life among priests. The text gives reasons and recommendations:

> In order that priests may find mutual support in their pursuit of the spiritual and intellectual life, that they may be able to work together in a manner more useful to their ministry, and that they may be delivered from the dangers that often arise from loneliness, some sort of common life or association of life must be encouraged among them. This may take different forms, depending on different personal or pastoral needs; for example sharing a house where this is possible, or eating together, or at any rate frequent regular meetings.[34]

In practice, as in virtually all the recommendations of the council documents, exactly the opposite has happened. Before the cultural revolution of the 1960s, it was still common for a group of priests to share a house and eat together, however unsatisfactory they found it. After that, priests became more and more determined to have their own homes, so that instead of promoting the 'common life', bishops tended to break up large parishes into small units, each served by a single priest living on his own. In some countries even curates within a single parish would each acquire his own separate house. With the disappearance of domestic servants, living alone came to mean, for the first time, literally living as the only person in the house. The 'dangers that often arise from loneliness' became endemic.

In some places groups of priests volunteered to set up 'team ministries', living together and sharing responsibility for the parish they were to serve. This could work well, until the bishop, in the regular autumn manoeuvres, replaced one member of the 'team' with someone else, who had not been part of the original group. Very quickly the 'moderators' of 'team ministries' became indistinguishable from traditional parish priests, and the other 'team members' reverted to thinking of themselves as curates. However successful a team ministry might be, if it depends solely on the good will of the bishop not to move priests around, it cannot be called a true community life. Once again the tendency was to break up these inchoate communities and set each priest alone in his own isolated home.

The 1983 Code of Canon Law preserved the same canons as the 1917 code regarding collegiate churches, although now the cathedral chapters have lost the function of advising the bishop (CIC 503–510). Some aspects of the old regulations survive; there are still particular statutes, remuneration on the occasion of celebrating the Office, a local superior and other officers as needed. But parishes are now definitely separated from chapters, and the bishop is to appoint a parish priest who need not be a member of the chapter. More importantly, the right of the bishop to make all appointments is preserved, together with the requirement that he appoint 'only priests who are of sound doctrine and life and who have exercised a praiseworthy ministry' (CIC 509). Without even the administrative function formerly exercised, chapters of canons are now no more than ceremonial gatherings of worthy and senior priests, chosen by the bishop.

Twenty-first Century Experiments

In the early 1990s Cardinal Lustiger initiated a new method of training priests for the Diocese of Paris. Seminarians are allocated to certain parishes, all within ten minutes' walk of the cathedral, where they are to live in community with the priests of the parishes. In the parish of Saint-Séverin for example there are four priests and eight seminarians, who eat together, share the housework and cooking (there are no paid staff) and celebrate Lauds and Vespers in common, sometimes Compline. Ten parishes now house eight seminarians in each, though not all are for the Diocese of Paris – one is for the Lebanon, one for a north Italian diocese, etc. On Thursdays the entire seminary gathers at Saint-Séverin for midday Mass, followed by lunch together.

Studies take place at the studium of the Ecole Cathédrale, immediately north of Notre-Dame, and are taught largely by diocesan priests, rather than the particular institutes (St-Sulpice, Eudistes etc) who had formerly taught in French seminaries. The small communities of seminarians make it possible to detect and deal with personal problems much more efficiently than in a large college.

After ordination the new priests are encouraged to continue the common life – defined as *la vie fraternelle*, rather than *communau-*

taire, which is a term used to include the entire parish. However there are 'problems of architecture', in that many parishes have provided entirely separate apartments for each of the clergy, and there remains a desire among priests, especially the older ones, for independence. Nevertheless among the new priests trained in the new way, the common life, with both prayer and meals in common, is taking form. The new Archbishop, Cardinal Vingt-Trois, now appoints clergy as a team, curé and vicaires together, rather than moving priests individually.

At present no other diocese in France is imitating the plan, although the ten suffragan sees to Paris are taking an interest and beginning to work together with the Metropolitan. The Bishop of Bellay-Ars is interested in the communal life, but the diocese being very rural, all that is possible at present is the grouping of neighbouring priests for occasional prayer and meals in common.[35]

In other countries we hear of a number of new projects of a similar nature, which are being operated with some success, though still the problem arises that the whole venture is entirely dependent on the goodwill of the bishop. Canon 509 still denies the members of anything calling itself a 'college' the right to choose their own new associates. As a result there are innumerable applications for some sort of status independent of the diocesan bishop, meaning the establishment of an institute of Pontifical Right, although the very real possibilities under the new Code of Societies of Apostolic Life, even of diocesan right, have not yet been fully explored, as we shall see.

Note
1. See R. Price, 'Pastoral Theology: a Fruit of the Enlightenment', in *The Pastoral Review*, vol. 3, 3 (May-June 2007), pp. 7–12.
2. F. S. Rautenstrauch, *Entwurf zur Eintrichtung der theologischen Schulen in den k. k. Erblanden*, Wien 1782.
3. McManners, *French Ecclesiastical Society under the Ancien Régime*, p. 290.
4. Pisani, *Congregations of Priests*, pp. 112–4.
5. McManners, *French Ecclesiastical Society*, p. 277.
6. Helyot, *Ordres Religieux*, II, p. 68.
7. Morand, *Sainte-Chapelle*, p. 240.
8. McManners, *French Ecclesiastical Society*.
9. Ibid., pp. 59–73.
10. Ibid., pp. 221, 256.
11. Langlois, *Essai Historique sur le Chapitre de Rouen*.
12. Ibid., pp. 69–70.
13. Ibid., pp. 31–40.

14. A. Bellenger, *The French Exiled Clergy*, Downside 1986, pp. 75–9.
15. Langlois, *Essai Historique sur le Chapitre de Rouen*, p. 70.
16. Ibid., p. 31.
17. Heyen, *St Simeon in Trier*, pp. 260–301.
18. D.I. 43, Rheingau-Taunus Kreis, p. xx.
19. Betz, *Collegiate Church of Our Lady at the Alte Kapelle, Regensburg*, pp. 5–6.
20. Boureau, *L'Oratoire en France*.
21. T. Mozley, *Letters from Rome*, London 1891, II, p. 108.
22. For all of this, see T. A. Birrell, 'Holzhauser and England'.
23. J. Champ, *William Bernard Ullathorne, a Different Kind of Monk* (Leominster, Gracewing, 2006), pp. 397, 400–4, 504.
24. Quoted in Ward, 'Manning and his Oblates', pp. 42–3.
25. E. S. Purcell, *Life of Cardinal Manning*, London 1896, II, p. 61.
26. Ward, 'Manning and his Oblates', pp. 46–7.
27. R. O'Neil, *Cardinal Herbert Vaughan*, London 1995, p. 187.
28. Westminster Archdiocesan Archives, *Constitutiones Congregationis Anglicæ Oblatorum S. Caroli*, 1877.
29. Mai, *850–Jahre Kollegiatstift zu Regensburg*, p. 34.
30. *Martyrologium Romanum*, 3 May, no. 12.
31. A. Reid, *Organic Development of the Liturgy* (Farnborough, St Michael's Press, 2004), p. 264.
32. Cistellini, *San Filippo Neri*, I p. 197.
33. See Murray, *Newman the Oratorian*, and the innumerable lives and studies of Newman.
34. *Presbyterorum Ordinis* § 8, in A. Flannery, *Vatican Council II, The Conciliar and post Conciliar Documents* (Leominster, Fowler Wright, 1981), vol. 1, p. 879.
35. Conversations with Canon (now Bishop) Jérôme Beau and others, 23 March 2006.

Chapter 14

Reaffirmation and Renewal

A new phase of church history opened in April 2005, the end of the period of radical discontinuity triggered by the Second Vatican Council of 1962–5. The present Holy Father, Pope Benedict XVI, has made it quite clear that the texts of that council may be understood only in terms of what he calls the 'hermeneutic of continuity'. It may no longer be seen as marking a decisive break with the past, but must be interpreted in accordance with the continuous development of Catholic doctrine and practice. The chaos of the 1960s and 1970s cannot be attributed to the council itself but rather to a spurious 'spirit' of the council (*das Konzils Ungeist*). The Holy Father's reading of the council has been aptly expressed as 'the spirit killeth, but the letter giveth life'. In this approach he has met with widespread approval and support, particularly from the younger generation, and a general mood of reform has spread through the world, even though a few influential senior churchmen still cling to the discredited ideas of the 1970s. As one reformist bishop from the Antipodes recently put it, 'They [the liberal bishops] are just going to have to get used to change.'

The text of the Second Vatican Council already quoted about the desirability of common life among the secular clergy (page 269 above) need not, therefore, be consigned to history. There is increasing interest in the idea of such a common life, not least because of the scandals caused by the behaviour of priests living alone. All over the world we hear of groups of priests attempting to found small communities on the ancient model. This explains the number of would-be Oratories (over thirty at present) as they search for a way of fulfilling this ideal within modern canon law. Certain bishops do actively promote the common life, notably as we have seen in Paris, but the lack of canonical structure means that any resulting communities are vulnerable to the whim of the next bishop. Part of the solution can only be achieved by the Holy See, with the necessary revision of canon law to liberate priests from being moved from place to place in too arbitrary a fashion. There is good precedent: the Sixth Council of Paris in 829, quoted in the 'Longer Rule', says 'Priests should not be sent about at random here and there, neither by bishops nor by other prelates.'[1] However, in anticipation of such a reform, there are real possibilities in the new Code of Canon Law, which should be better known and more often used. We have seen many different models of common life in the past, ranging from full community, with 'one refectory and one dormitory', to separate canonical houses, with only prayer in common. Our historical study of community life in the past is presented as an aid to finding acceptable models of clerical life in the future.

Colleges, Societies of Apostolic Life and Associations of Christ's Faithful

The 1983 Code of Canon Law provides three possible frameworks for communities of those who do not take vows: the collegiate church, the Association of Christ's Faithful, and the Society of Apostolic Life. As we have already seen, the age-old institution of collegiate church has been so curtailed that it is not a viable option for new foundations. The right of self-government has for all practical purposes been swept away, since all members of a collegiate church are now under the jurisdiction of the bishop, are selected by him, and are already such as have approved themselves to him by loyal service to the diocese. That is not really a 'community'. For a community to exist with stability, it is essential that the members of that community should have the right to choose the men who are going to come and share their life. All religious orders and institutes are entitled to select their own new members, or to dismiss them when appropriate. The necessary autonomy of every institute precludes the possibility that an outside agency such as a diocesan bishop could intrude members or take them away, especially if the ones being intruded are elderly senior clergy. Men of mature years who have lived alone for decades, however exemplary their conduct, cannot easily be brought to share the true common life. Further, for a real community to exist, it is essential that they should be able to train their own members, or at least ensure that they are trained in their own particular spiritual tradition. The sort of community of secular clergy that so many are clamouring for within the diocesan presbyterate cannot be found in the institute of a collegiate church as at present constituted.

Another possibility is a 'Public Clerical Association of Christ's Faithful'. These are described in Canons 282–320. In such an association 'Christ's faithful, whether clerics or laity, or clerics and laity together, strive with a common effort to foster a more perfect life, or to promote public worship or Christian teaching' (CIC 298). For any sort of community to begin to function, there must be at least three members (CIC 115, §2). An association can be established by the bishop (CIC 312, §2), but could put itself under the spirituality and direction of an existing institute (such as an Oratory), or a religious order, becoming in effect a residential group of brothers of the secular Oratory or members of a 'Third Order' (CIC 303, 311). It would need its own statutes, and the diocesan bishop would be responsible for ensuring they are observed (CIC 304–5, 314). He would also confirm the election of a 'moderator', or appoint him outright (CIC 317). This would create a real institute, a juridical person capable of holding property (CIC 313, 319), which could be self-governing in its internal life, and could select and form its own members (CIC 307, 309). (This could be an easy way of preparing a community for eventual establishment as an Oratory.) However, any association set up by a diocesan bishop can equally easily be suppressed by him or his successor (CIC 320 §2). The code does say 'for grave reasons', but no bishop will ever admit to acting without grave reasons: they could include the needs of parishes the other end of the diocese where he wishes to deploy the priests from the association, or a 'pastoral reorganisation' of parishes. In other words, an association is a very much less satisfactory halfway stage than a 'Society of Apostolic Life', which can only be suppressed by the Holy See. Accordingly, an association should only be attempted if the diocesan bishop is wary of establishing a society. (Obviously an association which achieved pontifical right is independent of the local ordinary (CIC 320 §1) but would be very difficult to establish except after a long period under diocesan right.)

The best option for community life in the new code is the 'Society of Apostolic Life', provided for by canons 731–46, and expounded in a useful handbook by Mgr Bonfils.[2] The Oratories of St Philip are individually Societies of Apostolic Life, of pontifical right, but they are not the only ones. Most of the others are missionary societies, with branches in many countries, but the code makes it quite clear that small communities of clerics or laymen and women can exist under this category, whether of pontifical or diocesan right. Even those of diocesan right have a surprising degree of stability, protection against arbitrary moves, and self-governance. Just as in the past many Oratories began life as *piae domus*, which sometimes existed for decades before reaching sufficient numbers and stability to supplicate the Holy See for canonical establishment, so in our own time groups that are still too small or too provisional for pontifical status could form a true community life with much less difficulty as a Society of Apostolic Life under the local bishop. The advantage of this approach, even provisionally, is that there would be a real community immediately, governed by statutes not by whim, and with the security that members cannot be moved away, nor can a future bishop suppress it without recourse to the Holy See. Candidates for the priesthood could, therefore, join such a Society of Apostolic Life with the confidence that they are joining a real institute, and could be trained for permanent membership of the society.

Societies of this nature must have their own constitutions and statutes (CIC 734 and 738), and the relationship between the diocese into which the priest was formerly incardinated and the new society must be regulated according to these constitutions. 'Living a fraternal life in common, in their own special manner, they strive for the perfection of charity through the observance of the constitutions' (CIC 731). In theory, therefore, it is perfectly possible for a bishop to establish a community of secular priests, living in common, and entirely self-governing, with a degree of stability and the right to maintain its own independent existence and select its own members, as long as he does not call it a 'collegiate church', and the members do not claim to be 'canons' or 'canonical clergy', although in historic terms that is precisely what they are.

In practice, recourse is usually had to the Holy See for a greater surety of stability. 'Societies of Apostolic Life' have recently been established in various places and for various purposes. Some are purely local, such as the St-Philipp Neri Institut in Berlin, established by the Holy See in 2004. This follows the ancient constitutions of the Oratory of St Philip, but without any legal association with other Oratories. Its unique status is partly due to the privilege of using the classic Roman liturgy (what Pope Benedict XVI calls the 'extra-ordinary use of the Roman Rite'). Other new 'Societies of Apostolic Life' are international, and operate with the specific purpose of preserving and extending the use of the same classic liturgy: such are the Fraternity of St Peter the Apostle, and the Institute of Christ the King. These international societies do not form permanent communities, since their members may move from place to place, and in this they are more like the French Oratory, practising the common life for the duration of the posting to each place, but subject to the major superior's right to move them on to a new place. However real community life is possible since new members are selected by existing members of the society, and moves are made by the authorities of the society, exactly as in an order of friars; they cannot be intruded or moved by a bishop outside the society.

The Oratory of St Philip Neri

In the search for a successful manner of living the common life, secular priests turn increasingly to the Oratories of St Philip Neri, which are now classed as Societies of Apostolic Life, and are indeed the oldest, most enduring and most widespread of them. The idea of the Oratory has a much wider scope than the specifically missionary societies, or those founded to promote a particular ministry or liturgy, since the purpose of an Oratory remains the sanctification of the laity by whatever means is appropriate to the time and the locality. On the other hand, its scope is limited by its fidelity to the vision of St Philip Neri. This is defined in the *Annuario Pontificio* as 'individual formation in spiritual culture and devotion, by means of instruction, personal contact, spiritual direction, the ministry of the confessional, accessible preaching and a liturgical apostolate, particularly among students and other young people'.[3] In other words it is not meant to be occupied exclusively in parish work. Almost alone among long-established forms of religious life, the Oratory has increased in numbers since the Second Vatican Council: of the eighty-one houses existing in 2009, thirty-two have been founded since 1965. Throughout the world groups of priests or seminarians inquire continually about the possibility of establishing a new Oratory, and in some cases these inquiries do develop into successful new foundations. At the 2006 Congress, the Procurator General reported that there were thirteen 'Communities in Formation', which were already in touch with the Oratorian Confederation, and had shown a real intention of proceeding towards canonical recognition as new Congregations of the Oratory. Beyond that there were nineteen 'projects of foundation', which varied from one or two priests with the vague intention of one day trying to start an Oratory, to communities of a dozen who had already begun to live a community life in the spirit of the Oratory constitutions. Twelve months later he was able to report that two of the 'Communities in Formation' had been established as Oratories, and that eleven such communities continued to progress towards establishment. However these included three which had only been 'projects' before, and of the previous list of 'communities' three have disappeared. Since the year 2000, two Oratories have become extinct, and some others, including recent foundations, have dwindled in numbers to the point that they can no longer operate as a 'collegial' community. This shows the rather volatile nature of some of these would-be Oratories, and raises the question of how many of the priests and seminarians concerned are genuinely inspired by the vision of St Philip Neri, and how many merely want to get away from the control of their bishops.

The international machinery constructed for the Oratory in the mid twentieth century is not really adequate to deal with the great numbers of applications now being received. Because of this, it is now becoming more difficult to establish a new Congregation of the Oratory from the beginning, and the officers of the Confederation are more wary of giving encouragement to groups who do not seem to have the spirit of St Philip at heart. That is not to say they do not have a future as an institute of some kind, only that the Oratory may not be the one appropriate. Hence the possibilities suggested above of an Association of Christ's Faithful or a Society of Apostolic Life.

Possibilities within the Diocesan Priesthood

Many, it would appear, are searching for a structure in which they can live the common life within a diocese, and with a degree of security against arbitrary disruption, while engaging in parish work or some specific ministry. In describing a possible manner of life for diocesan clergy, I cannot avoid being influenced by my own experience of the Oratory, a manner of life that does actually work. Different Oratories operate in different ways, and one can draw on the experience of many houses to show the possibilities that exist within a flexible structure. However I can also draw on my experience of life as a diocesan priest, a manner of life that does not work. Unless the aim is consciously to carry out the characteristic work of the Oratory in the manner of St Philip, groups would be better advised to find a benevolent bishop and inform him of the possibilities under canons 282–320, 731–46, and in particular canon 579. If the bishop be truly benevolent, there is no reason why different types of community may not be possible within the diocese. The past examples we have been examining suggest structures that might be valid in the future.

There are, broadly speaking, three models: full community life on the Chrodegang pattern, collegiate life on the medieval model, and associated canonical houses, as used by a post-medieval chapter. Different priests will find different models attractive: few will be able to live the full community life unless they are trained up to it, but many more might be happy with the other two models, which could also provide accommodation for retired priests, and the convalescent. There will always be a few who are genuinely better off on their own, and there will always be remote parishes and missions which are best served by hermit priests, but the eremitical vocation is rare.

Full Community Life

The first possibility is the true religious community, as described in the Chrodegang Rules, and as extant in the Oratory. In this, life is almost identical to that of a monastery, save for the absence of vows. This is the sort of community for which the status of Society of Apostolic Life is most appropriate.

In any community, new members must undergo a period of probation or 'noviciate', and are admitted to full membership by a vote of the existing members. Although not bound by vows, there must be an undertaking to abide by the statutes of the community, and to obey the officers elected or appointed to run that community. The evangelical counsel of obedience is exercised towards the collective decisions of the community, and towards the provost and other officers each in pursuit of their specific area of competence. Although in the Chrodegang Rules the superior of any community was directly appointed by the bishop, and apparently for life, it would seem more appropriate now if the members of the community could choose their superior, for a limited term. In a society of diocesan right, although the bishop or his representative presides over the election, it is not necessary for him to confirm it, and it takes effect on the authority of the society.[4]

In practice in the present day it is difficult to envisage a successful community unless all the members are able to vote on the major decisions which affect each of them, although a large community will probably need an inner working group to advise the superior on the day-to-day running of the house. The structure of the Chrodegang and Aachen rules, in which the bishop appoints the provost, and the provost makes all the decisions, will probably not work. In nearly all the medieval colleges the members made collective decisions, and this seems more appropriate for our age. Every community will need a clear understanding of who is in charge in the absence of the superior, in other words a vice-provost or similar, as well as a treasurer and a domestic bursar. Other offices will emerge as needed: librarian, archivist, novicemaster, sacristan, groundsman and so on, who could be appointed by the superior, or chosen by the meeting of all members.

Community life can be defined by four characteristics: prayer in common, sharing a common house, eating together, recreation together. Prayer in common must be the centre around which the life of the community revolves. Institutes of common life within a diocese will almost certainly want to celebrate at least part of the Office together, probably with the laity, but it could be advantageous to compose some sort of specific family prayers, for the community alone, that would help to cement them together as a unity. For this a private or 'domestic' chapel may be necessary, unless the house adjoins a suitable public church. In any case a domestic chapel is useful for private prayer and spiritual reading.

If members of the community have to serve a number of parishes on a Sunday, they will never be together at Mass, even at Christmas and Easter. It could be necessary, therefore, to choose one day each week for a community or 'conventual' Mass, at which all will be present. This could be followed by a general meeting, for business or for instruction, followed by a festive meal and recreation. Such a 'community day' would have to be a strict obligation on members, and pastoral work fitted around it, if community life is to flourish properly. It reflects the commitment which each member must have to every other.

The sharing of a common dwelling is the characteristic of a full community. To begin with, in a diocesan situation, this will be the presbytery of a central parish chosen for its suitability. In selecting a site, it is essential that there should be room for expansion, so that new buildings can be added when necessary. But the bishop should resist the temptation to sell off the presbyteries in the outlying parishes that will be served by the new community. In our time, there is a reasonable expectation that each member will have a sufficiently large private room, and in most countries private bathrooms are no longer unusual. The old common dormitory would no longer be appropriate, even for junior members. However in a full community there should be common areas, a recreation room, an informal sitting room, a library, workshops, and so on. For pastoral contacts a number of 'parlours' or private interview rooms are essential. Given the prevalent danger of time-wasting or worse on the internet, there is much to be said for a common 'Information Technology' room, where all computer work could be done in a public space, and great savings could be made on such things as printers. In general, members of the community, when not in their private rooms for prayer and study, should find their relaxation in the community rather than outside it. The maintenance and cleaning of the house would be a shared responsibility.

The common refectory is essential to full community life. At least once a day there should be a meal together, either midday or evening depending on the apostolate of the members. This should have a degree of formality, though not many houses these days preserve the ancient custom of reading during meals. Members of the community should take their turn at serving, and at reading if this is adopted. Circumstances will dictate whether a cook is employed, or whether members take turns at cooking. Experience has shown that it is not always cheaper to dispense with a professional cook, as individual members can be irresponsible in their shopping and wasteful in failing to take account of what is already in stock. For the community meal to be a true means of building up unity of purpose among the members, there should be restraint in the number of guests invited. A guest of one inevitably becomes the guest of all, so that some form of authorization for invitations is necessary.

The tradition of all ancient religious communities, whether vowed or unvowed, has always been that a portion of the house is set aside for the use of members only, and that outsiders are not introduced beyond necessity. This can take the form of an 'enclosure', within which guests may only be invited by permission of the community, and totally excluding children, or women other than the Council of Nicaea's 'mother, sister or aunt beyond reproach'. Most communities have felt it useful to restrict guests in the refectory to adult men. In the latter part of the twentieth century, many communities, including many Oratories, dispensed with all such rules, and opened the house to all comers. The results were not always edifying. Any new community would be well advised to decide on what portion of the buildings should be generally accessible for pastoral ministry, and what portion should be private to the community.

Collective recreation is another important part of community life. Traditionally this took the form of gathering in a relaxed way after the formal meal, for half an hour to an hour of friendly conversation, avoiding business or controversial topics. The validity of a vocation to community life is usually tested more at this 'recreation' than any other time. For a community to flourish, it is essential that no one stays away from the common recreation, since if any one begins to think his activities or his interests are more important than the building of community, he is clearly unsuited to full community life. As well as this collective recreation, a successful community will find opportunities for occasional excursions, cultural events and the like.

The problem of 'keeping residence' which exercised reforming councils so much in the past is perhaps less obvious today, but it is still important that members remain faithful to the common life. In the Chrodegang Rules there is no mention of holidays at all, whereas the medieval college statutes nearly always specify a maximum period that can be spent outside the community. These days it seems reasonable for members of a full commmunity to observe the same holiday allowance as the diocesan clergy in general. In England this tends to be a day off once a week, and a total of four weeks' holiday. Apart from these times, members should be resident, that is to say they should be present at community prayer, the formal meal and recreation every day. Pastoral responsibilities should be organized around the times that the community has appointed for these exercises, except of course for genuine emergencies.

If the evangelical counsel of obedience is adequately exercised by conforming to the daily demands of community life, the counsel of chastity is well safeguarded by the structure of community life. When priests get into difficulties, it is usually through loneliness, as the Second Vatican Council hinted. Life in community is a great help, and the rule of 'enclosure' can be a great safeguard. No structure is infallible, of course, and problems can arise in any circumstances, but there is no doubt that community life does make priestly life much easier.

The counsel of poverty is perhaps more difficult in an unvowed community. In a true religious order, where no one owns any private property at all, 'poverty' often means that you only have to apply to the monastic bursar to be given anything you could possibly want. In a community without vows, one has to live within one's means. If some members are notably richer than others, community life suffers, so that some moderation of the right to private property has always been found necessary.

If we may recapitulate what has gone before, in the Chrodegang Rules the principle was established of 'From each according to his means, to each according to his needs.'[5] Those who had private means were expected to contribute, either by making over their capital to the community while retaining the income, or at least by covering all their own expenses. Those without means were supported by the community. In medieval colleges a regular income for each member was provided either from individual prebends or from a common fund, and frequent reforms were made in the attempt to equalize the income. In many later colleges those with large private means could never be admitted, and membership would be forfeited if someone came into possession of a significant external income. In early modern congregations, such as the Oratory, those who had private means were expected to contribute at least the amount of their living expenses, preferably more. At all periods the community usually undertook to provide *victum et vestitum,* a food and clothing allowance, as well as accommodation within the community. In some cases priests were allowed to keep personal donations such as those given for offering Mass for a particular intention, as in the original Rule of Chrodegang, and the constitutions of the Oratory. In other cases all ecclesiastical income was to be pooled, including such donations, as in the Holzhauser Institute or the Oblates. Income from other sources, such as book royalties, salaries for teaching and the like, remained the priest's own, but most communities invited them to contribute a share to the common fund.

Applying all this to modern conditions, it is unlikely that many prospective members of new communities will be in possession of a large private income. Most will need to be supported from a common fund, and the first requisite in setting up a new community, therefore, will be the establishment of such a fund. In some countries generous private benefactors might set up a community with a single donation, though the danger would then be that the founder or benefactor could demand some say in how the community should run, like a medieval patron. More often, a community must begin with a diocesan parish, and try to support itself on the income of the parish. Each diocese will have guidelines on the amount each parish should contribute to the support of its priest, and it is perfectly reasonable for each parish served by a member of a community to contribute that amount. Other income may come from specific donations, which will increase as the community becomes established and people begin to reap the benefit of their pastoral care. It is for each community to decide whether Christmas and Easter collections, and donations given after a baptism, wedding or funeral should go to the common fund, or even whether Mass 'stipends' should also be held in common.

The individual member is entitled to his private income, if any, his salary if he is a teacher or chaplain, his royalties if he is a writer, his lecture fees and so on. In a full community, if that sum exceeds a reasonable amount he should be expected to contribute to the support of those who have no income. 'From each according to his means, to each according to his needs.'

A full community, as outlined above, will certainly need a written rule of life, to be approved at least by the diocesan bishop, if not by the Holy See. If the idea of communities within dioceses becomes widespread, a general rule applicable to all would be useful. Such was the *Institutio Canonica*, the Rule of Aachen, promulgated for use in all secular communities throughout the Empire. Models for such rules can be found all over Europe in the past thousand years, though perhaps one can recommend attention to the Constitutions of the Oratory (the original 1612 as well as the 1989 ones), and those of the Oblates of St Charles. Bonfils supplies a useful appendix outlining what would be necessary in drawing up such a set of statutes.[6] As circumstances vary from place to place and generation to generation, any individual community will need its own 'particular statutes', to apply the general rule to the particular case, as each medieval college had.

The Second model: Collegiate Life

Full community life is certainly not for everyone. In fact, unless priests are prepared for this way of life from their first training, it will usually be found very difficult if not impossible for them to join a community of the type described above, with its quasi-monastic rule of life. Many more might be attracted by something based more on the later medieval college. Here either a 'Society of Apostolic Life' or an 'Association of Christ's Faithful' would be the appropriate canonical framework.

As we have seen, colleges varied enormously in type, but very few seem to have insisted on the full community life. The surviving buildings make it plain that usually each member of the college had his own front door, opening into a small apartment, quite sufficient by the standards of the age for a private dwelling. However these apartments were often linked by a covered cloister walk, and the college did include some common rooms, especially a chapel and a dining hall.

This model would of course involve a specially designed building, with the attendant problems of finding a suitable site and the necessary funds. This implies a serious commitment from the diocese to establishing such a way of life. As in many of the medieval colleges, it might not be possible for the building to be very close to the church it is to serve. However the general design is very familiar to modern architects, used to designing a 'sheltered housing' complex. Ranges of apartments could be grouped around a central garden, linked up by a covered walkway, and communicating with offices, a chapel, a common sitting room and dining room, perhaps guestrooms that any member could request. Yet each apartment could be self-contained, with its own kitchen and bathroom, so that the priest has the privacy of his own home, and can come and go as he pleases.

The four principles of community life would be applied in a slightly different manner from that in a full community. Prayer in common, either in the domestic chapel or the nearby church, would still be essential. However, as in a late medieval college, it might not be necessary for all to attend every time, as long as there is a sufficient quorum to keep the Divine Office going with decency and decorum. As in the full community, there should be a community Mass once a week at which all should be present, with a 'chapter' meeting to resolve the business for the week to come. A common meal together, after Mass and chapter, and some time of recreation together before dispersing, would also follow naturally.

Although the life would be far less 'monastic' than in the full communities, the evangelical counsels would still need to be cultivated. Obedience would be to a local superior or provost, and there would still have to be a bursar, someone responsible for the maintenance of the community buildings, the organization of the regular common meal. Chastity would still be assisted by the fellowship that should develop between members of the college, safeguarded by the fact that in linked apartments it is difficult to come and go without being observed. Poverty would be less stringent than in a full community: a reasonable approach would be for each to be charged a theoretical 'rent' for the apartment, to cover common services and maintenance, such rent to come either from parishes or from earned income of some sort. This might include, for instance, a diocesan salary for curial work.

In modern conditions, there is much to be said for surrounding the college buildings with a secure wall or fence, with a porter on duty at the entrance, exactly as in the almost equally unsafe conditions of early medieval Europe. Car parking, gardens and all the residential buildings would then be secured from casual intruders, and in many areas of modern cities this degree of 'security' would make life much less stressful for all members.

The Third model: associated houses

A third, even looser, model of community life might be considered, for those who would find the 'sheltered housing' model too restrictive. In this case an 'Association of Christ's Faithful' would provide sufficient canonical structure. As in the greater post-medieval colleges and chapters, each priest would have his own house, quite detached, with its own garden and garage, and would run his own household quite independently. Yet the priests would form a true association by meeting regularly, perhaps once a month, for a collegiate Mass, a meeting to discuss imminent business, a meal together. All would be encouraged to be generous in covering for each other in cases of illness or during holidays, inviting each other for meals, or gathering on a Sunday evening for cards and whiskey. This would be slightly less than a 'college', slightly more than a 'deanery' as it exists at present. And here too, it might be appreciated, in rough areas, if the clergy houses were all within an enclosure with one securely guarded entrance. Again, a 'provost' would be necessary to supervise the limited degree of common life that would be practised in such an enclosure.

Recruitment and Training

It was characteristic of the first millennium 'minsters', as of the high medieval colleges, of the Oratory, the Oblates and all similar institutes, that they recruited and trained their own members. Experience has shown that where a community of priests can be seen to live harmoniously together, young men will be moved to offer themselves for training. Conversely, where priests are seen to be lonely and isolated, very few consider the priestly vocation attractive. It should be possible, therefore, for communities of priests within the diocesan structure, especially those we have called 'full communities', to accommodate young men aspiring to ordination.

If such men apply, they should be examined by the bishop in the normal manner to determine whether they are suitable for priestly training, but if they want to practice the common life, they should be assessed by a particular community to see if they are suitable for it. The best way of assessing future members has always been a period of time spent living in the house, to observe how the applicant relates to the others, and whether he is able to play his part in the life and work of the house. In the Oratory this period is called a 'noviciate' by analogy with the noviciates of religious orders, and it lasts three years. In the Oblates of St Charles it was two years. It might be difficult in modern conditions to extend the assessment process beyond one year, but that should be a year spent fully in the community, sharing the life, 'learning to drive, to cook and to pray'. At the end of that period the community meeting, in consultation with the bishop, may decide to recommend him for priestly training.

Academic studies for the priesthood have become assimilated to university courses, and therefore only occupy part of the year. During that part the student might have to live away from the community, in a seminary or Catholic university, but during the vacations he should be back in the community, except for a reasonable holiday period. A more mature student might be able to undertake his academic studies by 'distance learning', without having to leave the community house for more than a few weeks of the year. At some stage, if appropriate, he could be definitively joined to the community, or the bishop might take the opportunity of the rapid increase in priestly numbers to found a new community. If, on the other hand, he proves unsuited for full community life, he might usefully be deployed in one of the looser structures. Very few will be found to have the hermit vocation suitable for an isolated parish.

Pastoral Care and other works

In all models of community life for secular clergy, after the ceaseless round of prayer, members were expected to serve the people in preaching and sacrament. As we saw, one result of the late eighteenth-century 'Obfuscation' was that priests came to undervalue, or even deny, the value of prayer and sacrament, preferring to fill their time with activity for the social improvement of their people. We have surely progressed beyond that now, and can see that the essential work of the priest must still be prayer, preaching and administering the sacraments: everything else is to be fitted into spare time. Yet many priests still struggle under burdens of business and administration, properly the work of the laity, and parishes suffer accordingly. At least in England, most parishes are far too small to be viable, given the amount of administration that is now required. Without the resources to pay for professional secretaries, the priest finds himself attempting to do all the administration, while having to delegate the preaching and sacraments to lay people. That is another reason why few feel called to a model of priesthood which means a lifetime of administration and little contact with people. Community life can provide a solution, after other solutions have failed.

If six or seven parish priests lived together in a community, the parishes would easily be able to support them, at considerably less expense than if they had six or seven separate houses. Collectively they could employ one or two really good secretaries to handle all the business and administration, thus setting the priests free to preach and pray. This means that the bursar and domestic manager need not, indeed perhaps should not, be a priest, but a qualified layperson dedicated to serving the community. We should, however, remember how unsatisfactory the situation was at San Girolamo when the community was under the control of Teccosi, an outside layman (page 234 above). Lay staff, just like priests, should wish to serve, not to be served.

The first-millennium 'minsters' characteristically served an area of up to one hour's walk from the community house. It would not be absurd for a modern community to serve parishes within an hour's travel from the centre (though in modern traffic conditions, it might be quicker to walk than drive). The central community church, the 'minster' church, would obviously take on a more important role than the satellite parishes, and this could cause some resentment, unless it was already known to be the historic 'mother church' from which the other parishes were formed in recent decades. To begin with there would certainly be reservations among the people, who are accustomed to have their own priest living next to their own church, but once they realize that they are getting a much better service from a happy healthy priest, backed up by a supportive community, they will wonder why they ever tolerated the previous system. Each parish should still have its own dedicated priest – people very much dislike being served by a 'team' – but illnesses and absences would be covered by a familiar fellow member of the community rather than a stranger. Hospital night calls could be shared around the community in rotation, rather than falling always on one. Different priests could develop different skills, so that, for instance, one could be chaplain to all the schools, one to the nursing homes, and so on, for such institutions naturally serve people from more than one parish.

However, parish work is not by any means the only function of the priest. Some are needed for curial posts in the diocese, the canon lawyers, vicar general, chancellor and so on: they could certainly benefit from life in community, which would provide them with a home and enable them to keep in touch with pastoral reality by celebrating Mass for the people on a Sunday. There is also a place for scholars and writers among the clergy, able to teach in a seminary or lecture in adult education. A community could also provide a home for ill or retired priests, who might still wish to exercise a ministry in hearing confessions and celebrating the occasional Mass, but could be supported and encouraged by the younger clergy around them. A large community house could be a holiday home for an elderly isolated priest, or a refuge for his annual retreat. There are endless posibilities for a much more adaptable form of priestly life than can exist in the present system.

To begin with, grouping priests into communities might leave the outlying parishes feeling aggrieved. However as community life stimulates increased vocations to the priesthood, new communities could be formed back in those outlying areas. That is why the bishop must never sell off the properties around the satellite churches! Ultimately the development of a more satisfactory manner of priestly life will mean greatly increased congregations, and the long steady decline in church membership that we have seen since 1964 could at last be reversed.

Conclusion

All this may seem like wishful dreaming, projecting an impossible new system of priestly life with the hope that things will improve. Our historical study has shown that community life is indeed possible among secular clergy. We have been motivated by the desire to see what models of community life have existed in the past, what were their strengths, what were their weaknesses. By and large, the system worked, and it worked well. Communities came into being and survived for hundreds of years, during which the local church grew and flourished. They came to an end usually because of circumstances beyond their control, war and revolution. Sometimes they were destroyed by jealousy, as the curés conspired against the chapters in the Revolution, the Old Brotherhood undermined the Holzhauser Institute in England, the ordinary diocesan clergy resented the influence of the Oblates. No system can be devised which is immune from such perils, no legislation will succeed in eliminating jealousy or any of the other deadly sins. Nor can any system be set up which is infallible: there will always be casualties, there will always be the need for good will and determination to make the system work. However it does seem that there is a widespread interest at present in community life for secular clergy. Glib and simplistic models could easily be disastrous, which is why it is important to look carefully at what has been done in the past, to learn from its successes, and take warning from its failures.

We have described a model of priestly life which may seem strange to some, impracticable or idealistic to others. Only experience will tell whether it will be successful. It would be impossible to think of any model of diocesan priestly life that could be worse than the one we have at present. We may call on the experience of the past to redress the problems of the present, for the future has a traditional flavour.

Notes
1. Paris VI (829), book 3 canon 4; Mansi XIV, c. 597, also RL 6.
2. Bonfils, *Sociétés de Vie Apostolique*.
3. *Annuario Pontificio*, SCV 2006, p. 1498.
4. Bonfils, *Sociétés de Vie Apostolique*, p. 106.
5. RC 31, cf RB 34.
6. Bonfils, *Sociétés de Vie Apostolique*, pp. 169–74.

Bibliography

Amann, E., *L'Epoque Carolingienne*, vol. VI of A. Fliche and V. Martin (eds), *Histoire de l'Eglise* (Paris, Bloud & Gay, 1937).
Amann, E., and Dumas, A., *L'Eglise au pouvoir des laïques*, vol. VII of A. Fliche and V. Martin (eds), *Histoire de l'Eglise* (Paris, Bloud & Gay, 1940).
Amort, E., *Vetus Disciplina Canonicorum Regularium et Secularium*, 2 vols, (Venetiis, 1747; reprinted Farnborough, Gregg, 1971).
Bertram, J., *The Chrodegang Rules* (Aldershot, Ashgate, 2005).
Betz, K.-H., *The Collegiate Church of Our Lady at the Alte Kapelle* (Regensburg, Schnell & Steiner, 2007).
Billot, C., *Les Saintes Chapelles royales et princières* (Paris, Editions de Patrimoine, 1998).
Birrell, T. A., 'Holzhauser and England', in G. van Gemert and H. Ester (eds), *Grenzgänger, Litteratur und Kultur im Kontext, für Hans Pörnbacher* (Amsterdam, 1990), pp. 453–62.
Blair, [W.] J., *Anglo-Saxon Oxfordshire* (Stroud, Alan Sutton, 1994).
Blair, W. J. (ed.), *Minsters and Parish Churches, the local church in transition 950–1200* (Oxford, Committee for Archaeology, monograph no. 7, 1988).
Blair, [W.] J. & Sharpe, R. (eds), *Pastoral Care before the Parish* (Leicester, University Press, 1992).
Blair, W. J., *The Church in Anglo-Saxon Society* (Oxford, University Press, 2005).
Boden, G. H., *The History of Tong Church, College, and Castle*, (Wolverhampton, privately printed, *c.*1900).
Boniface, St, *The Letters of St Boniface,* trans. E. Emerton (New York, Columbia University Press, 2000).
Bonfils, J., *Les Sociétés de Vie Apostolique* (Paris, Cerf, 1990).
Boureau, R., *L'Oratoire en France* (Paris, Cerf, 1991).
Bowker, M., *The Secular Clergy in the Diocese of Lincoln 1495–1520* (Cambridge, University Press, 1968).

Bradshaw, H. and Wordsworth, C., *Statutes of Lincoln Cathedral*, 3 vols (Cambridge, 1892–7).
Brooks, Nicholas, *The Early History of the Church of Canterbury* (Leicester University Press, 1984).
Burgess, C. and Heale, M., *The Late Medieval English College and its Context* (Woodbridge, Boydell & Brewer, 2008).
Capecelatro, A., trans. T. A. Pope, *The Life of Saint Philip Neri, Apostle of Rome*, 2 vols (London, Burns and Oates, 1882).
Catto, J. I., *The Early Oxford Schools* (Oxford, University Press, 1984).
Cistellini, A., *San Filippo Neri, L'Oratorio e la Congregazione Oratoriana*, 3 vols (Brescia, Editrice Morcelliana, 1989).
Claussen, Martin, *The Reform of the Frankish Church* (Cambridge, University Press, 2004).
de Clercq, Carlo, *La Législation religieuse franque de Clovis à Charlemagne*, 2 vols (I Louvain, 1937; II Paris, Bibliothèque de l'Université, 1958).
Cook, G. H., *English Collegiate Churches of the Middle Ages* (London, Phoenix House, 1959).
Crusius, I. (ed.), *Studien zum weltlichen Kollegiatstift in Deutschland* (Göttingen, Vandenhoeck & Ruprecht, 1995).
Darlington, R. R., 'Ecclesiastical Reform in the Late Old English Period', *English Historical Review* 51, no. cciii (1936), pp. 385–428.
Deansley, Margaret, 'Early English and Gallic Minsters', *Transactions of the Royal Historical Society*, 4th ser. XXIII (1941), pp. 25–69.
Deanesley, Margaret, 'The Familia at Christchurch', in Little, A. G. and Powicke, F. M. (eds), *Essays in Medieval History Presented to Thomas Frederick Tout* (Manchester, University Press, 1925).
Deansley, Margaret, *The Pre-Conquest Church in England* (London, A. & C. Black, 1961).
Deraine, C., 'Chanoines', in *Dictionnaire d'histoire et de géographie ecclésiastique*, XII (Paris, Letouzey & Ané, 1953), cc. 353–405.
Dickinson, J. C., *The Origins of the Austin Canons and their Introduction into England* (London, SPCK, 1950).
Douglas, D. C., *The Domesday Monachorum of Christ Church, Canterbury* (London, Royal Historical Society, 1944).
Drage, Elaine, 'Bishop Leofric and the Exeter Cathedral Chapter (1050–1072). Re-assessment of the Manuscript Evidence.' Unpublished D.Phil. thesis, University of Oxford, 1978.
Dugdale, Sir William, *Monasticon Anglicanum*, ed. Caley, J., Ellis, H., and Bandinel, B., 6 vols in 8 (London, James Bohm, 1846).
Edwards, K., *The English Secular Cathedrals in the Middle Ages*

(Manchester, University Press, 1949).
Foot, S., *Monastic Life in Anglo-Saxon England, c.600–900* (Cambridge University Press, 2006).
Gadiel, M., *La Perfection Sacerdotale, ou la vie et l'esprit du serviteur de Dieu Barthélemy Holzhauser* (Paris-Lyon, Lecoffre Fils. & Cie., 1868).
Gallonio, A., *Life of Saint Philip Neri* (Oxford, Family Publications, 2004).
Ganz, D., *Corbie and the Carolingian Renaissance* (Sigmaringen, Thorbecke, 1990).
George, A., *L'Oratoire* (Paris, Bernard Grasset, 1928).
Gibbs, M., *Early Charters of the Cathedral Church of St Paul, London* (London, Camden Society 3rd series 58, 1939).
Goodall, J. A. A., *God's House at Ewelme* (Aldershot, Ashgate, 2001).
Haddan, A. W. and Stubbs, W., *Councils and Ecclesiastical Documents relating to Great Britain and Ireland* (Oxford, Clarendon Press, 1869–78).
Hall, R. and Stocker D., *Vicars Choral at English Cathedrals* (Oxford, Oxbow, 2005).
Hamilton Thompson, A., 'Notes on Colleges of Secular Canons in England', *Archaeological Journal* 74 (1917), pp. 139–239.
Hamilton Thompson, A., *The Cathedral Churches of England* (London, SPCK, 1925).
Hamilton Thompson, A., *The English Clergy and their organisation in the later Middle Age* (Oxford, Clarendon Press, 1947).
Hamilton Thompson, A., *The History of the Hospital and the New College of the Annunciation of St. Mary in the Newarke, Leicester* (Leicestershire Archaeological Society, 1937).
Harrison, F., *Life in a Medieval College, The Story of the Vicars-Choral of York Minster* (London, John Murray, 1952).
Hartzheim, J., *Concilia Germanica* (Köln, 1759).
Helyot, R. P., *Histoire des Ordres Religieux et Militaires* (Paris, 1792).
Heyen, F. J., *Das Stift St Simeon in Trier (Germania Sacra N.F. 41, Die Bistümer der Kirchenprovinz Trier; Das Erzbistum Trier 9)* (Berlin, 2002).
Hyma, A., *The Christian Renaissance* (Hamden, Conn., Archon Books, 1965).
Jeffery, Paul, *The Collegiate Churches of England and Wales* (London, Robert Hale, 2004).
Klingshirn, William E., *Caesarius of Arles, Life, Testament, Letters* (Liverpool, University Press, 1994).
Klingshirn, William E., *Caesarius of Arles, the Making of a Christian Community in late Antique Gaul* (Cambridge University Press, 1994).

Knowles, D., *The Monastic Order in England, 943–1216* (Cambridge, University Press, 1949).

Langefeld, Birgitte, *The Old English Version of the Enlarged Rule of Chrodegang* (Frankfurt, Paul Lang, 2003).

Langlois, P., *Essai Historique sur le Chapitre de Rouen pendant la Révolution (1789–1802)* (Rouen, Fleury, 1865).

Leclercq, H., 'Chanoines', in *Dictionnaire d'Archéologie Chrétienne et de Liturgie*, III (Paris, Letouzey & Ané, 1911), cc. 223–48.

Leesch, W., Persoon, E. & Weiler, A., *Monasticon Fratrum Vitae Communis* (Brussels, 1977–9).

Lesne, E., *Histoire de la Propriété Ecclésiastique en France, vol. VI, Les Eglises et les Monastéres* (Lille, Facultés Catholiques, 1943).

Mai, P., *850–Jahre Kollegiatstift zu den heiligen Johannes Baptist und Johannes Evangelist in Regensburg* (München, Schnell & Steiner, 1977).

Martène, E., *De Antiquis Ecclesiae Ritibus*, 2 vols (Venice, 1788).

Martyrologium Romanum, editio altera (Roma, Typis Vaticanis, 2004).

McKitterick, R., *The Frankish Church and the Carolingian Reforms, 789–893* (London, Royal Historical Society, 1977).

McManners, J., *French Ecclesiastical Society under the Ancien Régime, A Study of Angers in the Eighteenth Century* (Manchester, University Press, 1960).

Miller, M. C., *The Formation of a Medieval Church, Ecclesiastical Change in Verona, 950–1150* (Ithaca & London, Cornell University Press, 1993).

Morand, S.-J., *Histoire de la Sainte Chapelle* (Paris, 1790).

Morhain, E., 'Origine et histoire de la "Regula Canonicorum" de Saint Chrodegang', *Miscellenea Pio Paschini, Studi di Storia Ecclesiastica*, vol. I, *Lateranum* N.S. XIV (1948).

Murray, P., *Newman the Oratorian* (Leominster, Fowler Wright, 1980).

Nightingale, J., *Monasteries and Patrons in the Gorze Reform, Lotharingia, 850–1000* (Oxford, University Press, 2001).

Page, W., 'Some Remarks on the Churches of the Domesday Survey', *Archaeologia*, LXVI (1915), pp. 61–101.

Pisani, P., *The Congregations of Priests from the Sixteenth to the Eighteenth Century* (London, Sands, 1930).

Poggiaspalla, F., *La Vita Comune del Clero dalle origini alla Riforma Gregoriana* (Uomini e Dottrine 14, Roma, Edizioni di storia e letteratura, 1968).

Ponelle, L. and Bordet, L., *St Philip Neri and the Roman Society of his Times (1515–1595)* (London, Sheed & Ward, 1937).

Raines, F. R., *The Rectors of Manchester, and the Wardens of the*

Collegiate Church of that Town (Manchester, Chetham Society, 1885).
Rame, J., *Historians of the Church of York* (London, Rolls Series II, 1871).
Richards, J. D., *The Vicars Choral of York Minster, the College at Bedern* (York, 2001).
Saint Chrodegang, Communications présentées au colloque tenu à Metz à l'occasion du douzième centenaire de sa mort (Metz, Editions de Lorraine, 1967).
Sapientia Majorum, Documents concerning the history, customs and spirit of the Oratory (privately printed Port Elizabeth & Oxford, 2007).
Saul, N., *Death, Art and Memory in Medieval England* (Oxford, University Press, 2001).
Saul, N., *St George's Chapel Windsor in the Fourteenth Century* (Woodbridge, Boydell & Brewer, 2005).
Scarisbrick, J., 'Henry VIII and the Dissolution of the Secular Colleges', in C. Cross, D. Loades and J. J. Scarisbrick, *Law and Government under the Tudors* (Cambridge, University Press, 1988).
Schroeder, H. J. (ed), *The Canons and Decrees of the Council of Trent* (Rockford, Tan, 1978).
Schuster, Bl. Ildephonsus, *The Sacramentary* (London, Burns, Oates & Washbourne, 1924).
Siegwart, J., *Die Chorherren und Chorfrauengemeinschaften in der deutschsprachigen Schweitz vom 6 Jahrhundert bis 1160* (Studia Friburgensia, Neue Folge 31, Freiburg, Universitätsverlag, 1962).
Sonntag, F-P., CO, *Das Kollegiatstift St Marien zu Erfurt* (Leipzig, 1962).
Sparrow Simpson, W., *Registrum Statutorum et Consuetudinum Ecclesiae Sancti Pauli Londiniensis* (London, 1873).
Statutes of the Colleges of Oxford (London, HM Commissioners, 1895).
Stubbs, W. (ed.), *Memorials of St Dunstan* (London, Rolls Series 63, 1874).
Tanner, T., *Notitia Monastica* (London, William Bowyer, 1744).
Thompson, E. H., *The Life of M. Olier* (London, Burns & Lambert, 1861).
Veissière, Michel, *Une commaunité Canoniale au Moyen Age, Saint Quiriace de Provins (XIe-XIIIe siècle)* (Provins, Société d'histoire et d'archéologie de l'arrondissement de Provins, Documents et travaux 1, 1961).
Verheijen, Luc, *La Règle de Saint Augustin* (Paris, Etudes Augustiniennes, 1967).

de Vogüé, Dom Adalbert, *Le Régle de St Benoit* (Sources Chrétiennes 181, Paris, Editions du Cerf, 1972).

van Waesberghe, J. F. A. M., 'De Akense Regels voor Canonici en Canonicae uit 816.' Thesis for Doctorate of Letters in Catholic University of Nijmegen, 1967.

Wallace-Hadrill, J. M., *The Frankish Church* (Oxford, University Press, 1983).

Waltzing, J-P., 'Collegia', in *Dictionnaire d'Archéologie Chrétienne et de Liturgie*, III (Paris, Letouzey & Ané, 1914), cc. 2102–40.

Ward, D., 'Manning and his Oblates', in Fitzsimmons, J., *Manning, Anglican and Catholic* (London, Burns Oates, 1951), pp. 40–56.

Werminghoff, A., 'Die Beschlüsse des Aachener Concils in Jahre 816', *Neues Archiv für ältere deutsche Geschichtskunde*, XXVII (1901–2), pp 607–51.

Whitelock, D., Brett, M., and Brooke, C. N. L., *Councils and Synods, with other documents relating to the English Church I, 871–1204* (Oxford, Clarendon Press, 1981).

Wulfstan, *Homilies*, ed. D. Bethurun (Oxford, University Press, 1957).

Index of Names

(other than Popes)

Adalberon I, Archbishop of Metz 112
Adalberon II, Archbishop of Metz 109
Adalberon, Archbishop of Reims 113
Adalbold, Bishop of Utrecht 130
Adalmus, Bishop of Laon, 113
Aderaldus of Troyes 129
Ælfric, Archbishop of Canterbury 118
Ælfric, Abbot of Eynsham 116, 125, 126
Æscwig, Bishop of Dorchester, St 120
Æthelflaed, Lady of Mercia 115
Æthelred, King of Wessex 125
Æthelwine, Duke of Essex 119
Æthelwold, of Winchester, St 115, 117–18
Agnellus, Bishop of Rimini 46
Agobard, Bishop of Lyons 78
Alcuin of York 103, 106
Aldric, Bishop of Le Mans 90, 98
Alfer, Earl of Mercia 119
Alfred, King of Wessex 101, 103, 114
Alnwick, Bishop William 190
Altfried, Bishop of Hildesheim 100

Amalarius of Metz 88
Amand, Bishop of Utrecht 58
Ambrose of Milan, St 10, 12, 34–6
Amort, Eusebio 22, 33, 234
Angesis of St-Wandrille 88
Anghilram, Archbishop of Metz 64, 66, 67, 70, 77, 79, 106, 119
Anselm, Bishop of Alicante 134
Anselm, Bishop of Laon 99
Antoninus of Florence, St 185
Antony of Egypt, St 26–7
Appelius, Father 242
Aquablanca, Dean 150, 157
Arundel, Bishop Thomas 194
Ashton, Hugh 212
Astley, Sir Thomas 171–2
Athanasius, St 33–4
Athelstan, King of Wessex 115–16, 195
Atto, Bishop of Vercelli 109
Augustine of Canterbury, St 47
Augustine of Hippo, St 25, 36–8, 40, 61, 83, 84, 131, 134–5, 150 (*see also* Rule of)

Baldebert, Bishop of Basel 62
Baldock, Dean 147
Baldwin, Archbishop of Canterbury 167

Baronio, Cardinal Cesare 107, 235, 237
Basil of Caesarea, St 15, 33, 105
Baudin, Bishop of Tours 41
Bede, St 47, 53–4, 56, 103
Bek, Bishop Anthony 167–8
Bek, Bishop Thomas 168
Bellarmine, Robert, St 37
Benedict of Aniane, St 37, 81–2, 88, 134
Benedict of Mainz 106
Benedict of Nursia, St 33, 40–41 (*see also* Rule of)
Benno, Bishop of Meissen 99
Beornwald of Bampton, St 55
Beregisius of St-Hubert, St 65
Beren, *see* Birinus
Bernard of Clairvaulx, St 142
Bernardine of Siena, St 185
Bernwald of Hildesheim, St 130
Berowulf, Bishop of Würzburg 78
Bertram of Aquileia, Bl. 151
de Bérulle, Cardinal Pierre 244–6, 247, 259
Biancheti, Cesare 248
Birinus of Dorchester, St 55, 114
Birrell, T. A. 260
Blair, W. J. 55
Blithe, Geoffrey 190
Bonfils, Bishop Jean 275, 284
Boniface of Crediton, St 60–2, 64–5, 88
Borja family 221
Borromeo, Charles, St 236, 240, 261
Bourdoise, Adrien 246
Bouyer, Louis 260
Bowker, Margaret, 189
Bradshaw, Henry 147
Brictus, Bishop of Moray 149
Buch, Henri-Michel 248

Bugga 60
Burchard, Bishop of Worms 130
Burghersh, Bishop Henry 190
de Bus, César 244

Cacciaguerra, Buonsignore 221, 234
Caesarius of Arles, St 37, 38, 40, 41, 43, 67
Calasancz, Joseph, St 248
de Cantilupe, Bishop Nicholas 186, 190
Capecelatro, Cardinal 239
Capgrave, John 118–19
Carafa, Pietro 221
Caraffa, Cardinal Carlo 248
Carloman, King 65
Catherine of Genoa, St 220
Cassian, John, St 12, 30, 33, 40, 126
Cedd, St 57
Ceonwald, Bishop of Worcester 114
Charlemagne, Emperor 17, 77, 79, 84, 88, 96, 164
Charles the Bald, Emperor 89, 95–9
Charles the Fat, Emperor 100
Charles Martel 64
Charles I of England 245
Charles II of England 242, 246
Charles V of France 202
Charles VI of France 202
Chatillon, Jean 19–20
Cheetham, Robert 198
Chichele, Archbishop Henry 211
Childebert, King 41
Chrodegang of Metz, St 62, 64–6, 77–9, 88, 102, 104, 112, 131, 134, 176, 248 (*see also* Rule of)

Index of Names

Chrysostom, John, St 14, 34
Clément, M. 257
Cochini, Christian 17
Codrington, Thomas 242–3
Colet, Dean John 148, 193
Collier, Warden George 226
Columbanus, St 53
de Condren, Charles 245, 246
Condulmar, Gabriele 216–17
Consolini, Pietro 237, 245
Constantine I, Emperor 13–14
Correr, Antonio 216–17
Crescentius of Andernach 58
de Cretenet, M. 248
Crusius, Irene 129, 140
de Cucharmay, Etienne 165
Cuthbert of Lindisfarne, St 56
Cuthberth of Lyminge 54
Cyprian of Carthage, St 6–7, 19, 29

Dagobert, King 58
Denehard, Canon of Erfurt 62
Dereine, C. 89, 112
Dicul of Bosham 55
Diuma of Charlbury, St 55
Dryden, John 242
Dugdale, Sir William 178, 205
Dunstan of Canterbury, St 115, 116–20, 126
Dupanloup, Archbishop Félix 259, 260–1

Eadbald, King of Kent 54
Eadburg of Bicester, St 55
Ealdred, Archbishop of York 126
Eamberth, Canon of Erfurt 62
Eangyth 60
Eanswith 54
Ebbe of Abingdon, St 55
Ebbo, Archbishop of Reims 90
Edgar, King 116–19, 120, 126

Edward the Confessor, King 127
Edward the Elder, King 114, 116
Edward I of England 184
Edward III of England 168, 201, 203
Edward IV of England 192, 203
Edward VI of England 164, 208, 225
Egbert, Archbishop of York 59–60, 103
Elizabeth I of England 227
Emery, M. 253
Erlwin, Bishop of Cambrai 130
Ermoldus 89
Errington, Archbishop George 263
Ethelburga, St 54
Ethelheard, Archbishop of Canterbury 78
Ethelwald, King of Deira 57
Eudes, John, St 246
Eusebius of Caesarea 14
Eusebius of Vercelli, St ii, 34–5, 176
Everard of Cysoing, St, 100

Faber, Fr Wilfred 266
Fedeli brothers 235
Ferreolus, Bishop of Uzès 40
Flodoard 61
Francesco, Bishop of Gubbio 145
Francis of Assisi, St 17
Francis I of France 202, 215
Francis V of Spain 233
Freomund of Cropredy, St 55
Frideswide of Oxford, St 55
Frigdian of Lucca, St 41
Frotarius, Bishop of Tulle 90
Froude, Richard Hurrell 227, 229

Fulco, Archbishop of Reims 101, 103
Fulgentius, Bishop of Cagliari 39

Gaduel, Jean 260, 261
Gallonio, Antonio 239
Gaudentius, Bishop of Abitene 39
Gerard, Bishop of Toul 108
Gerson, Jean 189
Gifford, Bishop Bonaventure 243
Giso, Bishop of Wells 127
Giustiniani, Cardinal Lorenzo 216
Godehard, Bishop of Hildesheim 130
Godiva, Lady of Mercia 128
Grabon, Matthew 188–9
Grandisson, Bishop John 168
Gratry, Alphonse 259
Gray, Bishop William, 190
Gregory of Nazianzen, St, 34
Gregory of Tours 41
Grey, Lord George 202
Grignon de Montfort, Louis, St 248
Grimbald of Winchester 103, 114, 117, 120
Grimlaic of Metz 112
Groote, Gerard, Bl. 218–19
Grosteste, Bishop Robert 150
Gualterius, Abbot of Lestirps 130
Guerra, Matteo 240

Haistulf, Archbishop of Mainz 92
Hamilton Thompson, A. 140, 225
Harold Godwinsson, King 127
Harrison, Canon Frederick 191

Hedde, Bishop of Strassburg 62
Heenan, John Carmel Cardinal 263
Heinrich II, Bishop of Regensburg 160
Heinrich, Archbishop of Trier 111
Heinrich, Bishop of Würzburg 130
Henri the Liberal, Count 137, 174
Henri, Archbishop of Reims 143
Henrietta Maria, Queen 245
Henry II, Emperor 129–30, 160
Henry IV, Emperor 130
Henry VI of England 210
Henry VII of England 187
Henry VIII of England 202, 223–4, 225
Henry of Lancaster, Duke 180, 206
Herard, Bishop of Tours 98, 103, 106
Herive, Archbishop of Reims 113
Hermanus, Bishop of Nevers 91, 99
Hermanus, Bishop of Sherborne 127
Hetti, Bishop of Trier 90
Hildebrand, *see* Pope Gregory VII
Hincmar, Bishop of Reims 98–9, 103, 106
Hilary, Bishop of Arles 39
Hilary of Poitiers, St 37
Hofer, P. 242
Holzhauser, Bartolomäus, 241–3, 246, 258, 260–1
Howard, Philip, Cardinal 242
Hugh, Bishop of Lichfield 154
Hugh of Lincoln, St 150, 154

Index of Names

Hugh of St Victor 17
Hugues de Brète, Canon 173
Hywel Dda, Prince of Wales 115

Ignatius of Antioch, St 7, 14, 27
Ignatius Loyola, St 244
Isidore of Seville, St 8, 59, 77, 81, 83, 84, 86, 104, 105, 106
Ivo, Bishop of Chartres 134

James II of England 243
Jerome, St 3, 7, 19, 27, 32, 33, 81, 83, 84, 105, 134
John I of Portugal 217
John of Capistrano St 185
John, of Pontoise, Bishop 174
John of Tours, Bishop 128
John of Vicenza 217
Josef II, Emperor 250
Justin Martyr, St 6

Kennedy, Bishop James 212
Kentigern of Glasgow, St 45
Kettler, Bishop Wilhelm Emmanuel 260
Klüppel, Eckhard 187
Knowles, D. David 53, 78, 101, 118
Konrad, Archbishop of Cologne 144
Köth von Warscheid, Gerhard 233
Krenn, Bishop Kurt 264
Kuno of Regensburg, Bishop 159

Laberthonnière, Père 260
Lancaster, house of 201, 206
Lanfranc of Canterbury, St 149
Langefeld, Brigitte 79, 104, 106
Lawrence, St 25
Leduld, Abbot of Mouzon 113
Leidrad, Bishop of Lyons 78

Leofric, Bishop of Exeter 79, 126–7, 200
Leofric, Earl of Mercia 128, 149
Leonardi, John, St 241
Leuterius of Châlons 96
van der Leyen, Johan W. 233
Lietbert, Bishop of St Rufus 133
Longespee, Bishop Roger, 171
Longland, Bishop John 206–7
Louis the Fat, King of France 176
Louis the Pious, Emperor 80, 81, 89, 91, 95, 96, 98
Louis the Young, King of France 176
Louis II, Emperor 96
Louis V of France 113
Louis IX of France, St 176–7, 201
Louis XVI of France 254
Louis XVIII of France 253
Louis, Duke of Bourbon 178
Lothar, Emperor 96
Ludubert of Trier 62
Ludwig, King of Bavaria 160
Ludwig I, King of Bavaria 160
Lul, Bishop of Erfurt 62
Lustiger, Cardinal 270

Madalree of Verdun, St, 100
de Malebranche, Nicolas 245
Manasses, Bishop of Troyes 99, 129
Manning, H.E. Cardinal 261–3
Mansi, J.B. 189
Martin of Tours, St 35
Mary I of England 226–8
Maurice, Bishop of London 146
Medici family 221
Meinwerk, Bishop of Paderborn 130

Mentmore, Abbot Michael 179
Metcalf, Thomas 242
Moland, Bishop of Lichfield 156, 157
Montacute, Elizabeth 171
Morgan, John 242
Morhain, E. 83, 128
Mortimer, Edward, 204
Motta, Paolo 241

Napoleon I, Emperor 253
Neri, Philip, St, 221, 234–6, 240–1, 261
Newman, John Henry Cardinal 106, 227, 229, 265–6
Nicholas of Cusa, St 198
Nightingale, John 90
Nizier, Archbishop of Trier 41
Norwich family 201

Oda, Archbishop of Canterbury 115
Odo, Bishop of Beauvais 99
Odulphus of Utrecht, St, 99
Olier, Jean-Jacques 246–7
Osburg of Coventry, St 56
Osmund of Sarum, St 148, 150, 155
Oswald of Worcester, St 115, 118
Otto I, Emperor 112
Ouen of Rouen, St 58
Outrequin de St Léger, Canon 255

Pallu, François 247
Papczyński, Jan 248
Paphnutius, Abba 11–12
Papillant, Canon 256
Paradis, Marie-Léonie, Bl. 265
Parker, Matthew 225
Parr, Queen Katherine 225
Pateshul, Bishop Hugh 154, 156, 157
Paul of Tarsus, St 6, 12, 25
Paul, Bishop of Verdun 58
de Paul, Vincent, St 245, 246, 247
Paulinus of Nola, St 39
Pembrugge family, 204
Perrot, John, 242
Peter of Blois 163
Peter Chrysologus, St 39
Peter Damian, St 17, 85, 130–3, 140, 141, 177, 188, 248
Peter de Honestis 135
Pététot, Pierre 259
Philip III of France, le Hardi 177
Philip IV of France, le Bel 177, 184
Philip V of France, le Long 202
Philip VI of France 178
Piamun, Abba 30
Pippin, King 60, 61, 63, 65, 77, 80, 102
Pirmin, St 62, 64
Poggiaspalla, Ferminio 27, 30, 85, 130
Pole family 186, 208
Pollio, St 10
Pomerius, Julius 38–9, 59, 67, 72, 83, 84, 85, 131, 134
Possidius 38
Poullart, Claude 248
Prosper of Aquitaine see Pomerius

Quartermayne family 207
Quesnel, P. 246

Rabanus Maurus 92
Radbod of Dol 114
Radbod of Trier 111
Radulphus of Bourges, St 92, 98

Index of Names

Ratherius of Verona, St 103, 109–10, 176
Ratzinger, J. Cardinal ii
Rautenschrauch, Franz Stefan 250
Remigius, Bishop of Lincoln 147, 149
Remigius, Bishop of Strassburg 62
Richelieu, Cardinal 244, 246
Richerus Wasco, Deacon, 64
Riculf, Bishop of Soissons 98
Rigobert, Bishop of Reims 61
Robespierre, Maximilien 253
de la Rochefoucauld, Cardinal 255, 257
Roger, Earl of Warwick 171
Romilli, Archbishop 262
Romillion, P. 244–5
Rorico, Bishop of Laon 113
Rosa, Persiano 234
Rotherham, Archbishop Thomas 200
Ruysbroeck, Jan 218

de Sales, François, St 239, 244, 245, 246
Salmon, Bishop John 168
Saul, Nigel 140
Savonarola, Girolamo 221
Scarisbrick, Jack 224
Schuster, Ildefonso, Bl. 110
Semmler, Josef 89
Sergeant, John 243
Seymour, Edward 224
Sidonius, Bishop of Konstanz 62
Sigeher and Sigewand, Canons of Erfurt 62
Siegwart, J. 112, 129, 130
Sigismund of Burgundy, King 41
di Simeone, Enrique 217

Simon, Richard 245
Sindulfo, Bishop of Vienne 58
Socrates 11
Sonntag, Franz-Peter 140
Sozomen 34
Stephen, King of England 179
Stodilus, Bishop of Limoges, 96
Stonor, Sir John 205
Suhard, Cardinal 265
Swithin of Winchester, St 119
Symons, D. Thomas 118

Teccosi, Vicenzo 234, 288
Tertullian 6, 13
Tetradius, Bishop of Besançon 58
Theoderic, Archbishop of Trier 112
Theodore of Tarsus, St 54
Theodric, Bishop of London 115
Thibout II of Champagne 137
Thibout V of Champagne 174
da Thiene, Gaetano 221
Thomas Aquinas, St 18, 23
Thomas, Archbishop of York 148
Thurstan, Archbishop of York 143
Taio of Saragossa 83, 84, 88

Ubald, Bishop of Gubbio 142–3
Ullathorne Archbishop William Bernard 261

Valentinian, Bishop of Chur 41
Vaughan, Cardinal Herbert 262
Vaux, Lawrence 227
Veissière, Canon Michel 136–7, 174
Vingt-Trois, Cardinal 271
Vernaccia, Ettore 220

Wala, Bishop of Basel 62
Wallace-Hadrill, J. M. 23
Walter, Bishop of Hereford 127
Walter, Bishop of Orleans 99
de la Warre, Thomas 198
Waynefleet, Bishop William 210
Welfo, Duke of Bavaria 135
Werminghoff, Albert 88
White, Sir Thomas 228
Whittington, Sir Dick 208
Wienbert, Canon of Erfurt 62
Wihtred, King of Kent 54
Wilfred of Selsey, St 55
William I of England 146, 179
William II of England 149
William of Laneham 158
William of Malmesbury 126
Willibert, Bishop of Cologne 99
Wilmart, Dom 62–3
Wiseman, Cardinal Nicholas 261–2, 265
Wlfer, Earl of Mercia 56
Wolfgang, Bishop of Regensburg 112
Wolsey, Cardinal Thomas 148, 187, 193, 205, 210
Woodhead, Abraham 238
Wordsworth, Christopher 148
Wulfrad, Bishop of Bourges 98
Wulfred, Archbishop of Canterbury 78
Wulfsige, Bishop of Sherborne 116, 118, 125
Wulfstan of Worcester, St 116, 125, 126
Wykeham, Bishop William 209–10

Zeno of Verona, St 36
Zum Jungen, Emich Philipp 233
Zwentibold, King 112

Index of Popes

Alexander II (1061–73) 134, 149, 166
Alexander III (1159–81) 143
Alexander VI (1492–1503) 187

Benedict XVI (gloriously reigning) 273, 276
Boniface I (418–22) 149
Boniface IX (1389–1404) 216

Callistus II (1119–24) 142
Celestine III (1191–8) 143, 149
Clement I (90–99) 8
Clement IX (1667–9) 217
Constantine I (708–15) 59
Cornelius (251–3) 10, 29

Eugenius II (824–7) 100
Eugenius III (1145–53) 143
Eugenius IV (1431–47) 217

Gelasius I (492–6) 39, 42
Gelasius II (1118–19) 142
Gregory I (590–604) 42, 46–8, 61, 67, 83, 84, 103, 106, 149
Gregory II (715–31) 61, 106
Gregory V (996-9) 112
Gregory VII (1073–85) 129, 130, 132, 134
Gregory XII (1406–15) 217

Gregory XIII (1572–85) 235

Hadrian I (772–95) 17, 78, 84, 106
Hadrian II (867–72) 106
Hadrian IV (1154–9) 137
Honorius I (625–38) 55

Innocent I (402–17) 15, 80
Innocent III (1198–1216) 17
Innocent X (1644–55) 242
Innocent XI (1676–89) 242

John VIII (872–82) 100
John XII (955–64) 117
John XIII (965–72) 111
John XXII (1316–34) 211

Leo I (440–61) 15–16, 25, 129
Leo IX (1049–54) 132
Leo XIII (1878–1903) 264

Martin V (1417–31) 217

Nicholas I (858–67) 100, 106
Nicholas II (1059–61) 133

Paschal II (1099–1118) 129
Peter (33–68) 3, 5, 23–4
Pius V (1566–72) 217
Pius VII (1800–23) 257

Pius IX (1846–78) 260

Silvester I (314–35) 42
Siriacus (385–98) 9, 12, 14
Stephen II (752–7) 64

Urban I (222–30) 28–9, 135
Urban II (1088–99) 135
Urban III (1185–7) 159
Urban VIII (1623–44) 245

Xystus II (257–8) 25

Zacharias (741–52) 61, 65, 66
Zosimus (417) 9

Index of Places

(other than Councils)

Aachen 77, 79, 96–7, 112, 113, 164-5
Abergwili 168, 226
Abingdon 55
Agaunum 41
Aix la Chapelle see Aachen
Aix en Provence 239, 244–5
Altötting 264
Angers 160, 173, 253, 254–5, 256
Aquileia 36, 151
Arles 40
Arundel 188, 201, 202, 225
Aschaffenburg 169
Astley 171–3
Attigny 64
Austria 240, 250, 258, 264
Avignon 239

Bamberg 129, 160, 211
Bampton 55, 200
Banbury 207
Barcelona 89, 100, 129
Basel 62, 78
Bath 120, 128, 149
Battlefield 200
Bavaria 240, 241–3, 264
Bayeux 148
Beauvais 99
Bellay-Ars 271
Berkeley 202
Berlin 276

Bermondsey 59
Beverley 101, 116, 125, 126, 146, 179, 191, 194–6, 198
Bexhill, 56
Bicester 55, 136
Bingen 169
Birmingham 265–6
la Bisbal 111
Bishop Auckland 168, 194
Bishop's Stortford 178
Bleidenstadt 62, 113, 187, 233, 258
Bloxham 182
Bologna 248
Bosham 55, 174
Boulogne 191
Bourbon-l'Archambault 178
Bourges 201
Braga 217
Brasil 240
Brecon 226
Bridgenorth 164, 178
Brou 201
Buraburg 62
Burton on Trent 225
Bury St Edmunds 115

Cambridge 181, 210, 211, 212, 224, 228–9
Camerino 239
Canterbury 47, 54, 78, 118, 167

Carlisle 136
Châlons-sur-Marne 89, 96
Châteaudun 201
Charlbury 55
Chartres 111, 173
Cheltenham 89
Chester 115, 149
Chester le Street 101, 168
Chichester 146, 150, 191
Chiemsee 242
Cholsey 120
Christchurch 136
Chur 41, 90
Cirencester 136, 199
Cluny 107
Cobham 140, 198, 202
Colchester 136
Cold Norton 136
Cologne 111, 211
Compiègne 96–7, 112
Condom 245
Cotterstock 168
Coventry 56, 128, 167, 200
Crediton 114, 115
Cropredy 55

Denmark 223
Derby 165
Diedenhofen 96
Dorchester on Thame 55, 120, 136, 146, 147, 164
Dorpat (Tartu) 189
Dover 54, 174, 178
Durham 186

Edington 187
Eichstätt 62
Eisgarn 170, 264–5
Elmley 178
Ely 101, 176
Erfurt 62, 140, 169–70, 186, 211, 219
Eton 194, 209, 224

Evesham 115
Ewelme 186, 194, 199, 208
Exeter 115, 125–6, 164, 178, 190, 200
Eynsham 149

Fano 239
Fermo 101, 239
Ferrara 239
Flanders 240
Fleury 118
Florence, 221
Folkestone 54, 115
Fotheringay 201, 202, 203–4, 224, 225
France 243–8
Frankfurt am Main 96
Fréjus 239
Fresile 129
Fritzlar 62

Geisenheim 219
Geismar 169
Gellone 64
Genoa 217, 220
Germany 221, 223, 252, 256, 258, 267
Glasgow 150
Glastonbury 108, 115, 118
Gloucester 115, 116, 146, 164
Gnosall 178
Goa 240
Gorze 64, 90, 107, 112, 113
Grafton Regis 181
la Granja 233
Groenendaal 218
Gue-de-Maulny 178

Hackington 167
Halberstadt, 100, 223
Hampton Court, 205
Harzberg 130
Hastings 164, 174, 178

Index of Places

Hemingborough 186, 194
Hereford 125, 150, 157, 191
Herrenberg 219
Herrieden 100
Heytesbury 164, 226
Higham Ferrers 198, 199
Hildesheim 100, 129, 130, 143
Hippo Regius 37–8, 84, 134
Hoxne 115
Hull 186
Hullmartin 172

Ingham 187
Ingolstadt 211, 241
Ireland 53
Irthlingborough 194
Italy 252, 258, 265, 266

Kingston on Thames 200
Kirkby Beler 187
Koblenz 90, 112
Konstanz 62, 90
Kulm 219

Lanchester 167
Landshut 264
Langres 143
Laon 98, 113
Lecce 212
Leicester (Newarke) 178, 180, 185, 194, 199, 201, 202, 206–7, 224
Le Mans, 90, 98, 103, 106, 107
Leominster 101
Lichfield, 149, 156–7, 159, 167, 190–1
Liège 90, 126, 129
Limoges 96
Lincoln 120, 146, 147–51, 153, 158–9, 167, 190–1
Lingfield 202
Lisbon 217
Liverpool 227

London 90, 127, 128, 146–7, 155-6, 159, 167, 174, 176, 179, 186, 192, 193, 200, 208, 224, 227, 261–3, 266
Longuyon 41
Lorraine (Lotharingia) 125, 127
Lorsch 64
Lucca 129, 134, 142, 239
Lyminge 54
Lyons 78

Magdeburg 111, 112
Maguzzano 110
Maidstone 194, 198
Mainz 92, 111, 112, 169
Maldon 180
Malmesbury 115, 118
Manchester 198, 226–7
Marienthal 219
Marstoke 187
Maryvale 265–6
Mattsee 170, 264
Mattighofen 264
Mendham 115
Merewell 176
Mettingham, 178, 201
Metz 64, 66, 73, 78, 90, 103, 112, 113
Mexico 267
Middleham 226
Milan 36, 134, 236, 240, 262
Milverton 172
Minster in Sheppey 54
Minster in Thanet 54–5
Mockstadt 169
Monte Luco 182
Montpellier 245
Moray 149
Mottisfont 187
Mouzon 113
Murbach 62

Naples 236, 248
Netherlands 222, 223, 252
Nevers 99, 111
Newarke see Leicester
Norbury 169
North Creake 178
Norton Subcourse 201
Norwich 168
Nottingham 178

Ohrdruf 62
Olton 261
Orleans 173, 259
Oscott 261, 265
Ottery St Mary 168, 224
Oxford 55, 115, 136, 164, 171, 174, 178, 179, 180-1, 187, 210-11, 212, 224, 228-9, 266
Oxfordshire 226

Paddington 256
Padua 239
Palermo 217, 239
Paris 143, 151-2, 176-8, 201, 202, 211, 215-6, 233, 244-5, 246-7, 254, 265, 270-1, 273
Parma 217
Passau 166
Pastrana 233
Pisa 265
Poland 240, 248, 258, 267
Pontefract 164, 178
Portugal 240, 252, 258, 265
Prague 211
Provins 136-7, 165, 173-4

Quebec 265

Ramsbury 114, 125
Ramsey 118
Raveningham 201
Ravenna 10, 39

Reading 256
Reculver 54
Regensburg 96, 159, 164, 170, 197-8, 258, 264
Reichenau 62
Reims 103, 111, 113
Rettenbach 135
Reval (Tallinn) 189
Riga 189
Ripon 116, 118, 146, 179, 191, 197, 198, 227
Rochefort 256
Rome 46, 53, 110, 135, 143, 209, 217, 220-1, 234-7, 241, 245, 248, 263, 265-6, 288
Rotherham 200
Rouen 58, 148, 168, 255-7
Rufford 200

Saint Albans 179
Saint Andrews 211-12, 223
Saint-Arnulf 112
Saint Buryan 115
Saint-Denis 58, 64
Saint Endellion 226
Saint-Evre 90
Saint German's 114, 134
Saint Pölten 264
Saint-Séverin 41
Saint-Trond 64, 66
Saint-Wandrille 88
Salisbury 127, 146, 148, 150, 155, 190
Salzburg 242
Santa Maria in Portu 143
Sarum see Salisbury
Schönenwald 78
Scotland 201, 222, 223
Seekirchen 233-4, 264
Seéz 257
Selsey 55, 146
Sens 111
Sherborne 114, 118, 125, 146

Shottesbrooke 169
Shrewsbury 164
Sibthorpe 168
Siena 241
Soisy 137
Sonning 114
Southwell 125, 126, 146, 197, 227
Spain 240, 252, 258, 265, 267
Speyer 91, 112
Staindrop 202
Stoke by Clare 186, 204, 225
Stoke sub Hampden 178
Stone 56
Stonor 205, 226
Stowe 128, 149, 159
Strassburg 62
Sussex 55
Sweden 223
Switzerland 221, 223

Tattershall 199, 202, 207, 224
Tettenhall 115
Thame 207, 209, 256
Thionville 96
Tholey 41
Thonon 239, 244
Thornton 225
Tickhill 178
Tittmoning ii, 170, 241, 243
Tong 194, 204–5
Tormarton 169
Toul, 79, 90, 100, 113
Tours, 35, 41, 191
Trier 36, 41, 62, 90, 91, 111–12, 166, 198, 258
Troyes 111, 129
Turin 129
Tuxford 186
Twineham 136

Udine 151

Urgel 89, 129

Vaugirard 246
Venice 216–7
Verdun 79, 90, 95, 112, 113
Verona 36, 109–10
Vicenza 239
Vienne 142
Vincennes 202, 254
Volterra 129

Waltham 127, 136, 164
Warwick 164, 171, 178, 202
Wells 114, 125, 127, 128, 149, 159, 191, 193
Wenslow 194
Westbury on Trym 118, 119, 167, 198, 224
Westminster 168, 176, 178, 179, 201, 203, 224, 227, 261–3
Winchcombe 101, 118
Winchester 56, 114, 117, 119, 120, 174-6, 194, 209, 256
Windesheim 218–9
Windsor 164, 168, 178, 199, 201, 203, 224, 226
Wingfield 186
Wingham 167
Withybrook 172
Woking 59
Wolverhampton 119, 163, 227
Wolvey 172
Worcester 118, 167
Worms 91, 112
Wroxton 136
Würzburg 62, 78

York 116, 125, 126, 146, 148, 150, 157, 158, 166–7, 179, 191, 192, 206, 227

Zürich 112, 130, 222

Index of Councils and Synods

Aachen (813) 81; (816–7) 63, 80–90; (836) 91
Ænham (1009) 124
Agdé (506) 16, 43
Amesbury (928) 119
Angers (1365) 188
Aquileia (1181) 143
Arles (314 ?) 14; (813) 80
Augsburg (952) 109
Aure (994) 109
Auxerre (567) 44
Avignon (1337) 144n

Bergamo (908) 110
Bourges (1214) 144
Buda (1279) 145n

Calcuthae (787) 78
Calne (978) 109, 117, 119
Carthage I (394) 14–15
Carthage III (397) 7
Carthage IV (398) 7, 9–10, 42
Carthage V (c.400) 15
Châlons-sur-Marne (813) 80
Châlons-sur-Saône (873) 96
Clermont (535) 43
Cloveshoe (747 and 786) 60
Cologne (1260) 144
Compostella (1056) 129
Corbie (c.839) 92
Ctesiphon (414) 15, 42

Elvira (305 ?) 11–12, 14, 15
Epernay (846) 107
Esztergom (1114) 142
Etruria (1327) 144n, 145n

Fîmes (881) 96
Florence (1346) 144n, 145n

Gerona (517) 16, 43
Goslar (1019) 109
Gubbio (1303) 145n

Hungary (1268) 145n

Kirtlington (977) 119–20
Konstanz (1415) 188

Lateran III (1179) 143
Lateran IV (1215) 142, 144, 170
Liège (1287) 145n
Lombardy (1287) 144n
London (1214) 144; (1399) 188

Mainz (813) 77, 80; (888) 109; (1310) 145n, 212
Meaux (845) 95; (1245) 144n, 145n
Mérida (666) 59
Metz (753) 64; (888) 100

Index of Places

Milan (1311) 145n
Mont-Sainte-Marie (961 and 972) 113

Narbonne (1368) 188
Neocaesarea (314) 14
Nicaea (325) 11–12, 14, 40, 41–2, 66, 84, 116, 281

Orange (441) 10, 42
Orleans III (538) 44
Orleans IV (541) 44

Palermo (1388) 188
Paris (829) 91, 274; (1212) 144; (1346) 145n; (1429) 189
Pavia (876) 100; (1023) 109
Poitiers (1000) 109
Pontignone (876) 100

Ravenna (877) 100; (1314) 145n; (1317) 144n, 145n
Reims (813) 80
Rome (324) 42; (721) 106; (826 and 853) 100; (1059 and 1063) 132, 135
Rouen (1214) 144

Soissons (853) 96

Tarragona (516) 43; (1317) 212; (1329) 145n
Telepte (418) 15
Toledo (400) 15, 42; (531) 43; (589) 44; (633) 16, 58; (638) 58–9
Tours (567) 16, 44; (813) 80
Trent (1545–63), 7, 8, 153, 231–2, 247, 254, 255
Trier (1337) 145n
Trosby (909) 99, 109, 110
in Trullo (691) 17

Vaison-la-Romaine (529) 43
Vatican I (1869–1961) 260
Vatican II (1962–5) 269, 273, 277, 282
Venice (465) 43; (1438) 189
Ver (755) 64, 65

Winchester (975) 109, 119

Index of Subjects

Aachen, Rule of *see Institutio Canonica*
Ancrene Rewle 208
Apostles 23–5
Apostolic Canons 6, 13, 27
Apostolic Constitutions 6, 7, 13
Archconfraternity of Charity 220–1, 234
Associations of Christ's Faithful 275–6, 284, 286
Augustinian Canons 133, 136–7, 163, 171, 178–9, 216, 218–9, 248

Bartholomeans 234, 241–3, 258, 260–1, 283, 290
Bederns 158, 191, 194, 195–6
Béguines 189, 212
Berefellows 194–5
Bérullians see French Oratory
Brethren of the Common Life 189, 218–20

Calvinism 223
Canonesses 87
Canonici 42, 48–9, 58, 59–60, 80, 113, 142, 154–7, 165
Canons of Edgar 125
Cantors *see* Precentors
Capitula of Theodulf 103, 126
Carmelites 244

Cathars 17
Cathedral Chapters 146–57, 267
Celibacy 2, 9, 11–18, 36, 109, 116, 145, 282, 285
Celi Dé 57, 116
Cellerars 71, 86–7, 165
Chancellors 146, 148
Chantries 165
Chapter 68–9, 81, 105
Chums 16, 40, 45, 58
Civil Constitution of the Clergy 255–6, 257
Clementines 13, 22, 27
Clementine Schism 257
Clergy 1–10
Clerks of Pious Schools 248
Clerks Regular 218, 221
Code of Canon Law (1917) 267–8
Code of Canon Law (1983) 270, 274–7
Collegiate Churches 140–1, 146, 163–6, 224–9, 232, 254–5, 264–5, 267, 274, 288
Collegium 28–9
Commendam 244
Company of Mary 248
Confession 67, 69, 104
Confraternities 220–1
Congregation of Christian

Index of Subjects

Doctrine (Doctrinaires) 244, 252
Congregation of the Hearts of Jesus and Mary (Eudists) 246, 253, 270
Congregation of Holy Ghost 248
Congregation of the Holy Nail 241
Congregation of the Holy Trinity 241
Congregation of the Priests of the Mission 234, 247, 253
Congregation of St Gabriel 248
Congregation of St George 216–8
Congregation of St John 217–8
Congregation of St Joseph 241
Congregation of St Tiburius 234

Deans 90, 146, 148, 152, 157, 165, 169, 187
Death, Black 184–5
Devotio Moderna 216, 218–9
Dionysio-Hadriana 17, 83, 84, 106
Divine Office 67–8, 71–2, 86, 104, 175, 206–7, 235, 237, 239, 250–1, 256, 280, 285
Doctrinaires 244, 252
Domesday Book 127
Domus Episcopi 42–3, 44, 98
Donation of Constantine 23

Edict of Milan 29, 32
'Enlightenment' 250–1, 287
Eudists *see* Congregation of the Hearts of Jesus and Mary

Ferrets 228
Food and drink 70–1, 105, 147, 174, 177, 281
Fraternity of St Peter 276

French Oratory 234, 244–6, 252-3, 259–60, 277

Gallicanism 245
Goliards 111, 145
Gregorian Reforms 124, 128, 130, 137

Hermitages 181–2, 212
Holidays 282
Hospitals 178–80, 206–9
Hospitium 91

Institute of Christ the King 276
Institute of Secular Clergy *see* Bartholomeans
Institutio Canonica 81–90, 97, 100, 102–6, 108, 110, 125, 127, 129, 131–3, 134, 141, 147, 149, 151, 177, 280, 284
Isidorean Decretals 22, 42, 103, 106–7

Jansenism 245
Jesuits 244–5, 252

Lazarists 247
Lent 69–70
Lepers 143, 179
Little Oratory 239
Lutheranism 223

Matricula 44, 49, 73, 145
Milan Society for Foreign Missions 262
Mill Hill Missionaries 262, 263
Minor Clergy 7–11, 45, 68, 111, 145, 157–9, 165, 169, 172, 181, 198, 231, 256
Minor Corporations 157–60
Minsters 54–5, 56–7, 101–2, 125, 127–8, 288
Missionaries of Mary 248

Missionaries of St Joseph 248
Mission Society see
    Congregation of the Priests
    of the Mission
Monasticism 26–7, 32–3, 52–3,
    57, 103
Monastic Reform 185
Mulieres subintroductae 14

Nicolaism *see* Celibacy
Norbertines 135

Obedience 279, 282, 285
Oblates of St Ambrose 240, 261
Oblates of St Charles 261–3,
    284, 287, 290
Old Brotherhood ('Chapter')
    243, 289
Oratory of St Philip Neri 1,
    234-41, 244, 261, 265-7, 268,
    273, 275-6, 277-8, 279, 287
Oratory of Divine Love 220–1
Ordo Canonicus 53, 96, 113
Ordo Qualiter 103, 104

Petite-Eglise 257
Petrini 235
Pia Domus 268, 276
Pious Workers 248
Poverty 18–19, 39, 72, 129,
    131–2, 135, 141, 282–4, 285
Prebends 108, 140–1, 142,
    152–5, 164, 169–70, 172,
    173, 176, 188, 193–4, 255
Precentors 146, 148, 152, 165
Primicerius 59, 71, 79, 82, 90,
    110
Provinciale Anglicanum 189
Provosts (*Praepositi*) 45, 46, 71,
    78, 82, 86, 165, 176, 187,
    238, 239, 279, 285, 286

Regula Longior 102–6, 125–7,
    129, 133, 147, 274
Regular Clergy 48, 133
Regula Sancti Pauli 128, 146–7
Rule of Augustine 36–8, 67, 82,
    132, 134, 135, 137, 150, 179
Rule of Benedict 40–1, 48, 53,
    56, 60, 63, 66–7, 69, 81–3,
    86–7, 102–3, 135, 208
Rule of Berne 62–3
Rule of Chrodegang 65–74,
    77–9, 81, 82, 84–8, 90,
    102–5, 119, 133, 135, 141,
    152, 157, 208, 228, 279–80,
    283

Schools 57, 80–1, 82, 100, 143,
    148, 166, 169, 173, 180–1,
    209–12
Secular Clerks of Blessed
    Virgin 241
Seminaries 231–2, 244, 245–7,
    287
Simony 4, 109, 117, 132
Societies of Apostolic Life 247,
    262, 271, 274, 275–7,
    279–84
Society of the Foreign Mission
    of Paris 247
Sulpicians 246–7, 253, 270
Syrian Canons 42

Terrorism 252, 253
Theatines 221
Treasurers 146, 149

Vicars 147, 154–60, 165, 172,
    191–3

Wardens 165

www.ingramcontent.com/pod-product-compliance
Lightning Source LLC
Chambersburg PA
CBHW032017230426
43671CB00005B/121